WESTERN CIVILIZATION

EARLY MODERN THROUGH THE 20TH CENTURY

FIFTH EDITION

VOLUME II

Editor

William Hughes
Essex Community College

William Hughes is a professor of history at Essex Community College, in Baltimore County, Maryland. He received his A.B. from Franklin and Marshall College and his M.A. from the Pennsylvania State University. He continued graduate studies at the American University and the Pennsylvania State University. Professor Hughes is interested in cultural history, particularly the role of film and TV in shaping and recording history. He has written articles, essays, and reviews for *The Journal of American History, The New Republic, The Nation, Film and History,* and *The Dictionary of American Biography.*

Annual Editions
A Library of Information from the Public Press

Cover illustration by Mike Eagle

The Dushkin Publishing Group, Inc.
Sluice Dock, Guilford, Connecticut 06437

The Annual Editions Series

Annual Editions is a series of over forty-five volumes designed to provide the reader with convenient, low-cost access to a wide range of current, carefully selected articles from some of the most important magazines, newspapers, and journals published today. Annual Editions are updated on an annual basis through a continuous monitoring of over 200 periodical sources. All Annual Editions have a number of features designed to make them particularly useful, including topic guides, annotated tables of contents, unit overviews, and indexes. For the teacher using Annual Editions in the classroom, an Instructor's Resource Guide with test questions is available for each volume.

VOLUMES AVAILABLE

Africa
Aging
American Government
American History, Pre-Civil War
American History, Post-Civil War
Anthropology
Biology
Business and Management
Business Ethics
China
Comparative Politics
Computers in Education
Computers in Business
Computers in Society
Criminal Justice
Drugs, Society, and Behavior
Early Childhood Education
Economics
Educating Exceptional Children
Education
Educational Psychology
Environment
Geography
Global Issues
Health

Human Development
Human Resources
Human Sexuality
Latin America
Macroeconomics
Marketing
Marriage and Family
Middle East and the Islamic World
Nutrition
Personal Growth and Behavior
Psychology
Social Problems
Sociology
Soviet Union and Eastern Europe
State and Local Government
Third World
Urban Society
Western Civilization, Pre-Reformation
Western Civilization, Post-Reformation
Western Europe
World History, Pre-Modern
World History, Modern
World Politics

Library of Congress Cataloging in Publication Data
Main entry under title: Annual editions: Western civilization, vol. II: Early Modern Through the Twentieth Century.
    1. Civilization—Addresses, essays, lectures—Periodicals. 2. World history—Addresses, essays, lectures—Periodicals. Title: Western civilization, vol. II: Early Modern Through the Twentieth Century.
901.9'05   82-645823   ISBN 0-87967-780-5

Fifth Edition

Manufactured by The Banta Company, Harrisonburg, Virginia 22801

Editors/ Advisory Board

To The Reader

In publishing ANNUAL EDITIONS we recognize the enormous role played by the magazines, newspapers, and journals of the *public press* in providing current, first-rate educational information in a broad spectrum of interest areas. Within the articles, the best scientists, practitioners, researchers, and commentators draw issues into new perspective as accepted theories and viewpoints are called into account by new events, recent discoveries change old facts, and fresh debate breaks out over important controversies.

Many of the articles resulting from this enormous editorial effort are appropriate for students, researchers, and professionals seeking accurate, current material to help bridge the gap between principles and theories and the real world. These articles, however, become more useful for study when those of lasting value are carefully *collected, organized, indexed,* and *reproduced* in a *low-cost format*, which provides easy and permanent access when the material is needed. That is the role played by *Annual Editions*.

Under the direction of each volume's *Editor*, who is an expert in the subject area, and with the guidance of an *Advisory Board*, we seek each year to provide in each *ANNUAL EDITION* a current, well-balanced, carefully selected collection of the best of the public press for your study and enjoyment. We think you'll find this volume useful, and we hope you'll take a moment to let us know what you think.

What exactly are we attempting to do when we set out to study Western civilization? The traditional course in Western civilization is a chronological survey of sequential stages in the development of European institutions and ideas, with a cursory look at Near Eastern antecedents and a side glance at the Americas and other places where westernization has occurred. So we move from the Greeks to the Romans to the medieval period and on to the modern era, itemizing the distinctive characteristics of each stage, as well as each period's relation to preceding and succeeding developments. Of course, in a survey so broad (usually moving from Adam to the atom in two brief semesters) a certain superficiality seems inevitable. Key events whiz by as if viewed in a cyclorama; often there is little opportunity to absorb and digest the complex ideas that have shaped our culture. It is tempting to excuse these shortcomings as unavoidable. But to present a course on Western civilization that leaves students with only a jumble of events, names, dates, and places is to miss a marvelous opportunity. For the great promise of such a broad course of study is that by examining the great turning points or shifts in the evolution of our culture we can understand the dynamics of continuity and change over time. At best, the course can provide a coherent view of our traditions and offer the opportunity for reflection about everything from the forms of authority to the nature of humankind to the meaning of progress.

One way to bring coherence to the study of our civilization is to focus on what is distinctly "Western" about Western civilization. Much has been written about the subject. Vera M. Dean, for example, has argued, "There is no real differential between West and non-West except that created by the West's chronologically earlier acquisition of technology." She concludes that industrialization will shortly obliterate all differences between East and West.

Not all Western observers are so monolithic in their views. Arnold Toynbee, Herbert Muller, and F. S. C. Northrop, to mention just a few, have written with pride of the unique qualities of the West, while urging our civilization to learn from the East.

What about the Eastern perspective? The West, writes Zen philosopher D. T. Suzuki, is "analytical, discriminative, differential, individualistic, intellectual, objective, scientific, generalizing, conceptual, schematic, impersonal, legalistic, organizing, powerwielding, self-assertive, disposed to impose its will upon others." The East is "synthetic, totalizing, integrative, non-discriminative, deductive, non-systematic, intuitive, subjective, spiritually individualistic, and socially group-minded."

As students become attuned to the distinctive traits of the West, they develop a sense of the dynamism of history—the interplay of the forces of continuity and change. They begin to understand how ideas relate to social structures and social forces. They come to appreciate the nature and significance of conceptual innovation and recognize the way values infuse inquiry. More specifically, they develop an understanding of the evolution of Western ideas about nature, humankind, authority, and the gods, i.e., they learn *how* the West became distinctly Western.

Of course, the articles collected in this volume can't deal with all of these matters, but by providing an alternative to the synthetic summaries of most textbooks, they can help students acquire a fuller understanding of the dynamics of Western civilization and a clear sense of its unique components. This book is like our history—unfinished, always in process. It will be revised biennially. Comments and criticism are welcome from all who use this book. To that end a postpaid article rating form has been included at the end of the book. Do you know of any articles that could improve the next edition? With your assistance, this anthology will continue to improve.

William Hughes

Editor

Unit 1

The Age of Power

Seven selections trace the evolution of political power in early modern times. Topics include the European state system, the relationship between the rulers and their citizenry, relations between science and religion, and the art and architecture of the period.

The concepts in bold italics are developed in the article. For further expansion please refer to the Topic Guide and the Index.

Unit 2

Rationalism, Enlightenment, and Revolution

Eight articles discuss the impact of science, politics, music, economic thought, changing social attitudes, and the rights of women on the Age of Enlightenment.

The concepts in bold italics are developed in the article. For further expansion please refer to the Topic Guide and the Index.

Unit 3

Industry and Ideology: The Nineteenth Century

Five articles focus on the nineteenth century in the Western world. Topics include the working class, the industrial revolution, Karl Marx, and John Stuart Mill.

Unit 4

Modernism and Total War: The Twentieth Century

Ten selections discuss the evolution of the modern Western world, the beginnings of psychology, the Russian Revolution, the world wars, the Nazi state, and the effects of Europe's loss of economic and political dominance in world affairs.

The concepts in bold italics are developed in the article. For further expansion please refer to the Topic Guide and the Index.

The concepts in bold italics are developed in the article. For further expansion please refer to the Topic Guide and the Index.

Unit 5

Conclusion: The Human Prospect

Seven articles examine how politics, war, economics, and culture affect the prospects of humankind.

The concepts in bold italics are developed in the article. For further expansion please refer to the Topic Guide and the Index.

Topic Guide

This topic guide suggests how the selections in this book relate to topics of traditional concern to Western civilization students and professionals. It is very useful in locating articles which relate to each other for reading and research. The guide is arranged alphabetically according to topic. Articles may, of course, treat topics that do not appear in the topic guide. In turn, entries in the topic guide do not necessarily constitute a comprehensive listing of all the contents of each selection.

TOPIC AREA	TREATED AS AN ISSUE IN:	TOPIC AREA	TREATED AS AN ISSUE IN:
Art, Music, and Architecture	2 Philip II's Grand Design 5. The 17th-Century "Renaissance" in Russia 21. How the Modern World Began	**Industrial Revolution**	9. Meeting of Minds 16. Cottage Industry and the Factory System 17. When Karl Marx Worked For Horace Greeley
Business	11. The Commercialization of Childhood 16. Cottage Industry and the Factory System 24. The Big Picture of the Great Depression	**Labor**	16. Cottage Industry and the Factory System
		Middle Class	18. Samuel Smiles: The Gospel of Self-Help
Childhood	11. The Commercializaiton of Childhood	**Modernism**	21. How the Modern World Began
Colonialism/ Colonies	29. The War Europe Lost	**Philosophy**	6. Locke and Liberty 19. John Stuart Mill 21. How the Modern World Began
Democracy	36. Thoughts on Heroism	**Politics/Political Authority**	1. The Emergence of the Great Powers 2. Philip II's Grand Design 3. Conflict in Continuity 4. Louis XIV and the Huguenots 6. Locke and Liberty 7. From Boy-King to "Madman of Europe" 10. Prussia & Frederick the Great 26. The Nazi State: Machine or Morass? 27. Remembering Mussolini 30. Thinking Back on May 68 31. Paristroika 32. The Causes of Wars
Economics/ Economists	17. When Karl Marx Worked For Horace Greeley 24. The Big Picture of the Great Depression		
Enlightenment	10. Prussia & Frederick the Great 11. The Commercialization of Childhood 12. The First Feminist		
European State System	1. The Emergence of the Great Powers 2. Philip II's Grand Design 29. The War Europe Lost	**Religion**	2. Philip II's Grand Design 5. The 17th-Century "Renaissance" in Russia
Ideology	6. Locke and Liberty 19. John Stuart Mill 26. The Nazi State: Machine or Morass?		

TOPIC AREA	TREATED AS AN ISSUE IN:	TOPIC AREA	TREATED AS AN ISSUE IN:
Revolution	13. The Shot Heard Round the World 14. Was France the Fatherland of Genocide? 15. Counter-Revolution? Toulon, 1793 23. When the Red Storm Broke 30. Thinking Back on May 68	**Totalitarianism**	26. The Nazi State: Machine or Morass? 36. Thoughts on Heroism
Science	8. Galileo and the Specter of Bruno 9. Meeting of Minds	**War**	1. The Emergence of the Great Powers 7. From Boy-King to "Madman of Europe" 22. Sarajevo: The End of Innocence 25. Munich at Fifty 27. Remembering Mussolini 28. 1945 29. The War Europe Lost 33. How the Cold War Might End
Society	3. Conflict in Continuity 11. The Commercialization of Childhood 16. Cottage Industry and the Factory System 20. Sarah Bernhardt's Paris 24. The Big Picture of the Great Depression 28. 1945 35. Plagues, History, and AIDS	**Westernization**	5. The 17th-Century "Renaissance" in Russia
		Women	12. The First Feminist 20. Sarah Bernhardt's Paris
Technology	16. Cottage Industry and the Factory System	**Working Class**	16. Cottage Industry and the Factory System

The Age of Power

The early modern period (c. 1450–c. 1700) was a time of profound change for Western civilization. During this epoch the medieval frame of reference gave way to a recognizably modern orientation. The old order had been simply, but rigidly, structured. There was little social or geographical mobility. Europe was relatively backward and isolated from much of the world. The economy was dominated by self-sufficient agriculture. Trade, and therefore cities, did not flourish. There were few rewards for technological innovation. A person's life seemed more attuned to revelation than to reason and science. The Church both inspired and delimited intellectual and artistic expression. Most people were prepared to subordinate their concerns to those of a higher order—whether religious or social. Carlo Cipolla, a distinguished European historian, has given us an interesting capsulization of the waning order: "People were few in number, small in stature, and lived short lives. Socially they were divided among those who fought and hunted, those who prayed and learned, and those who worked. Those who fought did it often in order to rob. Those who prayed and learned, learned little and prayed much and superstitiously. Those who worked were the greatest majority and were considered the lowest group of all."

That constricted world gradually gave way to the modern world. There is no absolute date that marks the separation, but elements of modernity were evident throughout much of Western civilization by the eighteenth century. In this context the late medieval, Renaissance, and Reformation periods were transitional. They linked the medieval to the modern. But what were the elements of this emergent modernity? Beginning with the economic foundation, an economy based on money and commerce overlaid the traditional agrarian system, thus creating a more fluid society. Urban life became increasingly important, allowing greater scope for personal expression. Modernity involved a state of mind, as well. Europeans of the early modern period were conscious that their way of life was different from that of their forebears. In addition,

these moderns developed a different sense of time—for urban people clock time superceded the natural rhythms of the changing seasons and the familiar cycle of planting and harvesting. As for the life of the mind, humanism, rationalism, and science began to take precedence over tradition—though not without a struggle. The spread of Protestantism presented another challenge to orthodoxy. And, as economic and political institutions evolved, new attitudes about power and authority emerged.

The early modern period is often called an Age of Power, primarily because the modern state, with its power to tax, conscript, subsidize, and coerce, was taking shape. Its growth was facilitated by the changing economic order, which made it possible for governments to acquire money in unprecedented amounts—to hire civil servants, raise armies, protect and encourage national enterprise, and expand their power and influence to national boundaries and beyond.

Power, in various early modern manifestations, is the subject of the articles assembled in this unit. "The Emergence of the Great Powers" surveys the shifting international balance of power during the seventeenth and eighteenth centuries. "Conflict in Continuity in 17th-Century France" demonstrates the state's impact on the social hierarchy. The power of the state to impose religious uniformity can be seen in "Louis XIV and the Huguenots," while "Locke and Liberty" explores the philosopher's efforts to develop a political theory centered on liberty and property.

Looking Ahead: Challenge Questions

What were the philosophical justifications for the new political order?

How did various segments of society react to the emergence of the modern state apparatus?

How extensive were the modernizing tendencies of the era? What impact did they have upon the remoter sections of Europe, such as Russia?

How did the modern international order evolve?

Unit 1

The Emergence of the Great Powers

I

Although the term *great power* was used in a treaty for the first time only in 1815, it had been part of the general political vocabulary since the middle of the eighteenth century and was generally understood to mean Great Britain, France, Austria, Prussia, and Russia. This would not have been true in the year 1600, when the term itself would have meant nothing and a ranking of the European states in terms of political weight and influence would not have included three of the countries just mentioned. In 1600, Russia, for instance, was a remote and ineffectual land, separated from Europe by the large territory that was called Poland-Lithuania with whose rulers it waged periodic territorial conflicts, as it did with the Ottoman Turks to the south; Prussia did not exist in its later sense but, as the Electorate of Brandenburg, lived a purely German existence, like Bavaria or Württemberg, with no European significance; and Great Britain, a country of some commercial importance, was not accorded primary political significance, although it had, in 1588, demonstrated its will and its capacity for self-defense in repelling the Spanish Armada. In 1600, it is fair to say that, politically, the strongest center in Europe was the old Holy Roman Empire, with its capital in Vienna and its alliances with Spain (one of the most formidable military powers in Europe) and the Catholic states of southern Germany—an empire inspired by a militant Catholicism that dreamed of restoring Charles V's claims of universal dominion. In comparison with Austria and Spain, France seemed destined to play a minor role in European politics, because of the state of internal anarchy and religious strife that followed the murder of Henri IV in 1610.

Why did this situation not persist? Or, to put it another way, why was the European system transformed so radically that the empire became an insignificant political force and the continent came in the eighteenth century to be dominated by Great Britain, France, Austria, Prussia, and Russia? The answer, of course, is war, or, rather more precisely, wars—a long series of religious and dynastic conflicts which raged intermittently from 1618 until 1721 and changed the rank order of European states by exhausting some and exalting others. As if bent upon supplying materials for the nineteenth-century Darwinians, the states mentioned above proved themselves in the grinding struggle of the seventeenth century to be the fittest, the ones best organized to meet the demands of protracted international competition.

The process of transformation began with the Thirty Years War, which stretched from 1618 to 1648. It is sometimes called the last of the religious wars, a description that is justified by the fact that it was motivated originally by the desire of the House of Habsburg and its Jesuit advisers to restore the Protestant parts of the empire to the true faith and because, in thirty years of fighting, the religious motive gave way to political considerations and, in the spreading of the conflict from its German center to embrace all of Europe, some governments, notably France, waged war against their own coreligionists for material reasons. For the states that initiated this wasting conflict, which before it was over had reduced the population of central Europe by at least a third, the war was an unmitigated disaster. The House of Habsburg was so debilitated by it that it lost the control it had formerly possessed over the German states, which meant that they became sovereign in their own right and that the empire now became a mere adjunct of the Austrian crown lands. Austria was, moreover, so weakened by the exertions and losses of that war that in the period after 1648 it had the greatest difficulty in protecting its eastern possessions from the depredations of the Turks and in 1683 was threatened with capture of Vienna by a Turkish army. Until this threat was contained, Austria ceased to be a potent factor in European affairs. At the same time, its strongest ally, Spain, had thrown away an infantry once judged to be the best in Europe in battles like that at Nördlingen in 1634, one of those victories that bleed a nation white. Spain's decline began not with the failure of the Armada, but with the terrible losses suffered in Germany and the Netherlands during the Thirty Years War.

In contrast, the states that profited from the war were the Netherlands, which completed the winning of its independence from Spain in the course of the war and became a commercial and financial center of major importance; the kingdom of Sweden, which under the leadership of Gustavus Adolphus, the Lion of the North, plunged into the conflict in 1630 and emerged as the strongest power in the Baltic region; and France, which entered the war formally in 1635 and came out of it as the most powerful state in western Europe.

It is perhaps no accident that these particular states were so successful, for they were excellent examples of the process that historians have described as the emergence of the modern state, the three principal characteristics of which were effective armed forces, an able bureaucracy, and a theory of state that restrained dynastic exuberance and defined political interest in practical terms. The seventeenth century saw the emergence of what came to be called *raison d'état* or *ragione di stato*—the idea that the state was more than its ruler and more than the expression of his wishes; that it transcended crown and land, prince and people; that it had its particular set of interests and a particular set of necessities based upon them; and that the art of government lay in recognizing those interests and necessities and acting in accordance with them, even if this might violate ordinary religious or ethical standards. The effective state must have the kind of servants who would interpret *raison d'état* wisely and the kind of material and physical resources necessary to implement it. In the first part of the seventeenth century, the Dutch, under leaders like Maurice of Nassau and Jan de Witt, the Swedes, under Gustavus Adolphus and Oxenstierna, and the French, under the inspired ministry of Richelieu, developed the administration and the forces and theoretical skills that exemplify this ideal of modern statehood. That they survived the rigors of the Thirty Years War was not an accident, but rather the result of the fact that they never lost sight of their objectives and never sought objectives that were in excess of their capabilities. Gustavus Adolphus doubtless brought his country into the Thirty Years War to save the cause of Protestantism when it was at a low ebb, but he never for a moment forgot the imperatives of national interest that impelled him to see the war also as a means of winning Swedish supremacy along the shore of the Baltic Sea. Cardinal Richelieu has been called the greatest public servant France ever had, but that title, as Sir George Clark has drily remarked, "was not achieved without many acts little fitting the character of a churchman." It was his clear recognition of France's needs and his absolute unconditionality in pursuing them that made him the most respected statesman of his age.

The Thirty Years War, then, brought a sensible change in the balance of forces in Europe, gravely weakening Austria, starting the irreversible decline of Spain, and bringing to the fore the most modern, best organized, and, if you will, most rationally motivated states: the Netherlands, Sweden, and France. This, however, was a somewhat misleading result, and the Netherlands was soon to yield its commercial and naval primacy to Great Britain (which had been paralyzed by civil conflict during the Thirty Years War), while Sweden, under a less rational ruler, was to throw its great gains away.

The gains made by France were more substantial, so much so that in the second half of the century, in the heyday of Louis XIV, they became oppressive. For that ruler was intoxicated by the power that Richelieu and his successor Mazarin had brought to France, and he wished to enhance it. As he wrote in his memoirs:

> The love of glory assuredly takes precedence over all other [passions] in my soul. . . . The hot blood of my youth and the violent desire I had to heighten my reputation instilled in me a strong passion for action. . . . *La Gloire*, when all is said and done, is not a mistress that one can ever neglect; nor can one be ever worthy of her slightest favors if one does not constantly long for fresh ones.

No one can say that Louis XIV was a man of small ambition. He dreamed in universal terms and sought to realize those dreams by a combination of diplomatic and military means. He maintained alliances with the Swedes in the north and the Turks in the south and thus prevented Russian interference while he placed his own candidate, Jan Sobieski, on the throne of Poland. His Turkish connection he used also to harry the eastern frontiers of Austria, and if he did not incite Kara Mustafa's expedition against Vienna in 1683, he knew of it. Austria's distractions enabled him to dabble freely in German politics. Bavaria and the Palatinate were bound to the French court by marriage, and almost all of the other German princes accepted subsidies at one time or another from France. It did not seem unlikely on one occasion that Louis would put himself or his son forward as candidate for Holy Roman emperor. The same method of infiltration was practiced in Italy, Portugal, and Spain, where the young king married a French princess and French ambassadors exerted so much influence in internal affairs that they succeeded in discrediting the strongest antagonist to French influence, Don Juan of Austria, the victor over the Turks at the battle of Lepanto. In addition to all of this, Louis sought to undermine the independence of the Netherlands and gave the English king Charles II a pension in order to reduce the possibility of British interference as he did so.

French influence was so great in Europe in the second half of the seventeenth century that it threatened the independent development of other nations. This was particularly true, the German historian Leopold von Ranke was to write in the nineteenth century, because it

> was supported by a preeminence in literature. Italian literature had already run its course, English literature had not yet risen to general significance, and German literature did not exist at that time. French literature, light, brilliant and animated, in strictly regulated but charming form, intelligible to everyone and yet of individual, national character was beginning to dominate Europe. . . . [It] completely corresponded to the state and helped the latter to attain its supremacy, Paris was the capital of Europe. She wielded a dominion as did no other city, over language, over custom, and particularly over the world of fashion and the ruling classes. Here was the center of the community of Europe.

The effect upon the cultural independence of other parts of Europe—and one cannot separate cultural independence from political will—was devastating. In Germany, the dependence upon French example was almost abject, and the writer Moscherosch commented bitterly about "our little Germans who trot to the French and have no heart of their own, no speech of their own; but French opinion is their opinion, French speech, food, drink, morals and deportment their speech, food drink, morals and deportment whether they are good or bad."

But this kind of dominance was bound to invite resistance on the part of others, and out of that resistance combinations and alliances were bound to take place. And this indeed happened. In Ranke's words, "The concept of the European balance of power was developed in order that the union of many other states might resist the pretensions of the 'exorbitant' court, as it was called." This is a statement worth noting. The principle of the balance of power had been practiced in Machiavelli's time in the intermittent warfare between the city states of the Italian peninsula. Now it was being deliberately invoked as a principle of European statecraft, as a safeguard against universal domination. We shall have occasion to note the evolution and elaboration of this term in the eighteenth century and in the nineteenth, when it became one of the basic principles of the European system.

Opposition to France's universal pretensions centered first upon the Dutch, who were threatened most directly in a territorial sense by the French, and their gifted ruler, William III. But for their opposition to be successful, the Dutch needed strong allies, and they did not get them until the English had severed the connection that had existed between England and France

under the later Stuarts and until Austria had modernized its administration and armed forces, contained the threat from the east, and regained the ability to play a role in the politics of central and western Europe. The Glorious Revolution of 1688 and the assumption of the English throne by the Dutch king moved England solidly into the anti-French camp. The repulse of the Turks at the gates of Vienna in 1683 marked the turning point in Austrian fortunes, and the brilliant campaigns of Eugene of Savoy in the subsequent period, which culminated in the smashing victory over the Turks at Zenta and the suppression of the Rakoczi revolt in Hungary, freed Austrian energies for collaboration in the containment of France. The last years of Louis XIV, therefore, were the years of the brilliant partnership of Henry Churchill, Duke of Marlborough, and Eugene of Savoy, a team that defeated a supposedly invulnerable French army at Blenheim in 1704, Ramillies in 1706, Oudenarde in 1708, and the bloody confrontation at Malplaquet in 1709.

These battles laid the basis for the Peace of Utrecht of 1713–1715, by which France was forced to recognize the results of the revolution in England, renounce the idea of a union of the French and Spanish thrones, surrender the Spanish Netherlands to Austria, raze the fortifications at Dunkirk, and hand important territories in America over to Great Britain. The broader significance of the settlement was that it restored an equilibrium of forces to western Europe and marked the return of Austria and the emergence of Britain as its supports. Indeed, the Peace of Utrecht was the first European treaty that specifically mentioned the balance of power. In the letters patent that accompanied Article VI of the treaty between Queen Anne and King Louis XIV, the French ruler noted that the Spanish renunciation of all rights to the throne of France was actuated by the hope of "obtaining a general Peace and securing the Tranquillity of *Europe* by a Ballance of Power," and the king of Spain acknowledged the importance of "the Maxim of securing for ever the universal Good and Quiet of Europe, by an equal Weight of Power, so that many being united in one, the Ballance of the Equality desired, might not turn to the Advantage of one, and the Danger and Hazard of the rest."

Meanwhile, in northern Europe, France's ally Sweden was forced to yield its primacy to the rising powers of Russia and Prussia. This was due in part to the drain on Swedish resources caused by its participation in France's wars against the Dutch; but essentially the decline was caused, in the first instance, by the fact that Sweden had too many rivals for the position of supremacy in the Baltic area and, in the second, by the lack of perspective and restraint that characterized the policy of Gustavus Adolphus's most gifted successor, Charles XII. Sweden's most formidable rivals were Denmark, Poland, which in 1699 acquired an ambitious and unscrupulous new king in the person of Augustus the Strong of Saxony, and Russia, ruled since 1683 by a young and vigorous leader who was to gain the name Peter the Great. In 1700, Peter and Augustus made a pact to attack and despoil Sweden and persuaded Frederick of Denmark to join them in this enterprise. The Danes and the Saxons immediately invaded Sweden and to their considerable dismay were routed and driven from the country by armies led by the eighteen-year-old ruler, Charles XII. The Danes capitulated at once, and Charles without pause threw his army across the Baltic, fell upon Russian forces that were advancing on Narva, and, although his own forces were outnumbered five to one, dispersed, captured, or killed an army of forty thousand Russians. But brilliant victories are often the foundation of greater defeats. Charles now resolved to punish Augustus and plunged into the morass of Polish politics. It was his undoing. While he strove to control an intractable situation, an undertaking that occupied him for seven years, Peter was carrying through the reforms that were to bring Russia from its oriental past into the modern world. When his army was reorganized, he began a systematic conquest of the Swedish Baltic possessions. Charles responded, not with an attempt to retake those areas, but with an invasion of Russia—and this, like other later invasions, was defeated by winter and famine and ultimately by a lost battle, that of Pultawa in 1709, which broke the power of Sweden and marked the emergence of Russia as its successor.

Sweden had another rival which was also gathering its forces in these years. This was Prussia. At the beginning of the seventeenth century, it had, as the Electorate of Brandenburg, been a mere collection of territories, mostly centered upon Berlin, but with bits and pieces on the Rhine and in East Prussia, and was rich neither in population nor resources. Its rulers, the Hohenzollerns, found it difficult to administer these lands or, in time of trouble, defend them; and during the Thirty Years War, Brandenburg was overrun with foreign armies and its population and substance depleted by famine and pestilence. Things did not begin to change until 1640, when Frederick William, the so-called Great Elector, assumed the throne. An uncompromising realist, he saw that if he was to have security in a dangerous world, he would have to create what he considered to be the sinews of independence: a centralized state with an efficient bureaucracy and a strong army. The last was the key to the whole. As he wrote in his political testament, "A ruler is treated with no consideration if he does not have troops of his own. It is these, thank God! that have made me *considerable* since the time I began to have them"—and in the course of his reign, after purging his force of unruly and incompetent elements, Frederick William rapidly built an efficient force of thirty thousand men, so efficient indeed that in 1675, during the Franco-Swedish war against the Dutch, it came to the aid of the Dutch by defeating the Swedes at Fehrbellin and subsequently driving them out of Pomerania. It was to administer this army that Frederick William laid the foundations of the

soon famous Prussian bureaucracy; it was to support it that he encouraged the growth of a native textile industry; it was with its aid that he smashed the recalcitrant provincial diets and centralized the state. And finally it was this army that, by its participation after the Great Elector's death in the wars against Louis XIV and its steadiness under fire at Ramillies and Malplaquet, induced the European powers to recognize his successor Frederick I as king of Prussia.

Under Frederick, an extravagant and thoughtless man, the new kingdom threatened to outrun its resources. But the ruler who assumed the throne in 1715, Frederick William I, resumed the work begun by the Great Elector, restored Prussia's financial stability, and completed the centralization and modernization of the state apparatus by elaborating a body of law and statute that clarified rights and responsibilities for all subjects. He nationalized the officer corps of the army, improved its dress and weapons, wrote its first handbook of field regulations, prescribing manual exercises and tactical evolutions, and rapidly increased its size. When Frederick William took the throne after the lax rule of his predecessor, there were rumors of an impending coup by his neighbors, like that attempted against Sweden in 1700. That kind of talk soon died away as the king's work proceeded, and it is easy to see why. In the course of his reign, he increased the size of his military establishment to eighty-three thousand men, a figure that made Prussia's army the fourth largest in Europe, although the state ranked only tenth from the standpoint of territory and thirteenth in population.

Before the eighteenth century was far advanced, then, the threat of French universal dominance had been defeated, a balance of power existed in western Europe, and two new powers had emerged as partners of the older established ones. It was generally recognized that in terms of power and influence, the leading states in Europe were Britain, France, Austria, Russia, and probably Prussia. The doubts on the last score were soon to be removed; and these five powers were to be the ones that dominated European and world politics until 1914.

II

Something should be said at this point about diplomacy, for it was in the seventeenth and eighteenth centuries that it assumed its modern form. The use of envoys and emissaries to convey messages from one ruler to another probably goes back to the beginning of history; there are heralds in the *Iliad* and, in the second letter to the Church of Corinth, the Apostle Paul describes himself as an ambassador. But modern diplomacy as we know it had its origins in the Italian city states of the Renaissance period, and particularly in the republic of Venice and the states of Milan and Tuscany. In the fourteenth and fifteenth centuries, Venice was a great commercial power whose prosperity depended upon shrewd calculation of risks, accurate reports upon conditions in foreign markets, and effective negotiation. Because it did so, Venice developed the first systemized diplomatic service known to history, a network of agents who pursued the interests of the republic with fidelity, with a realistic appraisal of risks, with freedom from sentimentality and illusion.

From Venice the new practice of systematic diplomacy was passed on to the states of central Italy which, because they were situated in a political arena that was characterized by incessant rivalry and coalition warfare, were always vulnerable to external threats and consequently put an even greater premium than the Venetians upon accurate information and skillful negotiation. The mainland cities soon considered diplomacy so useful that they began to establish permanent embassies abroad, a practice instituted by Milan and Mantua in the fifteenth century, while their political thinkers (like the Florentine Machiavelli) reflected upon the principles best calculated to make diplomacy effective and tried to codify rules of procedure and diplomatic immunity. This last development facilitated the transmission of the shared experience of the Italian cities to the rising nation states of the west that soon dwarfed Florence and Venice in magnitude and strength. Thus, when the great powers emerged in the seventeenth century, they already possessed a highly developed system of diplomacy based upon long experience. The employment of occasional missions to foreign courts had given way to the practice of maintaining permanent missions. While the ambassadors abroad represented their princes and communicated with them directly, their reports were studied in, and they received their instructions from, permanent, organized bureaus which were the first foreign offices. France led the way in this and was followed by most other states, and the establishment of a Foreign Ministry on the French model was one of Peter the Great's important reforms. The emergence of a single individual who was charged with the coordination of all foreign business and who represented his sovereign in the conduct of foreign affairs came a bit later, but by the beginning of the eighteenth century, the major powers all had such officials, who came to be known as foreign ministers or secretaries of state for foreign affairs.

From earliest times, an aura of intrigue, conspiracy, and disingenuousness surrounded the person of the diplomat, and we have all heard the famous quip of Sir Henry Wotton, ambassador of James I to the court of Venice, who said that an ambassador was "an honest man sent to lie abroad for the good of his country." Moralists were always worried by this unsavory reputation, which they feared was deserved, and they sought to reform it by exhortation. In the fifteenth century, Bernard du Rosier, provost and later archbishop of Toulouse, wrote a treatise in which he argued that the business of an ambassador is peace, that ambassadors must labor for the common good, and that they should

never be sent to stir up wars or internal dissensions; and in the nineteenth century, Sir Robert Peel the younger was to define diplomacy in general as "the great engine used by civilized society for the purpose of maintaining peace."

The realists always opposed this ethical emphasis. In the fifteenth century, in one of the first treatises on ambassadorial functions, Ermalao Barbaro wrote: "The first duty of an ambassador is exactly the same as that of any other servant of government: that is, to do, say, advise and think whatever may best serve the preservation and aggrandizement of his own state."

Seventeenth-century theorists were inclined to Barbaro's view. This was certainly the position of Abram de Wicquefort, who coined the definition of the diplomat as "an honorable spy," and who, in his own career, demonstrated that he did not take the adjectival qualification very seriously. A subject of Holland by birth, Wicquefort at various times in his checkered career performed diplomatic services for the courts of Brandenburg, Lüneburg, and France as well as for his own country, and he had no scruples about serving as a double agent, a practice that eventually led to his imprisonment in a Dutch jail. It was here that he wrote his treatise *L'Ambassadeur et ses fonctions*, a work that was both an amusing commentary on the political morals of the baroque age and an incisive analysis of the art and practice of diplomacy.

Wicquefort was not abashed by the peccadilloes of his colleagues, which varied from financial peculation and sins of the flesh to crimes of violence. He took the line that in a corrupt age, one could not expect that embassies would be oases of virtue. Morality was, in any case, an irrelevant consideration in diplomacy; a country could afford to be served by bad men, but not by incompetent ones. Competence began with a clear understanding on the diplomat's part of the nature of his job and a willingness to accept the fact that it had nothing to do with personal gratification or self-aggrandizement. The ambassador's principal function, Wicquefort wrote, "consisted in maintaining effective communication between the two Princes, in delivering letters that his master writes to the Prince at whose court he resides, in soliciting answers to them, ... in protecting his Master's subjects and conserving his interests." He must have the charm and cultivation that would enable him to ingratiate himself at the court to which he was accredited and the adroitness needed to ferret out information that would reveal threats to his master's interests or opportunities for advancing them. He must possess the ability to gauge the temperament and intelligence of those with whom he had to deal and to use this knowledge profitably in negotiation. "Ministers are but men and as such have their weaknesses, that is to say, their passions and interests, which the ambassador ought to know if he wishes to do honor to himself and his Master."

In pursuing this intelligence, the qualities he should

cultivate most assiduously were *prudence* and *modéra-tion.* The former Wicquefort equated with caution and reflection, and also with the gifts of silence and in-direction, the art of "making it appear that one is not interested in the things one desires the most." The diplomat who possessed prudence did not have to resort to mendacity or deceit or to *tromperies* or *artifices,* which were usually, in any case, counter-productive. *Modération* was the ability to curb one's temper and remain cool and phlegmatic in moments of tension. "Those spirits who are compounded of sulphur and saltpeter, whom the slightest spark can set afire, are easily capable of compromising affairs by their ex-citability, because it is so easy to put them in a rage or drive them to a fury, so that they don't know what they are doing." Diplomacy is a cold and rational business, in short, not to be practiced by the moralist, or the enthusiast, or the man with a low boiling point.

The same point was made in the most famous of the eighteenth-century essays on diplomacy, François de Callières's *On the Manner of Negotiating with Princes* (1716), in which persons interested in the career of diplomacy were advised to consider whether they were born with "the qualities necessary for success." These, the author wrote, included

> an observant mind, a spirit of application which refuses to be distracted by pleasures or frivolous amusements, a sound judgment which takes the measure of things, as they are, and which goes straight to its goal by the shortest and most neutral paths without wandering into useless refinements and subtleties which as a rule only succeed in repelling those with whom one is dealing.

Important also were the kind of penetration that is useful in discovering the thoughts of men, a fertility in expedients when difficulties arise, an equable humor and a patient temperament, and easy and agreeable manners. Above all, Callières observed, in a probably not unconscious echo of Wicquefort's insistence upon moderation, the diplomat must have

> sufficient control over himself to resist the longing to speak before he has really thought what he shall say. He should not endeavour to gain the reputation of being able to reply immediately and without premeditation to every proposition which is made, and he should take a special care not to fall into the error of one famous foreign ambassador of our time who so loved an argument that each time he warmed up in controversy he revealed important secrets in order to support his opinion.

In his treatment of the art of negotiation, Callières drew from a wealth of experience to which Wicquefort could not pretend, for he was one of Louis XIV's most gifted diplomats and ended his career as head of the French delegation during the negotiations at Ryswick in 1697. It is interesting, in light of the heavy reliance upon lawyers in contemporary United States diplomacy (one thinks of President Eisenhower's secretary of state and

President Reagan's national security adviser) and of the modern practice of negotiating in large gatherings, that Callières had no confidence in either of these pref-erences. The legal mind, he felt, was at once too narrow, too intent upon hair-splitting, and too contentious to be useful in a field where success, in the last analysis, was best assured by agreements that provided mutuality of advantage. As for large conferences—"vast concourses of ambassadors and envoys"—his view was that they were generally too clumsy to achieve anything very useful. Most successful conferences were the result of careful preliminary work by small groups of negotiators who hammered out the essential bases of agreement and secured approval for them from their governments before handing them over, for formal purposes, to the *omnium-gatherums* that were later celebrated in the history books.

Perhaps the most distinctive feature of Callières's treatise was the passion with which he argued that a nation's foreign relations should be conducted by persons trained for the task.

> Diplomacy is a profession by itself which deserves the same preparation and assiduity of attention that men give to other recognized professions. . . . The diplomatic genius is born, not made. But there are many qualities which may be developed with practice, and the greatest part of the necessary knowledge can only be acquired, by constant application to the subject. In this sense, diplomacy is certainly a profession itself capable of occupying a man's whole career, and those who think to embark upon a diplomatic mission as a pleasant diversion from their common task only prepare disap-pointment for themselves and disaster for the cause which they serve.

These words represented not only a personal view but an acknowledgment of the requirements of the age. The states that emerged as recognizedly great powers in the course of the seventeenth and eighteenth cen-turies were the states that had modernized their govern-mental structure, mobilized their economic and other resources in a rational manner, built up effective and disciplined military establishments, and elaborated a professional civil service that administered state busi-ness in accordance with the principles of *raison d'état.* An indispensable part of that civil service was the Foreign Office and the diplomatic corps, which had the important task of formulating the foreign policy that protected and advanced the state's vital interests and of seeing that it was carried out.

BIBLIOGRAPHICAL ESSAY

For the general state of international relations before the eighteenth century, the following are useful: Marvin R. O'Connell, *The Counter-Reformation, 1559–1610* (New York, 1974); Carl J. Friedrich, *The Age of the Baroque, 1610–1660* (New York, 1952), a brilliant volume; C. V. Wedgwood, *The Thirty Years War* (London, 1938, and later editions); Frederick L. Nussbaum, *The Triumph of Science and Reason, 1660–1685* (New York, 1953); and John B. Wolf, *The Emergence of the Great Powers, 1685–1715* (New York, 1951). On Austrian policy in the seventeenth century, see especially Max Braubach, *Prinz Eugen von Savoyen,* 5 vols. (Vienna, 1963–1965); on Prussian, Otto Hintze, *Die Hohenzollern und ihr Werk* (Berlin, 1915) and, brief but useful, Sidney B. Fay, *The Rise of Brandenburg-Prussia* (New York, 1937). A classical essay on great-power politics in the early modern period is Leopold von Ranke, *Die grossen Mächte,* which can be found in English translation in the appendix of Theodore von Laue, *Leopold Ranke: The Formative Years* (Princeton, 1950). The standard work on *raison d'état* is Friedrich Meinecke, *Die Idee der Staatsräson,* 3rd ed. (Munich, 1963), translated by Douglas Scott as *Machiavellianism* (New Haven, 1957).

On the origins and development of diplomacy, see D. P. Heatley, *Diplomacy and the Study of International Relations* (Oxford, 1919); Leon van der Essen, *La Diplomatie: Ses origines et son organisation* (Brussels, 1953); Ragnar Numelin, *Les origines de la diplomatie,* trans. from the Swedish by Jean-Louis Perret (Paris, 1943); and especially Heinrich Wildner, *Die Technik der Diplomatie: L'Art de négocier* (Vienna, 1959). Highly readable is Harold Nicolson, *Diplomacy,* 2nd ed. (London, 1950). An interesting comparative study is Adda B. Bozeman, *Politics and Culture in International History* (Princeton, 1960).

There is no modern edition of *L'ambassadeur et ses fonctions par Monsieur de Wicquefort* (Cologne, 1690); but Callières's classic of 1776 can be found: François de Callières, *On the Manner of Negotiating with Princes,* trans. A. F. Whyte (London, 1919, and later editions).

Philip II's grand design for the glory of God and empire

Robert Wernick

Every messenger reaching the King of Spain's campaign headquarters swelled the scope of the success. The entire French force was destroyed at Saint-Quentin, half of it killed or wounded, the other half taken prisoner or on the run. The king's exultant generals, including the Duke of Savoy, were all for pressing on through the hundred undefended miles to Paris and wiping the French monarchy, a hereditary enemy, off the map. Philip II, whose official nickname was Prudentissimus, was not so sure. Great things were possible, he wrote to his father that evening, but characteristically he added *"si no falta dinero"* (provided the money holds out).

Of course it did not hold out, as it never seemed to when he needed it most. Philip was the richest man in the world. Every year his fleets brought him immense cargoes of silver and gold from the conquered kingdoms of the New World. But this was the 16th century; nobody had quite invented central banks or paper money. All that bright bullion pouring ashore in Cádiz seemed to ooze and trickle away between there and the battlefield. Master of half the world, Philip was at that moment short on cash and credit. Who was going to pay for the fodder for the hundreds of horses that would be needed to drag his guns over the wretched roads from Saint-Quentin to Paris?

So the battle, though it brought enormous prestige to the Spanish Army and led to a peace that lopped off a few towns from the kingdom of France, had no profound influence on European history. But it did lead to the creation of one of the great European monuments.

The battle was fought on the feast day of Saint Lawrence, August 10, 1557; during the fighting Philip's artillery set fire to the church of Saint Lawrence in Saint-Quentin. Being an extremely devout monarch, he felt a debt to this saint, martyred during the Roman persecutions by being roasted alive on a gridiron. Philip ascribed his victory at Saint-Quentin to the intercession of this saint, and ordered that his bones be rescued from the burning church. He then resolved to dedicate what would become the greatest building project of his reign to Saint Lawrence.

A place for grandeur and solitude

The site was chosen with great care, near the little mining village of El Escorial (Escorial has a lilting sound but means slag heap) close to the geographic center of Spain. It was high enough in the foothills of the Sierra de Guadarrama to have cool clean air in summer, as well as a splendid view stretching 30 miles across the dry, dusty Castilian plain to Philip's new capital city of Madrid. The mountains were full of wild pigs and deer for Philip to hunt, and good, hard, pyrite-flecked granite to be quarried nearby. It was a place for grandeur and solitude, a place where Philip could govern his empire and commune with his God. The building was called San Lorenzo de El Escorial and it was meant to stand alone on the mountainside, free from the ordinary distractions of courts and cities —the bustling summer resort that now sprawls at its feet was the product of a later, laxer century.

1. THE AGE OF POWER

The king had two architects of genius, Juan Bautista de Toledo and Juan de Herrera. From beginning to end, though, Philip watched over and approved every step of El Escorial's design and construction: the ground plan—a gridiron, perhaps to recall the instrument of Saint Lawrence's torture—as well as the unornamented, monumental style of its buildings.

Philip's plan began with one of the dying wishes of his father, Charles V, the Holy Roman Emperor: a suitably somber and majestic crypt in which, from his death onward, all the kings of Spain might be buried. Above the crypt Philip wanted a church. Around the church, in a great rectangle, he wanted a royal palace, a monastery, a library, a hospital and a center of learning. It was an immense undertaking, with 6-foot-thick walls, 9 towers, 88 fountains, 2,618 windows and 14 interior courtyards. The church in its center was really a private chapel for the king and his family, high officials of the court and resident monks of the order of Saint Jerome, but Philip wanted it to have a dome resembling that of St. Peter's in Rome.

The workers were well organized, well disciplined and well paid. Diego Suarez, one of the great adventurers of that age of adventure, writing his memoirs as an old man, recalled *el buen plato*, the good food that was served. No gambling or swearing was permitted on the construction site. The architects and engineers used laborsaving machinery like two-wheeled cranes and ingenious building methods such as working the stone at the quarry and transporting it direct to its proper place. The job was completed by 1584, in the incredibly short time of 21 years, and the result was hailed as the eighth wonder of the world.

Posterity would not be kind to the king or to his creation. For reasons of state and religion he did some dreadful things, but he did not seem to enjoy doing them. Many historians of the past 400 years, especially those writing in English, have had an anti-Spanish or anti-Catholic bias, and they have done their best to turn this most Spanish and Catholic of monarchs into some kind of monster. He was regularly portrayed as a pitiless, bigoted persecutor, who loved to see heretics writhing in the fire. They have painted him as the murderer of his own son (the Don Carlos characterized as a tragic hero in Schiller's play and Verdi's opera), who in real life was a homicidal maniac and whose death, though mysterious, is no longer generally attributed to Philip. With justice he has been blamed for the execution of the noble Flemish patriots Count Egmont and Count Horn, and made responsible for the assassination of William of Orange; but he has been questionably described as the would-be murderer of Queen Elizabeth I of England, and of his third wife, Elizabeth of Valois, whom he loved dearly and who actually died in childbirth. (He was, as a matter of fact, a devoted family man, tender and courteous to all his wives, even the temperamental frump Mary Tudor, Queen of England and Ireland from 1553-58 and still known as Bloody Mary.) He has also been viewed as a dull, plodding, bloodless bureaucrat who sat spiderlike in a dark cell weaving evil plots, who squandered the riches of Spain on grandiose projects like the "Invincible Armada" and the palace of the Escorial, leaving his country impoverished, depopulated, doomed to decay.

El Escorial's own reputation has hardly fared better. Art critics have often found it bare and sterile. In the middle of the 19th century a sprightly Argentine exile reported smugly that not 20 visitors a week came to this "barbarous and somber" pile, which Philip had constructed with the "sweat of Spain and the booty of war . . . so that two hundred friars could sing a *miserere* over freedom of thought, which he had assassinated." Baedeker, the guidebook from which generations of earnest 19th- and 20th-century tourists learned the proper opinions about the art of Europe, condemned the Escorial for "lacking the divine spark. . . . Philip II had the misfortune of belonging to an epoch which shone neither for creative force nor for taste."

Today we are not quite so censorious of 16th-century people for behaving in 16th-century ways. Thousands of visitors tramp through the Escorial every week, except those parts of it that still function as monastery and institution of higher learning. Tourists need feel no shame about admiring what is now recognized universally as a unique architectural masterpiece. They also—thanks to an ongoing exhibition opened in 1984 by Spain's Patrimonio Nacional to celebrate the 400th anniversary of the building's completion—can learn about the techniques of its construction, admire its treasures and gain some insight into the complex mind of its builder.

You can follow Philip II's life by looking at the portraits done of him, from the elegant Renaissance prince of 24 who posed for Titian in 1551, to the hollow-cheeked old man of the last years, dressed in somber black. None of the portraits reveals very much about his inner feelings, for Philip had been taught by Charles V to trust no one, and he became a master at keeping his thoughts and his plans secret. He was not an extrovert or daring combatant like his father. But he was enormously conscientious, doggedly faithful to his country and his church, and did his backbreaking duty as king for 42 years without a word of complaint.

Critics tend to overlook the sheer scale of the job thrust upon him when he was still in his 20s. He was lord and master of what today would be called a superpower. There were two superpowers in the 16th century—Turkey in the East, Spain in the West. Like his contemporary, Süleyman the Magnificent, Philip was responsible for running a huge multinational empire. His titles take up line after line on official documents: King of Castile, of Aragon, of Portugal, of the Indies (that is, most of Central and South America), of Jerusalem, of the Two Sicilies, Duke of Milan, Duke of Burgundy, Count of Flanders, Count of Holland—the list goes on and on. Just getting the news of what was happening in all these places took a maddening length of time, a minimum of two weeks from Brussels or Naples, six months from the Philippines, which in 1542 had been named for the 15-year-old heir to the throne by the Spanish explorer López de Villalobos. Every year he had to worry about the possibility of famine, plague, a Turkish invasion. He had to worry about Protestant rebellion in the Netherlands, Moorish rebellion in the south of Spain, Algerian pirates in the Mediterranean, English pirates in the Atlantic. He had to worry about his uncle Ferdinand I, the new Holy Roman Emperor, who had succeeded Charles V but was soft on heresy. He had to worry about religion and religious wars.

In an age when some rulers changed religion as easily as they did their coats, he was stubbornly faithful to the Roman Catholic Church. But what could he do about his slippery sister-in-law Elizabeth of England? She was a heretic, which was bad, but if he got rid of her, the throne would go to Mary Stuart, a good Catholic but married to a Frenchman, which was worse. When the cantankerous old Pope Paul IV called him a "putrid member" and "that little beast" and tried to take Naples away from him, what could he do but send an army against Rome?

He had to worry about the Indians in his new American domains. It had been decided that they had souls, but how best could they be saved? How could he support the monastic orders he sent there to convert them? He always had to worry about money. Three times the mighty King of Spain had to declare himself bankrupt.

No wonder he took his time about making decisions. Time and I can take on any other two, he liked to say. Historians have made fun of him for procrastinating his way past opportunities like that given him by the victory at Saint-Quentin. But he had his spectacular successes too, like the Battle of Lepanto in 1571, in which a Spanish fleet, with those of Venice and the Papal States, under his bastard brother Don John of Austria, destroyed the Turkish navy. It took considerable talent just to hold all his scattered dominions together during 42 years of war and crisis. When he died, in 1598, he left his son Philip III more territory than any other man has reigned over before or since.

In his quiet way he understood that such immense domains could not be ruled by the sword, as his father had tried to do by riding with his armies back and forth across Europe and even crossing to North Africa to besiege Tunis. He worked out for himself the way the modern state would have to be run—by paper. Every day, whatever other ceremonials required his royal presence—dances, bullfights, autos-da-fé—he spent hours reading state papers, recommendations by his council, reports from his spies, petitions from his subjects. They came to him on folio sheets with very wide margins, which he filled with scrawled notes, observations, corrections, suggestions and commands. As king he felt duty-bound to be interested in everything. He tells his ambassador in Rome to tell the Pope to mind his own business. He specifies the amount of lace to be worn on the court costumes of counts and barons. He warns the Duke of Medina Sidonia, commander of the Invincible Armada, that the English ships will unchivalrously fire cannonballs at him instead of closing in to fight it out with cold steel (but unfortunately he does not tell the Duke what to do about it). He approves the export of some Andalusian horses. He devises a detailed scenario for handling the Baron Montigny, a Flemish rebel convicted of high treason: garrote him in his prison cell, announce that he has died of fever, give him a handsome burial with 700 royal masses for the repose of his soul. (This is the Philip that history loves to hate.) He corrects his secretaries' errors of geography and spelling.

It was too much for any one man to do, but he did it anyway. He preferred doing it in the Escorial because, far away from the distractions of Madrid, he could get through four times as much paperwork in a day. It was a place mainly for work and prayer.

If it was the king's workplace, he regarded it as belonging first to God and second to Philip, and he made sure God got the lion's share of everything. Rising dramatically from the mountainside, the palace might have been expected to have its main facade facing the plain, to overawe visitors riding up from Madrid. Philip would have none of that; the church had to be oriented in the traditional way so the priest at the altar faced east, toward Bethlehem and Calvary. If that meant cramping the main entrance by putting it in the west wall facing the mountains, that was what had to be done. The church, built in the form of a Greek cross and surmounted by an immense cupola and dome, is central to the complex. The king's quarters are in an outthrust of the church on the east side.

Like the builders of the Italian Renaissance, Philip and his architects were seeking the classical harmonies of ancient Greek and Roman temples. The biggest courtyard in the Escorial, the one leading up to the church, measures 210 feet by 126 feet, the measurements given by the Roman architect Vitruvius as ideal for a space of this sort. The builders were going back beyond Vitruvius, however. They were heirs to a mystical tradition holding that the Universe is built on number and proportion. In the ceiling of the library is a painting showing ancient sages, Pythagoreans and naked gymnosophists of India constructing *anima*, the human soul, out of numbers.

Introducing these ideas to Spain was a revolutionary step. Traditionally, Spaniards—much of whose country had been occupied by the Moors for 700 years—covered their buildings with extravagant Moorish-style ornament. But here in the dry heartland of Castile,

1. THE AGE OF POWER

Philip was speaking for another Spain—austere, proud, dignified, devout. He wanted a building stripped to geometric essentials. Long before Mies van der Rohe, he had decided that less could be more. The Escorial is all cubes, spheres and pyramids—cubes symbolizing the solidity of the Earth; spheres symbolizing the perfection of heaven; pyramids, in the form of lines rising and converging to an invisible point, forming a connection between the two.

The south facade is a long, bare rectangle with 286 windows in regular rows. A window pattern on this scale is almost bound to be boring, even in the Versailles of Philip's great-grandson Louis XIV, even in the Seagram Building. But Juan de Herrera, with his subtle spacing of the rows of windows and the cornice overhanging the second row, the arcades upholding the terrace at the foot of the wall, the reflecting pool, conveys a sense of movement. The eye of the beholder is carried along as by a slow, formal Spanish dance.

The bareness of Escorial's facade was an exact reflection of the king's personal style. His bedroom and study, just off to the right of the high altar, are brick-floored and as austere as possible, with a door opening into the church, which itself is all aflame with marble, jasper, bronze and gold. The retable behind the altar was meant to be the most magnificent in the world, soaring 86 feet, with paintings in swirling dramatic colors by artists of the Italian Mannerist school.

There was no contradiction in Philip's mind between austerity and magnificence. In the palace, the throne he sat on was deliberately bare and simple, a campstool that his father had taken around on his campaigns. But the long hall leading to the throne room was lined with elaborate, specially commissioned paintings of some of his own most important battles.

Philip was a connoisseur of painting. When the monks of the Escorial sat down to supper in their refectory, Titian's *Last Supper* looked down on them from the wall. Philip was a patron of Titian's, as had been his father, and the king corresponded with the painter regularly and bought a number of paintings.

Philip's art collection, some of it inherited, was remarkably catholic. Next to Titian, he loved the often erotic, mystical fancies and sour human observation of Hieronymus Bosch. And when he wanted a picture and couldn't get it, he sometimes had it copied, meticulously and full size, and shipped to the Escorial. Whenever a collection was put on sale in Europe, his agents were there. He commissioned two El Grecos and collected a number of Northern Renaissance masters, among them Bosch, Hans Baldung Grien and Quentin Metsys. Even after being plundered by Napoleon, and after more than 150 of its paintings were carted off to the Prado in Madrid, the Escorial remains one of the world's great museums.

The salubrious air of the Escorial has done wonders for the works of art, which over the years have not had to suffer from the ailments common in polluted urban centers. Some of the palace rooms have been redone in elegant 18th-century style to please Bourbon kings who found Philip's structure too grim to suit them. These rooms contain their own treasures, including a superb series of tapestries created in the late 18th century illustrating daily life in Spain and woven from cartoons by the young Goya.

In the great vaulted hall of the library, with its frescoes by Pellegrino Tibaldi, the same air has kept the leaves of the books crisp and easy to turn for the past 400 years. It is probably the only library in the world today where books are put on shelves with their spines against the wall (common practice in the 16th century), so that clean mountain air can seep more easily between the gilded pages. When Philip assembled it, it was the greatest library in Europe, with some 4,000 volumes of his own and 5,000 more that he had gathered from monasteries and palaces around Spain. Many of its collections, including medieval Arabic and Hebrew manuscripts, are unique, so to this day scholars have kept coming. It also contains a large number of works that were condemned by the Inquisition. Had Philip not saved them, they might have disappeared entirely.

He has often been described as a prince of darkness, but the Escorial shows how much he loved light. Two rows of windows flood the library with sunshine in early morning and early evening, the best hours for study. Clear windows in the giant cupola light every corner of the church. The 14 interior courtyards, of varying proportions and sizes, make sure that every room in the palace, college or monastery receives its fair share. The sun was a physical blessing. The king insisted that the monks get the southern part of the building so they would be a bit warmer in winter.

Proclaiming the one true faith

The Escorial was a spiritual symbol of the faith he was sworn to uphold, the one that the Council of Trent had proclaimed to be the one true faith, *quod semper, quod ubique, quod ab omnibus* (because it was believed in forever and everywhere and by all men). It was also an ideal place from which to rule over half the world strictly according to the rules. It was hardly Philip's fault that they were changing. By the 16th century, the one true faith was no longer believed *ab omnibus*. It had been replaced by, in Philip's view, the detestable Protestant formula *Cujus regio ejus religio* (Each state to the religion of its ruler). And, though no one realized it at the time, the day of the 16th-century superpowers (sometimes known as the Age of Kings) was over. Spain and Turkey might continue to dazzle the world for another century or so but they had neither the manpower, nor the resources, nor the tough mercantile mentality needed to maintain themselves as great powers in the modern world. The Mediterranean, which was the center of their vital interests and had been the center of the civilized world for many centuries, was being turned into a backwater.

The struggle for the future control of the globe had moved north and west to troublesome countries that Philip did not understand. He had learned to hate the English climate in the three years when, by his marriage to Mary Tudor, he had been titular King of England. He hated the beefy, beer-guzzling nobles of Germany and the Netherlands who expected him to join in their swinish revels. He hated sending his men to fight a never-ending war against the Dutch in a gloomy land where, as one of his soldiers wrote, "there grows neither thyme, nor lavender, figs, olives, melons, or almonds . . . where dishes are prepared, strange to relate, with butter from cows instead of oil." Some historians have argued that the empire might have been easier to control if Philip had moved his capital to Lisbon or to Brussels where he and future monarchs would have been closer to the sea routes of the Atlantic. But he was never tempted.

Were he to come back to life today, he would not be pleased by most of 20th-century culture, but he would be happy that monks are still meditating and chanting in the Escorial, and that the college he founded is still in operation—its most distinguished graduate today is Juan Carlos, King of Spain, Philip's descendant in the 14th generation.

Philip was active, still filling the margins of his state papers, still hunting, into his 71st year. When his gouty leg swelled up to become useless and infection began to attack his arms, he said, "Since I must go to the Escorial anyway to fill my tomb, I might as well go there to die." He had himself carried on a litter, seven miserable, jolting days from Madrid.

A king's death was a public event in those days, like his birth and marriage, and for Philip it was only one more official ceremony to be gone through. His sufferings went on for 14 weeks and they were atrocious, his limbs rotting away, the doctors not daring to treat them or bandage them because of the pain, the smell so bad that courtiers found any excuse to stay away. He bore it without murmur, keeping open the little door to the church so he could hear the monks chanting for the salvation of his soul.

CONFLICT IN CONTINUITY

in so many words...
LANGUAGE & SOCIETY
1500-1900

IN 17th-CENTURY FRANCE

Service to the Crown might bring hereditary office and a title for the upwardly mobile of Louis XIV's France, but not acceptance by the traditional 'aristocracy of the sword'. Close scrutiny reveals attempts to incorporate a new breed of noble into an essentially static society.

Roger Mettam

Roger Mettam is senior lecturer in history at Queen Mary College, London, and author of the forthcoming *Images of Power: Social and Political Propaganda in Louis XIV's France* for George Philip.

DURING THE REIGN OF LOUIS XIII the definition of social groups was the principal preoccupation of French high society, and of the pamphleteers, jurists and theorists who put their services at its disposal. These often passionate debates were prompted by two long-term trends within the kingdom. First there were the attempts by the Crown to encroach upon some of the aristocratic and clerical privileges which hampered its tasks of protecting the realm, maintaining order and giving good justice, financing the government and increasing certain kinds of economic activity. Secondly there was the problem of incorporating a new and influential group, the bureaucracy (whose senior members claimed to be noble), into the traditional hierarchy of social categories.

Noblesse d'épée; the comte de Toulouse in the dress of a novice in the Order of the Holy Spirit.

In the early 1600s, the simplest and most generally accepted way of classifying French society was by recourse to the tripartite medieval division into Estates – the First Estate of the clergy, the Second of the nobility, and the Third which contained everyone else. The alternative term – the three 'orders' – was also frequently used but with no additional subtlety of meaning. The Estates-general, in which the representatives of all three orders came together at the behest of the king, met infrequently, and not at all between 1614 and 1789. At those gatherings, the petitions and the grievances of the nobility and the Third Estate had reflected provincial concerns. Those orders had acquired no national sense of purpose, any more than the varied and disparate French provinces felt themselves to be part of a single nation. Only the clergy continued to meet centrally in their *assemblées générales*, and even there the peripheral parts of the kingdom were

First published in *History Today*, February 1987, pp. 30-35. Reproduced by kind permission of History Today, Ltd., 83-84 Berwick Street, London W1V 3PJ England.

not represented. In contrast the provincial Estates still assembled regularly in some areas of France, including the large and important provinces of Brittany, Burgundy, Languedoc and Provence. In most of those gatherings, the three Estates participated on equal terms, although in Languedoc the meetings were constituted in the manner ultimately to be adopted for the Estates-general in 1789, namely that the Third was doubly represented and therefore was equal to the combined voting strength of the nobility and clergy.

As social categories, each Estate contained a wide variety of people. The First encompassed the regular orders of monks; the bishops, who were usually drawn from leading French aristocratic houses; and the lowly parish priests, who were often of similar background to their humble parishioners. At meetings of Estates or assemblies, the First was represented only by the higher clergy. The Second comprised all members of the *noblesse d'épée*, the sword-bearing nobles whose titles could be traced back, often over many centuries, to some outstanding act of service to the Crown, normally in the field of military valour. Here too there was a wide disparity between the great princely and ducal lines and the humble provincial noble. Nevertheless membership of these first two Estates carried considerable privileges for everyone, not least the exemption from most direct taxation. The ambitious bureaucratic nobility, so bitterly resented by the sword aristocracy, had no place in the Second Estate at the provincial or general Estates. Its only position in the traditional hierarchy was, to its fury, among the motley members of the Third.

The term *tiers état*, the Third Estate, had a variety of meanings, according to the context in which it was being used. In its largest sense, it included all laymen of non-noble status. At meetings of the provincial Estates its members were exclusively from the bourgeois élite, usually the mayors of certain towns who had themselves been elected by a narrow upper stratum of the citizenry. The term '*bourgeois*' was equally ambiguous. It might be used, according to the circumstances, as a description of all urban dwellers, or only the more substantial townsmen, or of an even narrower élite which had been granted the specific privileges of '*bourgeoisie*' – notably the right of exemption from certain taxes. The Parisian bourgeois, in this most restricted sense of the word, claimed as a privilege that when they were involved in litigation, no matter where the dispute had arisen, the case could be heard only by the courts of the capital city which alone had the power of jurisdiction over them, a piece of arrogance which was not accepted by proud provincial tribunals. To the citizen who had acquired the superior status of being bourgeois, the appellation was one of which he could be proud. Yet when the duc de Saint-Simon described Colbert, the minister of Louis XIV, as the son of a bourgeois, which was incidentally untrue as the Duke well knew, he intended it to be a vile insult.

These imprecise terms presented few problems for the men of the time, because their exact meaning was usually explained by the context in which they were employed. That did not prevent numerous squabbles among the members of each Estate, and between Estates, about the criteria of social status and the exact order of precedence to be adopted on private and public occasions. The king was undeniably at the head of the pyramid, but the exact configuration of those below was less certain. Cardinals and papal nuncios claimed a controversial degree of supremacy, as on occasion did illegitimate members of the present and the previous royal dynasty. There were also the 'foreign princes', who were French nobles but came from families which had once been, or sometimes still were in other parts of Europe, sovereign ruling houses. They acknowledged the supremacy of the French Crown but expected the non-royal nobles of the kingdom to defer to them. Within the native aristocracy there were conflicting theories about the gradation of the nobility, each family selecting that most suited to its own situation. The duc de Saint-Simon, who as a *duc et pair* was on the highest rung of the French aristocratic ladder, stressed rank rather than antiquity because his family had risen rapidly in relatively recent times. Others, perhaps only counts rather than dukes, but with a direct line of succession stretching back at least to 1400 – the date which conferred undoubted respectability on a noble house – preferred to claim that length of lineage was a more important yardstick of aristocratic worth than the current titles held by the family. Nevertheless they all agreed that the nobility was a military élite in origin, and that this remained its principal function in the kingdom. Service in the bureaucracy could not be a qualification for ennoblement.

Many of these disputed claims between and within the Estates led to prolonged lawsuits, and it was not uncommon for processions and ceremonies to be delayed or disrupted because the participants – clerical, noble, judicial and municipal – could not agree on the order in which they should speak in a debate, sit in an assembly or enter a building. Sometimes doorways had to be widened, rooms rearranged or new entrances constructed so that certain groups did not have to give way to others. On one occasion a corps of judges took clandestine steps during the hours of darkness and, when morning came and a procession was due to enter the chamber, the provincial nobles not only found that the judges were sitting in the places they claimed for themselves, but were locked in behind a newly constructed iron grille so that they could not be dislodged from their self-appointed position of precedence in the 'best seats'. It was accepted that a royal judge or an elected mayor was given added status by his office, which elevated him above his social position as an individual, but the extent of his rise up the hierarchy was a matter of contention both among rival office-holders and those whose families were of higher standing in society. Some historians have ridiculed these disputes, especially those among courtiers for apparently trivial courtesies in the elaborate etiquette of the court, but that is both unimaginative and anachronistic. These battles for ceremonial precedence were the outward manifestation of very real and deep rivalries, between individuals, families and institutions, about their social status and their administrative powers.

If such altercations were frequent and fervent, as well as having a long pedigree in preceding centuries, they

A prince of the church; the Cardinal de Bouillon (portrait by Rigaud).

their first office with money acquired through participation in commerce and industry, bourgeois pursuits which were forbidden by law to the nobility on pain of permanent loss of rank. Whereas the true noble was 'of the sword', carrying the weapon which symbolised his military origins and virtues, these new men were *noblesse de la robe*, their elevation dependent on the robes of their office. Thus they clearly worked for their living, which further disqualified them from any aura of nobility., The members of the *robe* had always tried to avoid this kind of criticism by adapting their lifestyle, so that it was more aristocratic. They abandoned commerce and purchased landed estates instead, built lavish town and country houses and in every way portrayed themselves as *'vivant noblement'* – living nobly. The sword nobles were not convinced by this propaganda.

The *noblesse de robe* was not slow to defend itself against the socially superior claims of the sword nobles, and the literary war raged – sometimes in short and pithy tracts but also in monumental histories of French institutions and society, compiled by partisan jurists who proclaimed their objectivity while subtly advancing the cause of either *robe* or *épée*. The upper levels of the bureaucracy, especially the judges of the *parlement* of Paris, which was the senior court of appeal in the kingdom, asserted not only that they were full members of the nobility but that they were high up in the noble hierarchy. The *parlement*, annoyed that its judges were not regarded as part of the Second Estate, went even further by insisting that it was superior to the entire Estates-general because it was traditionally the mediator between the king and all his subjects, whatever their rank. The *parlementaires* further denounced the usurpation of their legitimate functions by the ecclesiastical courts and rejected the right of the Holy See to interfere in the internal affairs of France. The *noblesse de robe* therefore castigated the existing First and Second Estates, and disdained to be included in the Third.

These fierce disputes about noble status did not prevent robe and sword from working together on matters of common interest, especially in the

were as nothing when compared with the problem posed by the new bureaucratic nobility, the *noblesse de robe*. These men had been accorded the titles and privileges of nobles by the Crown as a reward for service in the administration, a criterion for ennoblement which the military aristocracy could not accept. There had always been newcomers into the ranks of the sword, some of them acceptable because of their valour in battle, others not so but nevertheless irresistible because they were royal ministers or favourites. That was very different from the inclusion among the nobility of a large and totally unqualified group of office-holders. Even more offensive was that fact that, as the bureaucrats purchased their offices and now had the right to pass them on to their relatives, their whole family was claiming hereditary membership of the nobility. The old aristocracy was quick to denounce

these men as parvenus and bourgeois, however prestigious the offices they held. The only source of *noblesse* was military prowess, on one or many occasions, which led to the granting of an initial title by the monarch. After that the whole family observed the traditional aristocratic ethic of pursuing honour and glory, so that cumulative virtue was passed down the generations and was often rewarded with further hereditary grants of noble rank. The true aristocrat therefore had immense obligations to his Estate, and it was accepted that a noble who committed a base act should be punished more severely than a commoner guilty of the same offence, because *'noblesse oblige'*, and to know virtue and reject it was outrageous.

The bureaucratic nobles lacked military valour, antiquity of lineage and an appreciation of both honour and virtue. They had often purchased defence of social or provincial privileges against the encroachments of the central government. Fraternisation was also possible, and in Paris it was accepted that the *présidents* of the *parlement* were men of immense prestige and status, if by virtue of their office rather than their birth, and could properly be invited by the greatest aristocratic families to convivial occasions. As the judges were often highly intelligent, it was also appropriate to ask them to the *conversazioni*, on political, social and cultural issues, which were held in the salons of eminent noble hostesses. Yet, in a society where men entertained their equals and inferiors but never visited people of lower rank, it was extremely rare for a *parlementaire* to be host to a sword noble.

The threat to the nobility from the Crown and from Richelieu was of a different kind. The royal government knew that nobles were essential in the army, where they provided the entire officer corps, and in the maintenance of order throughout the kingdom – although at times of crisis they might foment revolt and behave treacherously. Richelieu made no attempt to undermine most of their cherished privileges, like the exemption of all nobles from most direct taxation. Many of these would have been as precious to the robe as to the sword, because the bureaucratic élite was undoubtedly noble in law, whatever older families might say. The minister

'The noble is the spider, the peasant the fly'; this Lagnier cartoon emphasises that noble power and riches were based on the sweat of the peasant's brow in Louis XIV's France.

Civic piety; the consuls of Narbonne, beneath their coats of arms and dressed in municipal robes (panel painting of 1600).

therefore chose to attack one aristocratic right which was positively disliked by the judges of the robe, the freedom of the noble to carry the sword and to decide causes of honour by means of the duel. The Crown maintained, and the judges willingly agreed, that only the royal courts could arbitrate in disputes between subjects, however highly born they might be. The edict forbidding duelling which Louis XIII issued in 1626 was neither the first nor the last royal pronouncement on this subject because the practice simply could not be eradicated, but each edict provoked a vigorous argument between the adherents of the monarchical and the aristocratic ideology.

In all the debates about the nature of nobility or the position of the Crown in the political and social hierarchy, the partisans did not try to define the precise middle ground between their opposing positions. Thus on duelling the noble camp stressed the paramountcy of honour and the royalists emphasised the total supremacy of the king. Neither side actually spelled out exactly what would happen when the monarch commanded a noble to act in a manner which he thought to be dishonourable. They contented themselves instead with uncompromising statements of their fundamental principles. This particular argument reached the literary heights when the tragedy of *Le Cid* by Corneille was added to the propaganda. The great tragedian was reasonably cautious in his defence of noble honour, but the champions of aristocracy declared that the play was a more overt justification of their position than it in fact was. Richelieu certainly regarded it as very anti-monarchical in tone, and it was with his support that Desmarets de Saint-Sorlin quickly countered with his own play *Roxane*, in order to present the royalist case to the theatre audiences of Paris.

There was one other important school of thinkers which joined in the controversy about nobility, and its members, who included Pascal, Nicole, La Mothe Le Vayer and the duc de La Rochefoucauld, came to more cynical conclusions. They denied that nobles, whether *robe* or *épée*, had any inheritance of accumulated virtue. The aristocracy was composed of ordinary human beings and, although a social hierarchy was a useful fiction for keeping the poor in order, intelligent men should recognise that this was a piece of political expediency and not the honouring of an intrinsically worthy élite. These writers do at least refer to the poorer elements of society, if in an unflattering way, and that is remarkable because most social theorists did not even consider them. The poor do sometimes appear in administrative documents, where they might be designated by their specific occupation if that were relevant to the context; or by blanket terms – the peasants, *'la lie du peuple'*, literally the dregs of the nation; or, if they had been seditious, as riff-raff, rabble, *'canaille'*. Only the Christian thinkers, like St Vincent de Paul and St François de Sales, really addressed the problem of poverty, and considered those so afflicted as souls in their own right.

Molière's plays keenly satirised social ambitions and manners in 17th-century France; contemporary illustration of a scene from 'Les Amants Magnifiques'.

In the years after Louis XIV took personal control of the government, on the death of Cardinal Mazarin in 1661, the fierce arguments about the new and old nobility died away. *Robe* and *épée* learned to live together, and had discovered some brief community of interest during the civil wars of the Frondes in 1648-53. Yet the main reason for the diffusion of these tensions was that Louis XIV was determined to discourage social mobility. Earlier in the century, favoured men had been elevated to high social rank, even if in small numbers, and this had caused great offence to those who were overtaken by them and to those who found such parvenus joining their own stratum. This would now

cease, both to avoid further provocation and because the rapid advancement of some individuals made others equally ambitious. Louis therefore ensured that favours were distributed evenhandedly among all meritorious candidates, but that no one should ever be given a post for which he was socially unsuited. Rapid mobility ceased, and a favoured bishop like Bossuet remained in the diocese of Meaux because he lacked the degree of nobility which was essential for one of the great archiepiscopal sees.

Only the small circle of royal ministers received more rewards than their social origins would have justified, and here too Louis refused to allow the excessive upward movement of previous reigns. Moreover these close advisers were very much at the mercy of the king and, if they fell from favour, their families would lose much of the prestige associated with ministerial power. A truly aristocratic house had its own prestige, acquired through careful planning of marriages and acquisition of offices over many generations. It hoped that the king would honour it further, but even if it was out of favour no monarch could take away its illustrious name and status. Louis knew that it was better to play off the powerful nobles against each other, rather than to rely on some and ignore others.

Although much was written about the dangers of rapid social mobility, it was always relatively rare in the seventeenth century. The passionate condemnations by noble writers of *mésalliances* – marriages between impoverished *épée* and wealthy *robe* houses – suggest that the practice was widespread, whereas it was always an uncommon occurence and became even less common under Louis XIV. No matter how empty the royal treas-

(Below) Honour at the stake; a duel between le chevalier de Guise and le baron de Luz, 1613.

ury, the king could always find money to save a sword family from the degradation of marrying into the bureaucracy. Most marriages were between spouses of remarkably similar backgrounds, their families seeking to consolidate their position within their own stratum rather than trying to enter a higher one. Each house hoped to have one or more patrons in the levels above, and clients in those beneath, but although these numerous and rival *clientèles* stretched across the social strata, this did not mean that many individuals drastically changed their own position in society. Slow and gentle advance was possible, especially as a reward for long service or increased expertise, but the French noble, judicial or municipal family was as much concerned to prevent rivals from rising as it was to improve its own fortunes.

On balance a static society was safer for everyone. That did not prevent some exceptionally wealthy bourgeois from building grand town houses and playing at being noble, but such display did not gain them entry into polite society. Much of the comedy in the plays of Molière rests on the stupidity of men who play a social role for which their background does not fit them. They always suffer humiliation because, as the playwright regularly points out, the upper levels of society are more clever, though not necessarily more pleasant, than those below.

Wealth was not a criterion in the delineation of social categories, although it was clearly useful to men of all ranks. The rich bourgeois could not buy himself into high society, but he could purchase an office and begin to climb up the bureaucracy towards ultimate membership of the *robe*. In the world of the sword nobility, it was generally agreed that the great aristocrats lived more lavishly than those lower down the ladder, and of course the king was the most splendid of all. This was symbolic display, and both monarch and aristocracy were quick to rebuke a lower noble whose ostentation was excessive for his rank. In contrast, when a family lacked the resources to sustain the appropriate style of living, it did indeed have to withdraw from society in Paris or in the important provincial centres and live quietly on its country estates, but it did not lose the lustre of its titles and offices. Its soirées and salons had ceased but its prestige remained. As Antoine L'Oisel had said earlier in the century, 'poverty is not a vice and does not disennoble'.

The First and Second Estates contained men of very different financial resources, from the extremely rich to the severely poor. Even in the *robe*, where money was essential for the purchase of ennobling offices, there were families of widely varying fortunes. Among the bourgeois, the municipal administrative élites were the most prestigious but were not always the wealthiest. There was no group in seventeenth-century social theory which was defined in terms of its financial resources.

In the final decade of the century, some new ideas began to be voiced, although they were not welcomed by most members of the privileged orders. Hereditary aristocratic rights were questioned, especially exemption from direct taxation, and it was suggested that all subjects should pay taxes according to their wealth. Birth still retained some importance, but merit should be the sole reason for advancement, for aristocrats as for everyone else. The pursuit of wealth by the bourgeoisie was to be praised, not despised, and hard work was to be lauded. Idleness, whether aristocratic or monastic, was a vice. Military prowess and the search for honour, so dear to the nobility, were responsible for the proliferation of wars and of widespread human misery. Luxury was an evil, and the poor deserved genuine help and consideration. If these novel arguments were fiercely rejected by most of high society, they could not be eradicated totally; but their subsequent history belongs to the next age, the Age of Enlightenment.

FOR FURTHER READING:
The arguments about nobility and social status in the first half of the seventeenth century are well summarised in Davis Bitton, *The French Nobility in Crisis, 1560-1640* (Stanford University Press, 1969). For the reign of Louis XIV, the best survey of social attitudes is contained in the more widely-ranging book of Antoine Adam, *Grandeur and Illusion: French Literature and Society, 1600-1715* (Weidenfeld and Nicolson, 1972). These two works are chiefly concerned with the opinions of writers – jurists, pamphleteers, playwrights and poets – but occasionally the nobles and other social groups voiced their own views. One such instance is described by J. Michael Hayden, *France and the Estates General of 1614* (Cambridge University Press, 1974). Lastly, the life-style and priorities of this aristocratic age are vividly revealed in Norbert Elias, *The Court Society* (Blackwell, 1983).

LOUIS XIV AND THE HUGUENOTS

Roger Mettam

HISTORIANS HAVE DEVOTED MUCH attention to the decision of Louis XIV, in 1685, to revoke the Edict of Nantes and thereby deny the French Protestants – the Huguenots – any role in his kingdom. The original Edict had been issued in 1598 by his grandfather, Henri IV, and was undoubtedly an uneasy compromise, designed to end the so-called 'wars of religion' which had divided Frenchmen since 1560. It insisted that the Roman religion was the true faith of the country, but it allowed the presence of Protestants, permitting them to become royal officials and to retain certain places of surety which they had the right to defend militarily. The Edict was therefore a recognition that none of the political and religious groups who had fought in the civil wars could achieve a total victory, and that an accommodation was vital. Yet to the moderate Catholics and to the extreme papalists, it went too far in its tolerance of these heretics, while to the Huguenots it was less than they had expected from a King who until recently had been the leader of their cause. Henri IV had been compelled to convert to Catholicism in order to secure his throne, but his Catholic subjects suspected his sincerity and the Protestants regarded his change of heart as a betrayal.

Further battles with the Huguenot minority dominated the subsequent reign of Louis XIII until, after the siege and fall of the last Protestant stronghold at La Rochelle, another agreement was reached in the 1629 *Grâce* of Alais, which severely restricted the access of Huguenots to offices and removed their right to garrison places of surety. Since that date, they largely ceased to be a problem for the French government. They played a conspicuous part in commercial and industrial life, showed no signs of disloyalty during the civil strife of the Frondes in 1648-53, and their only crime was therefore to be an heretical sect in the Catholic dominions of the Most Christian King, as the French monarchs always styled themselves.

Heterodoxy was always unwelcome in any monarchy where the power of the ruler rested partly on a religious basis, but the adherents of the RPR, the *religion prétendue réformée*, as it was generally known at the time, gave Louis XIV no reason to feel that he was harbouring an actively seditious group within his realm. If it was their mere existence which was offensive to this Catholic sovereign, then it might be expected that he would have taken action against them as soon as he took over the reins of power on the death of Mazarin in

1661. Yet nearly twenty years were to elapse before severe pressure was exerted upon the Huguenots to abjure their faith.

In his *mémoires* for 1661, Louis XIV listed the problems facing the crown on his assumption of personal power, and he devoted some time to the religious issues which concerned him. The Jansenists and the defiant Cardinal de Retz, with his militant supporters among the parish clergy of Paris, were all designated as dangerous elements in society, but the Huguenots were not even mentioned in this context. Later on in his text he does refer to them, and hopes that in the long term this heresy can be eliminated. Yet Louis stresses that this must be achieved by gentle persuasion and that the rights previously granted to this minority must be respected. It seems, therefore, that the decision to revoke the Edict of Nantes and force the Huguenots into submission was taken, not at the beginning of the personal rule, but at a much later date.

Historians have selected a number of villains on whom to blame this outrageous act of persecution, for that is the emotive language they have employed. To Protestant scholars, especially in England and the Netherlands, it bore the worst hallmarks of Catholic absolutism, but some French

First published in *History Today*, May 1985, pp. 15-21. Reproduced by kind permission of History Today, Ltd., 83-84 Berwick Street, London W1V 3PJ England.

writers have regarded it with little more favour. It caused the exodus from France of foreigners who had worked hard to boost French economic life, the exile of many Frenchmen who had been similarly industrious, and the loss of men with great military expertise, both in fighting and in the manufacture of new weaponry, most of whom now placed their talents at the disposal of enemy rulers. Worst of all, it did not solve the Protestant problem within the kingdom because, despite fierce and socially divisive persecution, stubborn enclaves of Huguenots remained in the frontier provinces until long after the death of Louis XIV in 1715, while many of those who had converted awaited their revenge.

Some chroniclers of these dramatic events have placed the principal responsibility upon the King himself. The Edict of Fontainebleau of 1685, which revoked the Nantes agreement, was based on the premise that, as the recent policy of conversion had been overwhelmingly successful, there was no further need for an edict of toleration because there were no Protestants remaining. Surely, it has been argued, the King did not really believe that. If he did not, then the revocation was clearly designed to countenance persecution. Yet kings are always at the mercy of their advisers, and perhaps it is they who should be blamed, either for misleading their sovereign or for being themselves misled about the number of converts. Madame de Maintenon, that most pious of royal mistresses, has also been suspected of influencing the King, as have his confessor and the other Jesuits. Some writers have singled out the war minister, Louvois, suggesting that he was reluctant to disband the army which he had assembled with such difficulty for the recent Dutch War of 1672-9 and saw a policy of forced conversion as a way of employing the troops in peacetime. Many have noted that the revocation came two years after the death of Colbert – the minister who had most valued the Protestants, both French and foreign, for their contribution to his plans for economic revival and expansion. Or was it a gesture by Louis XIV to appease the Pope, who had been increasingly irritated by the aggressively gallican approach of the King to his relations with the Holy

See, and might be somewhat mollified by a crusade against heresy?

Whatever the calculated risks of initiating the persecution of the Huguenots, there were a number of consequences which could not have been foreseen in 1685, even though historians have added them to the charges against Louis XIV when they have considered the revocation and its aftermath. First of all, Europe seemed peaceful. The Dutch War of 1672-9, in which the French had been forced to fight the Holy Roman Emperor, the King of Spain and many powerful German princes, when they had hoped to confront only the tiny Dutch Republic, had been far from successful for Louis XIV. Yet the following years had been more peaceful, and in 1684 the Truce of Ratisbon was signed by France, Spain and the Empire, which committed them to a further peace for twenty years. The French were therefore reassured that the Emperor had no aggressive designs against them, and would concentrate on the Turkish threat to his imperial lands. Another cause for celebration was the accession of a Catholic King, James II, to the throne of England, with no indication that he would be forced to vacate it a mere three years later. The next great European conflict, the Nine Years War of 1688-97, was not even thought to be likely. Also, the possible exodus of many Protestant Frenchmen was not envisaged, because the royal ministers were confident that their newly fortified frontiers were as capable of keeping citizens within France as they were adequate for preventing unwelcome enemeies from violating her territorial sovereignty.

Historical chance apart, the government was nevertheless guilty of complacency in its foreign policy during the 1680s. Louis had always protested the legitimacy of his diplomatic claims and his military adventures, but other powers had not been convinced. They saw him as an aggressive seeker after glory and new conquests, who was prepared to use the most brutal tactics in order to achieve his purposes. The French therefore grossly underestimated the desire of many other rulers to humiliate their nation. Similarly the Pope, far from praising the King of France for his resolute assault on heresy, regarded the revocation of the Edict of Nantes

as yet one more arrogant act by a sovereign who had been violating the rights and liberties of the Church for many years. Indeed this one action did more than any other to harm the reputation of Louis XIV in his own country and in many parts of Europe. It is obviously vital for historians to discover why such a repressive decision was taken and who was responsible for it.

* * *

If the Huguenots had been hardworking and docile subjects since 1629, the memory of their earlier misdeeds was still vivid. This was an age when much attention was paid to the history of France, and in particular to the reign of Henri IV and his success in ending the 'wars of religion'. In fact religion had been only one element in the sixteenth-century civil wars, although warring aristocratic factions and provincial separatists had adopted sectarian labels when they were politically convenient. The most enduring memories of Huguenot participation in those turbulent decades were that some of them had contemplated the dismemberment of the kingdom, hoping to establish a Protestant state in the southern and western provinces where they had been dominant; that they had also allied with foreign enemies of the crown; and that they had formulated political theories which were unashamedly revolutionary. To moderate Catholic Frenchmen, there was little to choose between the Protestants and the ultrapapists, for both groups seemed to owe their prime allegiance to an international system which appeared to threaten the government of France.

After the Massacre of St Bartholomew in 1572, Protestant writers had elaborated ideas of a social contract between king and people which could be revoked if the sovereign behaved in a tyrannical manner, in this case his persecution of religious creeds. Some even advocated tyrannicide, and further offended by insisting that society and government were purely civil creations, by and for the people, and that there was no divine basis for such political arrangements. Political theory was being secularised, even if it was to safeguard the liberties of religious minorities. In fact these ideas, some of which were also adopted by the ultra-papist opponents of Henri III and Henri IV, ceased to be voiced so militantly in the early seventeenth century. Yet the ministers of Louis XIII still regarded the Huguenots as potential republicans and tyrannicides, who denied the divine nature of kingship. Although many Protestant merchants and town councillors were more moderate and wanted to live in peace with their king, confirmed in their religious freedom by the Edict of Nantes, the more militant among them again negotiated with foreign powers in the 1620s and aroused royal doubts about their loyalty. Also there were still influential nobles associating with the Protestant rebels for more secular motives, as was demonstrated by the speed with which they defected to the royalist side when sufficiently persuasive bribes, financial or social, were offered to them. As much of Europe was already deeply involved in the Thirty Years War, and it was only a matter of time before France would have to take an active part in this conflict, Richelieu was keen to crush internal rebellion and stop treacherous negotiations with countries which would be certain enemies once hostilities commenced.

When the Huguenot insurrection was finally suppressed and the *Grâce* of 1629 was signed, Richelieu did not take steps to prevent the practice of the Protestant religion. He was prepared to tolerate many Huguenots because they were clearly invaluable for his own schemes of economic reorganisation and colonial expansion. It was only their free access to administrative office and their right to have places of surety which could no longer be allowed. Nevertheless a few of them did attain positions of high favour, including Hervart, who became one of the two intendants of the finances under Mazarin, and Turenne, who was an outstanding military commander during the reign of Louis XIV. In foreign policy Richelieu did not regard religion as an intrusive consideration, and he, like François I a century earlier, sought allies for purely strategic reasons. Where François had allied with the German Protestant princes and even with the Turk, Richelieu now cheerfully enlisted the aid of the Lutheran Swedish King, Gustav II Adolf.

The government policy of excluding Protestants from most administrative positions was supported by many other influential groups in France which were always hostile to heterodoxy. The judges of the Paris *parlement*, the senior law court in the realm, were as hostile to Protestantism as they were to any attempts by Rome to assert papal authority within the kingdom. Although the gallicanism of the *parlementaires* was prompted by different concerns – largely jurisdictional – from those of the King, they were staunchly Catholic moderates and wanted nothing to do with heresy. So the settlement of 1629 pleased many people, because it ensured that Huguenots could never be administratively dominant in the provincial cities.

At La Rochelle, as in many other towns, a Catholic municipal magistrature was imposed by Richelieu upon a merchant population, many of whose principal and richest members were Huguenots. This did not necessarily cause tension, because the mercantile and civic élites were not rivals on the same ladder of social advancement. The former dominated the economy, the latter the administration. Even in the 1660s, when foreign Protestants were enticed into France by Colbert, and were encouraged to establish much needed industries with the protection of royal monopolies and grants of privileges, the native middle class was seldom inflamed, for it had often shown itself to be uninterested in establishing innovative manufactures. Colbert was irritated by the amount of French trade which was shipped by the Protestant Dutch, instead of by the French mercantile marine which he was always trying to expand, but this problem could be solved by giving incentives to indigenous shipbuilders and merchants, by exclusive tariffs and ultimately by war in 1672. It did not require the persecution of the Huguenots and their foreign co-religionaries who had now become domiciled in France. In the 1660s their loyalty was to France, not to fellow Protestants abroad, and Colbert had the highest opinion of their worth.

It was in the later 1670s that the mood began to change, and when the Peace of Nijmegen ended the Dutch War in 1679 some Huguenots were already apprehensive about their future in the kingdom of Louis XIV although they had done nothing during the war to arouse suspicions of their disloyalty or of their sympathy for the Dutch cause. Some had complained that the international conflict was disrupting their trade, but Catholic merchants and provincial officials had also been outspoken on this same point. At first, much of the initiative for putting pressure on the Huguenots seems to have come spontaneously from certain provincial centres, although the Paris government seized this opportunity to reassert its views on the desirability of converting the RPR because it now saw that there was considerable support in some areas for this policy. Yet violent methods were still to be excluded.

The rising tension between the two faiths in some French towns was largely caused by the gentle proselytising tactics which the crown and its agents had been using for many years, the subtle approach which Louis XIV had advocated in his *mémoires* for 1661. Financial incentives featured prominently among these methods of persuasion, whether in the form of bribes offered to individuals or more general grants of fiscal relief to those who converted. The King and his ministers put direct pressure on leading courtiers, while in the provinces bishops, intendants and royal agents either carried out the wishes of the King or even anticipated them, in which case the monarch was quick to laud their efforts. Nevertheless these plans for conversion were implemented to varying degrees in different parts of the kingdom, depending on the enthusiasm of the bishops and intendants, and on whether the two faiths were coexisting amicably or were already at odds. Some towns were predominantly of one religion, others more evenly divided between the two, and whatever the ratio there was often no tension. Moreover some intendants exaggerated the number of converts because they knew that such information would please the King, and that the central government would not be able to verify their statistics. In 1679 it was reported that 3,000 had abjured during the last two years in Languedoc, and that 25,000 *écus* had been spent there since 1676 in order to encourage them to do so.

Many of those who were prepared to go through the motions of conversion continued to practice their former faith in secret. Yet it was not only members of the RPR who benefited from the financial concessions made to converts. A number of less than scrupulous Catholics also profited, because they declared first that they had always really been Huguenots and then that they were now converting to the true faith, thus qualifying for the rewards paid to 'nouveaux convertis'. Also, some of those responsible for examining the would-be abjurers were less strict than others in the tests of orthodoxy which they demanded. However false or genuine these conversions, they were extremely offensive to the average Catholic, who had been a loyal son of the church, but who was being offered no fiscal concessions. It was these former heretics who were now being rewarded for their apostasy.

As the decade neared its end, the crown, either of its own volition or on the advice of its provincial agents, began to make life more difficult for the Protestants. The provisions of the 1598 Edict were still upheld, but anything not specifically included in it could now become a target for repressive governmental decrees. As the Edict had been designed to solve certain problems, there were many aspects of daily life which it simply ignored. Many of these were now regulated, and in such a way that the Huguenots could be greatly harrassed and inconvenienced if Catholic officials in the localities chose to do so. Yet these irritations were as nothing beside the next stage in this policy of repression, the *dragonnades*, the billetting of dragoons on recalcitrant Huguenots. It was this decision which really caused alarm among the French Protestants and anger among their co-religionaries in other countries. Because it involved the army, it is this increase in brutality which historians have frequently attributed to the war minister, Louvois, and his father, Le Tellier.

The attitude to religion of Louvois was governed primarily by political considerations. Some Huguenots were dangerous, others were harmless, and a third group was positively useful. In the first category Louvois included all those involved in local disturbances, whether as instigators

or as victims, because he had a deep detestation of internal disorder. Also the presence of Huguenots in frontier provinces was very worrying, because they might ally with a neighbouring Protestant enemy in time of war. These peripheral areas of the kingdom were always troublesome and separatist, but heterodoxy made them more unreliable, and the minister accordingly instructed local officials to use all means, gentle and fierce, to eliminate it. Yet he positively welcomed the role of the Huguenots in industry, and especially in the manufacture of armaments. On the death of Colbert in 1683, Louvois was actually made the minister responsible for all such economic activities. There were also many members of the RPR in the enlarged army which Louvois and his father, had created, and which they did not want to see reduced too greatly after the 1679 Peace. About one-tenth of serving Frenchmen were Protestant, as were some of the crack troops of foreign origin, notably the splendid Swiss. Nor had Louvois any reason to doubt their loyalty and willingness to serve the King of France. He was therefore determined that these men should not fall prey to the growing desire of Louis XIV that his realm be purged of heresy.

HUGUENOT GLOSSARY

DEACONS – Calvinist deacons were laymen who organised poor relief, not (as in the Anglican Church) men in training for the ministry.
DRAGONNADES – the selective billeting of dragoons on Protestant households in order to achieve conversion, begun in 1681. Billeting involved paying soldiers' wages as well as accommodating them, and was commonly accompanied by threats and violence.
THE EDICT OF NANTES – was a 'perpetual and irrevocable' grant of recognition, protection and limited toleration to the Huguenots. It was revoked by the Edict of Fontainebleau of 1685.
JANSENISTS – were advocates of a strictly moral and austere form of Catholicism, and were consequently fierce enemies of the casuistical Jesuits. Also, Richelieu and Louis XIV wrongly suspected them of planning wider political subversion.
MAISONS DE CHARITÉ – refugee relief establishments in Soho and Spitalfields, places where food and other necessities were distributed.
THE MASSACRE OF ST BARTHOLOMEW – of August 1572, in which some 13,000 Huguenots were slain, was blamed on the King himself, and he was regarded thereafter by the Protestants as a tyrant.
UNITED PROVINCES – the northern provinces of the Netherlands, successful in winning independence from Spanish control in the sixteenth century, which became the Dutch Republic.
WALLOON – French-related language used in the southern provinces of the Netherlands, in the area now Belgium and the Franco-Belgian frontier region.

The war minister knew that he must make a serious attempt to reduce the number of Protestants in the army, in order to please his royal master, but he intended to do so by conversion rather than expulsion. Financial incentives were duly offered, and many soldiers did convert. As in civil society, a number of Catholics changed their religion twice in order to benefit from the scheme. Many of those abjuring their heresy were so blatantly insincere that priests began to refuse them entry to the Catholic communion, and Louvois was forced to write to the bishops, demanding that they instruct their clergy to receive anyone who wished to convert without pressing them too hard. His main purpose was to keep them in the army, asking very few questions about their convictions.

Far from wanting the *dragonnades* as a justification for the retention of a large peacetime army, Louvois had plenty of other tasks for his troops to carry out. Some particularly disorderly regiments had been disbanded at the end of the war, but considerable forces were needed to carry out the policy of *réunions*, by which Louis XIV hoped to 're-unite' with his kingdom certain neighbouring territories to which he claimed a frequently dubious legal right. Many soldiers were also working on the massive engineering projects associated with the embellishment of Versailles, especially the extensive river diversions to provide a constant water source for this garden of delights. The idea of *dragonnades* did not come from Louvois but from a provincial intendant, Marillac, in 1681, and the King welcomed it. The war minister undoubtedly provided the troops, but he continually exhorted the military administrators to ensure that the dragoons strictly observed all the rules of proper behaviour. He had been compelled to abandon his preference for gentle persuasion and acquiesce in a policy of forced conversion, but he was not prepared to condone brutality. Needless to say, the reservations of the minister were disregarded in some areas, and many hapless Huguenots experienced considerable savagery at the hands of troops who always had the reputation for lawlessness, against Protestants and Catholics alike.

Some Huguenots and foreign

1. THE AGE OF POWER

Protestants began to depart in 1680, and the exodus gathered in speed and volume until the revocation of the Edict, and beyond into 1686 and 1687. Louvois was appalled at the inability of the frontier guards to prevent their departure. He protected those foreigners who did remain, and in 1686 persuaded Louis to grant permission for Protestant merchants from other countries to trade freely within France. Regrettably few were inclined to do so, and even fewer Frenchmen responded to the invitation of the minister to return home. At least Louvois was able to prevail upon the King to exempt regiments of foreign origin, like the Swiss, from his new religious uniformity.

If some 300,000 Protestants fled from France, twice that number remained there. Most of these converted to Catholicism, but their sincerity could not be guaranteed and ministers were always worried lest they should rise up against their monarchical oppressor. In the difficult mountainous areas of the South, these fears became a reality on a number of occasions before the death of Louis XIV in 1715. Moreover, if the revocation of 1685 was actively supported by many bishops, judges, priests, nobles, town councillors and ordinary Catholic subjects, it was condemned by many others, some of whom were extremely lucid and vocal. It was not that they included numerous Protestant sympathisers, but they either deplored forced conversions on the grounds that they did not really save souls, or they lamented the departure of so many useful citizens from the kingdom. Among these critics were some senior and respected bishops, who not only protested loudly but refused to implement the policy of repression with any fervour in their own dioceses. Some of them said that it would have been better to reform the abuses in their own church before seeking to gain converts to it. Military commanders, provincial governors, courtiers and officials were all represented in these critical ranks, and many of these also failed to take the repressive measures which were required of them. In addition, pamphlets from Huguenots in exile were successfully smuggled into France, castigating Louis XIV in ever

more violent terms. Indeed some of these tracts were written within the kingdom itself, but with a false title-page which claimed a foreign place of origin in order to mislead the French police authorities.

A few of the Catholic critics within France blamed Louvois, but more popular targets were the Jesuits, Madame de Maintenon and certain high churchmen, in particular the Archbishop of Paris. Yet a number of them clearly implied, and a few openly stated, that the King himself had made a major error of judgment. This was an extraordinary assertion. The usual way of criticising the government was to praise the monarch and blame the ministers either for misadvising him or for acting without his knowledge. Very often the advisers were genuinely thought to be the culprits, for the sovereign was held in great awe. Now he was beginning to be personally blamed for a tyrannical act towards loyal and industrious subjects, and from then on the criticism would mount. Soon he would be censured for his wider religious policy, his aggressive diplomacy, his belligerence in war and his mistakes in the internal government of France.

Truly the revocation of the Edict of Nantes was a turning-point in the reputation of Louis XIV in France and Europe, and from that moment he would seem to have been less and less in control of events. Within ten years of 1685, his armies would be dangerously on the defensive, he would have submitted to the authority of Rome, and his kingdom would be both impoverished and disgruntled. Although not all his later problems can be blamed directly on the revocation, that act undoubtedly contributed greatly to the fervour with which his enemies flung themselves upon him in the wars ahead, increasing his difficulties still further.

Meanwhile, other countries benefited in many ways from the skills of the Huguenots, both practical and artistic. Yet they were not always popular with the societies they joined, because some were considered too successful and others became a burden upon their new homelands. An anonymous Englishman, writing in 1715, who had encountered them in England and in France, commented

on this state of affairs with some distaste. He noted that some had readily betrayed their faith in order to remain in their native land, while others showed an equally hypocritical zeal for their beliefs which thus ensured them a warm welcome in England. Once there, some of them acquired a degree of prosperity which had eluded them in France, and the English traders suffered in consequence. This contemporary observation underlines the fact that the *émigrés* were a varied group with regard to personal wealth. Many were prosperous merchants and craftsmen who easily transferred their operations to another land with which they often had economic links already. Others had been less successful in the French commercial and industrial world, but hoped to improve their position in a new location. Some were poorer because much of their wealth had been in land and it was difficult to turn this into capital which could then be transported abroad. Accordingly the landed Huguenots fled in smaller numbers, because many felt that they had no choice but to remain on their estates and disguise their faith.

As we reflect on the events of 1685 in this tercentenary year, it is certainly difficult to excuse Louis XIV for his policy of persecution. Yet the Huguenots were not all the guileless innocents which their propagandists would have us believed. Many abjured their faith and stayed at home, but some saw that there was an opportunity to advance themselves in Protestant countries which could not refuse to receive and protect them. Thus, among many of those who stayed in France or left for other lands, it was the business acumen for which they have always been renowned which governed their religious allegiance.

FOR FURTHER READING:

J.H.M. Salmon, *Society in Crisis: France in the Sixteenth Century* (Methuen, 1974); Mark Greengrass, *France in the Age of Henri IV: the Struggle for Stability* (Longman, 1984); David Parker, *The Making of French Absolutism* (Edward Arnold, 1983), and *La Rochelle and the French Monarchy: Conflict and Order in Seventeenth-Century France* (Royal Historical Society, 1980); H.G. Judge, 'Church and State under Louis XIV', *History* (October, 1960); Jean Orcibal, 'Louis XIV and the Edict of Nantes', in Ragnhild Hatton (ed.) *Louis XIV and Absolutism* (Macmillan, 1976).

THE 17th- CENTURY 'RENAISSANCE' IN RUSSIA

Lindsey A. J. Hughes

Russian culture underwent a series of changes in the seventeenth century that some historians have described as a delayed 'Renaissance' that preceded the dramatic Westernisation of his country by Peter the Great. Echoes of Western art and culture had, of course, reached Russia long since: for example, elements of classical antiquity inherited from Byzantium; a style akin to Romanesque to be found in the architecture of the twelfth century; and the late fifteenth- and early sixteenth-century Kremlin cathedrals and palaces built by Italians. But a number of factors, not least the 250-year long Mongol occupation and adherence to the Orthodox faith, had served to isolate Russia from the mainstreams of European culture. The result was that at the beginning of the seventeenth century Muscovy not only lagged behind the West in intellectual and scientific matters, but also had a more limited repertoire of art forms, most of which were harnessed to the service of the Church. This is not to underrate the achievements of Old Russian craftsmen, who made objects of great beauty, nor to overlook the indigenous folk tradition in wooden architecture and applied art, but merely to point to a state of affairs that increasingly conflicted with Russia's efforts to learn much needed military and technical skills from the West.

Changes in Russian art began not so much with the overt importation of Western devices as with the fossilisation of traditional forms. One senses this most clearly in the numerous mid-seventeenth-century churches, built after the centuries-old pattern of a cube capped by one or five domes, but with the builder's imagination lavished on the exterior decoration of carved brickwork, limestone and ceramics. Byzantine forms were frequently retained as mere tokens, as, for example, in domes of solid brick, rising from the roof with no connection to the interior. But now domestic and ecclesiastical buildings began to receive an increasingly uniform treatment, their facades divided into storeys by window surrounds, cornices and half-columns of Western-inspired design. In the 1680s a style by the name of Moscow or 'Naryshkin' Baroque appeared. Alongside conventional Orthodox church designs, symmetrically planned and decorated in Western style, there appeared novel centrally-planned churches composed of one or more towers of receding octagons. The decorative features of Moscow Baroque, including carved and stepped gables, 'strap-work' ornamentation, ornate window surrounds, portals and columns based on the Classical orders, have been traced to such diverse sources as the Ukraine, Byelorussia, Poland, the Low Countries, Germany and Italy.

In religious painting one observes, alongside a tendency towards intricate decorativeness and complex compositions, a more realistic approach to the depiction of the human face and body, nature and architecture. New genres appeared, including portraiture from live models, secular murals and canvasses for interior decoration, and precise engraving for architectural and other purposes. Parallel developments are found in literature, with the growing popularity of secular tales and the beginnings of poetry and drama. If one also takes into account an increase in the importation and translation of foreign secular books and the establishment of Russia's first seat of higher learning, the Moscow Academy, in 1687, it is not hard to see how the term 'Renaissance' might have some limited application to this period of Russia's cultural history, even in the absence of any clear awareness of the rediscovery of antiquity.

These and other developments can be attributed to a number of events and circumstances which served simultaneously to bring Muscovy closer to the West and to weaken old traditions and prejudices. The curtain raiser to the century, the Time of Troubles, which concluded with the election of Mikhail Romanov as Tsar in 1613, and had seen the country invaded by Poles and Swedes, underlined Russia's military backwardness. In the words of S. F. Platonov: 'The Time of Troubles showed the need for close contact with the West and the need for armies equipped and trained on Western lines.' Military needs were to set the tone of 'borrowing' for the century. In the classic formula of S. M. Soloviev, 'the new had to appear in the guise of directly useful objects . . . with craftsmanship'; but Russians could scarcely avoid the less tangible aspects of Western life, 'like children tricked into learning by toys'.

A further step along the path to secularisation was marked by the mid-century schism in the Russian Orthodox Church, when many of the faithful – the Old Believers – were alienated by Patriarch Nikon's reforms of Church texts and ritual, instituted in 1653 and aimed at restoring it to the original Byzantine model. In addition to weakening the Church's internal unity, the preparation of the reforms and the subsequent schism obliged the authorities to use the services of theologians, translators and teachers from the clergy of Muscovy's better educated Orthodox neighbours, notably the Ukraine and Byelorussia. Fear of the 'Latin and Lutheran' West also confirmed the Church in its efforts to improve its educational standards.

A third significant event was the annexation of the previously Polish ruled Left-Bank Ukraine to Muscovy in 1654, Kiev itself being temporarily secured in 1667 and in perpetuity from 1686. Political and religious contacts with this and other polonised regions formed an important element in seventeenth-century Westernisation.

"The 17th Century 'Renaissance' in Russia," by Lindsey A.J. Hughes, *History Today*, February 1980, pp. 41-45. Reprinted by permission of the author.

1. THE AGE OF POWER

It is against this general background, in a century which also saw intensified diplomatic ties with most Western states, that one notes a steady flow of foreign personnel into Muscovy, amongst them merchants, who had visited the country since the arrival of the English in 1553 and had established permanent colonies and warehouses in a number of towns. Some of them served the tsars as special agents, travelling abroad to recruit mercenaries and craftsmen, while others were licensed to set up manufactures, such as the Dutchman Andrew Vinius's Tula ironworks (1632), Johann van Sveden's Moscow paper mills (1660s), which employed 'the best masters of paper making from the German lands', and the textile mills set up by Paullson and Tabert in the 1680s. In 1687 another Dutchman, Daniel Hartmann, was granted special trading rights because since 1655 he had brought to Russia 'many fine wares, medicines and many kinds of weapon for infantry and cavalry at lower prices than ever before'. There was a growing demand for 'fine wares' of Western origin in court circles. Palaces and mansions, previously sparsely furnished, were adorned with furniture, mirrors, clocks, painted fabrics, portraits and prints of foreign origin or inspiration.

Increasingly the demand for such goods was met not only by importers but by foreign craftsmen on the spot. In 1679 Jacob Reutenfels, an envoy from Tuscany, remarked on the rising standards of Muscovite workmanship, which were achieved 'thanks to their dealings with foreigners, which become freer with every day'. But Frenchman Foy de la Neuville, visiting Moscow in 1689, remarked: 'Without the Germans, who are in Moscow in great numbers, they would be able to do nothing.'

One group of foreign experts whose skills were in great demand were architects, although the government's practical orientation meant that it was fortifications experts and civil engineers rather than exponents of palace and church building whose services were sought. This policy of employing foreign architects began with Tsar Mikhail summoning foreigners to reconstruct city walls and fortifications in the 1620s and continued to the end of the century when Peter I engaged engineers from Brandenburg to fortify Azov in 1696. Some foreigners were employed on less mundane projects. For example, in 1624-25, the Englishman Christopher Galloway built the fanciful upper section of the Kremlin Spassky tower and installed a clock, much to the delight of the royal family. At about the same time one John Taller or Taylor, presumed to have been an Englishman, carried out restoration work on some of the Kremlin churches, and in 1660-62 the Swedish 'engineer' Gustav Dekentin provided interior designs for a royal dining hall 'in the new foreign manner'. The first stone bridge over the Moskva River, built in about 1687, has been attributed to a 'Polish monk' and a handful of other buildings may tentatively be attributed to foreign authorship, but in general it appears that until Peter I's reign the overall design and construction of buildings remained in the hands of native masters. This is confirmed by the hybrid design of most seventeenth-century Russian buildings that, even when highly

Westernised in decoration, can rarely be traced directly to foreign prototypes.

Large numbers of craftsmen came to Russia from the Polish-Lithuanian borderlands, especially during the Russo-Polish Wars of 1654-67. In 1672 a special district of Moscow - the *meshchanskaya sloboda* - was allocated to these mainly Byelorussian foreigners and housed a number of petty traders and craftsmen. The most influential group was initially employed on two of Patriarch Nikon's grandiose buildings schemes - the Iversky Monastery on Lake Valdai and the Monastery of the Resurrection at New Jerusalem, begun in 1654 and 1656 respectively. The latter was intended as a symbol of both Nikon's own prestige and the power of the Orthodox Church, both soon to be undermined by the patriarch's personal downfall and the schism. In 1666 seventeen Byelorussian craftsmen, including six carpenters and five tile-makers, were transferred from New Jerusalem to the royal workshop in Moscow. These two bands of craftsmen, together with other fellow-countrymen, brought new artistic devices to Muscovy, the former specialising in a distinctive form of high relief Baroque carving, the latter in glazed ceramic that had been employed at New Jerusalem in the construction of Baroque window surrounds, portals and iconostases. In 1681 the woodcarver Klim Mikhailov became head of the 'carving and joinery' section of the Tsar's main workshop, the Armoury. In 1667-68 he and other Byelorussians prepared decorative carving for the new wooden royal palace at Kolomenskoe and later produced a number of wooden iconostases, or icon stands, of which at least one survives, dated 1683-85, in the main cathedral of the Novodevichy Convent. It is possible that the architectural components of icon stands - carved and twisted columns, profiled cornices - influenced the carved stone decoration of Moscow Baroque.

By the middle of the century the Moscow Armoury comprised a complex of workshops producing not only small arms but also a wide range of useful and decorative objects for the royal household. It has been described as a seventeenth-century Russian 'Academy of Arts'. Amongst its finest products were icons, many of them painted in the new manner. The best known painter of the Armoury school was Simon Ushakov (1626-86), whose works departed from old stylised conventions in their naturalistic treatment of the human face, use of light, shade and, to a lesser degree, perspective and realistic depiction of nature and objects. The main features of Ushakov's style can be seen in his 'Old Testament Trinity' (1671). Alongside icon painters, the Armoury employed secular artists, who worked on the interior decoration of palaces, portraits, engravings, banners, etc. In 1687-88 there were twenty-seven icon painters and forty secular artists. Some, like Ushakov who was also an accomplished engraver and portrait painter, worked in both genres. There are records of a number of foreign artists employed in the Tsar's service, including the Dutchman Hans Dieters, who arrived in 1642, and his fellow-countryman Daniel Wuchters who, in a petition of 1667, described his skills as 'the art of painting portraits and biblical themes in life size . . . and diplomatic pictures on canvas'. In 1670, Peter Engels, a 'master of perspective' from Hamburg, came to

Moscow and was hired for court projects. It is to these and other foreign artists, most of whom took pupils, that we may attribute the new interest in portrait painting in court circles, a genre hitherto frowned upon, if not specifically banned, by the Church. Those seventeenth-century personages who had their portraits painted or engraved included Tsars Aleksei (1645-76) and Fedor (1676-82), Tsarevna Sophia, regent from 1682-89, ministers of foreign affairs A. S. Matveev and Prince Vasily Golitsyn and Patriarchs Nikon and Joachim.

Apart from the tutelage of foreign artists, it is possible to trace new devices in art and architecture to foreign graphic material. One well-attested source is the illustrated *Piscator* Bible in its 1650 and 1674 Amsterdam editions, copies of which were owned by Armoury employees. Modified copies of its late Renaissance engravings are found in a number of seventeenth-century church frescoes. Foreign prints and broadsheets were brought into Muscovy by merchants and sold in the streets of Moscow and other towns. The Church authorities were highly suspicious of such prints and in 1674 Patriarch Joachim tried to ban their sale, complaining that merchants 'buy paper prints of German origin and sell these prints which are made by the German heretics, Lutherans and Calvinists, according to their own damned persuasion, crudely and wrongly'.

The first published translation of a Western architectural manual – Vignola's *Rules of the Five Orders of Architecture* – appeared only in 1709, but Muscovite libraries acquired a number of works on architecture and allied subjects. In 1637, for example, the Cannonmakers' Chancellery, which employed foreigners, sent several architectural works to the royal library. The collections of Tsar Aleksei, Tsar Feodor and Patriarch Nikon contained several titles on architecture, atlases and illustrated descriptions of foreign states and cities. Both the Armoury and the Pharmacy owned foreign books, but the most impressive repository was the Ambassadorial Chancellery, which amassed a large collection for the use of its staff. Sixteen works in French, Italian and German on architecture, carving, landscape gardening and fountains were acquired from the exiled director of the Chancellery, A. S. Matveev, in 1677, whilst further titles on palace and civic architecture were added in 1682-83. The Chancellery had its own workshops for the production of charters and manuscripts and its own architectural team.

Another source of influence was the Moscow Foreign or 'German' Colony which, apart from housing a number of hired men and their families from the Protestant states of Europe, also provided an interesting example of European town-planning. Founded in 1652, the colony was indicative of the growing numbers of foreign personnel, who hitherto had resided in the heart of the city, and of continuing attempts to isolate their 'harmful' influence. Bernard Tanner, who visited Moscow with a Polish delegation in 1678, reported that the inhabitants 'kept everything as neat and orderly as in German towns, quite unlike the Muscovite practice. They have built many houses, which are made with economy and skill'. By the late 1680s, when it was described by the Jesuit Georgius David, the colony appeared 'more handsome than other districts . . . It contains many fine stone mansions which the German and Dutch merchants have lately built as their residences.' By the time Hendrik de Witt made his engraving at the beginning of the eighteenth century, many of the buildings were of stone and included some of the most imposing palaces in Moscow, like the one built for Peter I's favourite, Franz Lefort, in 1697-98. There were Protestant churches in the colony, including those of the 'old' and 'new' Lutheran communities built in 1684 and 1694-95 respectively. There was no question, however, of Muscovites being introduced to Catholic Baroque through the colony as Catholics were not granted permission to erect a church until the very end of the century; nor, indeed, was the direct borrowing of non-Orthodox ecclesiastical designs to be expected. The official view was that the churches of 'heretics' were 'vile'. 'It is not seemly that either stone or wooden Latin or Lutheran churches should be built in the Muscovite state . . . Such heretical Lutheran or Latin buildings are profane and vile . . . an abomination of desolation on the sacred soil of the Holy Russian land', runs a tract of the 1680s, attributed to arch-conservative Patriarch Joachim of Moscow. The fact that the secular authorities tolerated such 'abominations', albeit safely tucked away in the Foreign Colony, shows how the needs of the State overrode the strictures of the Church. As is well known, the young Peter had no scruples about frequenting the colony and even his father Tsar Aleksei had applied to one of the colony's pastors for help in putting on the first court theatricals in the 1670s.

Seventeenth-century Russians acquired their knowledge of the West more from contacts at home than from travel abroad. The long and hazardous journey, official formalities and restrictions and simple fear of the unknown ensured that, until a number were forced to do so by Peter, few Muscovites ventured into Western Europe. With the exception of journeys to the Ukraine and Byelorussia, there is no evidence that Russian architects and craftsmen went abroad in pursuit of their careers. A number of potential patrons did, however, and it is interesting to record the comments of Tsar Aleksei's English physician Samuel Collins (1671), who writes:

> 'Since His Majesty has been in Poland and seen the manner of the Princes' houses there and ghess'd at the mode of their Kings, his thoughts are advanc'd and he begins to model his court and edifices more stately, to furnish his rooms with tapestry and to contrive houses of pleasure abroad.'

Aleksei had visited the Polish-ruled towns of Smolensk, Vilna, Polotsk, Vitebsk and others during the campaign of 1654-56 and subsequently Polish influence, mainly through the medium of Byelorussia, was evident in the interior and exterior decoration of new and refurbished palaces and in the output of the Armoury. Aleksei employed a Byelorussian churchman and writer, Simeon Polotsky, as court poet and tutor to his children.

Many diplomatic missions visited the West during the seventeenth century and, although there is little direct evidence of artistic borrowing via this route and frustratingly little in the way of diaries, travel accounts and personal letters, some impressions of Western art were recorded. A visit to Denmark in 1621 prompted the priest Ivan Shevelev to compose a 'Treatise on the Lutherans', in which he expressed disapproval of the worldly appearance of Danish churches decorated with military trophies and 'indecent' statues and paintings, 'the nakedness of the bodies bedecked with gold and silver and their secret places lasciviously and shamelessly exposed'. The realistic nude failed to gain currency in seventeenth-century Muscovy. Ambassador Vasily Likhachev, who visited Italy in 1659, was more favourably impressed. He thought the architecture of Leghorn 'very fine' and Florence 'wonderfully built with very lofty palaces'. Standard impressions recur in official reports of this kind; for example, Muscovites were amazed by the size of many buildings in the West, impressed by the predominance of stone edifices and intrigued by fountains and other mechanical curiosities. The far more numerous accounts written by foreign travellers to Russia are equally informative. Few failed to be impressed by the quantity of churches and their colourful interiors, but most were struck by the apparent uniformity of Byzantine patterns, lack of sophistication in the fine arts and, in particular, the low levels of science and learning. Adam Olearius from Holstein, who made several visits to Russia in the 1630s–40s, writes: 'They have images painted with oil upon wood, wretchedly coloured and ill-proportioned.' Jacob Reutenfels wrote: 'The churches are shown respect by all, for they are for the most part tall and elegantly built, but they cannot in any respect compare with our own for size and magnificence.' Georg Schleissing, who came to Russia with a delegation from Brandenburg in 1684, remarked disparagingly that there was as little comparison between Russian 'palaces' and those of Rome, Florence and Venice as 'between a fly and an elephant'.

Foreigners for the most part remained unaware of the changes taking place in seventeenth-century Russian culture, but in Russia itself leading churchmen were alive to the dangers of innovation. The Church authorities and Old Believers alike feared the 'cunning' of the West, its concern for legality, form and reason as opposed to intuitive Orthodox 'wisdom'. In the words of the Old Believer leader, Archpriest Avvakum, burnt at the stake in 1682: 'Even though I am untutored in words, yet I have wisdom, untutored in rhetoric and philosophy, yet I have the wisdom of Christ within me.' Avvakum complained that painters depicted Christ 'with a plump face, curly hair, fat arms and muscles, thick fingers and likewise thick lips and altogether make him look like a German, big-bellied and fat, except that no sword is painted on his hip'. Nikon himself personally destroyed icons that were too innovatory, commanding that they be painted 'according to the ancient tradition', and his successor Joachim warned that icons 'should be made according to the ancient Greek traditions and not from seductive Latin and German pictures'.

It is no coincidence that defence of these new trends came from the Armoury. Simon Ushakov himself produced a tract on icon-painting in which he compared art to the reflective properties of a mirror. His fellow painter Josif Vladimirov in a tract written *c.* 1665–66 appealed for better craftsmanship and a more positive attitude towards foreign art: 'How can you claim that only Russians are allowed to paint icons and that only Russian icon-painting may be revered whilst that of other lands should be neither kept nor honoured? When we see the image of Christ or the Mother of God printed or painted with great skill, be it by our own or by foreign artists, our eyes are filled with great love and joy.'

A similarly positive attitude towards foreign culture can be observed in a number of high-ranking Muscovites, whose patronage of the arts went beyond the customary commissioning of chapels and acquisition of religious objects. One such was Prince Vasily Vasilievich Golitsyn (1643–1714), head of the Ambassadorial Chancellery and the leading statesman of the regency of Peter's half-sister Sophia (1682–89). Golitsyn was well educated for his time and knew Latin and Polish. He was described by the Russian historian Klyuchevsky as a 'fervent admirer of the West' who abandoned 'many of the sacred traditions of Russian antiquity'. His Moscow mansion and adjoining church were in the Moscow Baroque style. Inside the rooms were fitted out with rich furnishings, mirrors, portraits and engravings of foreign origin and there was a large collection of foreign secular books. We can only speculate on the direct sources of Golitsyn's taste. As Chancellor, he was in constant contact with foreigners and, although he never visited the West, his service in the Ukraine from 1676–81 would have introduced him to that region's more Westernised culture. Under Golitsyn the Ambassadorial Chancellery had its own workshops that produced diplomatic charters, engravings and architectural projects.

Golitsyn's patroness Sophia herself commissioned a number of buildings in the Moscow Baroque style, including new churches and residences in the Novodevichy Convent. The Church of the Transfiguration (1687–88) is an intriguing example of the transitional style, conventionally five-domed but decorated with a harmonious framework of Classical columns and window surrounds, whilst the contemporaneous Church of the Assumption was modelled on a Ukrainian design. Another of Sophia's Ukrainian-inspired buildings was the Church of Prince Josaphat (1688) on the royal estate at Izmailovo, with three tower[s] placed from west to east. In an engravin[g] of the princess, dated *c.* 1687, the usua[l] Orthodox trappings of stylised roya[l] portraits are supplemented by seve[ral] Virtues represented by Classical figures.

Other patrons receptive to Wester[n] art forms include A. S. Matveev, th[e] boyar, Bogdan Khitrovo, who directe[d] the Armoury from 1654–80, a number o[f] Peter's maternal relatives, the Naryshkin[s] who commissioned Moscow Baroqu[e] churches, Peter's sister Natalia an[d] Prince Boris Golitsyn. Western innova[tions] tions were adopted or perceived onl[y] by a small élite, confined to court[,] government and church circles, yet th[is] does not detract from their significance[:] one of the criticisms levelled by historian[s] against the more consciously Westernise[d] culture of the eighteenth century is tha[t] it, too, was a veneer, under which ol[d] traditions, illiteracy and superstitio[n] survived almost unscathed. The differ[-] ence is that in the seventeenth century[] one is still dealing with sporadic influence[s] rather than with the systematic imitatio[n] and large-scale importation of craftsmen[] adopted by Peter and his successors. In[] Peter's reign Westernisation found its[] expression in secular culture – the civic[] buildings of St. Petersburg, portraits and[] engravings of Russia's military and naval[] exploits and of the Tsar in military attire[,] triumphal arches – whereas in the seven[-] teenth century Western-inspired devices[] were applied mainly to religious object[s] – such as churches, icons, frescoes[,] iconostases. It has been argued, notabl[y] by the nineteenth-century Slavophiles[,] that seventeenth-century Westernisatio[n] was a more 'natural' process than Peter'[s] violent changes, but it is as futile to[] speculate on probable developments[] without the intervention of Peter as to[] ponder the growth of Russian Western[-] style democratic institutions withou[t] the Bolsheviks. All that can be said is[] that Peter's reforms were not as un[-] heralded nor such a revolutionary break[] with an uneducated and inward-looking[] past as has sometimes been suggested.

NOTES ON FURTHER READING

G. H. Hamilton, *The Art and Architecture o[f] Russia*, 2nd edn., Penguin (Harmondsworth, 1977[)] and J. H. Billington, *The Icon and the Axe*, Weiden[-] feld and Nicolson (London, 1966). Lindsay A. J[.] Hughes, 'Western Graphic Material as a source o[f] Moscow Baroque Architecture', *Slavonic an[d] East European Review*, IV, 1977, 433–43 and 'Th[e] Moscow Armoury and innovations in 17th[] century Muscovite art', *Canadian-American Slavi[c] Studies*, forthcoming.

LOCKE AND LIBERTY

As an articulate champion of liberty and toleration, of common sense and healthy measure in all things, England's John Locke (1632–1704) became in many respects the guiding spirit for America's Founding Fathers. His perception that personal freedom requires the private ownership of property remains a cornerstone of American political thought. Nonetheless, Locke is a hazy figure to most Americans, even as they approach the 1987 bicentennial of the Constitution, which embraces many of his ideas. Here, Maurice Cranston reviews the man's life and work.

Maurice Cranston

Maurice Cranston, 65, a former Wilson Center Guest Scholar, is professor of political science at the London School of Economics. Born in London, he was educated in England at St. Catherine's College and Oxford. His books include John Stuart Mill *(1965),* Jean-Jacques, The Early Life and Work of Jean-Jacques Rousseau, 1712–54 *(1982), and the recently reissued* John Locke: A Biography.

Among the philosophers of the modern world, John Locke has always been held in especially high regard in America. His influence on the Founding Fathers exceeded that of any other thinker. And the characteristically American attitude toward politics—indeed, toward life—can still be thought of as "Lockean," with its deep attachment to the rule of law, to equal rights to life, liberty, and property, to work and enterprise, to religious toleration, to science, progress, and pragmatism.

Like the Founders, Locke had participated in a revolution—the bloodless Glorious Revolution of 1688–89, in which the English overthrew the despotic King James II to install the constitutional monarchy of William and Mary and confirm Parliament's supremacy. Locke had justified that rebellion in his writings with arguments against "unjust and unlawful force," arguments that were cited as no less powerful in the American Colonies during the 1770s.

Earlier philosophers had theorized about justice, order, authority, and peace. Locke was the first to build a system around *liberty*.

Locke's chief works—*An Essay Concerning Human Understanding, Two Treatises of Government*, and his first *Letter Concerning Toleration*, all published in London in 1689–90—spoke in terms that Thomas Jefferson, James Madison, and other Americans recognized. Men were created equal by God and endowed by Him with natural rights; the earth was given by God to men to cultivate by their own endeavors, so that each could earn a right to property ("the chief end" of society) by the application of his labor to the improvement of nature. In the New World, Locke's message received a warmer welcome than in crowded, feudal Europe.

The practical men who led the American Revolution and wrote the Constitution and the Bill of Rights recognized Locke as a Christian, like themselves, who had discarded nonessential dogmas and yet retained a pious faith in the Creator and in the Puritan virtues of probity and industry. Other European philosophers influenced the Framers' thinking: Montesquieu (1689–1755) contributed a republican element and Jean-Jacques Rousseau (1712–78) a democratic element, neither present in the constitutional-monarchist system of Locke. But the French philosophers, though they worked in a field prepared by Locke, did not have his hold on the American mind.

But who *was* John Locke?

Paintings, including a 1672 portrait by John Greenhill that Locke admired, show a tall, lean, and handsome man with a dimpled chin and large, dark, languorous eyes. He had asthma; one of his teachers, the great medical scientist Thomas Sydenham, urged him to rest much to conserve the "needful heat." A contemporary at Oxford called him a "turbulent spirit, clamorous and never contented," who

John Locke (1689) by Dutch painter Herman Verelst.

could be "prating and troublesome." The earl of Shaftesbury, his long-time patron, thought him a "genius."

So, apparently, did Locke. His self-esteem shows in the understated Latin epitaph he wrote for himself before he died at age 73. The plaque at the Essex church where he was buried describes him as merely a scholar "contented with his modest lot," who "devoted his studies wholly to the pursuit of truth."

Locke was never a candid man. He had an almost Gothic love of mystery. A Tory spy once wrote that at Oxford Locke "lives a very cunning unintelligible life"; he was often absent, but "no one knows whither he goes." In his letters and notebooks, he used ciphers and a shorthand system modified for purposes of concealment. Yet a picture emerges from these and other sources: Locke was one of the most adept, compelling, and idiosyncratic "new men" to rise in what he called "this great Bedlam," 17th-century England.

•••

John Locke was born on August 29, 1632, at Wrington in Somerset in the west of England, where modern commerce first began to challenge the old medieval order. His grandfather, Nicholas Locke, was a successful clothier. His less prosperous father, John Locke, was a lawyer and clerk to the local magistrates. His mother came from a family of tanners; she was 35 when her first child, the future philosopher, was born; her husband was only 26. The baby was baptized by

1. THE AGE OF POWER

Samuel Crook, a leading Puritan intellectual, and brought up in an atmosphere of Calvinist austerity and discipline.

England was Bedlam partly because of tension between the arrogant, authoritarian, and High Anglican King Charles and the increasingly assertive and Puritan House of Commons. In 1642, when Locke was 10 years old, the Civil War began between the Royalist forces (the Cavaliers) and the Parliamentary army (the Roundheads). The struggle was religious and social as well as political. The ultimately victorious Parliamentarians tended to be drawn not from the traditionalists of the Church of England and the leaders of feudal society, but from the Calvinists and Puritans, men from England's "new class" of rising merchants.

Among these were Locke's Devonshire cousins, named King, who rose swiftly from the trade of grocers to that of lawyers, and then via Parliament to the nobility itself. Young John, too, would benefit from England's great upheaval.

During the Civil War, his father was made a captain of Parliamentary Horse by Alexander Popham, a rich local magistrate turned Roundhead colonel. Popham became fond of his captain's son. When Westminster, the country's best boarding school, was taken over by Parliament, Popham found a place there for the boy.

That was the *first* stroke of fortune that would assist Locke's rise from the lower- to the upper-middle class—a group whose aspirations he may have reflected when, as a political philosopher, he gave the right to property first priority among the rights of man.

At Westminster, Locke was influenced by headmaster Richard Busby, a Royalist whom the Parliamentary governors had imprudently allowed to remain in charge of the school. By the time Locke won a scholarship to Oxford's premier college, Christ Church, which he entered at age 20, he was well ready to react against the rule of the Puritan "saints" at the university.* By 27, Locke had become a right-wing monarchist; by 1661, when he was 29, and the Restoration had put the deposed king's son Charles II on the throne, Locke's political views were close to those of the conservative thinker of the previous generation, Thomas Hobbes.

In a pamphlet Locke wrote at that time, he said that no one had more "veneration for authority than I." Having been born in a political "storm" that had "lasted almost hitherto," he had been led by the calm that the Restoration brought to value "obedience."

• • •

By his early 30s, Locke was less interested in politics than in medicine, a new subject at Oxford. During the summer of 1666, he chanced to perform a small medical service for a student's father, Anthony Ashley Cooper, the future earl of Shaftesbury and leader of the Whig party, champion of the rights of Parliament over the Crown.† Even then Shaftesbury, a wealthy Presbyterian, was a vocal political "liberal," the chief foe of measures designed by the Anglican majority to curb the freedom of religious Nonconformists. If Locke had not already come over to Shaftesbury's views, the earl must soon have pulled him across the last few hurdles.

At 35, Locke went to live at Shaftesbury's London house as his physician. After he saved the earl from the threat of a cyst of the liver, Shaftesbury decided that Locke was too talented to be spending his time on medicine alone, and work of other kinds was found for him. Thus began Locke's 15-year association with a powerful patron.

Gradually, Locke discovered his true gifts. First he became a philosopher. At Oxford he had been bored with the medieval Aristotelian philosophy still taught there. Reading French rationalist René Descartes first opened his eyes to the "new philosophy" that was providing the underpinnings of modern empirical science. Discussions with Shaftesbury and other friends led him to begin writing early drafts of the *Essay Concerning Human Understanding*, his masterpiece on epistemology, the study of how we know what we know.

Shaftesbury, short, ugly, and vain, shared Locke's interest in philosophy and science. He was pragmatic: Though anti-Catholic, he

thought that religious toleration would help unite the nation, the better to pursue the kind of commercial imperialism that was proving so profitable for the seafaring Dutch.

• • •

Charles II, though he favored toleration primarily for the sake of Catholic recusants, agreed with Shaftesbury. In 1672, the king made Shaftesbury his chief minister, lord high chancellor. But the two soon fell out. Shaftesbury came to believe that England's main rival in trade and her potential enemy was not Holland but France, while Charles II remained strongly pro-French. Ousted as the king's minister, Shaftesbury became his leading adversary.

Later, when Charles II refused to deny his brother, a professed Catholic, the right to succeed him as James II, Shaftesbury tried to get the House of Commons to make the succession illegal. The people, he said, had a right to say who should rule. When Charles resisted, Shaftesbury called on his allies to rebel. The plot was nipped, and in 1682 the earl fled to Holland, where he soon died.

Locke, too, went to Amsterdam. One year later he was expelled *in absentia* from his "studentship" at Oxford by the king's command. The next summer, after Charles II's death and James's accession to the throne, the duke of Monmouth led a failed rebellion against the new king. Locke, named by the government as one of Monmouth's agents in Holland, went into hiding as "Dr. van der Linden."

Locke's friends in Holland included many of those who plotted with the Dutch prince William of Orange to topple James II, who was indeed deposed in 1688. We do not know how deeply Locke was involved, only that he returned to London in 1689 with William's wife Mary, the new English queen.

These were the events behind Locke's most famous works.

By the time the *Two Treatises of Government* appeared, Englishmen had come round to Shaftesbury's view: They justified deposing James II not just because he advanced Catholicism, but also because he had tried to be an absolute monarch like France's Louis XIV. In his preface, Locke said that he hoped the *Two Treatises* would help "justify the title of King William to rule us." But he did most of the writing when Charles II was king. Then, the question of whether a people had the right to rebel against their ruler was not a backward-looking moral issue but a forward-looking moral challenge.

Thomas Hobbes wrote *Leviathan* (1651) to provide new reasons for men to obey kings. In the *Two Treatises*, Locke used Hobbes's "social contract" to justify revolt against despots.

Hobbes's social contract united men, whom he viewed as natural enemies, in a civil society with a common purpose. Locke did not see men as enemies. He took a Christian view. He argued that men were subject, even in a state of nature, to natural law, which was ultimately God's law made known to men through the voice of reason.

Hobbes's theory had simplicity: Either you are ruled or you are not ruled, either you have obedience or you have liberty, either you have security and fetters or you have chaos and danger. Neither condition is ideal, said Hobbes, but the worst government was better than none at all.

• • •

The Lockean analysis was less pessimistic.

Locke believed that men could be both ruled and free. While subject to natural law, men also had natural rights—notably rights to life, liberty, and property. These rights were retained when men contracted to form political societies. Instead of surrendering their freedom to a sovereign, as Hobbes suggested, men had merely *entrusted* power to a ruler. In return for justice and mutual security, they had agreed to obey their rulers, on condition that their natural rights were respected. Natural rights, being derived from natural law, were rooted in something higher than the edicts of princes, namely the edicts of God. They were "inalienable."

Locke's "right to revolution"—to reject a ruler who failed to respect natural rights—thus derived not only from the social contract but also from the supremacy of God's law to man's. People who might have misunderstood, or been unimpressed by, the social contract in abstract philosophy could appreciate the principle that God's law is higher than that of kings. And while Locke based his politics on

---

*The Oxford routine was still medieval. Undergraduates had to rise at 5:00 A.M. to attend chapel, and do four hours' work in Hall before supper at noon. Conversation with tutors, and among students in Hall, had to be in Latin. Students had to hear at least two sermons a day, and visit their tutors nightly "to hear private prayers and to give an account of the time spent that day."

†The name Whig seems to have come from *Whiggamore*, a term for "horse thief" used by 17th-century Anglicans or "Tories" to express scorn for Scottish Presbyterians.

LOCKE'S 'SHATTERED AND GIDDY' ENGLAND

The tremors that rocked John Locke's times echo in his letters. England's fissures—between Crown and Parliament, Anglicans and Dissenters, aristocrats and achievers, rich and poor—had left a "shattered and giddy nation," he wrote at age 27. Few men "enjoy the privilege of being sober."

During the century before Locke's birth in 1632, England's population almost doubled, topping five million in 1640. But with growth came several woes: rising prices, falling "real" wages, and poor harvests and frequent famines caused by a miniature global ice age that lasted from about 1550 to 1700. While England was a naval power, as the 1588 defeat of the Spanish Armada had shown, the Dutch were far ahead in turning maritime prowess to profit.

•

But business was becoming important: Retail shops created by a new breed of merchant began to replace the old market fairs. Abroad, firms chartered by the Crown traded English woolens and African slaves for West Indian molasses and sugar and American fish and timber; the East India Company (est. 1600) dealt in textiles and tea. Commerce had not (yet) remade England; if Locke's home county, Somerset, prospered from new industries (notably clothing), it was also plagued by such poverty that people, wrote one chronicler, "hanged themselves from want." But, slowly, medieval England was becoming the mercantile nation that, by the 18th century, would create the British Empire.

Authority was eroding. The Roman Catholic Church's supremacy had been broken by the Protestantism that had arrived via Martin Luther's Germany and Huldrych Zwingli's and John Calvin's Switzerland, and by King Henry VIII's 1534 creation of the Church of England. And while the peerage was still dominant, the expanding landed gentry and the new commercial class now had to be heard. By the early 17th century, as historian Lawrence Stone has noted, "respectful subservience [to aristocracy] was breaking down."

King Charles I (1625–49), was besieged by troubles. Suspected by his Protestant subjects of "popish" leanings, he waged an unpopular war in Europe and, later, failed to secure Parliament's support in his effort to quash rebellion in Scotland, leading to the Civil War in 1642. The pro-Parliament Roundheads tended to be Calvinists (Presbyterians), Puritans, or Protestant Nonconformists—the rising merchants and the gentry. The royalist Cavaliers were High Church or Catholic aristocrats. The 1648 triumph of the Parliamentary Army under (among others) the ardent Puritan, Oliver Cromwell, was to an extent a victory—and not the final one—of the "new" middle-class England. Soon after, the English did what most Europeans then considered unthinkable: They beheaded their king and established a commonwealth.

Within five years, Cromwell assumed absolute power. His Protectorate was austere. Fancy dress, amusements such as alehouses and horseraces, and lively arts such as theater were discouraged. The Puritan zealots who controlled Oxford, wrote one of Locke's contemporaries, enjoyed "laughing at a man in a cassock or canonical coat." They would "tipple" in their chambers, but would not enter taverns or permit such diversions as "Maypoles, Morrises [folk dances], Whitsun ales, nay, scarce wakes." So unpopular were Puritan efforts to impose moral discipline that most Englishmen joined Locke in hailing the Restoration of Charles II in 1660. But the monarchy would never be the same. After Charles's successor, James II, was deposed, William and Mary became England's first constitutional monarchs. Merriment returned to everyday life. At Oxford, nearly 400 taverns flourished, as did, said one critic, "easy manners, immorality, loose language, disrespect."

•

While Protestantism—particularly Puritanism—played a large role in 17th-century politics, its influence went further. In the arts, it infused the epic poem *Paradise Lost* (1667), John Milton's eloquent attempt to "justify God's ways to man." In science, the mental traits fostered by Protestantism—independence, individualism, skepticism of authority—were central.

Early in the century Francis Bacon had called for close scrutiny of the natural world, for the adoption of the experimental method, and for an inductive style of reasoning. Among those who heeded him were Isaac Newton, Robert Boyle, and William Harvey, the pioneering anatomist. All helped dispose of scholasticism, the medieval system of inquiry that proceeded, in Aristotelian style, by deduction from untestable assumptions. The "new science" that they espoused encouraged a radical reconsideration of all areas of thought—in political theory, in economics, and in philosophy itself. It was, of course, an upheaval to which Locke himself made vital contributions.

religion, his was not the astringent faith of the Catholics or of Calvin, but that watered-down Christianity later known as Modernism.*

Locke's writing during his stay in Holland included a travel journal. It revealed how he would visit some great cathedral or chateau, but then take an interest only in working out the exact dimensions. He detested ceremonies and show, which he thought irrational and wasteful, and was pleased to find that one of the best Dutch universities had nondescript architecture. It proved "that knowledge depends not on the stateliness of buildings, etc."

"Knowledge" is the key word. Locke's philistinism was no aberration. He wanted to get away from the imagination, from the vague glamour of medieval things, from unthinking adherence to tradition, from enthusiasm, mysticism, and glory; away from all private, visionary insights and down to the plain, demonstrable facts. This was central to his mission as a philosopher and reformer. His antipathy to poetry and imaginative artists was coupled with scorn for ivory-tower scholars who talk "with but one sort of men and read but one sort of books." They "canton out to themselves a little Goshen in the intellectual world where the light shines... but will not venture out into the great ocean of knowledge."

Locke's venturing made him a polymath, but he was in no sense a smatterer. True, his expertness was not equal in all the subjects he chose to study. Compared to his friends, chemist Robert Boyle and Sir Isaac Newton, the great physicist, he was an amateurish scientist. His knowledge of the Scriptures was questionable. Although he wrote influential essays on monetary policy, he could not appreciate the subtlety of other economists. But what was important in Locke's case was not his versatility, but that each department of knowledge was related in his mind to all the others.

In the *Essay Concerning Human Understanding*, Locke says in the opening "Epistle" that in an age of such "master builders" as Boyle, Sydenham, and "the incomparable Mr. Newton" it is "ambition enough to be employed as an under-laborer in clearing the ground a little and removing some of the rubbish that lies in the way of knowledge." Locke did much more than that: The *Essay* provides the first modern philosophy of science.

A recurrent word in the work is a Cartesian one, "idea." Locke's usage is curious. He does not merely say that we have ideas in our minds when we think; he says that we have ideas in our minds when we see, hear, smell, taste, or feel. The core of his epistemology is the notion that we perceive not *things* but ideas that are derived in part from objects in the external world, yet also depend to some extent on our own minds for their existence.

•••

The *Essay* attacks the established view that certain ideas are innate. Locke's belief is that we are born in total ignorance, and that even our theoretical ideas of identity, quantity, and substance are derived from experience. A child gets ideas of black and white, of sweet and bitter, *before* he gets an idea of abstract principles, such as identity or impossibility. "The senses at first let in particular ideas, and furnish the yet empty cabinet." Then the mind abstracts theoretical ideas, and so "comes to be furnished with ideas and language, the materials about which to exercise its discursive faculty."

In Locke's account, man is imprisoned in a sort of diving bell. He receives some signals from without and some from within his apparatus, but having no means of knowing which if any come from outside, he cannot test the signals' authenticity. Thus man cannot have any certain knowledge of the external world. He must settle for *probable* knowledge.

Locke's general philosophy has obvious implications for a theory of morals. The traditional view was that some sort of moral knowledge was innate. Locke thought otherwise. What God had given men was a faculty of reason and a sentiment of self-love. Reason combined with self-love produced morality. Reason could discern the principles of ethics, or natural law, and self-love should lead men to obey them.

Locke wrote in one of his notebooks that "it is a man's proper business to seek happiness and avoid misery. Happiness consists in

*Locke rejected original sin. He maintained in *The Reasonableness of Christianity* (1695) that Christ had come into the world not to redeem wrongdoing man, but to bring immortality to the righteous. Locke, a professed Anglican, here argued like a Unitarian, though he felt that word conjured up the unpopular image of a skeptical dissenter.

what delights and contents the mind, misery is what disturbs, discomposes or torments it." He would "make it my business to seek satisfaction and delight and avoid uneasiness and disquiet." But he knew that "if I prefer a short pleasure to a lasting one, it is plain I cross my own happiness."

For Locke, in other words, Christian ethics was natural ethics. The teaching of the New Testament was a means to an end—happiness in this life and the next. The reason for doing what the Gospel demanded about loving one's neighbor, etc., was not just that Jesus said it. By doing these things one promoted one's happiness; men were impelled by their natural self-love to desire it.

Wrongdoing was thus for Locke a sign of ignorance or folly. People did not always realize that long-term happiness could usually only be bought at the cost of short-term pleasure. If people were prudent and reflective, not moved by the winds of impulse and emotion, they would have what they most desired.

The preface to the English edition of the first *Letter Concerning Toleration* says, "Absolute Liberty, just and true Liberty, equal and impartial Liberty is the thing we stand in need of." Many people assumed these words to be Locke's; Lord King, a relative, made them an epigraph in a Locke biography. In fact, they were the words of the translator of Locke's original Latin, William Popple.

Locke did *not* believe in absolute liberty, any more than he believed in absolute knowledge. He thought the way to achieve as much as possible of both was to face the fact that they were limited and then to see what the limitations were. As he did with knowledge in the *Essay*, Locke focused on the liberty that men cannot have, to show the liberty they can achieve. The limits are set by the need to protect the life, property, and freedom of each individual from others, and from the society's common enemies. No other limits need be borne, or *should* be. Locke set men on the road to the greatest possible liberty by the method he used to set them on the road to the greatest knowledge—teaching the impossibility of the absolute.

•••

Locke guarded his anonymity with elaborate care. The *Essay*, which made him famous throughout Europe in his own time, was one of the few works that appeared under his own name. Most were published anonymously. When an English translation of the first *Letter Concerning Toleration* was issued in London, Locke protested that it had happened "without my privity."

Some of his secrecy stemmed from his days of hiding in Holland, some was for fun, some plainly neurotic. Some added a needed touch of romance to his relations with his women friends.

While Locke never married, he sought female affection and courted a formidable lot of professors' bluestocking daughters. Once, when he was 27, his father wrote to him of a Somerset widow who was "young, childless, handsome, with £200 per annum and £1,000 in her purse," but Locke would not settle down. His closest relationship with *any* person developed in 1682, when Locke, then 50, met Damaris Cudworth, the 24-year-old daughter of a Cambridge philosopher. They exchanged verses and love letters (signed "Philander" and "Philoclea"); he called her his "governess," a role that he was oddly fond of inviting his women friends to assume. Yet no union resulted, although the two were to remain close, even years after she married a nobleman and became Lady Masham.

Locke, as he wrote to an old friend, considered "marriage and death so very nearly the same thing."

Locke was careful with money. His detailed accounts show that during his 30s he had a modest income of about £240 a year from rental property in Somerset, in addition to stipends from Christ Church and profits from investments.* Once, when going abroad, he asked an uncle not to let his tenants know, "for perhaps that may make them more slack to pay their rents."

Locke's attentiveness to important people brought him not only lodgings—he had no home, being always the guest of various admirers—but job offers as well. He was once the Crown's secretary of presentations, a £300-a-year job involving ecclesiastical matters. He refused an ambassadorship in Germany, saying that the duties there more befitted someone who could "drink his share" than "the soberest man" in England. Shaftesbury made him secretary of the Lords Proprietors of Carolina, in which role he advertised for settlers (people who could behave "peaceably" and not use their "liberty" for "licentiousness") and helped write a constitution for the colony.†

•••

In his mid-60s, Locke became the dominant member of a new Board of Trade. Though the post paid £1,000 a year, Locke complained to a friend: "What have I to do with the bustle of public affairs while sinking under the burdens of age and infirmity?"

Among other things, Locke's board made linen-making the "general trade" of Ireland (partly to keep the Irish out of England's wool business). When pauperism became an issue, Locke argued that the problem was not "scarcity of provision or want of employment," but indiscipline and "corruption of manners, virtue, and industry." He urged (unsuccessfully) new laws for the "suppression of begging drones." Healthy men between 14 and 50 caught seeking alms should serve three years on navy ships "under strict discipline at soldier's pay." Boys and girls under 14 should be "soundly whipped."

Lady Masham explained that Locke was "compassionate," but "his charity was always directed to encourage working, laborious, industrious people, and not to relieve idle beggars, to whom he never gave anything." He thought them wastrels, and "waste of anything he could not bear to see."

Locke was 68 before he retired, to the Masham country house, to spend his last years writing a commentary on the New Testament.

Although Locke has sometimes been dismissed as an ideologue of the age of bourgeois revolutions, he is in many respects the 17th-century thinker whose teaching is most relevant to the concerns of our own time. During the 19th century, that great age of nationalism and imperialism, Locke's individualism seemed narrow and dated. But in the presence of the kind of despotic and totalitarian regimes that have emerged during the 20th century, Locke's defense of the rights of man has taken on a new immediacy. During World War I, Woodrow Wilson looked to Locke to justify the use of force against tyranny. When World War II posed an even more intense challenge to democracy, Winston Churchill proclaimed the aim of victory in Lockean terms, as "the enthronement of human rights."

Numerous declarations and covenants of human rights have since expressed the principles through which the West has sought to formulate its demand for freedom under law. That is something we have claimed not only for our fellow citizens, but (as Locke did) for all men—not an ideal of perfect justice, but a minimal standard to which any government can fairly be called upon to conform. We no longer expect every nation to govern itself as democratically as we do ourselves, but we do demand that they all respect human rights, and we can still look to Locke for the classic formulation of the philosophy that informs that demand.

Modern opinion has often sought to add to assertions of the rights of individuals, pleas for the rights of groups, economic, ethnic, racial, regional, or whatever. But again, that was anticipated by Locke when he argued for the toleration of dissidents and minorities. In his time, religious persecution was at issue; in ours it is political. But persecution as such has not changed its character, and the case for toleration that Locke worked out 300 years ago is no less pertinent today than it was then. It is, if anything, more urgent, since progress has made persecution more common, efficient, and cruel.

The "storm" of change in which Locke was born continues. So, remarkably, does the value of his ideas on how to deal with change, maintaining the maximum liberty and justice for all.

---

*Though no plunger, Locke did speculate with some success (as Shaftesbury had) in the slave trade and in sugar plantations in the Bahamas. He wrote at least some books for money, among them a volume on French grape and olive cultivation (something good has "come out of France"). The estate he left, worth close to £20,000, was no fortune, but not a pittance either.

†Rejecting a "numerous democracy," the document prescribed legislative power balanced between citizenry and a local aristocracy; freemen had to "acknowledge a God." Locke received membership in the Carolina aristocracy and some land. But the colonists, who began arriving in 1669, repudiated the Lords Proprietors; the aristocracy was never created, and Locke's land appears to have yielded no rent.

FROM BOY-KING TO 'MADMAN OF EUROPE'

YOUNG CHARLES XII WAS THE DRIVING FORCE OF THE GREAT NORTHERN WAR.

Gary K. Shepherd

Charles XII, the dynamic young king who led Sweden into the Eighteenth Century, is not nearly as well known today as his contemporary Peter the Great, Czar of Russia. In his own short lifetime, however, Charles also was a shaper of history. Both drawn and undeterred by the challenge of conquering Russia, he was in fact Peter's greatest foreign nemesis.

The French philosopher Voltaire described the two rival sovereigns as, "by common accord, the most remarkable men to have appeared in over 2,000 years." Otherwise, said Voltaire, he would not have written his own *History of Charles XII*. Considerable praise for a man who lived only to the age of 36.

Charles, raised from infancy to be king, was well-read and scholarly, an excellent organizer and even a reformer. He personally was an ascetic—he never married, and he seemed to prefer the life of the military campaign trail. He was reputed to be uncompromisingly honest, and yet skilled at the nuances of diplomacy. He was adept at choosing subordinates to run his country while he was absent, which he was for most of his reign. The domestic affairs of Sweden, however, did suffer for those long absences.

His tactics ranged from the impetuous to the downright insane at times—not for nothing was he known as the "Madman of Europe." Like Hannibal, he almost always was outnumbered in battle, and still he won—usually. Totally fearless, he was described as a beserker and a knight errant in one, and he could inspire his men to incredible heroic feats. Yet he was described by one contemporary as "gentle as a lamb, shy as a nun."

When Charles XII, great-great nephew of the famed tactician Gustavus Adolphus, came to power in 1697 at the age of 15, the Baltic Sea was virtually a Swedish lake. As well as his throne, Charles inherited from his father, Charles XI, an efficient army and bureaucracy that the elder king had labored most of his life to build. The new king was soon to need both—especially the army.

Wasting no time, Frederick IV of Denmark, Peter I of Russia and Augustus, elector of Saxony and king of Poland, entered into a secret alliance (1699) to curb Swedish power. They determined to take advantage of Charles' youth and inexperience with a relatively simple plan: Danish King Frederick would invade Swedish territory in the west, and, while he kept the Swedes busy, the Russians and Poles would attack in the east.

In April of 1700 the Danes launched their attack, to begin what was to become known as the Great Northern War. Frederick was confident his superior fleet would protect him from retaliation. Meanwhile, the Russians confidently invested Narva on the Baltic coast in October of the same year.

Under cover of a naval demonstration by a friendly British fleet, Charles surprised everyone by slipping into Jutland and threatening nearby Copenhagen to the south. Frederick was forced to return home, where the young Swedish king dictated peace terms. Having dispatched Denmark in six weeks, Charles then turned his attention to the rest of the coalition.

He arrived in the east before Peter was even aware of his approach, to relieve the siege of Narva (near the Gulf of Finland in Estonia of today). Charles had an army of only 8,000 men to attack an entrenched Russian force of 40,000. The odds of five-to-one didn't bother Charles, who proceeded to attack in a blinding snowstorm on November 30, 1700. "Now is the time, with the storm at our backs," he said. "They will never see how few we are." Charles routed the Russians, capturing more prisoners than he had men in his army.

Charles then concentrated on a campaign to unseat Augustus as Polish king. By mid-summer, 1701, he had defeated the Saxons and Russians at Dunamünde; he then occupied Warsaw in May of 1702. In July he and 12,000 men routed the Saxons and Poles (24,000) at Klissow, 110 miles southwest of Warsaw. He took Cracow three weeks later. On April 21, 1703, he defeated the Saxons at Pultusk, and on September 22 he subdued the fortress of

By Gary K. Shepherd; reprinted from *Military History*, August 1986, pp. 12-17, by permission.

35

Thorn. He next deposed Augustus and had Stanislaus Lecycznski, Palantine of Posen, crowned as king of Poland. In many of those engagements, Charles was outnumbered by two or three to one.

Meanwhile, the Czar Peter had not been idle. In 1702, Peter took Ingria along the Gulf of Finland. He then founded St. Petersburg on May 16, 1703. In July of 1704 he re-took Narva after a long siege and massacred the inhabitants. In 1705 a Russian force under Scottish general Ogilvie appeared at Pultusk in Poland, forcing Swedish commander Adam Lewenhaupt to fall back to Riga. Ogilvie then set up to winter in an armed camp at Grodno. Charles attempted to draw Ogilvie out, but the Scot refused to fight. Meanwhile, Augustus advanced to attack a small force under Karl Rehnskjold in preparation to fall upon Charles' rear. But Rehnskjold routed the Saxons at Fraustradt. Soon after, Ogilvie was forced to withdraw.

Peter then sued for peace, but Charles had decided to invade Russia—he said he would discuss peace terms when he took Moscow. On New Year's Day, 1708, having left 10,000 men in Poland to support Stanislaus, Charles crossed the Vistula with 44,000 men, the largest force he had ever commanded in the field.

In June, Charles forced the crossing of the Benezina and defeated a force of 20,000 Russians at Holowczyn. In September, he defeated a Russian army of 16,000 near Smolensk. At this point he was only ten days' march from Moscow. But the Swedes by now had encountered the same "scorched-earth" policy that the Russians were to use on later invaders, and they were running short of supplies. Charles ordered General Lewenhaupt from Riga to join him with 11,000 reinforcements and, more importantly, a large baggage train of supplies. Charles halted at Mogilev to wait for them.

Then, while Charles was at Mogilev, he received an emissary from the Hetman of the Ukrainian Cossacks, Ivan Mazeppa. Mazeppa, once an ally of Peter's, had fallen into disfavor and was seeking a way to free the Ukraine from Russian suzerainty. He promised Charles that if the Swedes came to the Ukraine, he would lead a general uprising and gather an army 100,000 strong. Charles, against the advice of his generals, marched to join Mazeppa—he left word for Lewenhaupt simply to catch up with him.

It was a disastrous decision. The Russians learned of the planned uprising, and a force under Prince Menshinkoff occupied Baturan, Mazeppa's capital, killing many of his supporters and capturing most of his money and supplies. Lewenhaupt's column was intercepted at Liesna by a superior force. The general and about 6,000 men managed to fight their way through, later to join Charles, but they had to abandon the baggage train and its fresh guns. Meanwhile, a force of 12,000 that was supposed to invade Ingria from Finland and burn St. Petersburg had found the city too well defended and retreated to the fortress of Viborg, with the loss of 3,000 men along the way.

As a result of his own setback, Mazeppa was able to raise only a fraction of the men he had promised. Nevertheless, Charles settled down to winter in the rich Ukraine, still confident. Nature then took a hand. The winter of 1708-09 was the worst in a century. The Swedish interlopers continued to fight and win battles, but they suffered terribly from the cold.

By spring, Charles had only 20,000 men, 2,000 of them too crippled to fight. The Zaporozhian Cossacks, at the instigation of Mazeppa, had rebelled, providing both extra troops and a diversion to draw Peter's attention. With supplies still a problem, Charles decided to besiege the city of Poltava on the Vorskla River, a storehouse for huge stocks of powder and supplies that also controlled the southern approach to Moscow. He invested the city in May, expecting a swift surrender, but the Russians reinforced the garrison and held out.

By June, Peter had subdued the Zaporozhian Cossacks and marched with an army of 60,000 to relieve the city. At that point, Charles had about 24,000 men, only about half of them Swedish. Peter crossed the Vorskla River and set up a fortified camp a few miles north of the city.

As was his style, Charles rode out to personally reconnoiter the enemy positions—he was wounded in the foot by a Russian patrol. Confined to a litter, he passed his active command to Field Marshal Rehnskjold. When Peter heard of his incapacity, he abandoned his policy of avoiding battle and moved his camp closer to Poltava.

Charles decided to attack the fortified camp on the morning of July 8, 1709. Lewenhaupt urged him to raise the siege, but Charles refused, leaving men behind to guard the city and remaining supplies. Only 12,500 were actually to be used in the battle. Because powder was so short, the men were to charge with fixed bayonets, their rifles empty, and only four cannon were taken along to support the attack. Charles was counting on a combination of speed and shock to force the Russians back onto their own ranks in helpless confusion.

The attack commenced at first light. The left side of the Swedish line, where Charles himself was carried into battle on a litter, charged through a series of redoubts built to defend the Russian camp, as had been planned. But the commander of the right wing stopped to take the Russian redoubts, and so became separated from the main force. In addition, the central column, under Lewenhaupt, received a garbled order that he thought meant for him to halt.

Peter had been on the point of fleeing but, encouraged by the sudden pause, took advantage of the reprieve to draw up a battle line of 40,000 men and 100 cannon in front of the camp. Charles decided to strike while the iron was hot, even though he had only 4,000 men available for the final charge, to be led by Lewenhaupt.

Despite the odds, the right side of the Swedish lines did manage to force the Russians back, turning some of the Russian guns upon their enemies. But they soon were riddled by the Russian guns and overwhelmed at either wing by Russians troops.

Some historians are surprised that Peter did not immediately pursue his defeated enemy, but the fact is the Swedish army was still largely intact, and still dangerous. When Charles and Lewenhaupt regrouped at Pushkonivka, below Poltava, they found they still had about 16,000 men. The Russian strategy, of course, would be to force them into the V formed by the intersection of the Vorskla and Dnieper Rivers to the south. For the moment, Charles would accommodate—he had to, anyway.

Charles began retreating south in the hope of reaching Turkish territory and from there to make his way back to

Poland to join Stanislaus. To Charles, surrender was impossible, not only because of his own sense of honor, but because he knew that if Mazeppa and his Cossack allies were captured they would be tortured and executed as traitors.

When his army arrived at the Dnieper River, however, there were not enough rafts to take the entire host across. It was determined that Charles and Mazeppa would cross with about 1,600 men and as many of the wounded as possible, while the rest of the army would fight its way south and rejoin them at Ochakov on the Black Sea. But the day after Charles left, the pursuing Russian force of about 8,000 caught the Swedish force left behind. Lewenhaupt, who had fought so well before, seems to have had a failure of nerve—he now surrendered his much larger force of 14,000 to the Russians.

Charles did make it to Turkish territory, not without some adventures on the way, and was warmly welcomed. Lacking an army to fight his battles, Charles turned to the pen—he soon convinced the Turks to declare war on Russia. Peter promptly invaded Turkish territory, where he, too, was subjected to a "scorched-earth" strategy, and was trapped by a far superior force.

The Turks negotiated a peace favorable to Turkey, but Charles was outraged that Peter had been allowed to escape. Charles' "encouragement" led to four more declarations of war, but nothing came of them. Finally the Turkish leadership tired of Charles' interference and ordered him arrested. After Russia and Turkey signed the Peace of Adrianople in 1714, Charles decided to leave. He made his way incognito through Turkish and Austrian territory to Swedish Pomerania.

Charles spent most of 1715 using a combination of diplomacy and military strategy to defend the remnants of Sweden's central European territories from a fresh coalition that now combined Russia, Denmark, Saxony, Prussia, Hanover and Great Britain against him. He was forced at last to take refuge in his own Sweden when the Pomeranian port of Stralsund fell after a long siege in December of 1715.

But Charles did not long remain idle. He immediately embarked upon a scheme to take Norway, then a part of Denmark, as compensation for the lands lost in the east. His first invasion was indecisive in outcome. He mounted a second and soon was besieging the fortress of Fredrikshald. He was out inspecting the siege works when he was shot through the head. He was killed instantly. At the time, December of 1718, he was 36 years old.

Amid rumors that Charles had been killed by Swedish fire, rather than Danish, Swedish resolve collapsed on the spot. In effect, the Great Northern War was over. The royal heirs to Charles (sister Ulrika and her husband, Frederick I of Hesse-Cassell) were forced to grant Stettin and western Pomerania to Prussia and Sweden's eastern Baltic territories to Czar Peter's Russia. By the Peace of Nystad, which followed argument over succession to the childless Charles, Sweden thus permanently lost Livonia, Estonia, Ingria and the Finnish province of Kershold with its strategic fortress of Viborg on the Gulf of Finland.

While Sweden vanished as a Baltic, even a world, power, Russia now took stage as a colossus with one foot firmly planted in Europe—still shaky, somewhat mysterious, but a colossal presence nonetheless.

Rationalism, Enlightenment, and Revolution

This unit explores facets of the Age of Reason (the seventeenth century) and the Enlightenment (the eighteenth century). These two phases of the Western tradition had much in common; both emphasized a faith in science, a belief in progress, and a skepticism toward much of the cultural baggage inherited from earlier periods. Yet each century marked a distinctive stage in the spread of rationalism. In the seventeenth century a few advanced thinkers (Locke and Descartes, for example) attempted to resolve the major philosophical problems of knowledge, i.e., to develop a theoretical basis for rationalism. The eighteenth century brought a continuation of that effort in the works of Kant and Hume, but there was a new development as well: Voltaire, Diderot, and others campaigned to popularize science, reason, the principles of criticism, and the spirit of toleration among educated people. Thus, the critical attitudes engendered by rationalism and empiricism in the seventeenth century were brought to bear upon familiar beliefs and practices in the eighteenth century.

Several articles in this unit show the advance of critical reason. Science, the model for many of the new intellectual attitudes, is treated in "Galileo and the Specter of Bruno." "Meeting of the Minds" shows how science inspired the eighteenth-century faith in progress. "The First Feminist" reviews Mary Wollstonecraft's arguments for "enlightened" treatment of women, while "The Commercialization of Childhood" explores the Enlightenment's impact upon child-rearing.

During the seventeenth and eighteenth centuries, no tradition seemed safe from criticism. Even the Bible was scrutinized for contradictions and faulty logic. Universities and salons became intellectual battlegrounds where advocates of the ancient classics (only recently restored and returned to favor by Renaissance humanists) confronted the stalwarts of modernity. But the struggle went beyond the battle of the books. Powerful religious and political institutions were subjected to the test of reason and were usually found wanting. The goal was to reorganize human society on a rational or enlightened basis, to develop a new morality based on reason, not authority.

Of course, rationalism was not confined to the seventeenth and eighteenth centuries, as any reader of Aristotle or Aquinas can attest. Nor did the influence of the irrational disappear during the Age of Reason. The period, after all, witnessed a great European witch craze and a millenarian movement (the Ranters) in England. And those who doubt that atavistic attitudes could surface among the rationalists need only explore Newton's interest in alchemy and Pascal's mysticism. As for the Enlightenment, many have questioned how deeply its ideals and reforms penetrated eighteenth-century society. Certainly the "enlightened despots" of the continent stopped short of instituting reforms that might have diminished their authority. (Sebastian Haffner documents this point in "Prussia & Frederick the Great.") And while the doctrines of the Enlightenment may be enshrined in the noblest expressions of the French Revolution, that great upheaval also witnessed mass executions and systematic efforts to suppress freedom of expression. The excesses of the Revolution are chronicled in "Was France the Fatherland of Genocide?" Still, as Herbert Muller has written, the Enlightenment "not only diffused knowledge but set up public standards of truth. Its principles were aboveboard, freely accessible to all men, and not dependent upon intuitive, mystical, or revealed truth."

In our century, with its mass atrocities, world wars, and nuclear weapons, it is difficult to sustain the Enlightenment's faith in reason. But even before our recent disillusionment, rationalism provoked a powerful reaction—romanticism. Romantics trusted emotions, distrusted intellect; they viewed nature not so much as a repository of scientific laws, but as a source of inspiration and beauty; they were preoccupied with self-discovery, not social reform; and often they drew upon the medieval experience, which rationalists generally disregarded, for their images and models. True, the dream of reason has survived the Romantic rebellion and the excesses of our era. It lives on in our modern programs of mass education and social uplift, which is to say that it is embodied in contemporary liberalism and that its prospects are precarious.

Looking Ahead: Challenge Questions

Why did the Church consider Galileo's writings to be dangerous?

How deeply did rationalism penetrate the lives of seventeenth- and eighteenth-century Europeans?

How did new views of human nature affect attitudes about womanhood and childhood, and alter the treatment of the insane?

What did Europeans make of the American Revolution?

What went wrong with the French Revolution?

Galileo and the Specter of Bruno

The two men are often honored as martyrs to science, but for Bruno astronomy was a vehicle for politics and theology. Galileo was tried partly because his aims were mistakenly identified with those of Bruno

Lawrence S. Lerner and Edward A. Gosselin

In 1633 Galileo Galilei was brought before the Roman Inquisition and charged with teaching that the earth moves. The ensuing trial engaged the full authority of the Roman Catholic Church in a scientific and theological dispute with the most important scientific figure of the day. As is well known, Galileo was forced to recant his scientific convictions publicly on the grounds that he had defended the Copernican view of the universe, a position condemned as "false and opposed to Holy Scripture" in 1616. The incident is now universally regarded as a critical event in the birth of modern science.

In 1600, well within living memory at the time of Galileo's trial, Giordano Bruno had also met his fate at the hands of the Roman Inquisition. Bruno too was a celebrated Copernican, but his penalty was much severer: he was burned at the stake. The careers and persecutions of Galileo and Bruno have been linked in two kinds of myth, which tend to confuse the two figures in curiously opposite ways. According to the first myth, both men challenged an ignorant and obscurantist Catholic church in a modern spirit of freedom, and both were martyred to their cause. In this context Bruno was seen as a kind of proto-Galileo, or perhaps a Galileo manqué. He was a proto-Galileo simply because he too espoused the Copernican system and suffered an extreme version of Galileo's fate. He was a Galileo manqué in that, lacking Galileo's scientific insight and genius, he resorted to speculative mysticism. There is a kernel of truth to this myth,

as there is to many others, but the historical record yields a much richer and more elaborate tale.

The second myth is almost the converse of the first: that Galileo was a kind of resurrected Bruno in that he, like Bruno, was perceived as a religious and political revolutionary. The second myth must not simply be dismissed as wrongheaded. Indeed, our investigations have convinced us that an understanding of its role in early 17th-century beliefs is essential to a more complete understanding of what might be called the climatological prehistory of the trial of Galileo. We shall argue that Galileo's troubles came about in part because his contemporaries distorted his novel way of thinking into the more traditional and better-understood categories articulated by Bruno.

The first myth, depicting Bruno as a failed Galileo, was popular in the 19th century and well into the 20th; its moral was congenial to the world view of the 19th-century liberal. The myth lends support to the appealing legend that when Galileo recanted his Copernican position, he was heard to mutter, "Eppur si muove" ("And yet it moves"). There is no evidence to support that incident, and the real Galileo is a poor fit in such a heroic role. He is grossly miscast as a Nathan Hale or a William Tell.

What about Bruno? How does he fit the first myth that he was a martyr to science? For simplicity we shall confine our discussion mainly to his first and most important work on the Co-

pernican system, *La Cena de le ceneri* ("The Ash Wednesday Supper," or *Supper* for short). It was written in Italian in 1584. At the time Bruno was a member of the London household of the French ambassador to England.

If one regards the work as an exposition of the Copernican system together with some other scientific topics, one can only puzzle over its notoriety. It appears to be a compendium of nonsense—a disorganized display of gross error connected by incomprehensible passages. Bruno has the Copernican model of the solar system wrong. He demonstrates total ignorance of the most elementary ideas of geometry, let alone geometric optics. He throws in scraps of pseudoscientific argument, mostly garbled, and proceeds to high-flying speculations that seem disconnected from the preceding or subsequent arguments. Even the diagrams do not always correspond to the accompanying discussions in the text.

But there must be more to it, and that deeper significance must have been evident to Bruno's contemporaries. If Bruno had merely been a fool, he might have met with laughter and derision but not violent enmity and vehement official response. The Roman Inquisition would surely not have gone to the trouble it did to silence and repress him: he was imprisoned for eight years and subjected to innumerable hearings and interrogations before he was finally executed.

Bruno repeatedly makes it clear that the *Supper* is really not about the Copernican system at all: it is only peripherally a work on natural science and it is emphatically not to be taken literally. In accordance with the title, its central subject is the nature of the Eucharist: the Christian ceremony of Communion. Bruno praises Copernicus in a qualified way as the light before a new dawn. He heaps scorn, however, on the anonymous author of the preface to Copernicus' work *De revolutionibus orbium coelestium,* for Bruno clearly recognizes that the preface is spurious: in a fit of caution it suggests

Copernican astronomy should be understood as a theory for calculation only and not as an account of physical reality. (Today scholars know it was written by Andreas Osiander, a Lutheran theologian who was one of Copernicus' students.)

For Bruno the value of the Copernican system lies not in its astronomical details but instead in its scope as a poetic and metaphoric vehicle for much wider philosophical speculation. The Copernican replacement of the earth by the sun at the center of the solar system is for Bruno a symbolic restoration of what he calls the ancient true philosophy; according to him, it is to this philosophy one must turn in order to understand the true meaning of the Eucharist.

The "ancient true philosophy" was Bruno's brand of Hermetism, a mystic view based on Neoplatonic writings of the second and third centuries A.D. In Bruno's day it was widely believed the author of these writings was the semidivine Hermes Trismegistus, said to be a contemporary of Moses. The Hermetic philosophy had supposedly been handed down through Orpheus, Zoroaster, Pythagoras, Plato and the later Greek philosophers, and separately through the Judeo-Christian tradition. In the process the "ancient true philosophy" had become debased and corrupted, which for Bruno accounted for the lamentable state of worldly affairs.

According to the Brunonian Hermetic view, man shares in divinity and is therefore at least potentially in constant communion with God. The universal divine principle is extended to the entities that make up the macrocosmic universe as well as to man. Thus both stars and planets (Bruno does not make a distinction) are animate and endowed with souls; they can be operated on magically to effect social and political change. Rediscovered and refurbished by Bruno, the "ancient true philosophy" would unfetter the divine essence within all men. Its power could heal religious and political wounds and give birth to a new golden age.

It is important to understand that Bruno's adoption of natural science to foster broader theological, ethical, social and political purposes was entirely characteristic of the Renaissance world view. For the people of the Renaissance science was literally a branch of philosophy, often called on to illuminate or illustrate a nonscientific issue. Intelligent and well-educated people often saw explicit and highly anthropocentric parallels between

GIORDANO BRUNO is depicted in this anonymous engraving made in the early 17th century, about two decades after Bruno was executed by the Roman Inquisition. It is the earliest rendering of Bruno known, but no source contemporary with Bruno's life is known; the likeness is probably spurious. Bruno is shown in the habit of the Dominican order to which he belonged, a connection he acknowledged to varying degrees at different times in his life. Bruno's Dominican name on the inscription is in its Latin form. (His given name was Filippo.) "Nolanus" refers to his birthplace, Nola, a suburb of Naples.

scientific knowledge and the other aspects of life. Bruno is typical of contemporary Hermetists in leaping to conclusions about the relation of human beings to God based on theories about the workings of the macrocosm—and vice versa.

As Bruno saw it, one inevitable consequence of a return to the "true philosophy" would be the recognition of the essential unity between the liberal Protestants in England and the liberal Catholics in France. The theme of unity is sounded throughout the *Supper;* for example, in the Ptolemaic system there is a fundamental distinction between the earth, which was considered stationary, and the planets and stars, which were supposed to move within concentric spheres above the earth. On the other hand, once the Copernican view is accepted, the moving earth and the moving stars enjoy a similar status. Indeed, Bruno populated an infinite universe with an infinite number of stars, all in motion and central to their surroundings in an equivalent way. In like manner, he proposed a framework in which the liberal Protestant and Catholic views on the Eucharist could be seen as essentially equivalent.

What were the implications of this view for contemporary politics? To maintain the balance of power, England had traditionally allied itself with either France or Spain, whichever was weaker. In the late 16th century Spain was strong and religiously orthodox. France was in the throes of a violent and protracted religious civil war, in which Spain supported the orthodox Guisard party against the Protestants. The moderate French king Henry III and his adherents were caught in the middle. Nevertheless, an alliance between the French moderates and England, which seemed desirable to both parties, was blocked by an official commitment of France to Catholicism. A bridge over religious differences would therefore have been of great value in fostering the alliance.

Bruno was convinced that a monarch inspired and enlightened by Hermetism could lead the world into a golden age under the guidance of the "true philosophy." His candidates for this role were successively Henry III, Elizabeth I of England and finally Henry IV of France. Indeed, two years after the publication of the *Supper* he confided to Guillaume Cotin, the librarian of the Abbey of St. Victor in Paris, that from 1582 to 1585 he had been a kind of intellectual ambassador from the liberal Catholics of Henry III to the liberal Protestant court of Elizabeth I. Bruno's later enthusiasm for

the prospects of Henry IV was so great that in 1591 he imprudently interrupted his wanderings across Europe to return to Italy. His ultimate aim in returning seems to have been the conversion of the pope himself to Brunonian Hermetism.

Bruno's rash behavior almost immediately led to disaster. He was arrested on trumped-up charges by the Venetian Inquisition and then imprisoned. A year later he was moved to Rome, where he was confined for another seven years. In prison Bruno was no real threat to the Papacy. He had no following, no money and no influence. In the normal course of events he might simply have remained in prison until he was dead or forgotten. His execution seems to have been the pope's side of a minor political quid pro quo with the Spanish Hapsburgs.

In disposing of Bruno both the Papacy and Spain were announcing to all concerned that there would be no toleration of challenges either to religious orthodoxy or to the political status quo to which orthodoxy was closely linked, a connection we shall explore further. Nevertheless, Bruno's philosophical heritage survived in the early 17th century in a loose constellation of beliefs, held by an unorganized group of intellectuals called Rosicrucians. The aims and hopes of the Rosicrucians for a return of Pythagoreanism were nurtured in 1613 by the marriage of Frederick V, elector of the Rhenish Palatinate, to Elizabeth Stuart, daughter of James I of England. The marriage, mystically called the "chemical wedding of the Thames and the Rhine," was supposed to presage a return to the golden age of Elizabeth I.

In 1618 Frederick and Elizabeth were elected king and queen of Bohemia, from time to time a center of religious liberalism and toleration. Almost immediately they were deposed by the Hapsburg Holy Roman Emperor; the incident was the opening salvo of the Thirty Years' War, which renewed the political and religious strife of the late 16th century. In the years immediately following there was a "Rosicrucian scare": a strong and irrational fear of Rosicrucian subversion in Catholic strongholds.

Such was the prevailing political and religious climate when Galileo's popular exposition of his own Copernican views, *Dialogue on the Two Great World Systems,* was published in 1632. The publication had profound significance for people whose memories of the religious conflicts of the late 16th century were fresh and detailed. In a political and religious atmosphere

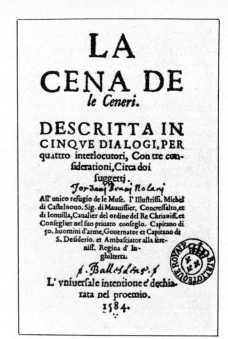

BRUNO'S STATEMENT of the Copernican picture of the universe is *La Cena de le ceneri* ("The Ash Wednesday Supper"); the title page from the book is shown. The work was written in Italian and published in England in 1584; an English translation by the authors of this article came out in 1977. The book is in the form of a debate centered on the Copernican system; Bruno's real objective was to extend Copernican ideas allegorically to theological and political speculation. The subtitle leads inexorably to the theme of unity emphasized throughout the work: "Described in five dialogues, by four interlocutors, with three reflections, on two subjects [dedicated] to the sole refuge of the Muses."

bearing a remarkable resemblance to that of the 1590's it was all too easy to confuse the aims of Galileo with those of Bruno. Hence the second and converse myth arises: in the public mind of 1633 Galileo became a revival, albeit an unwilling one, of the archetypal symbol of political and philosophical upheaval that Bruno had been three decades earlier.

We now know that Galileo's thinking was a radical departure from Renaissance thought. Indeed, it has often been maintained that Galileo's greatest contribution was his way of thinking about the physical universe. Unfortunately that was not necessarily clear to the great majority of his contemporaries. They were unable to understand not only his methods and his conclusions but also his aims and his intentions.

Compounding the lack of understanding was the fact that the late-Renaissance reader was predisposed to expect deliberately obscure writing.

Such obscurity was common, even when there was no external motive for it. In part its popularity is explained by a fondness for ornamentation and for elaborate elegance of expression. There was also a strong feeling that knowledge was for the initiate and that worthwhile understanding could be achieved only through much travail. The writing of Galileo's time is often full of multiple meanings, enabling the diligent reader to move from depth to depth. Such literary conceit was considered to be an appropriate reflection of the natural world, which yields pro-gressively deeper secrets to the diligent and gifted. Needless to say, Bruno employed this approach extensively.

Galileo emphatically did not write in such a manner, but it is much easier to appreciate this fact today than it was in the early 17th century. At that time there were some people inclined to believe his writing also concealed multiple levels of meaning; in particular, his *Dialogue* could readily be seen as a sequel to Bruno's *Supper*.

What are the grounds on which such a view was based? First one can list what might be called external literary reasons. Earlier Galileo had written a work called *The Starry Messenger,* whereas in the *Supper* Bruno called the stars "messengers of God." Furthermore, both Bruno's *Supper* and Galileo's *Letter to the Grand Duchess* had expressed similar attitudes toward Holy Scripture. Both works maintained that the Bible often speaks according to the common understanding of the people, and in so doing it may actually say things about nature that are not literally true. The view was eccentric enough to have caused Galileo and Bruno to be closely associated. Finally, it is worth mentioning that both Galileo and Bruno called the Copernican theory Pythagorean, a name often used synonymously with the politically unsavory term Hermetic.

Second, both Bruno's *Supper* and Galileo's *Dialogue* are remarkably similar in form. For example, both dialogues introduce courtly gentlemen and dogmatic Aristotelians as interlocutors. In both dialogues there is extensive discussion of a thought experiment in mechanics: If a stone is dropped from the top of the mast of a moving ship, where will the stone land on the deck? Both works also give the same correct answer: The stone will land at the foot of the mast. No matter that the points made by the thought experiment in the two works are entirely different, or that Bruno's arguments are garbled when they are taken in a purely physical way. A suspicious mind not inclined to physics would find it easy to confuse Galileo's intentions with Bruno's. Furthermore, both dialogues are written in Italian rather than in Latin. The reasons for this linguistic departure from contemporary scholarly convention are now known to be quite different, but again a suspicious reader might think in both cases the vulgar tongue was adopted in order to stir debate and intellectual dissent on the widest scale possible.

There is another and more global similarity in the form of the two works that could easily lead to the wrong conclusion about Galileo's intentions. In both works the Copernican system is defended in a nonmathematical and nontechnical way, completely ignoring the very details that make the system interesting and workable for the practicing astronomer. We have already shown that Bruno exploits the Copernican vision as a hieroglyph for his religious and reunionist aims. Galileo's dialogue is a purely philosophical and scientific work, but it too does not really defend the Copernican system in its then current form. Instead Gali-

ROBERT CARDINAL BELLARMINE played an important role in deciding Bruno's fate in 1600, and he personally admonished Galileo in 1616 not to hold to or defend the Copernican doctrine that the earth moves. It was clear to Galileo from the interview, however, that Bellarmine did not exclude the study of the Copernican view as a scientific hypothesis. Bellarmine's death before Galileo's trial in 1633 left an ambiguity in the position of the church as it had previously been stated to Galileo. This painting of Bellarmine is in the Roman church of St. Ignatius, where Bellarmine's remains are also kept.

leo widens his discussion to judge between his own philosophy of nature and the Aristotelian one. The *Dialogue* is thus opened to the suspicion that its chief aim lies below the surface, as is demonstrably the case for the *Supper*.

The close link between politics and religion we mentioned above underlies a third major reason for confusing Galileo with Bruno. Copernicanism was widely associated with revolutionary political and religious thought. In 1599 Tommaso Campanella, an apostate Dominican monk, led a revolt against Hapsburg rule in Calabria, in the southern part of Italy. Campanella's aim was to reestablish the famous ancient Pythagorean city of Croton in Calabria, but his revolt was quickly crushed and he spent the next 26 years in prison. During those years he was far from idle. In 1600 he wrote his *City of the Sun,* a distinctly Hermetic and Copernican work (although it was not Copernican in an astronomical sense). Within a few years of his arrest his jailers lost interest in him, and he was left in relative peace to write, which he did voluminously.

In 1616 Campanella learned that the Jesuit Robert Cardinal Bellarmine planned to admonish Galileo with respect to the dangerous theological implications of his scientific teachings. Campanella hastily wrote an *Apologia pro Galileo,* in which he attempted to show that Galileo's views were actually more rather than less in accordance with accepted theology than the Ptolemaic system was. The theological arguments presented by Campanella on this point bear strong similarities to those made by both Bruno and Galileo. To the possible later detriment of Galileo's case, the *Apologia* is the only work by Campanella in which Bruno is mentioned at all.

Campanella also wrote several letters to Galileo from prison. The letters make it clear that he viewed Galileo much as Bruno had viewed Copernicus: as a genius who heralded the dawn of the new truth without comprehending the philosophical significance of his discoveries. Such an attitude was almost certainly shared by others who were much less friendly to Galileo than Campanella was.

We strongly suspect that Galileo's close, if unwanted, association with Campanella was a major element in Galileo's eventual recantation. When Campanella was finally released from prison, he came into the pope's favor. In the late 1620's the Spanish grew increasingly angry with Urban VIII for following a partly se-

cret and rather clumsy pro-French policy. Consequently they engaged in psychological warfare that played on Urban's belief in astrology: astrologers predicted the pope's death with the solar eclipse of June, 1628, and later with the eclipse of December, 1630. Campanella was known to be a magus, or sorcerer, and so Urban enlisted his aid in performing antieclipse magic. The magic was apparently successful, because Urban did not die.

For a few years Campanella's suc-

cess admitted him to the confidence of the pope. It was necessary, however, to keep such magical operations a close secret. In 1600 the Jesuit Martin del Rio expressed an opinion of the church, in which many forms of magic were condemned. It would not do to let the public see the pope engaged in activity that was arguably heretical.

Campanella capitalized on the success of his antieclipse magic to put forward his Hermetic views, and to some degree he was successful. Indeed, at

THOMAS CAMPANELLA

De Larmessin, sculp,

TOMMASO CAMPANELLA, shown here in a 17th-century engraving by Nicolas de Larmessin the Elder, was an apostate Dominican monk who was imprisoned in 1599 for leading a revolt against the rule of the Hapsburgs in southern Italy. Tortured, starved and frozen while in prison, he nonetheless wrote voluminously about Hermetic and philosophically Copernican ideas. In 1616 he wrote his *Apologia pro Galileo* ("Apology for Galileo"), in which he argued that Galileo's views on astronomy were in accordance with orthodox Roman Catholic theology. Campanella later enjoyed the pope's confidence for a time, but he again fell from favor. He figures prominently in the confluence of events that finally brought Galileo to trial before the Inquisition. The motto *Propter sion non tacebo* recalls Campanella's zeal: "For the sake of the Heavenly City I will not keep still."

one point Urban authorized Campanella to found a college of missionaries, bearing the family name Barberini, which would convert the world to a "reformed," "natural" Catholicism. (Such adjectives were Hermetic watchwords.) Urban found Campanella's Hermetism congenial and was encouraged in his own purely political

pro-French policy. He entered into an alliance with France. In the meantime, however, the French had given their support to the Protestant Swedish king, Gustavus Adolphus. By 1632 the king's military successes had been so sensational that both the political viability of the Holy Roman Empire and the religious viability of the Roman

church throughout much of Germany were seriously threatened.

Thus the pro-French policy turned out to be too successful, and the growing hostility of the Hapsburgs could no longer be ignored. In such a political climate it is not surprising that Urban began to regard Campanella as a false prophet and all his teachings as dangerous. Since Campanella, Bruno, Hermetism and Copernicanism were all tangled together, it would have been a simple step in Urban's mind to link them with another eminent Copernican, Galileo. Given the proper background of fear and suspicion, this association and others could have inclined the pope and the Roman authorities to mistakenly regard Galileo as an antipapist, a religious liberal and perhaps a Hermetist.

DIALOGO
DI
GALILEO GALILEI LINCEO
MATEMATICO SOPRAORDINARIO
DELLO STVDIO DI PISA.

E Filofofo, e Matematico primario del

SERENISSIMO
GR. DVCA DI TOSCANA.

Doue ne i congreffi di quattro giornate fi difcorre
fopra i due

MASSIMI SISTEMI DEL MONDO
TOLEMAICO, E COPERNICANO;

*Proponendo indeterminatamente le ragioni Filofofiche, e Naturali
tanto per l'vna, quanto per l'altra parte.*

CON PRI   VILEGI.

IN FIORENZA, Per Gio:Batifta Landini MDCXXXII.

CON LICENZA DE' SVPERIORI.

TITLE PAGE from Galileo's *Dialogue on the Two Great World Systems* is decorated with a printer's colophon, or emblem, that depicts three fish swimming after one another in a circle. The unintended symbolism of the emblem caused a furor within the Roman church. The fish were assumed to be dolphins—albeit without justification to the modern eye—and the dolphins were immediately taken as a representation of Hermetic and Brunonian ideas condemned by the church. In the contemporaneous context of the Thirty Years' War the emblem was also interpreted as a symbol of philosophical and theological support for the French side. The motto of the emblem, *Grandior ut proles* ("Greater than the offspring"), was misinterpreted to imply that Galileo was extending the work of Bruno by harking back to a superior predecessor, perhaps Apollo, Pythagoras or Hermes Trismegistus. Such figures were associated with the officially discredited Hermetic philosophy.

There was a fourth reason for the Renaissance confusion of Galileo with Bruno, which seems peculiar to the modern mind. On the title page of Galileo's *Dialogue* his printer, Giovanni Batista Landini, had added a colophon, or emblem, which depicted three dolphins swimming after one another in a circle [*see illustration, this page*]. The emblem could be—and was—construed in an extremely damaging sense. In a letter to a friend of Galileo's in Florence, Galileo's Roman disciple Filippo Magalotti gives an account of an interview with Father Niccolò Riccardi. Riccardi was a Florentine who had risen high in the papal bureaucracy to become Master of the Sacred Palace, that is, the pope's theologian. Magalotti writes in part:

"On Monday morning...the most reverend Father...came to seek me.... Then he proceeded to disclose another reason for wishing to have...the *Dialogue*.... Under the seal of secrecy he told me that great offense had been taken at the emblem which was on the frontispiece.... On hearing this, I burst out laughing...and said I thought I could assure him that Signor Galileo was not the man to hide great mysteries under such puerilities and that he had said what he meant clearly enough. I declared that I believed I could affirm that the emblem was the printer's own. On hearing this, he appeared greatly relieved and told me that, if I could assure him that such was the case...the result would be most happy for the author."

The dolphin was a fairly common element in Renaissance emblematics, but the emblem in the *Dialogue* was not a standard cliché. The quest for its "real" meaning was one of the factors that stirred up the first unease about the work in Rome. Riccardi was favorably inclined toward Galileo, and his agitation, together with his implication that the entire case against Galileo depended on the colophon, shows how important it must have been. It was not uncommon to convey arcane messages through symbols. The Roman authorities were led to suspect that Galileo and Landini had together contrived the emblem to hide a message, or perhaps to act as a key or a summary of the work that was to follow.

A suspicious nature could devise connotations of the emblem that were particularly dangerous to Galileo. First the dolphin was associated with the shrine of the god Apollo at Delphi. In Greek mythology Apollo was the father of Asclepius, who was one of the major figures of the Hermetic myths. Furthermore, in Homer's *Iliad* Apollo had been the leading divine supporter of the Trojans, and one of the Trojan survivors, Francus, was the legendary founder of the French royal line. To reinforce the speculation, the word "dauphin" is etymologically related to "dolphin." In the context of the Thirty Years' War such a linkage of France and Troy might be open to serious misinterpretation: as a passing of the mantle of Apollo—or in Christian terms the passing of the Holy Spirit that confers authority on the pope—from Rome to the rising collateral lineage of the Trojans in France.

All such speculation later evaporated. After an embarrassing delay Magalotti was finally able to give Riccardi another, earlier Landini book with the same colophon. By that time, however, the fat was in the fire: Riccardi was off in full cry over the theology of the *Letter to the Grand Duchess,* to whose existence in manuscript Magalotti had clumsily called attention. We have already mentioned some of the difficulties raised by the *Letter;* from then on Galileo's adversaries had more substantial issues to chew on.

We can now describe how the spurious association of Galileo with the Hermetic tradition meshed with contemporaneous political reality and gave a powerful initial impetus to the judicial machinery in which Galileo was caught. Urban VIII preferred to avoid the opposing extremes of religious orthodoxy and Counter-Reformation enthusiasm. His political and personal inclinations led him on a course clear of Spain and thus toward France. As we have mentioned, however, his actions had stirred growing anger among the Spaniards.

In 1631 Gaspare Cardinal Borgia,

the Spanish ambassador to the Holy See, put increasingly heavy pressure on the pope for positive support of the Spanish cause. Urban recognized the danger of growing Spanish hostility, and he declared his readiness to try to dissuade France from an alliance with Sweden. In spite of this move, in March of 1632 Borgia openly attacked the pope in consistory, the meeting of the cardinals. Urban was furious, but he held his peace for fear of an open rupture with Philip IV of Spain.

To mollify Spain, Urban might have moved against France, but such a move would have risked an open break with the French church. The only course open to him was to make a nonsubstantive but strongly symbolic gesture. He could publicly sacrifice a person associated with the pro-French policies and the Hermetic philosophy from which he badly needed to dissociate himself. Campanella was the obvious choice. He was clearly connected not only with the pro-French policy but also with its underlying philosophy. Besides, he was expendable.

But Campanella knew too much. If strong and direct action were taken against him, the unedifying story of a pope who practiced heretical magic would certainly have come out. The next-best choice was Galileo. His association with Campanella in the public mind is underscored by the fact that the writer of the preliminary report of the committee investigating the *Dialogue* at first penned in Campanella's name instead of Galileo's and then had to erase it.

Given even these demanding circumstances, Urban might well have searched further for a scapegoat inasmuch as he had long held Galileo in high regard. Unfortunately, with singularly bad timing Galileo had managed to hurt Urban's feelings. The pope had argued that God could have accomplished his ends in infinitely many ways; as he put it to Galileo, "You must not necessitate God." Because Urban knew of Galileo's Copernican views, he had instructed Galileo not to make any definitive choice between the Ptolemaic and the Copernican systems. Galileo followed the instructions to the letter: the *Dialogue* ends with a passage disclaiming any choice between the two positions. The disclaimer, however, is clearly hypocritical, and Urban's views are put into the mouth of the dogmatic and dullwitted Simplicio. Consequently Urban was not unwilling to make a sacrifice of Galileo when one was needed.

Hence three strands are seen to converge. The political situation demand-

ed a sacrifice. Galileo's writings, interpreted by men who were intelligent but out of touch with his real intent, made him a likely candidate. His supposed mocking of the pope deprived him of Urban's goodwill at a crucial moment. The Hermetic misinterpretation of his writings had been able to launch events that were later sustained by other forces.

One of the least convincing of the traditional explanations for Galileo's troubles has been that his trial went forward because of the pope's personal animosity. Urban's feelings alone would not have led him to set the immense machinery of the Inquisition against Galileo. The enormous disparity between the social and the political positions of Urban and Galileo would have made such a response to a personal affront entirely inappropriate. Our extension of the accepted explanation for the trial shows how Urban's strong reaction can be understood. Given the exigencies of the state and the fact that Galileo seemed to fill a political need, the momentary agreement between this need and Urban's personal pique made things go badly for Galileo.

One can also understand the ambiguities of Urban's later treatment of Galileo. Galileo was old and in poor health when he was summoned to Rome, but even when he lost his sight, Urban angrily refused to mitigate his conditions of house arrest. Yet Urban never tried to interfere with the continued lionization of Galileo, even by princes of the church. Nor did Urban make any attempt to interfere in any effective way with Galileo's freedom to publish, which he surely would have done if he had regarded Galileo as dangerous outside the context of the Spanish policy. Once Galileo had served the purpose of being a symbolic victim, Urban's further actions seemed to stem from mere personal anger rather than official enmity.

Galileo thus became a symbolic victim in an age that set great store by symbols, just as Bruno had before him. He was a victim of pan-European reputation and high visibility, and his exemplary punishment again taught the lesson of 1600: that anti-Hapsburg, pro-French, religiously conciliatory policies were heretical or at least close to it. A caricature of Galileo was concocted from the real man by his enemies and the circumstances of the moment, and so it was a resurrected Bruno who went before the Inquisition in 1633 to furnish a myth around which an existing moral could be woven.

Meeting of Minds

The quaintly-named Lunar Society was short lived and had no
more than some dozen members. Yet, reports JOHN
TIMSON, it probably changed the map of industrial Britain

John Timson

THE SECOND HALF of the
18th century in Britain
witnessed intense scien-
tific and cultural activity.
It was a time when all
things seemed possible. Progress
was not only inevitable but, to most
people, eminently desirable.
Changes were taking place in science, industry, literature and society
which would in many ways shape
the future not only of Britain but of
the whole world.

It was the age of the learned
amateur who had an intense interest
in and curiosity about natural phenomena which had little to do with
seeking personal fame or fortune.
Most of those involved were already
wealthy or had professions which
gave them a comfortable living.
There were few professional scientists or inventors and men believed
they were uncovering the laws of
nature for the benefit of mankind as
a whole. These amateurs had the
time, the money and the intellectual
ability to carry out scientific experiments or to build new inventions in
a disinterested manner rarely possible since then.

Industrialists like Matthew Boulton and Josiah Wedgwood developed and marketed ideas and
inventions which were either their
own or which they had obtained
from their friends and colleagues.
They did not have the large, professional research and development
departments of modern industry.
Frequently there was little understanding of the processes involved

whether natural or artificial. It was
a pragmatic age and most of the
time they worked on trial and error.
The questions they asked were: is it
true, can it be repeated? Or, of an
invention: does it work, is it useful?

It was also a time when many
learned societies were founded.
Some, like the Lichfield Botanical
Society, had no more than three
members but still managed to publish new discoveries during their
short lives. Others like the Philosophical Society of Derby, founded
in 1783, would last much longer
and, as with similar societies in
other cities, would be a useful
meeting place for the educated men
of the area well into the 19th
century.

One of the most important and
influential of these bodies was the
one known as the Lunar Society,
founded about 1766 by Dr. William
Small, Matthew Boulton and Dr.
Erasmus Darwin. Its name referred
to the members' habit of meeting on
days near the time of the full moon
so that they would have light to ride
home by in safety after the meetings. Inevitably to some its members became known as the lunatics.

William Small died at the early
age of 41 in 1775 and both his
practice and his place in the Lunar
Society were taken by Dr. William
Withering, the Chief Physician at
Birmingham General Hospital. He
was a botanist as well as a physician
and in 1776 published *A Botanical
Arrangement of all Vegetables
Naturally Growing in Great Britain*.

He pioneered the use of foxglove
(digitalis) in the treatment of
dropsy.

Like many members, Withering
was something of an eccentric. He
lived his last years in his library
which he kept at a constant temperature of 65°F believing this to be
essential for his health. This led to a
wit of the time saying that, 'The
Flower of Physic is indeed Withering.'

The Lunar Society was a small,
informal group of about a dozen
members, each being allowed to
bring one guest to the meetings
which were held in the members'
homes. The society kept no minutes, published no journal and did
not seek to establish itself as a rival
to other learned societies. Its members had in common no more than a
liking for discussion about the latest
scientific discoveries and inventions, current literature and the
social questions of the day. They
had no common philosophy or
ideology and included practising
Christians and atheists, republicans
and monarchists, supporters and
opponents of the French and American revolutions.

Although the society could confer no honours and had no formal
standing in either the scientific or
academic worlds, many of the leading thinkers of the day were glad to
accept invitations as guests. Probably the most frequent guest was
Josiah Wedgwood. Others were
two of the leading scientists of the
time, Sir Joseph Banks the botanist

From *Heritage: The British Review*, April/May 1987, pp. 40-42. Copyright © 1987 by Heritage Publications.

and explorer, who was President of the Royal Society, and Sir William Herschell the Astronomer Royal.

Then there were John Smeaton, the civil engineer who achieved fame by building the concrete Eddystone Lighthouse, and John Wilkinson, the iron master who came to be, by his own orders, buried in an iron coffin. The society also entertained distinguished foreign guests.

Presiding over the society like a tribal patriarch was the great 18th-century polymath Erasmus Darwin, the grandfather of Charles Darwin. Erasmus was born in 1731 near Newark, Nottinghamshire. After studying medicine at Cambridge and Edinburgh he set up his practice in Lichfield and became one of the most eminent physicians of his day. It is said that he declined an offer of appointment as physician to King George III. Darwin was interested in anything and everything from canals and steam engines tô education and poetry. He was one of the great generalist amateurs unlike his more famous grandson who spent his entire life in the study of natural history.

Although Darwin did not specialise he was a never ending source of ideas and suggestions. His practice did not give him sufficient free time to follow up more than a very few of his ideas. Some were developed by fellow members, others which he designed on paper were (like those of Leonardo da Vinci) quite beyond the technology of his time.

Darwin delighted in unorthodox thoughts and at the meetings of the society he found people who were at least willing to listen even when they did not agree with him. It is clear that Erasmus Darwin had some notion of the theory of organic evolution which his grandson would later present to the scientific world with massive supporting evidence. To Erasmus, however, the idea of evolution was just a suggestion thrown out almost casually in one of his poems, and which he perhaps intended to be the start of a discussion, no more.

One of the society's most important functions was that it brought together scientists and industrialists and provided a forum where new and possibly useful concepts could be discussed. It also provided the opportunity for mutually advantageous friendships to form. When Josiah Wedgwood's pottery business was being developed Darwin not only gave Wedgwood advice on

some of the chemistry involved but also designed for him a horizontal windmill which was successfully built and used to grind pigments. Darwin even suggested the name 'Etruria' for Wedgwood's new works because he believed that Wedgwood had rediscovered the ancient Etruscans' secrets in the art of pottery. Wedgwood was certainly one of the most enterprising manufacturers of the time and left a fortune of nearly one million pounds. His eldest daughter Susannah married Darwin's son Robert. They were the parents of Charles Darwin.

It was through the Lunar Society that the partnership of Matthew Boulton and James Watt was formed. Watt, a rather shy and diffident young man, confided his ideas for the improvement of steam engines to Darwin who had already suggested improvements himself. Darwin quickly realised that the young Scot's ideas were far better than his own.

The steam engines in use before Watt were large, inefficient and only too liable to break down. Watt's improvements combined with Boulton's financial resources and business acumen resulted in the production of the world famous Boulton-Watt engines which were to be the power behind much of the Industrial Revolution. Wedgwood, who at one point lent Boulton £5000 towards their development, used Boulton-Watt engines at Etruria.

The society often met at the country residence of Samuel Galton, Great Barr House, near Sutton Coldfield, about eight miles from Birmingham and twelve miles from Lichfield. Galton was a prosperous businessman who was particularly interested in optics and colours. He was the first to put forward the idea of there being three primary colours. Galton's son, Samuel Tertius, married Darwin's daughter Violetta. One of their sons, Sir Francis Galton, was one of the most original thinkers of the 19th century who made many pioneering contributions to statistics, psychology and human genetics.

Richard Lovell Edgeworth was one of the more eccentric members. He invented several new kinds of carriage including one with a sail, a turnip cutter, and an umbrella for haystacks. Although his inventions were often less than practical he was awarded the gold and silver medals of the Society for the Encouragement of Arts for them. Darwin also

believed in stimulating invention and at one time lent Edgeworth £1,000 — a very considerable sum at the time. One of Edgeworth's more successful ventures was the construction in Ireland of a bog drainage scheme designed by Darwin. Edgeworth was also interested in education, not surprising since he had 22 children and served for six years as a Royal Commissioner on Irish Education. In 1800 he suggested that 'secondary schools' be established throughout Great Britain.

It was Edgeworth who introduced Thomas Day to the society. Day was a writer who was to become famous as the author of *The History of Sandford and Merton*, a moral tale read to three generations of British children. He died in 1789 after being thrown from a horse which did not respond to his theories of control by kindness. His widow asked another member, James Keir, to write Day's biography.

Keir was one of Darwin's oldest friends. They had met at Edinburgh University as students. Keir spent 11 years as a regular soldier before retiring with the rank of captain and taking up the study of industrial chemistry. In 1768 he went to live at West Bromwich and eventually founded the Tipton Alkali Works which were second only to Matthew Boulton's works at Soho in their use of the latest technology. The modern chemical industry can be said to have begun with Keir's factory. At the meetings of the society Keir often acted as chairman.

Probably the most eminent scientist member was Joseph Priestley. Like most of his Fellows he was an amateur scientist. He was a Unitarian minister and has a permanent place in the history of science as the discoverer of oxygen in 1774. Priestley was a prolific experimenter and also discovered ammonia, nitrous oxide, hydrogen chloride and sulphur dioxide. His open sympathy for the French Revolution made him unpopular in Birmingham where an angry crowd sacked his house on 14 July 1791.

After this happened Priestley left Birmingham for London and resisted the efforts of the other members to return. He said, however, that he could find no substitute for the society in London or elsewhere. In 1793 he published his *Experiments on the Generation of Air from Water* which he dedicated to the members of the Lunar Society. In

1794 Priestley emigrated to America where he founded the First Unitarian Church in Philadelphia. He died there in 1804.

The religious beliefs of members ranged from Keir's orthodox Christianity through Priestley's Unitarianism and Darwin's agnosticism to the militant atheism of John Baskerville. Strangely, Baskerville, who was a printer and the inventor of the typeface which bears his name, was well known in his day for his superbly printed Bibles.

Not everyone admired the Lunar Society. William Blake, famous for his hatred of the 'dark satanic mills,' had little sympathy for a group of men dedicated to the advancement of industry, science and invention. This led Blake to write a satire of the society which he called *Island in the Moon*. Yet Blake had contributed illustrations to Darwin's two volume poem, *The Botanic Garden*, which in spite of its title was partly devoted to the praise of industrial progress and forecast future inventions.

Samuel Johnson could sit in the Mitre Tavern in London and say 'There is more learning and science within the circumference of where we now sit than in the rest of the Kingdom.' Clearly he had little time for the Lunar Society. Perhaps Johnson, who had become one of the recognised leaders of intellectual life in the capital, resented the esteem in which Darwin and other members were held in the West Midlands and beyond. Darwin in particular had become the centre of cultural life in Lichfield which was Johnson's home town. This did not please Johnson, who after a brief visit said he had found Lichfield 'intellectually barren.'

Darwin's view of Johnson is perhaps reflected in a line from one of his poems where he wrote 'Johnson grinds poor Shakespeare's bones for bread.' The two men met a number of times but did not get beyond a frosty politeness in public. Both were famous for their conversation and were used to being the centre of attention. Clearly there was not room for both of them in the same town.

The Lunar Society did not survive its founder members. Indeed, when Darwin moved from Lichfield to Derby in 1781 and found it difficult to attend the meetings, the society had lost its driving force. Considering its short life and limited membership it had a remarkable influence on Britain as a whole and the West Midlands in particular. Through the ideas exchanged at its meetings and the contact and friendships made there, the foundations of heavy industry were laid in the Birmingham area. Had the society not existed the industrial map of Britain might well have been very different. More importantly, perhaps, the development of the Industrial Revolution might have taken place more slowly. Marriages between the children of its members, who might otherwise not have met, produced two of the greatest scientists of the 19th century. The course of history was changed by an informal, ephemeral society of about a dozen members who liked to ride home in the moonlight.

Prussia & Frederick the Great

An Historical Essay

Sebastian Haffner

"The King is the first servant of the state (*der Konig ist der erste Diener des Staates*)": these words of Frederick the Great are well-known. What is not so well-known is that the King of Prussia, who spoke and wrote French more often and better than he did German, originally said "*domestique*" and not "*serviteur*"—"*le premier domestique de l'etat*", the first flunkey of the state. That sounds very different and reminds us of another of Frederick's remarks: "How I detest this work to which the blind accident of my birth has condemned me!. . ."

Frederick was by nature an aesthete, a philosopher (today he would probably be called an "intellectual") and a humanist. This explains the terrible conflict he had during his time as Crown Prince with his father, the pious, good-natured Frederick William I, who in the service of his state had become the mean, hard-hearted "Soldier King." The King's son loathed his uniform at first—later it was to be his exclusive dress—and called it a "death-frock (*Sterbekittel*)."

The flute-playing, the love of art, the anti-Machiavellianism positively oozing with philanthrophy, the enthusiastic friendship with Voltaire, the rash humanitarian concessions when he assumed power—the abolition of torture (with exceptions); "The Newspapers must not be interfered with"; "In my state everyone can seek salvation after their own fashion"—all this is not a mask or a generous mood, this is the real Frederick, his original character. He sacrificed it to the "detestable work" to which he saw himself condemned—to put it more precisely, to the Prussian notion of the state, the *Staatsrason,* which demanded of him that he engage in power-politics, that he wage war, fight battles, seize territory, break alliances and treaties, forge money, get the utmost out of his subjects and his soldiers and not least out of himself—in short—that he be the *Konig von Preussen.*

Consequently, he grew bitter. He did not become a tyrant like his father, but he did become an icy cynic, a malicious tormentor to those around him, loving no man, loved by no man, sullen and indifferent towards his own person, unkempt, unclean, always in the same worn-out uniform, still brilliant, but filled now with an inconsolably nihilistic spirit, deeply unhappy below the surface; yet at the same time never idle, always at work, always on duty, indefatigably discharging his detestable work, a great King to his dying breath—with a broken soul.

One tends to be repelled by first impressions of Frederick; but when one studies him in more depth, one does fall under his spell, and he evokes a feeling which one cannot call love, but which is possibly stronger than love. The same is true of his state—the state he and his father created. A crudely-fashioned rational state, without the charm of Austria, the elegance of Saxony, the natural traditions of Bavaria, one might even say (paraphrasing Robert Musil): *ein Staat ohne Eigenschaften,* a state without qualities. And yet, as they say in Prussia, "not without its good points (*nicht ohne*)." A state where concern for the Army and the need for military efficiency to guarantee survival determined all financial, economic and social policies (rather modern and progressive for their time) as well as the degree of humanity.

The Army swallowed up the state budget; so higher taxes were necessary; higher taxes however needed a growing economy; so economic development was encouraged. Economic growth however meant an increase in the population, so immigration was tolerated; and if this happened to be humanitarian into the bargain (by helping the oppressed Protestants in France and Austria), so much the better. Classical Prussia and its great King, who governed it from 1740 to 1786, did not arouse enthusiasm abroad so much as aversion—but it did win respect. Even if Frederick the Great did risk the state and military power his father had built up, he was lucky; he won his big gamble.

Frederick took Silesia away from the Austrians and West Prussia from the Poles—both without any legal or moral pretext—and in doing so finally gave his state a connected body of territories. His truly great achievement, however, was that he managed to defend his Silesian prize in the Seven Years War against a coalition of three great European powers, Austria, France and Russia; an achievement which actually went far beyond the military capabilities of the still small and impoverished state of Prussia. It was this achievement that first enabled Prussia to take its place in the circle of major European powers, albeit as the last and least of its members.

Prussia, both in its creation and in its rise to greatness, is wholly the child of the European epoch between the Thirty Years War and the French Revolution. In no other period could this state have had such a stunning career. Previously there had only been two real powers in Europe. All the other states had to line up on one side of the long-term conflict betweens these two: the Habsburgs and the French Bourbons. But for the 140 years since 1648 the Continent had resembled a stock exchange where the shares of power were continually fluctuating. There was always a war being fought somewhere. In this period war was almost the normal state of affairs. For ordinary citizens at any rate, this was a more or less tolerable state of affairs, because it was only the armies that waged war. It was only to be expected that with so many wars being fought, provinces and countries would continually change hands.

Against this background Frederick's plundering of foreign countries does not look quite so spectacular as it would if judged according to present-day practices. Prussia was doing no more in Silesia and West Prussia than France had done in Alsace, Sweden in Pomerania, Bavaria in the Pfalz, and others had done or were doing elsewhere. And moreover, in the case of West Prussia, there was the excuse that Prussia really did need this connecting piece between Pomerania and East Prussia. Admittedly it did not need Silesia. With its annexation Prussia pushed forward into regions over which it really had no claim. Silesia had belonged under the Bohemian crown to Austria for centuries, and Austria at the bottom of its heart was never to forgive its loss. With this lasting enmity Frederick encumbered his state with a heavy burden which far outweighed the territorial gain.

Why did he do it? As everyone knows, it was more or less the first thing he did. He came to the throne in the summer of 1740. In December he summoned his armies to Silesia "to a rendezvous with glory." Why?

The vague claims of heritary entitlement which he could make at best were too thin to be taken seriously even as a motive let alone as a justification. His own explanations at the time are outrageous. He wrote in a letter in 1740:

> "The satisfaction of knowing my name would be in the newspapers and later in the history books, seduced me into doing it. . . ."

And a year later in a draft of *A History of My Times:*

> "The possession of battle-ready troops, a well-filled state treasury and a lively disposition: these were the real reasons which moved me to war."

But one must not take this entirely seriously. Self-irony and welf-mockery were part of Frederick's character. For his real reasons for waging war were in fact somewhat more serious. What "seduced" him was a uniquely favourable opportunity.

The reigning Habsburg had died in October 1740 without a male heir. The succession of his daughter Maria Theresa to the throne was open to dispute—or at least recognition of her should not be without its price: Silesia, for example. And why not first take the price demanded and negotiate later after gaining possession? The opportunity was favourable because in 1740 Silesia was stripped of all Austrian troops. Austria had only just ended a rather unfortunate war with the Turks with a rather unfortunate peace settlement. Frederick wrote in *A History of My Times:* "After the conclusion of this peace, the Austrian army was in a totally disorganised state. . . .The army was both exhausted and disheartened. After the peace settlement most of its troops remained in Hungary." So for the time being Austria was clearly in a state of military defencelessness and open to political blackmail. Frederick could not resist the opportunity of making such an enormous territorial gain.

That is far from political morality, and one cannot call it politically far-sighted either. But that is how things were done in the 18th century. It is significant that in the War of Austrian Succession, which Frederick's raid unleashed, it was not the victim Austria, but the aggressor Prussia which immediately found allies: France, Bavaria, and Saxony. They all wanted to exploit this momentary weakness of Austria. The fact that Prussia had openly exploited it to seize territory did not in the least deter them from joining forces.

In fact it was Frederick who a year-and-a-half later left his allies in the lurch with a cynical smile and unscrupulously agreed to the separate peace settlement, when Austria, under pressure, conceded to him its rights over Silesia. Then when Austria subsequently began to gain the upper hand again over the coalition of countries which had been weakened by Frederick's withdrawal, Frederick broke the freshly concluded peace treaty in the same cold fashion in which he had made it and declared war again in 1744, only to break his alliance with the coalition for the second time in 1745, when Austria once again ate humble pie. The Austrian War of Succession finally ended in 1748 after eight fruitless years for all the participants—except for Prussia who already had her sheep safely in the fold. A French diplomat remarked at the time "*Nous avons tous travaliie pour le roi de Prusse* (We have all been working for the king of Prussia). . . ."

2. RATIONALISM, ENLIGHTENMENT, AND REVOLUTION

That is how things were done politically in those days. Frederick's Silesian policy was undoubtedly unscrupulous power-politics, but *skrupellose Machtpolitik* was the style of the period. This is made even more apparent by the so-called First Partition of Poland in which he subsequently took West Prussia. The fact that in 1772 in peace-time three great powers simply agreed to cut three convenient pieces off a country that lay between them, was not seen as a monstrous act at the time. Whether the author of the idea was originally Russia or Prussia is still disputed today. Maria Theresa of Austria, who to begin with still had a few scruples, then also decided to get in on the act, so as not to end up empty-handed. Frederick commented: *"Sie weinte, aber sie nahm:* (She wept, but she took her share. . . .)"

A characteristic comment. Frederick the Great was a cynic. He was no more unscrupulous than other politicians of his day, but he differed from them in that he did not disguise his unscrupulousness. On the contrary, he actually took pleasure in openly calling his deeds by the nastiest terms he could find for them. It is difficult to say whether he did this out of mere vainglory or out of inner desperation over his "detestable work." But as a politician Frederick's cynicism presented him with a handicap, and together with his recklessness in the Seven Years War it nearly cost him his neck. He was not a great or masterful politician. His greatness lay elsewhere.

Frederick was intelligent, inventive and many-sided, with not only political and military talents, but rather a highly-gifted dilettante in an unusual number of fields. Just as his thoroughly respectable musical compositions never came close to the greatness of Bach, and his still highly readable writings never achieved the level of Voltaire, as a politician and strategist he never possessed the "ingenious" penetrating insight and the sureness of touch which mark out the greatest. On the contrary: time and again, at least in the first half of his long reign, Frederick was a decided opportunist, a *Hasardeur.*

During this period he acquired the double glory due to a successful statesman and a victorious general. For the Germans of the later Prussian *Kaiserreich* he seemed to embody Chancellor Bismarck and Field Marshal Moltke in a single person. But Frederick emerges unfavourably in such a comparison. Bismark's wars and Moltke's campaigns, whatever else may be said about them, are absolute masterpeices of planning and execution. Bismarck never began a war without first carefully isolating his opponent and putting him in the wrong. Frederick carelessly put himself in the wrong in his three Silesian wars; in the Seven Years War he foolhardily attacked a vastly superior coalition from a position of isolation. In every war, Bismarck knew from the beginning how he could reach peace again with advantage; Frederick never did. He just gambled.

Here the general and the statesman were one. Moltke's campaigns are methodically worked out, carefully deliberated operations. Frederick's battles are, with few exceptions, strategic improvisations, and often desperate gambles. After the defeat at Kunersdorf (1759), Prussia's position was hardly less desperate than it was to be 47 years later after Jena. The fact that the state did not collapse after Kunersdorf, as it did after the defeat by Napoleon, is only partly Frederick's own doing.

He only really acquired the title "the Great" (*Friedrich der Grosse*) in the last three long and terrible years of the Seven Years War, not through any genius, but through extreme steadfastness, resilience, and imperturbability when all hope seemed lost. He possessed an unlimited stoic capacity for suffering, an inner deadness which resisted every blow of fate. This king, who had begun as a frivolous "darling of fortune" (his expression, *Schosskind des Glucks*), showed in misfortune the bearing of a Red Indian being martyred at the stake. Therein lies his true grit. The fact that greatness was finally rescued and rewarded by a stroke of fortune—a new monarch succeeding to the Russian throne and shifting Russia's alliances—in no way detracts from it.

But it is time to take a somewhat closer look at the history of the Seven Years War. This war, the showpiece of "Prussia's Glory", is so overgrown with myths that one can barely perceive its true course any more. The Germans of the 20th century have oriented themselves around these myths in two World Wars—with terrible consequences, as we know.

First, the events leading up to the war. The outbreak of war was preceded by what people at the time called a "diplomatic revolution", a somersault-like turn-about in the traditional system of alliances. Prussia had achieved its conquest of Silesia in alliance with France, and since that time the Franco-Prussian partnership and the enmity between France and Austria had become permanent fixtures.

But things did not stay that way. The old continental rivalry of France and Austria was increasingly superseded by a new rivalry between France and England, with highly urgent disputes to settle in America, Canada and India. Frederick underestimated this new constellation when he sealed the treaty of Westminster with England in January 1756. He miscalculated in two respects. He hoped England would divert Russia from its long-standing alliance with Austria or at least hold it in check—a vain hope; and he calculated that France's opposition to Austria was intractable. But there he was mistaken; France took offence. And that gave Austria the chance to bury its old feud with France and to ally itself in turn with France against Prussia: the second "diplomatic revolution" of the year 1756.

Austria had never resigned itself to the loss of Silesia. Its alliance with Russia had already served to prepare the way for a future reconquest. The new Triple Alliance of Austria-France-Russia could broaden its aims even further: the reduction of Prussia to the March of Brandenburg; and the distribution of the rest of its possessions amongst the allies. Why shouldn't Prussia be divided up just as Poland was later on?

Frederick's situation was serious. His new ally England was a long way off, the prospective English theatres of war lay even further away—in India and Canada. He had to cope with three opponents single-handed, every one of which was stronger than he was.

He decided on a preventive war. But—with characteristic "Fritzian" audacity—he made at one and the same time a war of conquest out of the preventive war. Frederick's Political Testament of 1752 contains the following sentences:

> "Of all the countries in Europe those of most immediate interest to Prussia are: Saxony, Polish Prussia, and Swedish Pomerania. Saxony would be the most useful."

Frederick began the war by attacking and occupying Saxony without a declaration of war, and capturing the Saxon army. Thenceforth the Saxons had to pay Prussian taxes, which were collected by Prussian officials, and the King of Prussia incorporated the captured Saxon army into his own army. (The Saxon soldiers nevertheless deserted when they could.)

The conquest of Saxony was not much use to Frederick anyway. Admittedly he was able to invade Bohemia the following spring, but an Austrian army equally strong and eager for action was already waiting for him there, and the battle near Prague—the biggest so far of the century—was only what Schlieffen used to call an "ordinary victory" for the Prussians. The Austrians retreated in good order, dug themselves in in Prague, and a relief army was on its way. Frederick had to split up his army to avert the relief of Prague, and to risk for the first time an offensive battle while he was outnumbered: at Kolin, with 33,000 Prussians against 54,000 Austrians. He lost, had to abandon the siege of Prague, and withdraw from Bohemia. His attempt to surprise the enemy with a preventive war had failed.

In fact the war itself seemed already lost, for now the adversaries came from all sides. The French advanced through Thuringia, the Austrians took back Silesia which was poorly defended, and the Russians occupied East Prussia, which was not defended at all. But now the Prussians showed what they could do. Up and down, and back and forth, in all directions they took on each opponent individually, still with the same small but superb army, and won three magnificent victories, on each occasion against a numerically superior enemy: in the late autumn of 1757 at Rossbachk against the French, at Leuthen in Silesia against the Austrians, and in the summer of 1758 at Zorndorf in the Neumark against the Russians. These three battles made Frederick famous and popular throughout the world: a David who had coped with three Goliaths!

But he didn't really cope with them in the long run. Frederick's splendid little army gradually bled to death, and the replacements that he remorselessly levied and

enlisted no longer had the quality of the cuirassiers of Rossbach and Zorndorf and of the grenadiers of Leuthen. At Kunersdorf-on-the-Oder, where the Prussians risked a decisive battle in 1759 against the combined forces of the Austrians and the Russians, they suffered a crushing defeat. That saw the end of their successful all-round defence. From now on Prussia could only wage a delaying war of attrition.

It seems miraculous that Prussia was able to do this for three hopeless years. But it becomes less miraculous if one visualises the character of 18th-century wars. In those days wars were not people's wars. The citizen felt the effects all right: in higher taxes, devalued money, and wider conscription. But the countryside was not ravaged, the fields were cultivated and the harvests gathered in, business continued as usual, and the scholars let nothing upset the course of their controversies.

It was also remarkable how easily conquered and defeated countries and provinces adapted themselves to the respective shifts of power as a matter of course. The Saxons conscientiously paid their Prussian taxes; the Silesians readily paid homage to their Empress when they were occupied by the Austrians, and then just as readily paid homage to their King when the Prussians returned; the East Prussians paid homage to the Tsarina. The war passed over people's heads; they ducked and let the storm pass. Only for the soldiers was the endless war hard, terribly hard; but they stood under iron discipline. And the vast hopeless struggle was hard for the harassed King of Prussia, who needed a new inspiration every day in order somehow to survive.

Deliverance arrived at the beginning of 1762 with the death of the Russian Tsarina. Her successor, a rather confused man and an enthusiastic supporter of Frederick, not only made peace immediately but allied himself with his idol; and the Russian army swopped fronts. This Tsar, Peter III, was assassinated the same year, and his by no means grief-stricken widow and successor Catherine (later called the Great) revoked the Prussian alliance. But she remained at peace, and the other allies now also inclined more and more to peace. Their coffers were empty, their armies exhausted, the Franco-English war was decided, and dogged Prussia was obviously not going to be killed off.

This resulted in the peace of Hubertusburg—a peace brought about by exhaustion, which left everything just as it was. Saxony was restored again, Silesia remained with Prussia; so did East Prussia of course. It seemed that nobody had gained anything, and they had all been fighting for nothing.

But in reality this drawn game was a triumph for Prussia: it had held its own against three major powers.

Had it thereby become a major power itself? That was still a matter of doubt for a long time to come. Frederick himself in any case always remained conscious of the fact that, despite all martial glory, he had only just got away with it by an improbable stroke of luck. He had already stated after the Second Silesian War that he would not tackle so much as a cat for the rest of his life. After the Seven Years War he put that into practice. He returned to the priciples of his father, to made Prussia internally strong without dissipating this strength by using it to excess. His foreign policy after 1763 became—like that of his father—cautious, modest and defensive once again. Its sole anxiety was to prevent Austria from ever becoming too powerful in the empire again (by the acquisition of Bavaria for instance); otherwise seeking contact, now chiefly with Russia.

"It is worth cultivating the friendship of those barbarians": this was Frederick's political maxim, which he observed to the end of his days and which Prussia too mostly observed later on, for almost a century, to its own advantage. But this was not true power politics.

The Prussia that Frederick left behind was a European curiosity: a small major (or semi-major) power, which looked like a Turkish sabre on the map: long and curved like a worm, almost nothing but borders; in addition, scattered possessions in the German west, which could not be defended in case of war. Prussia in the later years of Frederick was, strictly speaking, still without a solid basis of power, or even existence; just terribly prickly, with a stubborn instinct of self-preservation and with that dreadful army, the grenadiers of Leuthen and Torgau, which the whole of Europe had not been able to handle a quarter-of-a-century ago. As long as its great old man, *der alte Fritz*, was alive and as long as he, with his new-found caution, left others in peace, people also preferred in God's name to leave Prussia in peace.

But Prussia's successes in the 18th century were not only due to the "genius" of Frederick the Great, not only due to favourable external circumstances and their skilful exploitation, and not only due to the success with arms and military efficiency. They were due above all to the fact that throughout the century Prussia was in such total accord with the spirit of the age, the *Zeitgeist*. This "rational state" was tailor-made for the Age of Reason. A state and nothing but a state, raceless, rootless, abstract, an administrative, judicial and military system construed from the spirit of the Enlightenment, "Prussia" could be displaced and transferred almost at will, and as it were slipped over the heads of any nations, races, and regions whatsoever. A popular rhyme of the period runs:

Niemand wird Preusse denn aus Not.
Ist er's geworden, dankt er Gott.
(No man turns Prussian but for the rod.
Once he is one, he thanks God.)

This Prussian rational state did not merely have a hard, metallic, mechanical face. It also had a cool liberality, justice and tolerance, which was none the less gratifying for its subjects because it was primarily founded on indifference. No witches were burnt in Prussia any more (as was still quite common elsewhere); there were no forced conversions and religious persecutions; everyone could think and write what he wished; the same law applied to everybody.

The millions of Poles, for example, who were incorporated by Prussia between 1772 and 1795, were no worse off in Prussia than they were before; if anything they were better off. There was no thought of "Germanising" them, which became the sad practice much later on, in the time of Bismarck and even more so in the post-Bismarck period, in the German Reich. And if anyone were to suggest to an 18th-century Prussian that he should deal with the Poles in the way Hitler did in the 20th century (or the way Poland subsequently dealt with those Germans placed under its jurisdiction) he would have been stared at as if he were mad.

The Poles who had become Prussians were neither treated as "sub-human" nor disposed of as alien elements; no interference whatsoever was made in their language, customs, and religion. On the contrary, they were (for instance) given more primary schools than ever before, with teachers who had to speak Polish as a matter of course. Polish serfdom was superseded by the milder Prussian hereditary subordination; and as far as the Polish upper classes were concerned, posts in the Prussian administration and posts as officers were open to them, and many Polish aristocrats became for generations not merely loyal but prominent Prussians. One of them sadly declared later, after 1871, that the Poles could have become Prussians any time, but never Germans.

One was not a Prussian by nature, as one was a Pole, a Frenchman, an Englishman, a German, or even a Bavarian or Saxon. Prussian nationality was more interchangeable than any other. This abstract statehood, rooted in no particular nation or race, but applicable at will so to speak, was Prussia's strength.

This 18th-century state demanded no enthusiasm from its subjects; it did not appeal to love of the Fatherland, national fervour, or even to tradition, but exclusively to their sense of duty. The highest Prussian order, the Black Eagle, bore the words: *Suum cuique*— To each his own. An apt state motto, even more apt if it were translated: "To each his duty."

The state set a tasks to every citizen, from the King to the poorest subject; it strongly obliged him to perform that task; and every class had a different task. One had to serve the state with money, another with blood, some also with "brains" (*Kopfchen*), but all with hard work. Performance of one's task was in Prussia the first and highest commandment and at the same time it entirely justified everything else: anyone who did his duty was not committing a sin, whatever he might be doing. A second commandment was certainly not to be sorry for oneself; and a third, much weaker one, was to be— perhaps not exactly good (that would be overdoing it), but decent to one's fellow citizens. One's duty to the state came first. It was possible to live with this substitute for religion, and even to live an orderly and decent life—as long as the state that one served remained orderly and decent. The limits and dangers of the Prussian religion of duty only became apparent under Hitler.

But—what was it all for? Prussia urged its subjects to perform their duty, but what duty did it actually perform itself? Everyone had to serve the "Prussian idea": what idea did Prussia serve? We cannot detect one: no religious idea, no national idea, no idea of the sort which is nowadays called ideological This state only served itself, served its own preservation which, as things stood geographically, inevitably also meant its expansion.

Prussia was an end in itself; and to its neighbours it was from the beginning a danger and a threat. It was possible to imagine Europe without it; and it is small wonder that many people wished it out of the way when it made itself so alarmingly strong and then made use of this strength under Frederick the Great—rapacious use, as one must observe in all objectivity. In the wars of Frederick the Great, right, *das Recht*, is almost always on the side of his enemies. And yet Frederick is the hero of these wars, and his injustice pales beside his heroic exploits. History is unjust like that sometimes.

Prussia did not have to exist. The world was able to do without it. It wanted to exist. Nobody had invited this small country into the circle of the major European powers. It obtruded itself, and it forced its way in. But the way it did so for half a century—with spirit, cunning, impudence, spite and heroism—is a spectacle worth contemplating.

The Commercialization of Childhood

In eighteenth-century England, picture books, playthings, and educational gimcracks became a thriving business: a trend that has continued from that time to this

J. H. Plumb

A new attitude toward children developed in England during the eighteenth century, an attitude that spread as easily to Boston, New York, and Philadelphia as it did to Birmingham, Leeds, and Glasgow. It was a gentler and more sensitive approach to children, one that was part of a wider change in social attitudes: a growing belief that nature was inherently good, not evil, and what evil there was derived from man and his institutions. The dominant attitude toward children in the seventeenth century had been autocratic, even ferocious: "The new borne babe," Richard Allestree wrote in 1658, "is full of the stains and pollutions of sin which it inherits from our first parents through their loins."

From birth, English children were constrained. They spent their first months, sometimes a year, bound tightly in swaddling clothes. Their common lot was fierce parental discipline. Even a man of such warm and kindly nature as Samuel Pepys thought nothing of beating his fifteen-year-old maid with a broomstick and locking her up for the night in his cellar, or whipping his boy-servant, or boxing his clerk's ears. Of two hundred manuals on child rearing prior to 1700, only three, those by Plutarch, Matteo Palmieri, and Jacopo Sadoleto, did not recommend that fathers beat their children.

In 1693 John Locke finally gave expression to what was clearly a new and more liberal attitude toward child rearing and education in *Some Thoughts Concerning Education.* This was by far his most popular book; it was reprinted nineteen times before 1761 and was as well known in America as in England. Locke believed in arousing the child's interest in education by a system of esteem for those who did well, and shame for those who were reluctant to learn. He disapproved of the time-honored method of flogging boys into learning, a sentiment that was already widespread but to which his authority gave added force. He was equally opposed to bribing the child to work through material rewards:

"The *Rewards* and *Punishments* then, whereby we should keep Children in order, *are* quite of another kind; and of that force, that when we can get them once to work, the Business, I think, is done, and the Difficulty is over. *Esteem* and *Disgrace* are, of all others, the most powerful Incentives to the Mind, when once it is brought to relish them. If you can once get into Children a Love of Credit, and an Apprehension of Shame and Disgrace, you have put into them the true Principle." As well as arguing for a more liberal attitude toward the child, Locke also pleaded for a broader curriculum in schools. He believed education should fit man for society as well as equip him with learning; hence he pressed for lessons not only in drawing but also in French. He opposed teaching languages by a rigid grounding in grammar and urged that Latin be taught by the direct method, as it would had it been a living language.

After Locke, education of children increasingly became social rather than religious. Greater emphasis was placed on its usefulness in the child's future life in society. Although a knowledge of the classics was still regarded as the mark of a gentleman, more and more small schools, run for a profit, provided a far more practical education—in bookkeeping, penmanship, the English language, foreign languages, mathematics, navigation, surveying, geography, and the use of globes. It was this type of education, not the grammar schools, that flourished vigorously in the eighteenth century.

By 1740, and perhaps before, children were no longer regarded as sprigs of old Adam, whose wills had to be broken by the rod. Nor was education regarded as a genteel accomplishment; boys and girls were being educated in order to play effective and successful roles in an aggressive commercial society. And because commercial opportunities everywhere abounded, parents were willing to invest, as never before, in the education of their children. Naturally enough this had a profound influence on the production of children's books.

Books by which children could be taught had existed from the first days of printing—alphabets, grammars, and the like—but few were designed specifically for children. Authors and publishers made very little attempt to entice the young mind with attractive and compelling illustrations and typography. It should be remembered that fairy stories, ballads, riddles, and fables were intended as much for adults as for children. Indeed, Aesop was not specifically adapted for children in England until 1692, when Sir Roger L'Estrange produced his edition.

The late seventeenth and early eighteenth centuries saw the beginnings of new attitudes toward children's literature and methods of learning to read. In 1694, "J. G." published *A Play-book for children, to allure them to read as soon as they can speak plain. Composed of small pages, on purpose not to tire children, and printed with a fair and pleasant letter. The matter and method plainer and easier than any yet extant,* which was, for once, a true statement in a blurb. The author states in his preface that he wishes to "decoy Children into reading." The book has wide margins and large type; its language is simple and concrete and mostly within the compass of a child's experience. It did well enough to be reprinted in 1703, by which time a few other authors, noticeably William Ronksley, were attempting to find methods and materials more suitable for very young children.

Ronksley believed in teaching by verse according to the meter of the Psalms—first week, words of one syllable, the next week words of two syllables, and so one. And he used jokes, riddles, and proverbs to sugar his pills. Even so, his and other innovative children's books of Queen Anne's reign were designed, quite obviously, to be chanted, to be learned by the ear rather than by the eye. They were meant more for teachers and parents to teach with than for a child to enjoy. Similar books were slow to appear, and it is not until the 1740's that the change in style of children's literature becomes marked. The entrepreneurial noses of Thomas Boreman and John Newbury twitched and scented a market for books written specifically for children that would be simple to produce and enticing to the eye. Of course, it was not quite as simple as that. Children do not buy books; adults do.

So the new children's literature was designed to attract adults, to project an image of those virtues that parents wished to inculcate in their offspring, as well as to beguile the child. By their simplicity, these alphabet and reading books also strengthened parents' confidence in their ability to teach their children to read at home. The new children's literature was aimed at the young, but only through the refraction of the approving parental eye.

By the 1740's and 1750's the market was there, ready to be exploited, and no man was quicker to seize the opportunity than John Newbery, whose *Little Pretty Pocket-Book,* published in 1744, captured the public imagination. Until the early nineteenth century Newbery's family continued to produce quantities of children's literature. Each decade the number of titles grew, and the most popular books were reprinted over and over again. The range was exceptional—from simple books for reading, writing, and arithmetic to *The Newtonian System of Philosophy Adapted to the Capacities of young Gentlemen and Ladies. . .Lectures read to the Lilliputian Society by Tom Telescope.*

The latter book is crystal-clear and the examples are exceptionally apposite. Its attitudes toward the universe, humanity, philosophy, and the natural sciences would have drawn cheers from the Encyclopedists. It is not only a brilliantly produced book for adolescent children, but it also gives us a novel insight into how the ideas of the Enlightenment were being disseminated through society. How ideas are transformed into social attitudes is a most complex problem, and social historians have almost all neglected the influence of children's literature in changing the climate of ideas. *Tom Telescope* therefore deserves a closer study.

There are six lectures. The first is on matter and motion, quite brilliantly explained. The second deals with the universe, particularly the solar system, and also with the velocity of light. Tom Telescope then moves on to atmosphere and meteors, and to mountains, particularly volcanoes, and earthquakes, and to rivers and the sea. Minerals, vegetables, and animals follow, and the final lecture is on the natural philosophy of man—his senses, the nature of his understanding, and the origin of ideas, with a great deal on optics, including the prism, and a section on pleasure and pain. The book is relatively brief—only 125 pages—but is wide-ranging, giving a simple outline of the most advanced attitudes toward the universe and man's place in it. God is present through his works and also as the divine wisdom that reason, if pursued, will ultimately reveal to mankind.

The philosophic attitude is purely Lockian, as the science is entirely Newtonian. "All our ideas, therefore," says Tom Telescope, "are obtained either by *sensation* or *reflection,* that is to say, by means of our five senses, as *seeing, hearing, smelling, tasting,* and *touching,* or by the *operations of the mind* [upon them]."

Although packed with lucid scientific information, the book has many asides, allegories, and stories that plead for a compassionate humanity, particularly toward animals. Tom's plea is based on the new attitude that cruelty to animals is improper. Cruelty between animals is necessary to sustain the animal world; hence cruelty, in this aspect, is a part of divine wisdom. But necessity alone permits human cruelty toward animals in the shape of killing and eating. Wanton cruelty is reprehensible, particularly to young animals and, above all, young birds. Most detestable of all is the taking or destruction of eggs (a common theme in eighteenth-century children's books).

Tom has no patience, however, with those who put kindness to animals before that to their fellow men. Tom's lecture reminds his hostess, Lady Caroline, of her neighbor Sir Thomas, whom young Tom has seen treat animals well if they please, "but rave, at the same time, in a merciless manner, at poor children who were shivering at his gate, and send them away empty handed." Another neighbor, Sir William, "is also of the same disposition; he will not sell a horse, that is declining, for fear he should fall into the hands of a master who might treat him with cruelty; but he is largely concerned in the slave trade (which, I think, is carried on by none but *we good Christians,* to the dishonour of our *coelestial Master*) and makes no difficulty of separating the husband from the wife, the parents from the children, and all of them. . .from their native country, to be sold in a foreign market, like so many horses, and often to the most merciless of the human race." Kindness to animals, yes, but greater kindness to human beings is the burden of Tom's final lecture.

Tom Telescope had an extraordinary success. Within a few weeks of its publication in 1761, it was on sale in Norwich and was being advertised there in the newspapers. A new edition was required in 1762, a third edition in 1766, and a fourth in 1770. All together there were at least ten editions by 1800. It is difficult, however, to be in any way certain of the size of these editions. Newbery printed fifteen hundred copies of his juvenile edition of Dr. Johnson's *Idler;* but there were editions of ten thousand for his very popular *Little Pretty Pocket-Book.* Doubtless the editions of *Tom Telescope* varied, the second probably much larger than the first, which, following Newbery's usual practice, would be small to test the market. By conservative estimate, the book probably enjoyed a sale of twenty-five to thirty thousand copies between 1760 and 1800, but the number could be far higher. Hence Lockian and Newtonian ideas, combined with a compassionate humanity, were being widely disseminated among the middle-class young.

Newbery's success with *Tom Telescope* did not go unnoticed, and the range of books on science designed for children grew. *A Museum*, published about 1750 and containing essays on natural history and the solar system, had run to fifteen editions by 1800. The Reverend Samuel Ward completed twelve such volumes on *The Modern System of Natural History* in 1776. In the same year, *Mr. Telltruth's Natural History of Birds and of Animals* was written for very young children—it too was full of the reasonableness of nature. And it cost only sixpence. In 1800 one publisher advertised thirty-eight books for children, covering the arts and sciences; of these, fifteen were scientific and only two dealt with religion. Geography, history, and the classics were rapidly adapted to the needs of juvenile readers.

Newbery and other publishers also produced quantities of moral tales, more beloved, one suspects, by parents than by children. Through Edward Augustus Kendall, the Newberys produced new types of fables, derived from the ballad of Cock Robin, in which birds develop human attributes, converse freely among themselves, and offer their own criticisms of human failure and shortcomings. Kendall wrote *The Swallow, The Wren, The Canary, The Sparrow*; and their themes are simple—cruelty to birds, taking eggs, breaking up nests, and caging finches are the marks of an evil boy. Cruelty is wicked, humane behavior laudable. Charity and benevolence will not only make a child happy but bring him the proper social rewards.

A similar burden is echoed in the potted biographies of eminent children and in the examples of historic characters held up for the edification of youth. The themes of most of them are avoidance of cruelty, violence, brutality, and the development of innocent virtues like obedience, sensitivity, a love of nature, and therefore of reason, which naturally leads to industry, benevolence, and compassion. Nothing was regarded as more edifying than the death of a model child.

Augustus Francis Emilian, perhaps the most nauseating boy in all children's literature, takes twelve pages to die in *Juvenile Biography,* a translation of an eighteenth-century French novel. After being on the point of death for more than thirty-six hours, Emilian rallies sufficiently at the last moment to say, although with painful effort, "What grieves me most is to quit you Mamma, as well as not to have lived long enough to be useful to my country." Not surprisingly, "At these immortal words a rattling in the throat stifled the half-articulated words." However, death did not come for another page and a half.

Even in the enlightened eighteenth century, there continued a savage, macabre streak in attitudes toward childrn. (Corpse viewing—practiced at Wesley's school at Kingswood—was thought of as salutary.) Yet, the desire to entertain, delight, and instruct children had disguised, if not obliterated, much of the heavy moralizing. Between 1780 and 1800, though, the moral note gets stronger. Mrs. Sarah Trimmer was the most formidable of children's writers at that time, and Mrs. Trimmer was not light of heart. The works of Mrs. Trimmer and Mrs. Anna Barbauld, another gentlewoman who produced countless instructive and moralistic tales, covered the shelves of the Newbery bookstore when Charles Lamb and his sister Mary went there in 1802. Lamb, himself a writer of children's stories, wrote indignantly to Samuel Taylor Coleridge: " 'Goody Two Shoes' is almost out of print. Mrs. Barbauld's stuff has banished all the old classics of the nursery; and the shopman at Newbery's hardly deigned to reach them off an old exploded corner of a shelf, when Mary asked for them. Mrs. B.'s and Mrs. Trimmer's nonsense lay in piles about. Knowledge insignificant and vapid as Mrs. B.'s books convey, it seems, must come to a child in the *shape* of *knowledge,* and his empty noddle must be turned with conceit of his own powers when he has learnt that a Horse is an animal, and Billy is better than a Horse, and such like; instead of that beautiful Interest in wild tales which made the child a man, while all the time he suspected himself to be no bigger than a child. . . .Think what you would have been now, if instead of being fed with Tales and old wives' fables in childhood, you had been crammed with geography and natural history!"

Nevertheless, the contrast in the range of what was available for children between, say, 1700 and 1800, is vivid. By 1800 there was no subject, scientific or literary, that did not have a specialized literature designed for children—often beautifully and realistically illustrated, at times by such distinguished book illustrators as Thomas Bewick. The simpler textbooks—for reading, writing, and arithmetic—were carefully designed, with large lettering, appropriate illustration, and a small amount of print on a large page; and there were books for very young children, such as *A Pretty Plaything for Children.* Novels specifically written about children for children began with *Sandford and Merton,* by Thomas Day. And the arts, as well as letters, were catered to—Master Michael Angelo's *The Drawing School for Little Masters and Misses* appeared in 1773, and there were books designed to teach children the first steps in music. As with adult books of the same era, less prosperous children could buy their books a part at a time. Nor was it necessary to buy the books; they could be borrowed. By 1810, there was a well-established juvenile library at 157 New Bond Street. Some owners of circulating libraries even maintained a special section for children.

As well as becoming far more plentiful, children's books also became cheaper. John Newbery used every type of gimmick to extend his market. With the *Little Pretty Pocket-Book* he offered—for an extra twopence— a ball for the son or a pincushion for the daughter. He used new types of binding that did not stain, and he even tried giving a book away when the purchaser bought the binding. He advertised his books in every possible way—rarely did a parent finish one of his books without finding in the text a recommendation to read others. He sensed that there was a huge market ready for exploitation, and he was right.

Within twenty years children's books were a thriving part of the Newcastle printer's trade; indeed, educational books attracted a very large number of provincial printers in the late eighteenth century, for they were well aware of the hunger of shopkeepers, tradesmen, and artisans for education, not only for themselves, but also, and most emphatically, for their children. The printers of Philadelphia did not lag behind those of the English provinces; they were some of the earliest in the field of children's literature outside London. In 1768 Shorhawk and Anderton, principally a firm of druggists,

advertised "a very great choice of books adapted for the instruction and amusement of all the little masters and mistresses in America." (John Newbery was also the proprietor of the famous Dr. James's Fever Powder, which he plugged remorselessly in his books: the relationship between the marketing of children's books and patent medicines was always close.)

By 1800 children's books had become very cheap; those costing a penny were plentiful, and this was at a time when books in general, because of inflation, had increased in price by 25 per cent. Nevertheless, Oliver and Boyd of Edinburgh turned them out by the score under the title of *Jack Dandy's Delight.* They published forty at sixpence, twenty-six at twopence, forty at one penny, and forty at a halfpenny. The penny books were well printed and delightfully illustrated. Only the poorest families of unskilled laborers could not afford a halfpenny. Like Thomas Paine's *The Rights of Man,* children's literature was within the range of the industrious working class, and particularly of those families whose social ambition had been stirred by the growing opportunities of a new industrialized society— more and more clerical jobs were available, and more and more parents were willing to make sacrifices to secure them for their children. Middle-class parents had begun to buy children's books in quantity.

From 1700 onward, the intellectual and cultural horizons of the middle-class child, and of the lower-middle-class child, had broadened vastly. There was an air of modernity about a great deal of his reading, a sense that he belonged to a new and exciting world. The same was true of a child's education, both the formal, so long as grammar school was avoided, and the informal. Itinerant lecturers in science, usually accompanied by complex electrical apparatuses, were exceptionally popular. Although their courses were mainly for adults, more often than not they offered cheap tickets for children. Indeed, this became a common practice for public amusements that were also partly educational.

The range and variety of such amusements may be demonstrated by looking at what was available at Leeds, a prospering industrial and commercial city of Yorkshire, during the summer months of 1773. In April families at Leeds were regaled by Mr. Manuel of Turin with his display of automatons, including an Indian lady in her chariot moving around the table at ten miles an hour and the "Grand Turk, in the Seraglio dress, who walks about the table smoking his pipe in a surprising manner." All the automatons, of course, were accompanied by mechanical musical instruments.

After Mr. Manuel, Mr. Pitt arrived with his principal marvel, a self-moving phaeton that traveled at six miles an hour, climbed hills, and started and stopped with the touch of a finger. He also brought along his electrifying machine, his camera obscura, his miraculous door that opened inside, outside, left, or right by the turn of a key. All this for one shilling. The phaeton either wore out, broke down, or proved too expensive to move, for it was dropped by Pitt, who continued for some years to travel the Midland circuit of Nottingham, Leicester, Coventry, and so on, but only with his scientific apparatus. Quite obviously he made a tolerable living from his traveling show.

On August 10 the attraction at Leeds was geographic, as a model of the city and suburbs of Paris arrived at the town hall. It covered eighteen square feet and was extremely elaborate. Viewing began at nine in the morning and closed at eight in the evening. In September a spectacular, double-column advertisement with woodcuts announced the arrival of Astley's circus, with prices, as usual, at a shilling for front seats, sixpence for back, but Astley warned that boys trying to climb in would be taken care of by guards. He also brought along with him his famous "Chronoscope," an apparatus for measuring the velocity of projectiles.

The emphasis was on marvels, curiosities, usually mechanical or optical ones, that were new and remarkable. Hence children were given a keen sense of a new, developing, and changing world in which mechanical ingenuity and electricity and science in general played an active part—a totally different cultural atmosphere from the one their grandparents had lived in. Their cultural horizons, too, were widened by the availability of music to listen to in festivals and concerts, the cheapness of musical instruments, and the plentiful supply of music teachers. Art materials were to be found in every provincial town, and so were drawing masters, who taught in the home as well as in the school. Prints of old masters and modern artists were a commonplace of life. Visually, it was a far more exciting age for children than ever before.

Through most of these amusements, however, ran the theme of self-improvement and self-education. The same is true of indoor games as well as outdoor excursions. Playing cards had long been used to inculcate knowledge—largely geographic, historical, and classical. One of the earliest packs, from about 1700, taught carving lessons—hearts for joints of meat, diamonds for poultry, clubs for fish, and spades for meat pies. But more often than not these were imports, usually from France. The eighteenth century witnessed a rapid increase in English educational playing cards, so that almost every variety of knowledge or educational entertainment could be found imprinted on their faces. The majority of booksellers, provincial as well as metropolitan, stocked them. Some cards were designed for the education of adults, or at least adolescents, but there were packs, very simply designed, for young children so they could play and learn at the same time. One pack, for example, taught the first steps in music.

After playing cards, one of the earliest educational games to be developed was the jigsaw puzzle, seemingly an English invention by the printer-bookseller and young entrepreneur John Spilsbury, who in 1762 produced dissected maps for the teaching of geography. These enjoyed an immediate, perhaps a phenomenal, success, and by the mid-1760's Spilsbury had thirty different jigsaw maps for sale. Unfortunately he died young—in his twenties—but what he had launched quickly proliferated, not only in the teaching of history, geography, and morals, but also purely for fun, though even these puzzles tended to have a moral message of self-improvement.

The principal publisher of educational games became John Wallis, whose firm began to flourish in the 1780's and lasted until 1847, during which time it dominated the field of educational games, some of which were extremely complex. In the seventeenth century, Pierre du Val had used gambling games, with painted boards and dice, to teach geography and history; indeed, it has been said that Louis XIV learned his lessons this way, for the French court and aristocracy of the seventeenth century had no inhibitions about children gambling. In England the first dice game played on a painted board for instruction seems to have been invented by John Jefferys in 1759. His game was called A Journey through Europe, or The Play of Geography, and the players moved along a marked route according to the throw of their dice. This proved very popular and spawned a host of similar games, some of extreme complexity, such as Walker's Geographical Pastime exhibiting a Complete Voyage Round the World in Two Hemispheres, which must have taken hours to play. There were also card games, often employing a rebus, which were extremely popular for teaching spelling, extending the vocabulary, and quickening the wits.

By the early nineteenth century, in spite of the novelist Maria Edgeworth's fulminations about their uselessness, almost as many kinds of educational toys were available as there are today. There were complex mechanical toys—water mills, printing presses, looms—which could be assembled and made to work. There were cheap inflatable globes, complicated perspective views, and toy theatres with movable scenery and actors, on which whole plays could be acted and reacted from the scripts provided. There were scientific toys, camera obscuras and the like, made cheaply for children. By that time, too, there were large quantities of toys on the market whose educational value was present, if secondary—Noah's arks, animal farms, soldiers and forts of every variety for the potential soldier, and of course, dolls and doll houses. These varied from the extremely cheap—cutouts in paper with brightly colored interchangeable clothes—to elaborate models with wax or earthenware faces, jointed bodies, and complete wardrobes. And in London there were, by 1800 at least, two shops that specialized in making rocking horses. In 1730 there had been no specialized toy shops of any kind, whereas by 1780 toy shops abounded, and by 1820 the trade in toys, as in children's literature, had become very large indeed.

Children, in a sense, had become luxury objects upon which their parents were willing to spend larger and larger sums of money, not only for their education but also for their entertainment and amusement. Indeed, by the second half of the eighteenth century, the most advanced radicals had become deeply concerned by the growing indulgence of parents toward their children, particularly the waste of money on useless toys. Maria Edgeworth denounced dolls and doll houses, had no use for rocking horses, and strongly disapproved of stuffed lambs, squeaky pigs and cuckoos, and all simple action toys. She was for a pencil and plain paper, for toys that led to physical exercise—hoops, tops, and battledores—and for a pair of scissors and paper for a girl to cut out her fancies with. Later, boys should be given models of instruments used by manufacturers—spinning wheels, looms, paper mills, and the like. The interest in Maria Edgeworth's long discussion of toys lies in the huge variety that obviously abounded in the 1790's—a variety not as extensive, of course, as today's, but reflecting our world rather than the world of seventeenth-century England.

Whatever the attitudes of parents, or of educational reformers, children had become a trade, a field of commercial enterprise for the sharp-eyed entrepreneur. The competition was fiercest, the ingenuity greatest, in children's literature and in indoor games that taught as well as amused. Both fields were remarkably inventive, and their most important feature was that they encouraged teaching in the home. They were so skillfully designed, so beautifully illustrated, that they gave confidence to parents as well as children by the ease with which they could be used. Ease of comprehension was as important as the delight of the contents, and books that combined both had an enduring success generation after generation. The most permanent effect of this revolution in children's literature was to marry text and illustration. Like all true marriages, that has proved indissoluble.

The First Feminist

In 1792 Mary Wollstonecraft wrote
a book to prove that her sex was as intelligent
as the other: thus did feminism
come into the world. Right on, Ms. Mary!

SHIRLEY TOMKIEVICZ

The first person—male or female—to speak at any length and to any effect about woman's rights was Mary Wollstonecraft. In 1792, when her *Vindication of the Rights of Woman* appeared, Mary was a beautiful spinster of thirty-three who had made a successful career for herself in the publishing world of London. This accomplishment was rare enough for a woman in that day. Her manifesto, at once impassioned and learned, was an achievement of real originality. The book electrified the reading public and made Mary famous. The core of its argument is simple: "I wish to see women neither heroines nor brutes; but reasonable creatures," Mary wrote. This ancestress of the Women's Liberation Movement did not demand day-care centers or an end to woman's traditional role as wife and mother, nor did she call anyone a chauvinist pig. The happiest period of Mary's own life was when she was married and awaiting the birth of her second child. And the greatest delight she ever knew was in her first child, an illegitimate daughter. Mary's feminism may not appear today to be the hard-core revolutionary variety, but she did live, for a time, a scandalous and unconventional life—"emancipated," it is called by those who have never tried it. The essence of her thought, however, is simply that a woman's mind is as good as a man's.

Not many intelligent men could be found to dispute this proposition today, at least not in mixed company. In Mary's time, to speak of *anybody's* rights, let alone woman's rights, was a radical act. In England, as in other nations, "rights" were an entity belonging to the government. The common run of mankind had little access to what we now call "human rights." As an example of British justice in the late eighteenth century, the law cited two hundred different capital crimes, among them shoplifting. An accused man was not entitled to counsel. A child could be tried and hanged as soon as an adult. The right to vote existed, certainly, but because of unjust apportionment, it had come to mean little. In the United States some of these abuses had been corrected—but the rights of man did not extend past the color bar and the masculine gender was intentional. In the land of Washington and Jefferson, as in the land of George III, human rights were a new idea and woman's rights were not even an issue.

In France, in 1792, a Revolution in the name of equality was in full course, and woman's rights had at least been alluded to. The Revolutionary government drew up plans for female education—to the age of eight. "The education of the women should always be relative to the men," Rousseau had written in *Emile*. "To please, to be useful to us, to make us love and esteem them, to educate us when young, and take care of us when grown up, to advise, to console us, to render our lives easy and agreeable: these are the duties of women at all times, and what they should be taught in their infancy." And, less prettily, "Women have, or ought to have, but little liberty."

Rousseau would have found little cause for complaint in eighteenth-century England. An Englishwoman had almost the same civil status as an American slave. Thomas Hardy, a hundred years hence, was to base a novel on the idea of a man casually selling his wife and daughter at public auction. Obviously this was not a common occurrence, but neither is it wholly implausible. In 1792, and later, a woman could not own property, nor keep any earned wages. All that she possessed belonged to her husband. She could not divorce him, but he could divorce her and take her children. There was no law to say she could not grow up illiterate or be beaten every day.

Such was the legal and moral climate in which Mary Wollstonecraft lived. She was born in London in the spring of 1759, the second child and first daughter of Edward Wollstonecraft, a prosperous weaver. Two more daughters and two more sons were eventually born into the family, making six children in all. Before they had all arrived, Mr. Wollstonecraft came into an inheritance and decided to move his family to the country and become a gentleman farmer. But this plan failed. His money dwindled, and he began drinking heavily. His wife turned into a terrified wraith whose only interest was her eldest son, Edward. Only he escaped the beatings and abuse that his father dealt out regularly to every other household member, from Mrs. Wollstonecraft to the family dog. As often happens in large and disordered families, the eldest sister had to assume the role of mother and scullery maid. Mary was a bright, strong child, determined not to be broken, and she undertook her task energetically, defying her father when he was violent and keeping her younger brothers and sisters in hand. Clearly, Mary held the household together, and in so doing forfeited her own childhood. This experience left her with an everlasting gloomy streak, and was a strong factor in making her a reformer.

At some point in Mary's childhood, another injustice was visited upon her, though so commonplace for the time that she can hardly have felt the sting. Her elder brother was sent away to be educated, and the younger children were left to learn their letters as best they could. The family now frequently changed lodgings, but from her ninth to her fifteenth year Mary went to a day school, where she had the only formal training of her life. Fortunately, this included French and composition, and somewhere Mary learned to read critically and widely. These skills, together with her curiosity and determination, were really all she needed. The *Vindication* is in some parts long-winded, ill-punctuated, and simply full of hot air, but it is the work of a well-informed mind.

Feminists—and Mary would gladly have claimed the title—inevitably, even deservedly, get bad notices. The term calls up an image of relentless battle-axes: "thin college ladies with eyeglasses, no-nonsense features, mouths thin as bologna slicers, a babe in one arm, a hatchet in the other, grey eyes bright with balefire," as Norman Mailer feelingly envisions his antagonists in the Women's Liberation Movement. He has conjured up all the horrid elements: the lips with a cutting edge, the baby immaculately conceived (one is forced to conclude), the lethal weapon tightly clutched, the desiccating college degree, the joylessness. Hanging miasmally over the tableau is the suspicion of a deformed sexuality. Are these girls man-haters, or worse? Mary Wollstonecraft, as the first of her line, has had each of these scarlet letters (except the B.A.) stitched upon her bosom. Yet she conformed very little to the hateful stereotype. In at least one respect, however, she would have chilled Mailer's bones. Having spent her childhood as an adult, Mary reached the age of nineteen in a state of complete joylessness. She was later to quit the role, but for now she wore the garb of a martyr.

Her early twenties were spent in this elderly frame of mind. First she went out as companion to an old lady living at Bath, and was released from this servitude only by a call to nurse the dying Mrs. Wollstonecraft. Then the family broke up entirely, though the younger sisters continued off and on to be dependent on Mary. The family of Mary's dearest friend, Fanny Blood, invited her to come and stay with them; the two girls made a small living doing sewing and handicrafts, and Mary dreamed of starting a primary school. Eventually, in a pleasant village called Newington Green, this plan materialized and prospered. But Fanny Blood in the meantime had married and moved to Lisbon. She wanted Mary to come and nurse her through the birth of her first child. Mary reached Lisbon just in time to see her friend die of childbed fever, and returned home just in time to find that her sisters, in whose care the flourishing little school had been left, had lost all but two pupils.

Mary made up her mind to die. "My constitution is impaired, I hope I shan't live long," she wrote to a friend in February, 1786. Under this almost habitual grief, however, Mary was gaining some new sense of herself. Newington Green, apart from offering her a brief success as a schoolmistress, had brought her some acquaintance in the world of letters, most important among them, Joseph Johnson, an intelligent and successful London publisher in search of new writers. Debt-ridden and penniless, Mary set aside her impaired constitution and wrote her first book, probably in the space of a week. Johnson bought it for ten guineas and published it. Called *Thoughts on the Education of Daughters*, it went unnoticed, and the ten guineas was soon spent. Mary had to find work. She accepted a position as governess in the house of Lord and Lady Kingsborough in the north of Ireland.

Mary's letters from Ireland to her sisters and to Joseph Johnson are so filled with Gothic gloom, so stained with tears, that one cannot keep from laughing at them. "I entered the great gates with the same kind of feeling I should have if I was going to the Bastille," she wrote upon entering Kingsborough Castle in the fall of 1786. Mary was now twenty-seven. Her most recent biographer, Margaret George, believes that Mary was not really suffering so much as she was having literary fantasies. In private she was furiously at work on a novel entitled, not very artfully, *Mary, A Fiction*. This is the story of a young lady of immense sensibilities who closely resembles Mary except that she has wealthy parents, a neglectful bridegroom, and an attractive lover. The title and fantasizing contents are precisely what a scribbler of thirteen might secretly concoct. Somehow Mary was embarking on her adolescence—with all its daydreams—fifteen years after the usual date. Mary's experience in Kingsborough Castle was a fruitful one, for all her complaints. In the summer of 1787 she lost her post as governess and set off for

London with her novel. Not only did Johnson accept it for publication, he offered her a regular job as editor and translator and helped her find a place to live.

Thus, aged twenty-eight, Mary put aside her doleful persona as the martyred, set-upon elder sister. How different she is now, jauntily writing from London to her sisters: "Mr. Johnson . . . assures me that if I exert my talents in writing I may support myself in a comfortable way. I am then going to be the first of a new genus . . ." Now Mary discovered the sweetness of financial independence earned by interesting work. She had her own apartment. She was often invited to Mr. Johnson's dinner parties, usually as the only female guest among all the most interesting men in London: Joseph Priestley, Thomas Paine, Henry Fuseli, William Blake, Thomas Christie, William Godwin—all of them up-and-coming scientists or poets or painters or philosophers, bound together by left-wing political views. Moreover, Mary was successful in her own writing as well as in editorial work. Her *Original Stories for Children* went into three editions and was illustrated by Blake. Johnson and his friend Thomas Christie had started a magazine called the *Analytical Review*, to which Mary became a regular contributor.

But—lest anyone imagine an elegantly dressed Mary presiding flirtatiously at Johnson's dinner table—her social accomplishments were rather behind her professional ones. Johnson's circle looked upon her as one of the boys. "Wollstonecraft" is what William Godwin calls her in his diary. One of her later detractors reported that she was at this time a "philosophic sloven," in a dreadful old dress and beaver hat, "with her hair hanging lank about her shoulders." Mary had yet to arrive at her final incarnation, but the new identity was imminent, if achieved by an odd route. Edmund Burke had recently published his *Re-flections on the Revolution in France,* and the book had enraged Mary. The statesman who so readily supported the quest for liberty in the American colonies had his doubts about events in France.

Mary's reply to Burke, *A Vindication of the Rights of Men,* astounded London, partly because she was hitherto unknown, partly because it was good. Mary proved to be an excellent polemicist, and she had written in anger. She accused Burke, the erstwhile champion of liberty, of being "the champion of property." "Man preys on man," said she, "and you mourn for the idle tapestry that decorated a gothic pile and the dronish bell that summoned the fat priest to prayer." The book sold well. Mary moved into a better apartment and bought some pretty dresses—no farthingales, of course, but some of the revolutionary new "classical" gowns. She put her auburn hair up in a loose knot. Her days as a philosophic sloven were over.

Vindication of the Rights of Woman was her next work. In its current edition it runs to 250-odd pages; Mary wrote it in six weeks. *Vindication* is no prose masterpiece, but it has never failed to arouse its audience, in one way or another. Horace Walpole unintentionally set the style for the book's foes. Writing to his friend Hannah More in August, 1792, he referred to Thomas Paine and to Mary as "philosophizing serpents" and was "glad to hear you have not read the tract of the last mentioned writer. I would not look at it." Neither would many another of Mary's assailants, the most virulent of whom, Ferdinand Lundberg, surfaced at the late date of 1947 with a tract of his own, *Modern Woman, the Lost Sex.* Savagely misogynistic as it is, this book was hailed in its time as "the best book yet to be written about women." Lundberg calls Mary the Karl Marx of the feminist movement, and the *Vindication* a "fateful book," to which "the tenets of feminism, which have undergone no change to our day, may be traced." Very well, but then, recounting Mary's life with the maximum possible number of errors per line, he warns us that she was "an extreme neurotic of a compulsive type" who "wanted to turn on men and injure them." In one respect, at least, Mr. Lundberg hits the mark: he blames Mary for starting women in the pernicious habit of wanting an education. In the nineteenth century, he relates, English and American feminists were hard at work. "Following Mary Wollstonecraft's prescription, they made a considerable point about acquiring a higher education." This is precisely Mary's prescription, and the most dangerous idea in her fateful book.

"Men complain and with reason, of the follies and caprices of our Sex," she writes in Chapter 1. "Behold, I should answer, the natural effect of ignorance." Women, she thinks, are usually so mindless as to be scarcely fit for their roles as wives and mothers. Nevertheless, she believes this state not to be part of the feminine nature, but the result of an equally mindless oppression, as demoralizing for men as for women. If a woman's basic mission is as a wife and mother, need she be an illiterate slave for this?

The heart of the work is Mary's attack on Rousseau. In *Emile* Rousseau had set forth some refreshing new ideas for the education of little boys. But women, he decreed, are tools for pleasure, creatures too base for moral or political or educational privilege. Mary recognized that this view was destined to shut half the human race out of all hope for political freedom. *Vindication* is a plea that the "rights of men" ought to mean the "rights of humanity." The human right that she held highest was the right to have a mind and think with it. Virginia Woolf, who lived through a time of feminist activity, thought that the *Vindication* was a work so true "as to seem to contain nothing new." Its originality, she wrote, rather too optimistically, had become a commonplace.

Vindication went quickly into a second edition. Mary's name was soon known all over Europe. But as she savored her fame—and she did savor it—she found that the edge was wearing off and that she was rather lonely. So far as anyone knows, Mary had reached this point in her life without ever having had a love affair. Johnson was the only man she was close to, and he was, as she wrote him, "A father, or a brother—you have been both to me." Mary was often now in the company of the Swiss painter Henry Fuseli, and suddenly she developed what she thought was a Platonic passion in his direction. He rebuffed her, and in the winter of 1792 she went to Paris, partly to escape her embarrassment but also because she wanted to observe the workings of the Revolution firsthand.

Soon after her arrival, as she collected notes for the history of the Revolution she hoped to write, Mary saw Louis XVI, "sitting in a hackney coach . . . going to meet death." Back in her room that evening, she wrote to Mr. Johnson of seeing "eyes glare through a glass door opposite my chair and bloody hands shook at me . . . I am going to bed and for the first time in my life, I cannot put out the candle." As the weeks went on, Edmund Burke's implacable critic began to lose her faith in the brave new world. "The aristocracy of birth is levelled to the ground, only to make room for that of riches," she wrote. By February France and England were at war, and British subjects classified as enemy aliens.

Though many Englishmen were arrested, Mary and a large English colony stayed on. One day in spring, some friends presented her to an attractive American, newly arrived in Paris, Gilbert Imlay. Probably about four years Mary's senior, Imlay, a former officer

in the Continental Army, was an explorer and adventurer. He came to France seeking to finance a scheme for seizing Spanish lands in the Mississippi valley. This "natural and unaffected creature," as Mary was later to describe him, was probably the social lion of the moment, for he was also the author of a best-selling novel called *The Emigrants*, a farfetched account of life and love in the American wilderness. He and Mary soon became lovers. They were a seemingly perfect pair. Imlay must have been pleased with his famous catch, and—dear, liberated girl that she was—Mary did not insist upon marriage. Rather the contrary. But fearing that she was in danger as an Englishwoman, he registered her at the American embassy as his wife.

Blood was literally running in the Paris streets now, so Mary settled down by herself in a cottage at Neuilly. Imlay spent his days in town, working out various plans. The Mississippi expedition came to nothing, and he decided to stay in France and go into the import-export business, part of his imports being gunpowder and other war goods run from Scandinavia through the English blockade. In the evenings he would ride out to the cottage. By now it was summer, and Mary, who spent the days writing, would often stroll up the road to meet him, carrying a basket of freshly-gathered grapes.

A note she wrote Imlay that summer shows exactly what her feelings for him were: "You can scarcely imagine with what pleasure I anticipate the day when we are to begin almost to live together; and you would smile to hear how many plans of employment I have in my head, now that I am confident that my heart has found peace . . ." Soon she was pregnant. She and Imlay moved into Paris. He promised to take her to America, where they would settle down on a farm and raise six children. But business called Imlay to Le Havre, and his stay lengthened ominously into weeks.

Imlay's letters to Mary have not survived, and without them it is hard to gauge what sort of man he was and what he really thought of his adoring mistress. Her biographers like to make him out a cad, a philistine, not half good enough for Mary. Perhaps; yet the two must have had something in common. His novel, unreadable though it is now, shows that he shared her political views, including her feminist ones. He may never have been serious about the farm in America, but he was a miserably long time deciding to leave Mary alone. Though they were seprated during the early months of her pregnancy, he finally did bring her to Le Havre, and continued to live with her there until the child was born and for some six months afterward. The baby arrived in May, 1794, a healthy little girl, whom Mary named Fanny after her old friend. Mary was proud that her delivery had been easy, and as for Fanny, Mary loved her instantly. "My little Girl," she wrote to a friend, "begins to suck so manfully that her father reckons saucily on her writing the second part of the Rights of Woman." Mary's joy in this child illuminates almost every letter she wrote henceforth.

Fanny's father was the chief recipient of these letters with all the details of the baby's life. To Mary's despair, she and Imlay hardly ever lived together again. A year went by; Imlay was now in London and Mary in France. She offered to break it off, but mysteriously, he could not let go. In the last bitter phase of their involvement, after she had joined him in London at his behest, he even sent her—as "Mrs. Imlay"—on a complicated business errand to the Scandinavian countries. Returning to London, Mary discovered that he was living with another woman. By now half crazy with humiliation, Mary chose a dark night and threw herself in the Thames. She was nearly dead when two rivermen pulled her from the water.

Though this desperate incident was almost the end of Mary, at least it was the end of the Imlay episode. He sent a doctor to care for her, but they rarely met again. Since Mary had no money, she set about providing for herself and Fanny in the way she knew. The faithful Johnson had already brought out Volume I of her history of the French Revolution. Now she set to work editing and revising her *Letters Written during a Short Residence in Sweden, Norway, and Denmark,* a kind of thoughtful travelogue. The book was well received and widely translated.

And it also revived the memory of Mary Wollstonecraft in the mind of an old acquaintance, William Godwin. As the author of the treatise *Political Justice,* he was now as famous a philosophizing serpent as Mary and was widely admired and hated as a "freethinker." He came to call on Mary. They became friends and then lovers. Early in 1797 Mary was again pregnant. William Godwin was an avowed atheist who had publicly denounced the very institution of marriage. On March 29, 1797, he nevertheless went peaceably to church with Mary and made her his wife.

The Godwins were happy together, however William's theories may have been outraged. He adored his small stepdaughter and took pride in his brilliant wife. Awaiting the birth of her child throughout the summer, Mary worked on a new novel and made plans for a book on "the management of infants"—it would have been the first "Dr. Spock." She expected to have another easy delivery and promised to come downstairs to dinner the day following. But when labor began, on August 30, it proved to be long and agonizing. A daughter, named Mary Wollstonecraft, was born; ten days later, the mother died.

Occasionally, when a gifted writer dies young, one can feel, as in the example of Shelley, that perhaps he had at any rate accomplished his best work. But so recently had Mary come into her full intellectual and emotional growth that her death at the age of thirty-eight is bleak indeed. There is no knowing what Mary might have accomplished now that she enjoyed domestic stability. Perhaps she might have achieved little or nothing further as a writer. But she might have been able to protect her daughters from some part of the sadness that overtook them; for as things turned out, both Fanny and Mary were to sacrifice themselves.

Fanny grew up to be a shy young girl, required to feel grateful for the roof over her head, overshadowed by her prettier half sister, Mary. Godwin in due course married a formidable widow named Mrs. Clairmont, who brought her own daughter into the house—the Claire Clairmont who grew up to become Byron's mistress and the mother of his daughter Allegra. Over the years Godwin turned into a hypocrite and a miser who nevertheless continued to pose as the great liberal of the day. Percy Bysshe Shelley, born the same year that the *Vindication of the Rights of Woman* was published, came to be a devoted admirer of Mary Wollstonecraft's writing. As a young man he therefore came with his wife to call upon Godwin. What he really sought, however, were Mary's daughters—because they were her daughters. First he approached Fanny, but later changed his mind. Mary Godwin was then sixteen, the perfect potential soul mate for a man whose needs for soul mates knew no bounds. They conducted their courtship in the most up-to-the-minute romantic style: beneath a tree near her mother's grave they read aloud to each other from the *Vindication.* Soon they eloped, having pledged their "troth" in the cemetery. Godwin, the celebrated freethinker, was enraged. To make matters worse, Claire Clairmont had run off to Switzerland with them.

Not long afterward Fanny, too, ran away. She went to an inn in a distant town and drank a fatal dose of laudanum. It has traditionally been said that unrequited love for Shelley drove her to this pass, but there is no evidence one way or the other. One suicide that can more justly be laid at Shelley's door is that of his first wife, which occurred a month after Fanny's and which at any rate left him free to wed his mistress, Mary Godwin. Wife or mistress, she had to endure poverty, ostracism, and Percy's constant infidelities. But now at last her father could, and did, boast to his relations that he was father-in-law to a baronet's son. "Oh, philosophy!" as Mary Godwin Shelley remarked.

If in practice Shelley was merely a womanizer, on paper he was a convinced feminist. He had learned this creed from Mary Wollstonecraft. Through his verse Mary's ideas began to be disseminated. They were one part of that vast tidal wave of political, social, and artistic revolution that arose in the late eighteenth century, the romantic movement. But because of Mary's unconventional way of life, her name fell into disrepute during the nineteenth century, and her book failed to exert its rightful influence on the development of feminism. Emma Willard and other pioneers of the early Victorian period indignantly refused to claim Mary as their forebear. Elizabeth Cady Stanton and Lucretia Mott were mercifully less strait-laced on the subject. In 1889, when Mrs. Stanton and Susan B. Anthony published their *History of Woman Suffrage,* they dedicated the book to Mary. Though Mary Wollstonecraft can in no sense be said to have founded the woman's rights movement, she was, by the late nineteenth century, recognized as its inspiration, and the *Vindication* was vindicated for the highly original work it was, a landmark in the history of society.

THE SHOT HEARD ROUND THE WORLD

HENRY FAIRLIE

"Here once the embattled farmers stood
And fired the shot heard round the world."
—Hymn sung at the completion of the Battle Monument
Concord, July 4, 1837

The claim in Emerson's line is expansive. Can it be true that the shot was heard round the world—when there were no satellites, no television, no radio, no telephone? Let us see.

It then took from five to six weeks for news to cross the Atlantic. (The first regular passenger service between England and the colonies was instituted in 1755.) Thus the news of the "battles" of Lexington and Concord, fought on April 19, 1775, appeared on May 29 in the London press, from which the French papers, as usual, took their news of America; and from them the press in the rest of Europe picked up the story. By June 19 it appeared in a newspaper as far away as St. Petersburg. Similarly the news of the Declaration of Independence was first published in a London newspaper on August 17, 1776; a week later it appeared in papers in Hamburg, on August 30 in Sweden, and on September 2 in Denmark. The actions in Lexington and Concord had been no more than skirmishes in two villages whose names Europeans can never have heard before. Yet the news excited editors across Europe, and they knew it would arouse their readers. The saw *at once* the size of the event.

In 1775-76 the French Revolution had not sounded its tocsin to the peoples of Europe. Most of them lived under the rule of a few absolute monarchs: Louis XVI in France; Maria Theresa (as dowager empress) and her son Joseph II in Austria and the Holy Roman Empire; Frederick the Great in Prussia; Catherine the Great in Russia; and Christian VII in Denmark. It was the age of the "enlightened despots," who genuinely had the welfare of their subjects at heart, but though they proclaimed the right of their peoples to be well governed, they did not acknowledge their right to govern themselves. The only monarch who had (sourly) learned the ABCs of freedom was, paradoxically, the one against whom the colonists were rebelling. The English were far freer than any peoples on the Continent. But the English reaction to the news from America is more interesting if we know how the shot was heard on the other side of the English channel.

Maria Theresa had ascended the throne in 1740 at the age of 23. Even then she realized that the old order could not survive, and set about instituting a series of effective reforms. Her scarcely less remarkable son, who succeeded his father as co-regent in 1765, produced the most thought-out exposition of the duties of an enlightened despot. They received the news of the Declaration at about the same time it reached London, and two weeks before it found its way through the heavy censorship into the daily press in Vienna. Taking a dim view of popular uprisings, Maria Theresa expressed to George III her "hearty desire to see the restoration of obedience and tranquility in every quarter of his dominions," and Joseph told the British ambassador, "The cause in which England is engaged . . . is the cause of all sovereigns who have a joint interest in the maintenance of due subordination . . . in all the surrounding monarchies."

The rulers feared that their subjects would see the American action not as a rebellion against a rightful monarch in his own territories—there had been plenty of rebellions against European sovereigns—but as the proclamation of a revolutionary doctrine of universal application, as the Declaration indeed announced it to be. Thus, although the Declaration was at last allowed through the censorship in Vienna, when the *Wienerisches Diarium* the next year explained the War of Independence as a clash between two political principles—monarchy and popular sovereignty—Maria Theresa was outraged, even though the paper had covered itself by printing an editorial saying that this view of the rebellion was mistaken.

Similarly, when the news of Lexington and Concord got through the censors into the *Sanktpeterburgskie Vedemosti*, the Americans were, in deference to the Empress Catherine, firmly called "rebels." In 1780, when Catherine read the Abbé Raynal's history of Europe's dominions overseas and came to his chapter on the American Revolution, she wrote to a friend: "The American record is filled with declarations in which there is too little that is reasonable and too much that is unbecoming impertinence."

2. RATIONALISM, ENLIGHTENMENT, AND REVOLUTION

IN BELGIUM, which was then under the rule of Austria, it was clear that the subjects of the enlightened despots might take the American "impertinence" as an example. From as early as 1766, when the *Gazette des Pays-Bas* in Brussels reported the remonstrations of colonial assemblies in America, the Belgian press followed American affairs intently. In four Belgian newspapers and journals the Maryland Constitution was printed in 1777, the Massachusetts Constitution in 1780, some of a collection of the constitutions of all 13 states in 1783, Virginia's Code of Civil and Criminal Laws in 1786, and in the following year the U.S. Constitution in full. This steady flow of news (including the reports of the war and of American victories) could only stir up the middle class in Belgium. They enjoyed neither national independence nor a constitution guaranteeing any basic political rights, while each day the Americans were remaking their political and civil society before the eye of the world. By 1787 a strong movement for independence and a new constitution was growing in Belgium.

In the debates that were provoked in Europe we can see how the shot was heard. We can follow them (as they were conducted in the press) through the 25 or so out-of-the-way historical monographs, memoirs, and so on, that are the main source of this story. Throughout the debates a constant appeal was made to the example of America. Liberty had been crushed in Poland, was struggling in Holland, said Lambert d'Outrement, a lawyer in Liege, but it had been maintained in England, and triumphed in America: "What will be the lot of the Austrian Low Countries?" There could be only one answer. Belgium would try itself. Toward the end of 1789 the States-General of the Austrian Netherlands deposed Joseph II and proclaimed the *United States* of Belgium. The Belgian Declaration of Independence (and the equivalent declarations of the provinces of Belgium, like the states in America) followed the American Declaration faithfully. In the Manifeste de la Province de Flandre (1790), "the Course of Human Events" became "*un Concours de circonstances . . . extraordinaires,*" and continued: "*En conséquence . . . au juge suprême de l'Univers . . . a droit d'être un Etat libre et indépendant*"—almost word for word the American original.

Thus, although the French Revolution had by then erupted, the inspiration was coming from America. The working people of Europe, it was said in the Belgian debates, must inevitably look to America. They had learned that conditions for the likes of them were better there, and many were emigrating. A telling use was made of America's distance from the mother country, since Belgium, like many of the territories of the Austrian Empire, was remote from the imperial capital and government in Vienna. Moreover when, during the War of Independence, the absolute monarchs of Europe entered into relations (and even alliances) with the Americans, they were in effect endorsing revolution. The monarchs might say that the American Revolution was intolerable, but by their actions they were telling their peoples that revolution was not a crime, but as d'Outrement said, "*un beau monument élevé à la liberté.*"

THE SIGNIFICANCE Europeans attached to America was underlined by the deftness and even courage with which editors across the Continent managed to circumvent the censorship. In 1775-76 Denmark was a significant power. It included Norway (and Greenland, a Norwegian possession), Schleswig and Holstein, Iceland, and three West Indian islands, St. Croix, St. Thomas, and St. John (which were later sold to the United States). Given the insanity of Christian VII, it was governed by a court party as an enlightened despotism, and as usual a significant part of the extensive bureaucracy was the ever watchful censorship.

On August 23, 1776, the *Altonaischer Mercurius* (a German-language newspaper published in Altona in Holstein) printed an edited version of the Declaration, which was then translated and printed at the top of the front page of the *Kiobenhavske* [Copenhagen] *Tidender*, the newspaper with the largest circulation in Denmark. In both papers it appeared uncut as far as the sentence "The History of the present King of Great-Britain is a History of repeated Injuries and Usurpations, all having in direct Object the Establishment of absolute Tyranny over these States." The trouble was that the intermittently insane George III was one of the demented Christian's closest allies. So in the above sentence, the words "King of Great-Britain" were replaced by "the present ministry of Great Britain." But the Declaration continued with the long list of grievances against George, and it was all too likely that any Danish reader would have begun ticking off in his mind his own grievances against the Danish monarchy. Ingeniously, the *Mercurius* solved the problem by publishing the Declaration in two halves, the second (with the grievances) appearing on August 26, in which all the references to King George were replaced by the anonymous "*Er*" (he). This appeased the censors; it cannot have fooled the readers.

How different it was in the New World. Over in the West Indies, the only Danish newspaper, the *Royal Danish American Gazette*, published (significantly) in English, printed the complete Declaration as early as August 17, even placing it prominently on the front page, which was otherwise reserved for advertising. The Danes in the colonies seemed themselves to have become Americans.

It was not only the editors in Denmark (and elsewhere), nosy for news, who were excited by the events in America. As early as October 22, 1776, A. P. Bernstorff, the great Danish minister for foreign affairs, wrote to a friend: "The public here is extremely occupied with the rebels [in America], not because they know the cause, but because the mania of independence in reality has infected all the spirits, and the poison has spread imperceptibly from the works of the philosophes all the way out to the village schools." Those last eight words, from such a source, tell us something we need to know.

So does a firsthand glimpse of the popular mood in Copenhagen. The *Aftenpost* carried a column—as we would now call it—by one Edmund Balling, describing life in the city; it sounds like a city column by Jimmy Breslin or Mike Royko. Balling dropped into alehouses, which he described as "our political schools of Fencing, those bourgeois Art of War Listening Rooms, where our little Politici, during a Glass of Ale, a Pinch of Snuff and a Pipe of Tobacco," tossed about the issues of the day. At the end of 1776 he found them debating the War of Independence. One said the Americans were rebels, and "ought to be beaten over the Forehead like Bullocks"; another countered that "the English ought to be thrashed"; a third had no doubt that the English had got "something to chew on"; and a sausage-stuffer called it an "accursed War" because the rice from South Carolina had become so dear, and what could he now stuff his sausages with in place of meat? On January 12, 1778, Balling told of a man entering an alehouse (after reading the news, one guesses, of Burgoyne's defeat): "Good evening, Gentlemen! Ha! Ha! Have we the newspapers? Well, what does England say now? . . . Yes, this War will likely make a rather considerable Change in Europe."

As in Belgium, the impact did not lessen even after America achieved its independence. In 1820 a Danish civil servant, C. F. von Schmidt-Phiseldeck, called the Fourth of July "this forever memorable day." And in our own time a Danish historian has said that "the Declaration of Independence had a decisive impact on the course of events leading to the attainment in 1849 of Denmark's first democratic constitution."

BUT AS WE come across the editors, their newspapers, and their readers, the European response is telling us something very important about the American Revolution itself. It was carried in the colonies and overseas by the assertiveness of the American middle class. One of George III's more apt comments was that his sovereignty was being challenged by a lot of "grocers." Marx was really saying no more when he declared that "the American Revolution sounded the tocsin for the European bourgeoisie," and gave "the first impulse to the European Revolution." Lenin later said the War of Independence was "one of those great, truly liberating, truly revolutionary wars"—something that cannot be said of the revolution he wrought in Russia.

Two vigorous merchant cities—Hamburg and Dubrovnik—illustrate the response of a newly aggressive merchant class in Europe. Hamburg was a free port, as most of its dock area still is (its official name even now is the Free and Hanseatic City of Hamburg), and since the Reformation had been the proud refuge of Protestants, other dissidents, and refugees. Ports are naturally liberal, being used to strangers, with their different cultures and ideas. When the Declaration was published in the *Staats und Gelehrte Zeitung*, its citizens naturally sympathized with the colonies in their claim to be a free trading nation, with which Hamburg could expand its commercial ties (as it did after the war), greatly reinforcing its prosperity. Completing the story, another cargo would eventually stream through Hamburg: a vast number of immigrants to the New World from Russia and Eastern Europe. Dubrovnik had risen to be a powerful merchant republic in the Middle Ages, and had existed since then (virtually independent) under the protection, in suc-

cession, of Venice, Hungary, and Turkey—until Napoleon, with his usual disrespect for history, abolished the republic in 1806, the same year in which he occupied Hamburg. Again, far away on the Adriatic, the citizens of a strong merchant port were stimulated by the news from America, a point made in a book published by the city of Dubrovnik to celebrate the bicentennial of the Declaration.

IT IS the response of the middle class in Europe that throws light on the attitudes in England. To the ruling class in England the Declaration of Independence did not herald the dawn of a new age, or introduce new abstract principles of freedom and equality that had a universal application. In fact, it seemed to them less of a threat than it did to the ruling monarchs on the Continent, since they enjoyed many of the freedoms the Americans were claiming. It was to them a very local document, a list (as indeed it was) of very local grievances. Neither it nor any shot, in their view, was heard round the world. Both had been aimed, after all, at them; and on the whole they took it like gentlemen.

Here was a war in which the First British Empire, as it is known to history, was falling, and it is natural we should wish that the author of *The Decline and Fall of the Roman Empire*, who was a member of Parliament throughout the war, had offered a long historical perspective or a few grand philosophical reflections on so great an event. But Edward Gibbon's attitude was not only devious; it was corrupt, even if in the accepted manner of the day. No one can blame him for wishing to write the great book, or for wishing to receive some patronage as he labored at his task. He looked, of course, to the government for an appointment, and accepted the post of one of the Lords Commissioner of Trade and Plantations. With this sinecure, his voice and vote were bought by George III and his ministers, which makes one appreciate even more the king's dig at him one day, "Scribble, scribble, scribble, eh, Mr. Gibbon?"

At the end of the difficult parliamentary session in 1775, Gibbon was glad to get away, saying that "having saved the British I must destroy the Roman Empire." But this little jest was capped by an American. Horace Walpole reported with delight in a letter in 1781: "Dr. [Benjamin] Franklin . . . said he would furnish Mr. Gibbon with materials for writing the History of the Decline of the British Empire." A lampoon went the rounds in London during the war. Attributed to Charles James Fox, a dauntless leader of the opposition and staunch friend of the Americans, two verses ran:

> King George in a fright
> Lest Gibbon should write
> The history of England's disgrace
> Thought no way so sure
> His pen so secure
> As to give the historian a place.
>
> His book well describes
> How corruption and bribes
> O'erthrew the great empire of Rome;

2. RATIONALISM, ENLIGHTENMENT, AND REVOLUTION

And his rantings declare
A degeneracy there
Which his conduct exhibits at home.

We do not get wit like that from our politicians now.

Whether in Gibbon's own jest, Franklin's quip, or Fox's lampoon, there is nothing to suggest that the governing class in London could work itself into any great passion over the American war—neither the supporters nor the opponents of the American cause. (Though the consummate and by then aged orator William Pitt, for whom Pittsburgh was named, reinforced his impassioned philippic in defense of the American colonists by collapsing unconscious on the floor of the House at the end.)

WE ALSO KNOW how the American news was received outside London. In December 1775 the daily journal of the Rev. James Woodforde (a country parson in Weston, Norfolk, of ordinary loyalty to the Crown) gave "notice of a Fast being kept on Friday next concerning the present war between America and us." Note that the colonists are not called subjects or rebels, as on the Continent, but *America*, as if they were already a nation. The war then seems to have aroused little interest until there was another official Day of Prayer in 1780, for it was by then clear that God was not pulling his weight. So the good parson "read the proper prayers on the Occasion, but there was no sermon preached. My Squire and Lady at the Church. . . . Sister Clarke, Nancy, Sam and myself all took it into our heads to take a good dose of Rhubarb on going to bed." Rhubarb is an astringent purgative—a very English way of disposing of the news of fresh disasters, rather like taking a "nice cup o' tea" in the Blitz.

In 1781 he recorded the news that "Cornwallis and his whole army . . . are all taken by the Americans and French in Virginia." That is all; not dismay, no commotion, no anger. When it was all over, the news of the Treaty of Versailles was a "joyful" event, though England had suffered a great defeat and lost a vast possession. There remained only the aftermath, an entry as late as December 9, 1785: ". . . to a poor soldier laterly [sic] arrived from America that had been wounded & is now ill gave 1 [shilling] and 6 [pence]"—a neglected veteran of an unpopular, unsuccessful war.

Throughout the war we could have found Horace Walpole at home in London, writing to his friends the letters that now fill 36 volumes in the Yale edition. One of Europe's most intelligent and cultivated men, he chose (happily for us) to be a spectator of great events rather than an actor in them. He returned again and again to the American question, urbane, tart, and outraged. Why are we in America? he asked, as 200 years later he might have asked about Vietnam. "We could even afford to lose America," he wrote as early as March 28, 1774. After Washington's victory at Trenton he wrote: "What politicians are those that have preferred the empty name of *sovereignty* to that of *alliance*! and forced subsidies to the golden age of oceans and commerce." The Americans, he pointed out to a friend,

"do not pique themselves upon modern good breeding, but level at the officers, of whom they have slain a vast number." This savage amusement at the fact that the Americans "impertinently" fired on English officers is a wholly accurate reflection of "the amazing heights which pro-Americanism could reach in London," as one researcher found it in even the popular novels of the day. The Boston Tea Party was to him the symbol of English official stupidity: "Mrs. Britannia orders her senate to proclaim America a continent of cowards, and vote it should be starved unless it drink tea with her."

By the end of 1777 Walpole was writing: "We have been horribly the aggressors." A week after the capitulation at Yorktown, but before he had news of it, he proclaimed: "The English in America are as much my countrymen as those born in the parish of St. Martin's in the Field; and when my countrymen quarrel, I think I am free to wish better to the sufferers than to the aggressors; nor can I see how my love of my country obliges me to wish well to what I despise. . . . Were I young and of heroic texture, I would go to America." It is clear from all the evidence that the English people as a whole could not have their hearts in a war against their "countrymen."

BUT THERE WAS one exception to this generally unexcited and unideological response in England, and it is illuminated by the reaction on the Continent. The merchants of the City of London and of other expanding cities of the new middle class in England identified their own interests closely with those of the colonists. The London press, almost without exception, was the voice of this class. With the introduction of the tax on the colonists' trade in molasses and sugar in 1764, the *London Chronicle* at once reported from the west coast port of Bristol, which depended on the American trade, that "the principal merchants of the city intend to support with all their interest the independent free trade of the American colonies." In the numerous and remarkably free English newspapers we can trace how this argument from interest developed steadily into an ideological assertion. As the Americans, during those extraordinary ten years from 1765 to 1775, worked out the philosophical grounds on which they would claim independence, the English merchant class found itself examining and then adopting the same arguments.

In resisting taxation "without representation" by the English Parliament, the Americans (those "grocers") argued that in *English custom* and "natural law" there was a power above Parliament—in short, the Constitution in revolutionary thinking, in the work of the Founding Fathers, and forever afterward in the mind of America. The idea that Parliament was sovereign was then a fairly new development, and there were many at home who objected to it, but it was the American colonists who clarified the issue by their dogged resistance. Moreover, the English middle class had its own doubts about the justice of the parliamentary system as it then existed. The Industrial Revolution was reaching its flood, and beyond London many of the rising middle-class cities such as Manchester and Sheffield were not represented at all. So the American cry of "no taxation without representation" drew a strong echo from them.

When the news of the Boston Tea Party reached England, the *London Packet* called such resistance lawful and even honorable against "tyrannic" measures. After Lexington and Concord the *London Evening Post* said that "the prevailing toast in every company of true Englishmen is, 'Victory to the Americans, and re-establishment to the British Constitution.'" (No one was arrested or imprisoned in England for supporting the Americans.) Thus in England as in Europe the American cause had been translated into a universal cause—by a rising class. The American Revolution represented the spontaneously international ideology of this class, which was feeling its strength in Europe, growing assertive in England, and already established in America, even able to organize and arm itself for war.

Of all the dramatic assertions in the Declaration of Independence, none is more "impertinent" than the assurance with which the 13 colonies said they had decided to "assume among the Powers of the Earth, the separate and equal Station" to which they were entitled. Yet the presumption was not as great as it seems. As early as 1765 a correspondent in the *London Magazine* said: "Little doubt can be entertained, that this vast country will in time become the most prosperous empire that perhaps the world has ever seen." This was widely appreciated, and both the English and Europeans were aware of the rapid increase in America's population, and of Franklin's estimate that it would double every 25 years. Shortly after Lexington and Concord the *Chester Chronicle* quoted Bishop Berkeley's poem, "Westward the course of Empire takes its way."

ONCE THE NEWS of the fateful shot reached the courts of Europe, the monarchs were alert to the effect the American rebellion might have on the balance of power in Europe. George III at once dispatched a personal envoy to Catherine the Great, to request fewer than 20,000 Russian troops for help in suppressing the American insurrection. But Catherine did not have a high opinion of George, and refused to supply any soldiers or to make the treaty that Britain wanted. She and her government were extremely well informed about American affairs, and on receiving news of the Declaration, the counselor of the Russian Embassy in London wrote to the Russian foreign minister, N. I. Panin, saying that both it and the prosecution of a formal war against Britain "offer evidence of all the courage of leadership" in America.

King George had no better luck in Vienna. Austria had been allied with France since 1756, but by 1775 it was exhausted by the Seven Years' War, and urgently trying to resist the rise of Prussia in the east under Frederick the Great. Maria Theresa saw that Austria needed to secure its position in the west by friendship with both England and France, and by 1776 wished to revive her earlier friendship

with England. In 1777 she wrote to her daughter Marie Antoinette (who had none of her inquiring intelligence or even savvy, and paid the price at the guillotine) that the "war in America" troubled her, as well it might since it pitted France and England against each other. She therefore skillfully maintained Austria's neutrality throughout the war, and forbade both English and American recruiting in Hapsburg lands.

This response of the European monarchs—Denmark also remained neutral, in spite of its alliance with England and its far-flung shipping and trading interests—was the clearest recognition that America had indeed become a new nation on something like equal terms with the oldest and most imperious in the Old World, at once acting and being accepted on the stage of Europe as one of the "Powers of the Earth."

It must be remembered that the enlightened despots were significant figures of the Enlightenment; Catherine corresponded regularly with Voltaire. There was therefore nothing particularly remarkable in the fact that the chief assistant to Panin as the Russian foreign minister was D. I. Fonvizin, whose plays boldly satirized the Russian aristocracy and the institution of serfdom. When Fonvizin traveled through Europe in 1777-78, he met Benjamin Franklin at a *rendez-vous des gens de lettres*, calling him in a letter to his sister "the glorious Franklin." (Franklin wrapped the European intellectuals around his little finger.) Another Russian, commenting on this meeting, wrote: "The representative of the young enlightenment of Russia was an interlocutor with the representative of young America." The excitement at such a meeting demonstrates yet another way in which the new United States, a child of the Enlightenment, impressed itself on Europe as already a mature nation.

THE STORY of how the shot was heard round the world carries obvious instructions. Any notion that the War of Independence was only a rebellion falls to the ground. Both rulers and their subjects saw it as a revolution of universal appeal. The dynamism of that appeal was derived from the fact that the Americans had already built a great trading nation and created not only a strong middle class in the process, but a society that as a whole was middle-class in its temper and energy. What is more, as a result of the preparation between 1765 and 1775—ten of the most creative years in political thinking in the history of the world—the Americans entered the War of Independence with a profound political philosophy that immediately lit fires round the world. They are not yet extinguished.

The names of two unknown villages, Lexington and Concord, became household words even as far as Dubrovnik and St. Petersburg. And on any Fourth of July one cannot help thinking of the few minutemen who took their stand on a bridge and sent the drilled Redcoats running with their tails between their legs back into Boston.

Was France the Fatherland of Genocide?

Laurent Ladouce

Laurent Ladouce is a lecturer at the Sorbonne who has written widely on liberation theology.

When Michel Baroin, the president of several insurance companies and a Freemason, was asked a few months ago to preside over the organization of the bicentenary of the French Revolution, many Frenchmen rejoiced: It was wise, so it was thought, to choose a man known for his moderation, his ecumenical ideas, his lifetime dedication to promoting dialogue and mutual understanding among ideological and political opponents. Baroin himself declared that he would make the bicentenary an occasion for national reconciliation.

After all, the spirit of the times seemed to favor this noble idea of a national reconciliation. In 1987, two years before the anniversary of its famous Revolution, France is celebrating the millennium of the crowning of Hugh Capet, the first "French" king and founder of a dynasty of French monarchs that was interrupted in January 1793 with the decapitation of King Louis XVI, during the Revolution. Furthermore, the unusual "cohabitation" between a socialist president and a conservative prime minister seems to encourage dialogue and reconciliation. In 1988, the French will have to elect a new president and this event will take place right between the millennium and the bicentenary celebrations.

For all these reasons, one may easily guess Baroin's satisfaction when he was appointed for this particular task. Sadly, however, destiny was not on his side: Baroin tragically disappeared in a plane accident a few weeks after he was chosen.

Had he survived, it remains doubtful that he would have achieved national reconciliation around the symbolism of the Revolution. Intellectual and moral forces both make such a reconciliation extremely problematic. If the Revolution is the source of French republican institutions, if it is seen to mark the frontier between the feudal age of injustice and inequality and the new era of social mobility and freedom, does that mean that we have to celebrate the entire French Revolution? Do we also have to celebrate the Reign of Terror, which bears at least some resemblance to modern totalitarian practices?

So, answered Edgard Faure, former president of the National Assembly and former minister of education, who was asked to succeed Baroin after his death. Faure's "wise suggestion" is that we should celebrate the French Revolution only in its first phase, between 1789 and 1792. But, some historians have pointed out, this is precisely the period when the king was still in power. In all honesty, can we celebrate the earliest phase of the Revolution as the founding event of the French Republic?

Actually, much work faces Faure. As we approach the year 1989, more and more books are being published by French authors that completely destroy the myth that has been patiently built by generations of historians of the French Revolution and taught to millions of children throughout the world. In particular, the Marxist scheme of a revolutionary transition between feudalism and capitalism is not supported by the facts. Ideas, not economic factors, seem to have guided the course of the French Revolution; among these ideas, Tocqueville pointed out, "the first ignited and the last extinguished was anti-religious passion. Never was anti-religion a general passion, ardent and aggressive, but in France." Tocqueville's observations are backed by statistics. They show that the clergy, not the aristocracy, was the first victim of the revolutionary terror. More than a class struggle between those who had and those who had not, the Revolution was a struggle over ideas, a metaphysical struggle between the Christian conception of man, nature, and history and the atheistic worldview of the eighteenth century philosophers. In recent years a few authors have shown that the French Revolution reached its climax with Robespierre's attempt to replace the old religion with the new one of state-incarnated Reason.

This, however, is not enough to destroy the myth of the French Revolution. Many "progressive" thinkers and historians still approve or justify the anti-religious fervor of the revolutionaries. They are thus challenged by a recent discovery made by a 32-year-old historian, Reynald Secher. Secher presented a remarkable doctoral thesis at the Sorbonne, subtitled, "The Franco-French genocide." His thesis demonstrates that the inhabitants of the Vendée region, after they surrendered to the Republican armies in 1793, were systematically exterminated in 1794 by order of the convention led by Robespierre. About 117,000 civilians—including women, and children—were massacred, in order that the "race" of Vendeans be obliterated as a hindrance to the progress of the Revolution.

For Secher, there is nothing "scandalous" about his discovery. "The scandal," he says, "is that the truth has been hidden from the French people for two hundred years." The implications of his work are far reaching. France, which claims to be the Fatherland of the Universal Declaration of Human Rights, may also have initiated what Pierre Chaunu has called "the first ideological genocide of modern times."

THE PROBLEM OF REVOLUTIONARY GENOCIDE

But was there a genocide? And was it ideological? The scandal of Secher's thesis started when it was published as a book and the young author appeared on the famous literary television program *Apostrophes*, which is seen every Friday evening by millions of French viewers; the episode serves as a paradigm for the kind of intellectual revisionism that has allowed the events in the Vendée to be erased from history.

On the program Secher's critics did not deny what was contained in his book. They argued that the terrifying facts he exposed in his book were the logical and almost inevitable result of The Reign of Terror. Some even remained reluctant to condemn the 1794 slaughter. They insisted that the word "genocide" was an inappropriate appellation for two reasons: 1) Etymologically, "genocide" means the systematic extermination of a racial, ethnic or religious group. In the case of Vendeans, we cannot speak of a racial or ethnical group such as the Jewish victims of Nazism. 2) Moreover, they insisted, the term genocide was coined in 1944 to describe the destruction of European Jewry. It therefore cannot be used retroactively.

A few months after his television appearance, Secher made a new discovery that he used in answering his opponents. In 1796, two years after the events in the Vendée, a historian named Babeuf had called the extermination "Populicide." Also, various testimonies Secher discovered indicate that the sinister Pol Pot, ideologue and leader of the Khmer Rouge, had thoroughly studied the methods used by the Republicans against Vendeans when he was a student in Paris.

But, one might ask, what is new in Secher's discoveries? After all, no less than fourteen thousand books have already been published about the Vendée insurrection and its brutal repression. Secher concedes that "much was said about Vendée." Nonetheless, he notes that

until now, we have had only partisan responses from the right and from the left. The documents indicate the events in the Vendée were not taken seriously. Furthermore, it was said that there were no documents. My work and my "discoveries" are based on documents that had never been analyzed scientifically, simply because the University was reluctant to do so.

These are not the decisive arguments. The real contribution of Secher was to show that the suppression of the Vendée was not accidental. It had been systematically planned and executed by those who wished to eradicate the inhabitants. The fact that the very name of the Vendée was abolished by the convention and replaced by the name of *Vengé*, which literally means "avenged," proves as much. Clearly, Pierre Chaunu is correct when he speaks of an ideologically motivated genocide. "Robespierre believed that he had the monopoly on the truth," Secher says. "The source of this truth was the law voted by the [democratic] convention. All those who opposed this truth were declared outlaws." Secher also quotes Robespierre: "The first motto of our policy is that we should lead the people by Reason and the enemies of the people by terror. This terror is nothing else but immediate and severe justice."

According to Secher, the Vendeans have been the victims of a double injustice. First, they were brutally suppressed in 1794. They have also been considered by generations of historians as "reactionary," unmitigated "enemies of the Republic," which is largely inaccurate. The Vendeans, like many others, had first welcomed the Revolution with enthusiasm. They then started to revolt against injustices that they had to endure, particularly the state's persecution of their priests. Actually, Secher explains, the Vendeans, in their insurrection against the brutality of the Republic, called on the very principles of the Declaration of Human Rights, written in 1790. They appealed to article 35: "When the government violates the rights of the people, insurrection is for the people the most sacred right and the most essential duty."

The repression of the rebellious Vendée took place during two different periods. First, there was a civil war between the Vendeans and the Republican army. After the defeat of the Vendeans in December 1793, it was decided to methodically exterminate them. The Vendeans were then

> France, the Fatherland of the Declaration of Human Rights, also initiated "the first ideological genocide of modern times."

73

called a "race," which made them appear like the planned victims of genocide. This planned process of extermination included women and children, the former because they were the "reproductive furrow" and the latter because they were "future bandits." The extermination was proposed as early as April 1793, but voted on only in the months of August and September.

The genocide took various forms. The Republicans began by poisoning the wells and the rivers with arsenic, but abandoned this course as too risky. They then poisoned the air and infected the cattle. In a second phase, they used the famous guillotine, but it was too costly, since the executioner had to be paid for each victim. Republicans also thought of shooting their intended victims with bullets, but then decided that the Vendeans were not worth being killed with bullets. In a third phase, the extermination process was conducted by three complementary actions: 1) A committee was charged to loot the entire region; 2) A flotilla of boats was charged with killing all the people living near the Loire River (particularly the inhabitants of Nantes); 3) "Infernal columns" were then sent out to seek survivors in order to kill them immediately or to bring them to special camps where they would soon die.

The drownings on the Loire River provide the most vivid images of the event. Both paintings and eyewitness accounts describe the inventive cruelty used to exterminate the population. The victims were packed on boats that were sunk in the middle of the river after being destroyed with axes. The carrier who organized the drownings voiced delight in contemplating what he called the "patriotic baptism" or the "big glass of the devout." Also used in this mass execution was what one carrier termed "the

> How many fell victim to this genocide? Using different methods, Secher has fixed the number at 117,000.

Republican wedding," whereby naked men and women were tied together in an obscene posture; These included not only married couples, but also fathers with daughters, and priests with nuns. During the fall of 1793, the Loire drownings accounted for 4,800 deaths. Secher has also shown that crematoria were used for exterminating the Vendeans. Since the ovens of the bakers were not big enough, the revolutionary executioners built immense furnaces in the countryside. Other reports tell of the skin of the Vendeans being used to make clothes or drums.

How many fell victim to this genocide? Using different methods, Secher and his colleagues have fixed the number at 117,000. This was about 15 percent of the Vendée's entire population. In some cities, 50 percent of the houses and buildings were destroyed —up to 80 percent in the town of Bressuire. In his investigations concerning the appraisal of the material losses, Secher has challenged another accepted idea about the Vendée.

Many historians have tried to find the roots of the insurrection in the excessive poverty of the region. According to documents available to Secher, however, the Vendée was reputed to be among the richest agricultural areas of France before the Revolution. The fact that the Republican armies, which managed to hold off foreign armies, suffered many casualties from the Vendeans and had difficulty in defeating them proves that the Vendeans were not only rich but also extremely well organized.

In his study of the Vendean insurrection, Secher has paid great attention to the religious factor. Prior to the Revolution, the Vendée was not exceptionally religious, but its clergy was well educated and energetic. The persecution of their priests started in 1790, when the Parliament voted in the Civil Constitution of the clergy. The priests were obliged to pledge allegiance to the state and required to be "citizens before they were priests." Priests and bishops could be elected by all active citizens, including Protestants, Jews, and nonbelievers. Clerical resistance to these measures was particulary strong in the Vendée. The nonjuring priests who wanted to remain faithful to Rome and to the Pope sought refuge among relatives who finally laid down their own lives trying to protect them. After the Revolution began, the Vendeans turned to the Catholic Church as their communal center. For this reason, they have sometimes been compared to the Irish and the Polish. Like the Poles under the Russians and the Irish under English, the Vendeans paid dearly for their religious-cultural loyalties. Secher's work, which has thrown into even greater contention the already threatened bicentenary celebration of the French Revolution, shows how high that price was.

COUNTER-REVOLUTION?
TOULON, 1793

William S. Cormack
and
Michael Sydenham

William S. Cormack is a postgraduate research student at Queen's University, Kingston, Ontario.

Michael Sydenham is Professor of modern history at Carleton University, Ottawa, and author of *The First French Republic* (Batsford, 1974).

ON AUGUST 27TH, 1793, WHEN THE revolutionary republican government of France was struggling desperately to defend the frontiers against the armies of the First Coalition, the great naval base of Toulon was suddenly surrendered to the British. Accepting an offer of military alliance from Admiral Hood, the commander of the British fleet which was blockading the port, the Toulonnais also accepted a restoration of the monarchy, formally recognising Louis XVII, an imprisoned child, as their king. Thus at one stroke the Republic lost its principal naval base and the bulk of its naval forces in the Mediterranean.

This event, which has been called the greatest single disaster to befall France in the whole course of the Revolutionary War, came at a time when the Republic was in imminent danger of defeat and disintegration. In March, social and religious tension in western France had already led to a savage civil war in which the republican armies were repeatedly routed by 'The Royal and Catholic Army of the Vendée'. Moreover, even committed republicans were deeply divided throughout the rest of the country. Where some relatively moderate men held it imperative to maintain order and legality, others believed that the emergency demanded extraordinary and even violent action.

Although there were infinite variations in this widespread conflict, the

'Blowing up the French Ships of War' — a scene from the siege of Toulon by the revolutionary government in December 1793, after the port had been surrendered to the British four months earlier.

First published in *History Today*, October 1987, pp. 49-55. Reproduced by kind permission of History Today, Ltd., 83-84 Berwick Street, London W1V 3PJ England.

moderates were generally strong in the Sections, the urban electoral assemblies, whereas the extremists usually dominated the political clubs, the Popular or Jacobin Societies. As the military situation deteriorated, as prices soared and food became scarce, this dissension deepened, becoming a struggle to secure or maintain control of the local administrative councils; and a further civil war began in the early summer of 1793, when the more extreme revolutionaries in Paris, notably the Montagnard deputies, seized control of the National Convention. Since this new phase of revolution coincided with the acquisition of power by the moderates in such great cities as Bordeaux, Lyon and Marseille, their attempt to suppress extremism was easily represented as 'federalism', a repudiation of national authority and national unity, the cardinal revolutionary crime. Furthermore, since men of property, conservatives and even reactionaries were naturally attracted to the side of moderation, the 'Federalist Revolt' was believed by Montagnards and Jacobins to be the outcome of a great counter-revolutionary conspiracy.

This whole situation indeed seemed to afford the Royalists and the Allies a wonderful opportunity to act decisively against the Revolution. More particularly, the revolt of Toulon and its subsequent surrender to the British could have provided the Allies

The execution of Louis XVI in January 1793 (from a contemporary print) — the signal for the unleashing of the most extreme phase of the Revolution, presided over by Revolutionary Committees during the Reign of Terror (below).

The spectacular defection of France's principal naval base to the British should be seen less as a master-stroke by forces of reaction and more as the anguished response of local moderates to the Revolution's extremes.

with a strategic foothold in southern France. Admiral Hood certainly felt that he had a tremendous chance, and the British Minister at Genoa, Francis Drake, wrote: 'No event of this war has so much tended to bring about a safe and honourable peace.' Conversely, the news from Toulon had immediate repercussions in Paris, where it was one direct cause of the decision of the National Convention to declare Terror to be 'the order of the day'. Used as a dramatic justification for the suppression of all opposition to the Revolutionary Government, the surrender was seen as a classic example of treasonable reaction. Thus on September 10th Jeanbon Saint-André, the cold and enigmatic naval expert in the Committee of Public Safety, attributed the disaster to a vast and sinister conspiracy. Linking the treason at Toulon to the widespread 'Federalist Revolt', and associating this with the activities of those outlawed deputies whom the Montagnards had expelled from the Convention, he saw all as allied to Royalist Counter-Revolution.

This contemporary Jacobin explanation has had great influence on subsequent historical writing. Ultraroyalist historians have seen Toulon's revolt solely in terms of royalism, and the conspiracy thesis has been incorporated into the standard 'revolutionary' accounts of the surrender. Thus a royalist *coup* is seen as following a 'federalist' rising, with counter-revolution finding willing allies among the officers of the French fleet. Much of this is evidently illusory. There was no connection between the Revolt of the Vendée and the resistance of the cities to extreme Jacobin-

ism. The complete failure of the royalists and the allies to exploit the situation either in western or in southern France is in itself conclusive evidence of the absence of any master-plan, plentiful though incoherent plotting may have been. Moreover, 'royalism' acts as a smoke-screen through which the local conflict that actually led to revolt in towns like Toulon can be seen only in hazy and distorted form. A bitter internal struggle for control of Toulon lay behind its revolt, and it was the interaction of that conflict with parallel divisions in the naval forces, not a 'royalist conspiracy', which explains the surrender to Hood.

In Toulon, positions of local power had been acquired during the Revolution of 1789 by an *élite* of notables which included wealthy property-owners, merchants and lawyers. Before long, however, the influence of these notables was challenged by elements espousing more radical social and political ideas. If the notables initially controlled the Municipality of Toulon and the Departmental Administration of the Var, their opponents' power was based in the Club Saint-Jean, the popular society which was affiliated with the Jacobins in Paris.

In 1791-92 the situation changed dramatically, for the Jacobins of Toulon won control of the municipality and gained the support of the National Guard. Strife between moderates and extremists then focused on a struggle between the Club and the Municipality on the one side and the Departmental Administrators, together with the Judges of the Criminal Tribunal, on the other. This conflict reached a frightful climax in July 1792. The Jacobins gathered support from nearby villages and, on July 28th, surrounded the *hôtel du Département* with an armed force. A contemporary who witnessed the event, Louis Richard, described the appalling massacre which ensued: some administrators were hung from lamp-posts; others were cut to pieces as they fled through the streets; and half the people of Toulon cowered in fright behind closed doors. The killings continued that night and the following day. Then, to fill the vacancies in the Department and the Criminal Tribunal, the Municipality named men of its own choice. Thus the Club

came to control all the authorities in Toulon. Yet its victory was not simply one of local Jacobins over local officials, for the whole town was deeply divided. July 1792 should be seen as the date upon which Revolutionary extremists won political control of Toulon by violence.

In 1793, however, the extremists' monopoly was broken. In May growing pressure from Marseille, where the moderates' power was increasing steadily, combined with awareness of feelings of outrage in Toulon to move the extremist administration to make a concession. Seventy-three notables, including priests, ex-nobles and many naval officers who had been arrested as counter-revolutionary 'suspects', were released. This at once led many Toulonnais to express the hope that the city's electoral assemblies, the Sections, which had not met since September 1792, would be reopened. The authorities in Toulon, however, were determined not to allow this, being well aware that the assemblies would be a power-base for their opponents. Events at Marseille, where the resurgent Sections had first defied the Jacobins and then, in June, closed down their Club, well showed what would happen. The Toulon administration therefore announced that the penalty of death would be exacted of anyone who called for the reopening of the Sections, and on July 12th the Jacobin Club staged an armed procession through the city to end all such demands. This march of intimidation proved to be the catalyst for a revolt by the Sections.

Violence and arbitrary measures had characterised the extremist regime in Toulon, and it was the threat of further violence which prompted the Jacobins' opponents to act. The evidence strongly suggests that it was a coalition of moderates, both royalist and republican, who engineered the opening of the Sections. Fear of a repetition of the horrors of the previous summer forged this alliance, and its goal was to overthrow the Jacobin Club and regain control of Toulon: it was not, as both Montagnards and ultra-royalists later claimed, intended to effect a royalist counter-revolution.

On the evening of July 12th a large group of Toulonnais, fearful of imminent violence, gathered at the Church

The Jacobins — whose Paris headquarters, insignia and a typical member are seen here — were the vanguard of the extreme Left in the Revolution; their seizure of Toulon in late 1792 was deeply resented by moderate elements in the town.

entrusting executive decisions to a General Committee of the Sections.

The attitude of the National Guard was but one manifestation of the extent to which extremism had lost popular support. When, expressing the ideas of popular democracy, the Jacobins had seized power in 1792, they had been supported by artisans, shopkeepers, sailors and, most importantly, workers from Toulon's Arsenal, the naval base. Soon, however, the new regime had begun to suppress popular effervescence and to demand a return to strict discipline in the dockyards to expedite the mobilisation of the Fleet, which was becoming more vital as war escalated. The alienation of the workers which resulted was then aggravated by a general decline in the standard of living. Furthermore, the regime in Toulon became politically isolated. The triumph of the Sections in Marseille, a city with which the people of Toulon had close links, had given the moderates great encouragement; but the Jacobin Municipality, which was also critical of the government of France by a minority of the Convention in Paris, could not afford to disavow that government. Having alienated its own people by its violence, it had only the backing of a remote national authority, itself of dubious legality.

The first acts of the new Sectionary regime were meant to consolidate its power and to crush opposition. Measures were immediately taken to suppress the Jacobin Club. The National Guard was reorganised and the Criminal Tribunal was replaced. Further, the Sections purged the Administrations in Toulon, naming a new Municipality and suspending the Departmental Directory. Yet republican forms and institutions were maintained, and this in itself is an indication that at this time moderates, both republican and royalist, were working together to re-establish regular and responsible government.

Having celebrated their unity with their brothers in Marseille, the men of the Sections in Toulon refused to obey a decree from the Committee of Public Safety ordering the naval embargo of that 'rebellious' city. The General Committee of the Sections considered the orders to blockade Marseille both illegal and 'contrary to the sacred interest of the Republic',

of the Minimes. A petition demanding that the Sections be opened was signed and presented to the Municipality. To the chagrin of the Jacobins, the National Guard, which they had

formerly been able to dominate, was virtually unanimous in its support of the demand. The character of the Guard had indeed changed, for many sailors and arsenal workers had been pressed to return to their work in the dockyard, and the shopkeepers and artisans who remained were apparently as fearful as anyone of a new round of disorder. Thus, with the support of the National Guard, the Sections were reconstituted, and declared themselves permanent,

Dedicated interventionist or pragmatic opportunist? Admiral Sir Samuel Hood, commander of the British fleet at Toulon.

and the Kingdom of Naples, and to blockade or defeat the Toulon Fleet. Co-operation with French rebels was an unforeseen possibility. Ostensibly sent to procure free passage for food supplies, the true purpose of the Marseillais delegation to the British fleet was to negotiate for military support. Marseille also encouraged the Toulonnais to enter an alliance with the British, and on August 24th Hood delivered a Proclamation and a Preliminary Declaration to the General Committee in Toulon. Although the Admiral was prepared to support the rebel cities with his fleet, his offer was conditional upon their declaring for a restoration of the monarchy:

> If a candid and explicit declaration in favour of monarchy is made at Toulon and Marseille, and the standard of royalty hoisted, the ships in the harbour dismantled, and the port, and forts [put] provisionally at my disposition, so as to allow of the egress and regress with safety, the people of Provence shall have all the assistance and support his Britannic Majesty's fleet under my command can give.

Hood, like the British Government, saw the restoration of some sort of reformed monarchy as essential to securing a peace settlement. Although it is likely he could not conceive of the option of moderate republicanism, he did not seek to impose a return to the *ancien régime*, as is shown by his later approval of Toulon flying the Tricolour.

On the night of August 24th the General Committee called an extraordinary session of the Toulon Sections to reach a decision on Hood's proposition. A heated debate ensued, great resistance being voiced to the idea of an alliance with the English. However, sentiments of national antipathy and distrust were outweighed by recognition of Toulon's dangerous position. Food supplies were low. Refugees from Marseille, which would fall to Carteaux the following day, were streaming into Toulon, bringing stories of Republican atrocities which seemed to show what the Toulonnais could expect from a vengeful Convention. Moreover, the Sectionary regime was threatened by internal enemies. Since July 12th and 13th the extremists had been subdued but not eliminated. The danger of a Jacobin resurgence in a time of crisis was evident in an abortive uprising by

and it asserted that Toulon had united with Marseille to save France from anarchists. These sentiments, which had motivated the Sectional revolt and over which Toulon broke with National Authority, were elaborated in an 'Address to all Citizens of the French Republic.' The Address denounced the Jacobins in Toulon and presented a tableau of their crimes, which had culminated in their violent opposition to the reopening of the Sections. The Address, however, went beyond the local situation to express the Sections' repudiation of the Revolutionary Government in Paris as illegitimate and bloodthirsty, and to state their devotion to the ideal of a constitutional republic:

> We desire a republic one and indivisible, and this they have never wanted to organise. We desire a constitution, fruit of wisdom and reflection, and they

propose to us only a phantom of government which will propagate factions and anarchy, and leave the ship of State tossed ceaselessly by the tempestuous seas of popular insurrections.

On July 27th, the Marseillais Departmental Army was routed at Avignon by the troops of the Convention under General Carteaux, who had been sent to crush the rebels. Desperate for supplies and threatened by the approach of the avenging forces of the Revolutionary Government, Marseille dispatched deputies to Admiral Hood, the British naval commander. Hood had been sent into the Mediterranean with a formidable Battle squadron and had been operating off the French coast since mid-July. His mission was to co-operate with Allied forces in the Mediterranean theatre, principally coming to the aid of the Sardinians arsenal workers on August 20th which occurred during the execution of two prominent Jacobins. The Workers' Committee in the arsenal, established under the previous regime and deeply suspicious of the Sections, instigated a riot in an attempt to prevent the executions. The significance of the uprising, which was frustrated by the firm stand taken by the National Guard and marine troops, was recognised by the contemporary witness M.Z. Pons: 'How can a city, stripped of everything and racked by internal war, withstand a siege?'

Thus the acceptance of British support and the proclamation of the Monarchy should not be seen as a successful Royalist *coup*. Toulon was isolated and the Sectionary regime was threatened from within by its extremist rivals who were in sympathy with the forces of the Convention marching against the city. Adoption of the monarchy was conditional on entering into an alliance with Hood, which was the only alternative to submission to the Montagnard government. Moreover, in the Declaration accepting Hood's offer, Toulon proclaimed the constitutional monarchy, not a restoration of the *ancien régime*. Thus it was not ultra-royalists who had prevailed, but the same coalition of moderates, both republican and royalist, who had dominated Toulon since July 13th.

The negotiations with Hood, however, encountered a formidable obstacle: resistance to the 'treason' from the French fleet. Since the early period of the Revolution the naval base at Toulon and the ships of the French navy at anchor in the harbour had been an arena for the local struggle, in which control of the Mediterranean fleet was one of the highest stakes. Extremists had sought support among sailors and arsenal workers. Moreover, they saw the officers of the navy, most of whom were nobles, as enemies of the Revolution and supporters of their moderate rivals. Not only was insubordination encouraged among crews of the squadron, but more direct assaults were made against naval commanders. In December 1789, the commanding officer at Toulon, comte d'Albert de Rions, was threatened by an angry crowd and then arrested by the National Guard. His successor,

Jean-Baptiste de Glandèves, was also seized by extremists in 1790, being accused of counter-revolutionary sentiments. Finally in 1792, following the massacre of Departmental administrators, the naval commander, Joseph, marquis de Flotte, was murdered along with several other officers. Using such violent intimidation, the extremists came to dominate Toulon's naval establishment just as they had the civil authorities.

As well as undermining discipline and attacking officers' authority, the Jacobin regime tried to control all aspects of naval operations in Toulon. In June 1793, they demanded a fleet sortie to challenge Spanish warships, and even urged French sailors to force their commanders into accepting such an operation. The precedent of local interference in the navy was thus set by the Jacobins; the Sectionary regime merely continued the pattern, the defiance of the Revolutionary government's orders to quarantine Marseille being the principal example of this local interference. When the General Committee was formed it was affiliated with the chiefs of the navy in Toulon: *contre-amiral* Trogoff, commander of the squadron; *contre-amiral* de Chaussegros, *commandant d'armes*: and *l'ordonnateur civil* Puissant. The General Committee claimed that naval officers would not comply with the embargo on Marseille; yet the commanders, whose correspondence was being opened, were apparently under pressure from the Sectionaries. The moderate regime was seeking to control the naval establishment, which had been receiving little support or guidance from Paris.

The defiant opening of the Sections on July 12th and 13th was accepted by the French squadron: by not intervening, the navy implicitly supported the *coup*. This was another indication of how isolated the previous regime had become. However, neither the crews nor all the officers were solidly behind the new one. Recognising its tenuous hold on the Fleet, the General Committee drew up an 'Address to the French Squadron' to try to head off resistance to Hood's offer. The Address stated the necessity of adopting the monarchy and assured the fleet of the generous assistance of the English admiral.

However, this Address and the news that the Sections had agreed to

surrender the fleet to the English was received with shocked indignation. Petitions demanding defence of the port were soon circulated among most of the warships. Moreover, while Admiral Trogoff was in conference ashore, the squadron declared his second-in-command, *contre-amiral* Saint-Julien, to be commander-in-chief. Saint-Julien then called for the capture of key harbour fortresses held by the Sections. Alarmed by the escalating resistance, the General Committee sent proclamations to the new Admiral and to the entire fleet. The proclamation to the fleet expressed both the justifications for allying with Hood and the ideological motivations behind the moderates' break with the Convention. It stated that Toulon would always hope to take the part of France:

> But, citizens, part of the Nation abandons us at this moment; they leave us lacking supplies, funds, support of all kinds; armies menace us; and what would be the result of the success of their attacks? Our return under the shameful yoke of the factious and of the assassins.

The document addressed to Saint-Julien informed the admiral that Toulon had made peace with the English under honourable conditions for the good of the city and all of France. Furthermore, he was warned that if the Fleet opposed the will of the Sections, 'force would be repelled with force.'

Saint-Julien was outraged by this ultimatum and declared that he would bombard the city if it attempted to impede his defence against the English. Displaying his determination, he ordered the squadron to anchor in line-of-battle, in position to sweep the harbour entrance. In Toulon, preparations were made in deadly earnest for what appeared an inevitable confrontation.

Yet the Fleet was still deeply divided and, despite Saint-Julien's bellicose manoeuvre, it was not firmly resolved to give battle. Many historians and contemporaries have alleged that this division occurred along regional lines, the crews from Toulon and Mediterranean ports supporting the Sections and the English alliance while those from Atlantic ports were prepared to fire on the city. Other accounts suggest that the fleet was divided by political affiliation, with republicans pitted against royalists, and this interpretation usually portrays loyal republican sailors in conflict with counter-revolutionary commanders.

In fact, despite the obsession of the Montagnard government and many historians with Royalist conspiracy, the divisions in the fleet were not clear-cut. The schisms, which were not fundamentally between officers and men, had been produced by Toulon's indigenous conflict and its continual intrusion into the affairs of the squadron. Moral anguish led to the dispatch of a message to the General Committee which illuminates the terrible dilemma in which the Sections had placed the fleet. The crews had sworn never to bear arms against Frenchmen:

> But never will we consent to dishonour ourselves by allowing our enemies entrance to Toulon so long as we will be present. To reconcile our oaths with the honour which is precious to us and which we desire to preserve untarnished at peril of our lives, this is what we propose to you.

The truly divisive question was not acceptance or rejection of the monarchy, but whether or not to follow Toulon in its planned surrender to the National Enemy.

Saint-Julien attempted to reopen negotiations, but the General Committee was more determined than ever. The admiral knew while most of the Fleet could be ordered to engage the English, few ships would obey a command to fire on Toulon. As a last expedient to preserve the squadron, Saint-Julien proposed that his ships demand from the Toulonnais a safe-conduct to sail to another French port. When this was not accepted unanimously, Saint-Julien personally visited the ships-of-the-line, striving to inspire the crews to fight to the death rather than to allow the enemy to enter the harbour.

But the admiral's time had run out and resistance in the fleet was collapsing. During the night of August 27th desertion aboard the French ships became general, so that by dawn several vessels were almost completely abandoned. As the British fleet offshore prepared to come into port, Admiral Trogoff raised his command flag aboard a frigate in Toulon's inner harbour and signalled the French squadron to rally to him. Saint-Julien made his own signal, ordering the

fleet to clear for action and prepare to repel the enemy. However, the will to resist had evaporated and the warships soon obeyed Trogoff's signal, leaving only three or four deserted vessels in the great harbour. Hood's ships were thus able to drop anchor without firing a shot.

Despite the tremendous strategic opportunity offered by the surrender of Toulon, the British, and the allied troops who supported them, would occupy the port for less than four months. Co-operation between the member states of the coalition against Revolutionary France was never great and the Toulon campaign was no exception. There was constant friction and little co-ordination between British, Sardinian, Neapolitan and Spanish forces. More seriously, the British Government, always reluctant to interfere directly in French internal affairs, vacillated over whether to commit itself fully to the endeavour, with the result that Hood never received necessary reinforcements from England. As for the French army besieging Toulon, it was strengthened considerably in October when the rebellious city of Lyon fell to Republican forces: this freed much-needed troops for the struggle to the south.

On December 17th the French, led in part by a young artillery officer named Napoleon Bonaparte, launched a decisive assault on the fortress dominating the high peninsula which separated the two roadsteads to Toulon's harbour. The fleet being vulnerable to Republican cannon fire, Hood was forced to evacuate on December 19th, and he ordered that the French ships be burned before departure. Over seven thousand Toulonnais supporters escaped with the allies, while those remaining faced the terrible vengeance of the Convention. Perhaps eight hundred 'federalists' perished in mass firing squads between December 20th-23rd, and another three hundred were later tried and executed by a Revolutionary Commission. Toulon itself was given a new Republican name: *Port-la-Montagne*. Thus apart from the long-term consequences of the destruction of the warships (a matter of considerable complexity) the revolt of Toulon did not prove so disastrous for France as had been feared. There, as else-

where, national unity was reestablished by violence and terror.

The story nevertheless illustrates an important and ill-appreciated aspect of the times. Ever since the Revolutionary government's condemnation, most accounts of the surrender have portrayed the naval commanders at Toulon (aside from Saint-Julien) as confirmed counter-revolutionaries. In particular, Admiral Trogoff has been charged with obeying secret Royalist orders. The Admiral's anguished correspondence with the Minister of the Navy, however, suggests that the Government was losing control of the navy and that Trogoff was desperate for direction. Since the early days of the Revolution, Paris had neglected the navy in Toulon and had continually upheld the Jacobin Club in its conflicts with naval commanders. Trogoff's letters to the minister were not answered and the admiral was left to cope as best he could with the local political situation. He had asked to be replaced – hardly the action of a royalist conspirator – but carried on in his command despite difficult circumstances and the threat of a superior enemy. Until shortly before the surrender to Hood, Admiral Trogoff hoped to preserve the fleet for France.

As the Revolutionary government's control over the fleet slipped away, local influence had increased. The squadron and naval base at Toulon became a battleground in the city's internal struggle between Revolutionary extremists and political moderates. Reluctantly, officers and men were drawn in and forced to take sides. Yet the situation involved more than a municipal power struggle; it had become a manifestation of the nation-wide conflict over what France was to become.

This conflict had direct implications for individual loyalty. The Montagnard government, having rejected legitimacy in favour of authority based upon naked power, had presented the Mediterranean fleet with a dilemma: how to reconcile a sense of national loyalty to the absence of a consistent or recognisable focus for this loyalty. When faced with their ultimate crisis, both Admirals at Toulon acted from devotion to France. The opposing courses they chose reveal the tragedy of this dilemma.

Industry and Ideology: The Nineteenth Century

The early years of the nineteenth century were marked by the interplay of powerful countervailing forces. The French Revolution and industrialization provided the impetus for political, economic, and social changes in Western civilization. The ideals of the French Revolution remained alive in France and inspired political movements in other parts of Europe as well. Industrialization brought material progress for millions, particularly the burgeoning middle class, but often at the expense of the great mass of unskilled workers who were victims of the low-paying, impersonal factory system. Shifting demographic patterns created additional pressure for change. It had taken all of European history to arrive at a population of 180 million in 1800. Then, in the nineteenth century, Europe's population doubled, causing major migrations on the continent, typically from the countryside to the cities, and sending waves of emigrants to America, Australia, and elsewhere. By 1919 about 200 million Europeans had resettled elsewhere.

But forces of continuity were at work also. Notwithstanding the impact of industrialism, much of Europe remained agrarian, dependent upon the labor of peasants. Christianity remained the dominant religion and, for the moment, the institution of monarchy retained the loyalty of those who wanted to preserve an orderly society. In addition, millions of Europeans, having experienced more than enough turbulence during the French Revolution and Napoleonic era, were willing to embrace even the most reactionary regimes if they could guarantee peace and stability.

The interplay of tradition and change raised vital new issues and generated fundamental conflicts in politics and thought. Of necessity the terms of political discourse were redefined. The century was an age of ideologies—conservatism, with its distrust of untested innovations and its deep commitment to order and tradition; liberalism, with its faith in reason, technique, and progress (often measured in material terms); various forms of socialism, from revolutionary to utopian, each with its promise of equalitarianism and economic justice for the downtrodden working class; and nationalism, with its stirring call for patriotism, unity, and independence for the nationalities of the world. Even Darwinism, the great scientific paradigm of the era, was misappropriated for political purposes. Transformed into Social Darwinism, it was used to justify the dominance of Western nations over their colonies. Popular misconceptions of evolution also reinforced prevailing notions of male supremacy.

In sum, the nineteenth century, for those who enjoyed economic and political status, was the epitome of human progress. For the rest, many of whom shared the materialist outlook of their "betters," it was a time to struggle for a fair share of the fruits of progress.

Several articles in unit 3 explore the dynamics of economic, technological, and scientific change. The social impact of these changes is addressed in "Cottage Industry and the Factory System" and "Sarah Bernhardt's Paris." Major nineteenth century ideologues are treated in "When Karl Marx Worked for Horace Greeley," "Samuel Smiles: The Gospel of Self-Help," and "John Stuart Mill and Liberty."

Looking Ahead: Challenge Questions

What were the causes and consequences of industrialization?

Why was it so difficult for laboring classes to organize for the purpose of improving wages and working conditions?

Karl Marx, Samuel Smiles, and John Stuart Mill were eminent Victorians, yet their perceptions of 19th-century England varied greatly. How would you account for these differences?

What, if anything, does the career of Sarah Bernhardt reveal about the place of women in France during the nineteenth century?

Unit 3

COTTAGE INDUSTRY AND THE FACTORY SYSTEM

Duncan Bythell

AT THE CENTRE OF MOST PEOPLE'S picture of Britain's industrial revolution in the nineteenth century stands the dark, satanic mill, where an exploited and dispirited army of men, women and children is engaged for starvation wages in a seemingly endless round of drudgery: the pace of their labour is determined by the persistent pulse of the steam engine and accompanied by the ceaseless clanking of machines; and the sole beneficiary of their efforts is the grasping, tyrannical, licentious factory master, pilloried by Charles Dickens in that loud-mouthed hypocrite and philistine, Mr. Bounderby. Crude and exaggerated though this image is, it depicts very clearly the main features of the pattern of production which became widespread in the manufacturing industries, not only of Britain, but also of the other advanced countries, by the end of the nineteenth century. For it highlights the emergence of the factory, where hundreds labour together under one roof and one direction, as the normal type of work-unit; it stresses the new importance of complex machine-technology in the process of production; and it emphasises that, because ownership of these machines, of the building which houses them and the engine which drives them, rests with the private capitalist, there exists an unbridgeable gulf between him and his property-less wage-earning employees.

This system of production, which is usually assumed to have been pioneered and rapidly adopted in Britain's textile industries around the end of the eighteenth century, did not, of course, emerge in a wholly non-industrial world. The popular picture suggests that it replaced – or rather, brutally displaced –

an earlier type of organisation, variously referred to as 'the domestic system', the 'outwork system', or simply as 'cottage industry', which differed totally from the factory system. Whereas the latter concentrates workers under one roof in an increasingly urban enviroment, the former disperses employment into the homes of the workers, most of whom live in the countryside. Although the modern mill is filled with the factory master's costly machinery, the domestic workshop houses simple and traditional hand-tools – the spinner's wheel, the weaver's loom, the cordwainer's bench, the nail-maker's forge, and the seamstress' humble pins and needles – which actually belong to the worker. And whilst the factory system implies clear class division, with the wage-earner firmly subordinated to, and perpetually at odds with, his employer, the domestic system gives the head of the household an independent, quasi-managerial status, which enables him to control his own time and to direct, in a 'natural' fatherly way, the efforts of his family team.

The unspoken assumption is that, in the undisciplined, fulfilling, and relatively classless world of cottage industry, the common man was certainly happier, even if he was materially worse off, than his grandson. Only in the last desperate phase, when the dwindling band of domestic handworkers found themselves competing hopelessly against the new generation of factory machine-minders, is the idyllic image tarnished; and the haunting picture of the doomed handloom weaver, striving in his cellar to match the output of his wife and children who have been forced into the factory, reinforces the notion that, between old and new systems, there is nothing but contrast, conflict, and competition.

Any concept of historical change based on snapshots taken on separate occasions tends to emphasise difference and discontinuities. In the caricature of the domestic and factory systems just presented, they appear to be completely antithetical. Yet on closer examination the story of most industries which 'modernised' in the course of the nineteenth century is full of important elements of *continuity* and *complementarity* between the factory and the pre-factory stages of their development; and it is on these two dimensions, rather than on the stark contrasts suggested by the traditional stereotype, that I want to focus attention.

Let us consider continuity first. A number of historians have recently suggested that the existence of the domestic system of production in such industries as textiles was one of the main features

Factory spinning

 From *History Today*, April 1983, pp. 17-23. History Today, 83-84 Berwick Street, London W1V 3PJ. Reprinted by permission.

stinguishing the pre-industrial onomies of Europe from the Third orld countries of today; and although ey prefer the abstract concept of roto industrialisation' to the well-tablished and perfectly adequate term omestic system', they are essentially aiming that the industrial revolutions the nineteenth century could not have ken place without the prior develop-ent of a form of production which, in eir view, was to provide both the pital and the labour needed for odern industrial development.

In making this claim, proponents of e theory of 'proto industry' are draw-ig attention to one of the most impor-nt, but often misunderstood, features f the classic domestic system – the fact at it already showed a clear distinction etween the capitalists who controlled it d the wage-earners who depended pon it for their livelihood. For the omestic system, no less than the factory stem which replaced it, was a method f mass-production which enabled weal-y merchant-manufacturers to supply t only textile fabrics, but also items as verse as ready-made clothes, hosiery, ots and shoes, and hardware, to dis-nt markets at home and abroad. In der to do so, they, like the factory asters who followed them, bought the propriate raw materials and hired age-labour to convert them into nished products. The pay roll of some these merchant-manufacturers could n into many hundreds: in the late 30s, for example, Dixons of Carlisle, tton manufacturers, employed 3,500 ndloom weavers scattered over the rder counties of England and Scotland d in Ulster; a decade or so later, Wards Belper, hosiers, provided work for me 4,000 knitting frames in the coun-es of Derbyshire, Nottinghamshire, d Leicestershire; and as late as the 870s, Eliza Tinsley and Co. put out ork to 2,000 domestic nail- and ain-makers in the west Midlands.

To service and co-ordinate such large d scattered forces required an elabo-te system of communication and con-ol in which the key figures were the ents – variously known as 'putters-t', 'bagmen', and 'foggers' – who were e equivalents of the modern supervisor r shop-floor manager. Certainly, the orkers whom these great men emp-yed generally owned their own tools, though in the case of an elaborate piece f machinery like the knitting frame ey often had to hire it; and most of

them worked on their own premises – although, again, it was by no means rare for the individual weaver, knitter, or nail-maker to rent space and tools in another man's shop. But except in a few minor rural trades like straw-plaiting and lace-making in the south and east Midlands, they neither provided their own raw materials, nor had they any interest in marketing the goods they helped to make. They were, in short, wage-earners who happened to own some of the tools of their trade. But the trade in which they worked was organ-ised by capitalists; and far from making goods to sell to local customers, they were often, all unknowing, supplying the wants of West Indian slaves and North American frontiersmen.

The crux of the argument about con-tinuity between domestic and factory systems of mass-production turns on whether it was actually the case that the firms which set up the first modern factories in a particular industry were already active in it on a putting-out basis, and whether the last generation of domestic workers transformed them-selves into the new race of factory hands. Of course, no one is maintaining that continuity was direct and complete in every single industry or region where such a transition occurred: indeed, there were areas such as East Anglia or the Cotswolds where the change-over sim-ply did not take place, and where a once important industry gradually van-ished as the old domestic system dwin-dled and died. But where 'modernisa-tion' did happen in traditional outwork industries in the course of the nineteenth century, as it did in the textile industries of Lancashire and Yorkshire and in the hosiery trade of the east Midlands, his-torians seem to be agreed that it was existing firms which played a leading role, albeit cautiously and belatedly in some instances, in setting-up the factory system and in embodying some of their capital in buildings and machines; in other words the fortunes made, and the expertise in marketing and managing acquired, in the old system of produc-tion were important in enabling the new system to develop.

There is less agreement, however, as to how far the existing hand-workers in any particular industry really did shift over to the factory. The theory of 'proto industry' suggests that the domestic sys-tem had created a country-dwelling but landless proletariat in many ways at odds with the traditional rural society around

them: they had only a minimal involve-ment in the agrarian economy, and were therefore rootless and prone to migra-tion; they possessed manual skills irrelevant to farming activities; and as wage-earners, they were obliged to respond to the pressures and the oppor-tunities of a market economy in which the price of survival was adaptability. In terms of both work-skills and mental outlook, that is to say, they were already well-equipped to form the first genera-tion of the modern industrial labour force.

But did this actually happen? The traditional picture suggests not, because it depicts a stubborn refusal to come to terms with changed circumstances and, indeed, a downright hostility to 'machinery' which, in the Luddite movement of 1811-16 in the Midlands and the various outbreaks of loom-smashing in Lancashire and elsewhere, sometimes erupted in violence. Clearly, the worker's readiness to change with the times depended partly on age, and partly on opportunity. Case studies based on census returns for Lancashire weaving villages during the crucial phase of transition in the middle of the nineteenth century suggest that, once a powerloom shed had been started loc-ally, the younger married men were ready enough to take work in it, but that the elderly were either reluctant to do so, or were debarred by the employer, and therefore stuck to the handloom. But until there was a mill virtually on the spot, most of these villagers believed they had little option but to stick to the handloom, and for want of other oppor-tunity they continued to bring their children up to it. Probably the most important strand of continuity in the labour force was in fact provided by the children of the last generation of hand-workers: by and large, a trade dies out because it stopped recruiting sometime before; and the demise of occupations like handloom weaving was finally assured when families were willing and able to put their offspring into some-thing different, instead of forcing them to follow automatically in father's foot-steps.

By highlighting the division between capital and labour which characterised the domestic no less than the factory system of production, and by consider-ing the continuity which this engen-dered, the new theory of 'proto industry' has pinpointed certain popular miscon-ceptions about the nature of cottage

3. INDUSTRY AND IDEOLOGY

industry. First of all, it must be clear that when economic historians refer to 'outwork' or 'cottage industry' they are *not* talking about a world where each family simply makes manufactured goods for its own use – although in even the most advanced societies elements of the home-made and the do-it-yourself survive. Nor are they discussing the self-employed craftsman or genuine artisan – the village shoe-maker and tailor, or the more sophisticated urban wig-maker or cabinet-maker – who produced and sold 'one-off' goods directly to the order of their local customers, and whose successors are still to be found in some parts of the modern economy. Indeed – and this is a second error which needs to be corrected – in the strict sense they are not dealing with 'skill' or 'craft' at all. As a method of mass-production, the greater part of cottage industry involved the

The weaver at his domestic hand loom (above) contrasts sharply with work on a factory power loom (below).

making of plain, simple, inexpensive goods by hands which, although they became more nimble and adept with experience, had neither needed nor received much initial training. Weaving heavy woollens and hammering nails and chains required a certain strength; but weaving plain calico, knitting coarse stockings, sewing buttons on shirts, plaiting straw, and sticking matchboxes together with glue called for neither brain nor brawn. A seven-year apprenticeship to learn the 'mysteries' of most domestic industries was unnecessary, when the work merely involved the monotonous repetition of a few simple

movements of the fingers; and because the work was unskilled and undemanding it was considered particularly suitable for women and children. Domestic industry, like factory industry, involved the worker in much mindless drudgery; the chief difference was that, in working at home with hand-tools, the wage-earner could go at his or her own pace, instead of having to keep up with the steam engine.

Thirdly, just as we need to abandon the notion that the domestic system was all about skilled craftsmen, so we must reject the idea that it was predominantly about 'men' at all. One of the advantages

which the old terms 'domestic system' and 'cottage industry' have ove 'proto industry' is that they suggest a important feature which old-styl mass-production shared with the earl textile mills: a domestic or cottage work shop called on the efforts of housewif grandparents, and children of bot sexes, as well as those of the household head. Thus the average weaving or kni ting family would run two or three loom or frames, and in addition would opera any ancillary machinery needed to pr pare or finish the work. Because worked as a team, the domestic wor unit could also practice division labour, so that each member coul specialise on just one stage in th sequence of production. Like any othe family business, a workshop involved i the domestic system was a collectiv enterprise to which all contributed wh could: and only when the househol included no children old enough to d even the simplest tasks did it depend fo its income on what a man could earn b his own unaided efforts. Because th capitalist-controlled outwork industri made particular use of women's an children's labour in this way, fema workers were generally in a clear majo ity in the work force; and in the mas production section of the needlewo trades, where outwork remained pa ticularly important until late in th nineteenth century, and which includ men's tailoring and shirt-making as w as dress-making and lace stitching, th preponderance of women was especial striking.

Fourthly, we must not imagine tha in a capitalist controlled industrial sy tem such as outwork was, relations be ween masters and operatives wer marked by much sweetness and ligh Since the main tie between them was th cash nexus, disputes about wages cou be frequent and bitter. Most employe in the industries which used the dome tic system operated in a tough compet tive environment, and their likely rea tion to a spell of bad trading condition would be to cut the piece-rates they pa their workers. Most of the scattere rural outworkers were disorganised an docile, and could offer little, if an resistance; and in any case, for wome and children a pittance was deeme better than no work at all. But the ad men – especially those who lived in th towns, and did the better-class wo which needed more strength or skill were another matter. They had a cle onception of the work and wages roper for a man, and they were better ble to take collective action against nderpaying masters and weak-willed lacklegs who broke the conventional ules.

As a result, at different times in the ate eighteenth and early nineteenth cenuries, fierce strikes broke out in such owns as Manchester, Coventry, Barnley and Norwich, major centres of andloom weaving; among the urban ramework knitters of Nottingham and eicester; and among the nail-makers of he Black Country. At a time when

formal trade unionism was a shadowy affair, and in difficult political and economic circumstances, some at least of Britain's industrial outworkers played their part in sustaining patterns of collective bargaining which, *faute de mieux*, sometimes involved great violence; whilst the support these disgruntled men gave to the various campaigns for parliamentary reform between the 1790s and the 1850s has been frequently noted by historians.

Once we have abandoned such misconceptions about the nature of the domestic system as it had come to exist

by the end of the eighteenth century, it is easier to see the similarities and the points of continuity between it and the factory system which was eventually and gradually to supersede it. And when we realise that the domestic system, far from being some prehistoric monster which expired when the first cotton factory was built, actually expanded and persisted in many industries and regions until well into the second half of the nineteenth century, we become aware, not only that the two types of mass-production overlapped in time, but also that they complemented each other,

(Above left) The Domestic Rope Maker; from *The Book of Trades*, 1804. (Above right) Making ropes by Huddart's Machinery.
(Below left) An outworker making pins at home: (below right) a needle pointer at work in a factory in Redditch, Worcester.

rather than competed. The textile industries usually occupy the forefront of any discussion of the domestic and factory systems; and in view of their wide geographic dispersal, their rapid expansion, and the hundreds of thousands they had come to employ by the late eighteenth century, this is entirely appropriate. But because, starting with the spinning branch of the British cotton industry in the 1770s, it was in these industries that the complete triumph of the factory system was achieved earliest, attention has been deflected from the many other trades – particularly shoe-making, clothing, and some branches of hardware – where the domestic system actually became more, rather than less, important. For although the first half of the nineteenth century saw the disappearance into the factory first of spinning and then of weaving in Lancashire and Yorkshire, it also witnessed the expansion of mass-production by outwork methods in the ready-made clothing trades and in the boot and shoe industries. And apart from the fact that these growing industries increased output by traditional rather than modern methods, there were other, less expansionary trades – such as Midlands hosiery and Black Country nail-making – which remained fossilised at the 'domestic' stage of development until well after 1850. In addition, the latter part of the nineteenth century actually saw a number of new, small-scale manufactures, such as paperbag and cardboard-box making, establish themselves as cottage industries. Thus, if outwork had more or less disappeared from the staple textile industries by the 1850s, it was more firmly entrenched than ever in and around many of the industrial towns of the Midlands and the south of England, and, above all, in what were to become known as the 'sweated trades' of London. Why was this?

The pioneering experience of the textile industries suggests some of the answers. Contrary to popular belief, even in the cotton industry, the transition from the domestic to the factory system was a slow, piecemeal affair, which took three generations; and in wool, linen and silk, the process was even more protracted. The reason was simple: the first power-driven machines of the 1770s revolutionised *spinning* only; and by making it possible to produce thread on a scale and at a price which would have been inconceivable in the days of the spinning wheel, they simply created a good deal more work for a great many more work-

ers – in this case, the weavers – at the next stage in the production process. And so long as enough extra weavers could be found at wages the employers were prepared to pay, there was no need to think of replacing the handloom with some labour-saving device, as yet uninvented. Thus between 1780 and 1820, the growth of spinning factories marched *pari passu* with a vast increase in the number of handloom weavers' shops; and technical progress in one section of the industry merely led to the multiplication of traditional handwork in associated sections.

The Croppers of the West Riding of Yorkshire were much involved in the machine-wrecking Luddite movement of 1812.

The same thing was to happen in other industries later: when lace-making was mechanised in Nottingham from the 1820s, there was a consequent increase in the amount of stitching, finishing and mending for hand-sewers in their homes; when machines were first used to cut out the components of a stock-sized shoe or coat, they made more unskilled assembly work for domestic workers; and even when the sewing machine had transformed the traditional needlework trades, it did not necessarily drive them out of the home into the factory, because, as a compact, hand-powered, and relatively inexpensive tool, it could be used in a domestic workshop as effectively as in a large factory. In all these ways, factory and domestic systems often co-existed and complemented each other in a given industry. Since it was rarely either possible or necessary for new techniques to be

introduced simultaneously at every stage in the process of manufacture, flexible combinations of centralised factory work at one stage, and cottage industry at the next, were perfectly practicable.

There was often a regional dimension to the co-existence of these two types of mass-production, and it was here that elements of competition emerged between them. In the classic case of cotton weaving, for example, the handloom survived as the dominant machine in some parts of Lancashire for almost a generation after it had largely given way to the powerloom in others: in large towns such as Stockport, Oldham and Blackburn, factory production was taken up in the 1820s by manufacturers who already operated spinning mills, but it made little progress in the small towns and villages of north-east Lancashire, such as Padiham, Colne and Hagate before the 1840s. In part, this reflected local differences in the availability of labour and capital, for the more remote rural areas were richer in the former than in the latter. But independent of such regional differences, there was also a qualitative side to this 'staggered' adoption of the powerloom, because the early, clumsy factory looms could cope better with the plain types of cloth than with fancy or patterned goods. Other industries were later to show similar disparities in the rate at which different districts and sections adopted new techniques: for example, the boot and shoe industry of Leicester

Merchants in the Cloth Hall, Leeds in 1814. Merchants used cottage industries as a method of mass-production to supply their buyers.

...eems to have relied more on factory production and less on outwork than did that of Northampton in the second half of the nineteenth century; whilst in the 1890s, cottage industry was more apparent in the ready-made clothing trade of London than in that of Leeds.

In short, the domestic system of mass-production in British industry took a long time a-dying during the nineteenth century. It might expand in one trade at the very time that it was contracting in another; in some industries, it could enjoy a harmonious co-existence with factory production for many years, whilst elsewhere it might struggle on in arduous competition for a generation or more. Why was this? How could this technically primitive form of large-scale production remain viable for so long in important parts of the world's first industrial economy?

To find the answer, we must try to fathom the minds of the entrepreneurs in the different industries, as they calculated how best, in a complex and competitive world, to get their goods to market with least cost and least trouble to themselves. A manufacturer who had grown up with the domestic system as the dominant mode of production in his trade would need strong inducements to abandon it, because under normal circumstances it offered him many advantages. If his employees provided their own tools and workrooms, he himself was spared the need to tie up his own capital in bricks and mortar and in machinery; and in times of periodic trade depression or slack seasonal demand – and most of these industries were subject to one or other of these risks, if not, indeed, to both of them – it was the worker, not his employer, who suffered when plant and equipment were standing idle. It was not that these great merchant-manufacturers lacked capital – indeed it required remarkably little fixed capital in most of these industries to build or rent a small factory and fill it with new or second-hand machinery; nor was it generally the case that appropriate new techniques were not available – the time-lag between invention and adoption of a new machine is a recurrent feature in many of these trades; it was rather the case that their capital under the domestic system was embodied in unused raw materials, goods 'in the make', and stocks in the warehouse.

Nevertheless, because it involved more sophisticated machinery, the application of power, and the construction of large, purpose-built work premises, the factory system of production was capital-intensive, rather than labour-intensive. By contrast, what an employer had to rely on to keep cottage industry viable was an abundance of cheap, unskilled, and unorganised labour. So long as he could find enough workers who had no choice but to take his work at the wages he was prepared to offer – no matter how low these might be – he could meet his production targets and reap his expected profits. From the late eighteenth to the late nineteenth centuries, there were many regions of Britain which could provide just such supplies of labour: a high and sustained rate of population increase, together with the greater commercialisation of agriculture, tended to create pools of unemployed or under-employed workers in many rural areas; and in so far as these impoverished country people moved off to the towns in search of more work and better wages, they often merely added to the chaos and confusion in the unskilled urban labour markets.

But what kept the domestic system alive after the mid-nineteenth century more than anything else was the continued availability – long after most adult men had deserted these low paid, dead-end jobs – of female and child labour: incapable of collective self-defence, and often deliberately ignored by their better organised menfolk; accustomed to regarding any earnings, however minute, as a worthwhile contribution to family income; and often only able to work on a part-time or casual basis – they were ideal for many employers' purposes. And in a perverse way, because it thrived on family labour, the domestic system actually helped to perpetuate its own labour force: because cottage industry, by enabling the whole household to earn, acted as a great inducement to early marriages and large families, and thus contributed to the 'population explosion' which was so important a feature of Britain's industrial revolution.

Because labour could be much cheaper in one part of the country than in another, an old-fashioned employer who stuck to outwork could still hope to compete with his more ambitious and enterprising fellows elsewhere who had switched over to factory production. Only in the last quarter of the nineteenth century did a combination of new circumstances – including rural depopulation, compulsory schooling (which both kept young children out of the labour market and widened their horizons), rising real incomes (which made small supplementary earnings less essential to a family), and more 'chivalrous' male

Gathering Teasels in the West Riding of Yorkshire, an aquatint after George Walker. Teasels are still used to raise the nap on woollen cloth.

(Below) *The Preemer Boy*, 1814; aquatint after George Walker. 'Preeming' is detaching, with an iron comb, the bits of wool on the teasel.

only stay in business if they themselves adopted American methods of production. Both the cotton manufacturers of the 1820s and the boot and shoe manufacturers of the 1890s had to overcome strong opposition from workers still suspicious of machinery and still attached (in spite of the precarious economic position in which it left them) to the domestic system: but once the entrepreneurs in any industry had concluded, for whatever reasons, that the disadvantages of cottage industry outweighed the benefits, its days were numbered.

From the worker's point of view, even if we forget the caricature, the dark satanic mill offered an uninviting prospect; but it is hard to escape the conclusion that the domestic system was in many ways even less agreeable. Even where cottage workers were not directly competing with factory workers – and I have suggested that it would be wrong to put too much emphasis on this side of the story – most of them were poorly paid, and likely to be alternately overworked and under-employed. Worst of all, they were subject to all kinds of abuses, not only from employers and their agents, but often from heads of households and fathers of families who connived, however reluctantly, in the exploitation of their own wives and children. Men may have been unwilling to accept the separation of home and workplace which the gradual replacement of the domestic system by the factory system involved: but in its long-term implications for family life, it was probably one of the most beneficial, as well as one of the most fundamental, of all the changes brought about by the industrial revolution.

attitudes towards women as workers – help gradually to eliminate some of the sources of cheap labour and thus undermine one of the domestic system's chief props.

Changes in market conditions, as well as the increasing difficulty of finding suitable labour, could also be instrumental in persuading entrepreneurs to abandon old-style mass-production in favour of the factory. When, for example, attractive new export markets opened up

for the English cotton industry in Latin America in the early 1820s, Lancashire manufacturers knew that they would be better able to increase output by introducing powerlooms than by seeking out more handloom weavers at higher wages; and when, more than two generations later, British boot and shoe manufacturers were faced with an 'invasion' of their own home market by cheap mass-produced, factory-made American imports, they recognised that they could

FOR FURTHER READING:
D. Bythell, *The Sweated Trades* (Batsford, 1978); J. L. and B. Hammond, *The Skilled Labourer* (London, 1919); G. Stedman Jones, *Outcast London* (Oxford University Press, 1971); P. Kriedte, H. Medick and J. Schlumbohm, *Industrialization before Industrialization* (Cambridge University Press, 1981); D. Levine, *Family Formation in an Age of Nascent Capitalism* (Academic Press, 1977); J. M. Prest, *The Industrial Revolution in Coventry* (Oxford University Press, 1960); E. P. Thompson, *The Making of the English Working Class* (Gollancz, 1963; Penguin Books).

When Karl Marx Worked for Horace Greeley

William Harlan Hale

William Harlan Hale has written a biography of Horace Greeley.

On Saturday morning, October 25, 1851, Horace Greeley's New York *Tribune*, entrenched after a decade of existence as America's leading Whig daily, appeared with twelve pages rather than its usual eight. The occasion was too noteworthy to be passed over without comment by the paper itself. So a special editorial was written—probably by Greeley's young managing editor, the brisk, golden-whiskered Charles A. Dana—to point it out.

Besides a "press of advertisements," the editorial ran, this morning's enlarged paper contained "articles from some foreign contributors that are especially worthy of attention." Among these were "a letter from Madame Belgioioso, upon the daily and domestic life of the Turks, and another upon Germany by one of the clearest and most vigorous writers that country has produced—no matter what may be the judgment of the critical upon his public opinions in the sphere of political and social philosophy."

Turning the pages to see who this most clear and vigorous German might be, readers glanced past such items as a "Grand Temperance Rally in the 13th Ward"; a Philadelphia story headlined "Cruelty of a Landlord—Brutality of a Husband"; a Boston campaign telegram announcing a Whig demonstration "in favor of Daniel Webster for President." Then they reached a long article entitled "Revolution and Counter-Revolution," over the by-line, Karl Marx.

"The first act of the revolutionary drama on the Continent of Europe has closed," it began upon a somber organ tone: "The 'powers that were' before the hurricane of 1848, are again the 'powers that be.'" But, contributor Marx went on, swelling to his theme, the second act of the movement was soon to come, and the interval before the storm was a good time to study the "general social state . . . of the convulsed nations" that led inevitably to such upheavals.

He went on to speak of "bourgeoisie" and "proletariat"—strange new words to a readership absorbed at the moment with the Whig state convention, the late gale off Nova Scotia and with editor Greeley's strictures against Tammany and Locofocoism. "The man goes deep—very deep for me," remarked one of Greeley's closest friends, editor Beman Brockway of upstate Watertown, New York. "Who is he?"

Karl Marx, a native of the Rhineland, had been for a short time the editor of a leftist agitational newspaper in Cologne until the Prussian police closed it down and drove him out. At thirty, exiled in Paris, he had composed as his own extremist contribution to the uprisings of 1848 an obscure tract called the

PHOTOGRAPH OF KARL MARX FROM BETTMANN ARCHIVE

From *American Heritage*, April 1957, pp. 20-25, 110-111. Copyright 1957 by American Heritage, a division of Forbes Inc. Used by permission.

3. INDUSTRY AND IDEOLOGY

Communist Manifesto. At least at this moment it was still obscure, having been overtaken by events and forgotten in the general tide of reaction that followed the surge of 1848 abroad. Thrown out of France in turn as a subversive character, he had settled in London, tried unsuccessfully to launch another left-wing journal there, spent the last of his small savings, and now was on his uppers with his wife and small children in a two-room hovel in Soho, desperately in need of work.

The following week Karl Marx was in the *Tribune* again, continuing his study of the making of revolutions. And again the week after that. "It may perhaps give you pleasure to know," managing editor Dana wrote him as his series of pieces on the late events in Germany went on, "that they are read with satisfaction by a considerable number of persons and are widely reproduced." Whatever his views might be, evidently the man could write. Next he branched out and wrote for Greeley and Dana on current political developments in England, France, Spain, the Middle East, the Orient—the whole world, in fact, as seen from his Soho garret. News reports, foreign press summaries, polemics, and prophecies poured from his desk in a continuous, intermixed flow, sometimes weekly, often twice-weekly, to catch the next fast packet to New York and so to earn from Greeley five dollars per installment.

This singular collaboration continued for over ten years. During this period Europe's extremest radical, proscribed by the Prussian police and watched over by its agents abroad as a potential assassin of kings, sent in well over 500 separate contributions to the great New York family newspaper dedicated to the support of Henry Clay, Daniel Webster, temperance, dietary reform, Going West, and, ultimately, Abraham Lincoln. Even at his low rate of pay—so low that his revolutionary friend and patron, Friedrich Engels, agreed with him that it was "the lousiest petty-bourgeois cheating"—what Marx earned from the *Tribune* during that decade constituted his chief means of support, apart from handouts from Engels. The organ of respectable American Whigs and of their successors, the new Republican party, sustained Karl Marx over the years when he was mapping out his crowning tract of overthrow, *Das Kapital.*

In fact, much of the material he gathered for Greeley, particularly on the impoverishment of the English working classes during the depression of the late 1850's, went bodily into *Das Kapital.* So did portions of a particularly virulent satire he wrote for the *Tribune* on the Duchess of Sutherland, a lady who had taken the visit of Harriet Beecher Stowe to London as the occasion to stage a women's meeting that dispatched a lofty message of sympathy to their "American sisters" in their cause of abolishing Negro slavery. Marx scornfully asked what business the Duchess of Sutherland had stepping forth as a champion of freedom in Amer-

ica, when at home she herself was living off vast Scottish estates from which not so long ago her own family had driven off 3,000 tenant families and burned their villages in order to turn the land back to pasture lands and ducal hunting preserves.

The *Tribune* was not only Marx's meal ticket but his experimental outlet for agitation and ideas during the most creative period of his life. Had there been no *Tribune* sustaining him, there might possibly—who knows?—have been no *Das Kapital.* And had there been no *Das Kapital,* would there have been a Lenin and a Stalin as the master's disciples? And without a Marxist Lenin and Stalin, in turn, would there have been . . . ? We had best leave the question there. History sometimes moves in mysterious ways.

Few episodes in journalism seem more singular and unlikely than this association of the frowning ideolo-

gist of Soho on one hand and, on the other the moon-faced, owlish Vermont Yankee known affectionately to legions of readers in North and West as "Uncle Horace" as he traipsed around the country on the steamcars with his squeaky rural voice, his drooping spectacles, his carpetbag, and his broad-brimmed white hat. It is startling enough today that their careers should ever have become intertwined. What is even more odd in retrospect is the degree to which they did. Although Marx filed well over 500 pieces to the *Tribune,* just how many there were nobody knows, since many were "spiked," killed and forgotten, while others were cut up and cannibalized, and still others were taken over bodily and printed without his by-line as leaders in the special precincts of Greeley's own editorial page. Precisely which of Marx's pieces were so used only a process of deduction and guesswork can tell, since no copies were kept. Today, scanning the *Tribune*'s files, one cannot be sure whether the voice one encounters thundering on its most famous page is that of the great Greeley himself or that of his rabid man in London, Herr Doktor Marx.

And the puzzle goes one step further. Even on those occasions when a *Tribune* contribution is clearly labeled as by Karl Marx, one cannot be sure that it really was written by Marx at all. Managing editor Dana, who conducted the office's day-to-day dealings with its London correspondent, evidently believed that whatever Marx sold the *Tribune* as his own really was his own. But today we know better. From Marx's immense correspondence with his acolyte, financial angel, and amanuensis, Friedrich Engels (still published for the most part only in the original German) we can discover something his American employers at the time never suspected, namely that much of what they bought as by "Karl Marx" was actually ghostwritten by the ever-helpful Engels.

Not one word of the opening article which the *Tribune* heralded as being by this "clearest and most vigorous" of German writers, Karl Marx, was penned by Marx at all. Nor was anything he sent to the paper under his own name for the next six months or so. Even after that, what was really Marx's and what was Engels' is a question that remains to be explored by Ph.D.'s in search of occupation. But all that matters is that much of what the *Tribune*'s subscribers in the 1850's took to be the work of Greeley was the work of Marx, and what they took to be the work of Marx was often that of an unknown assistant in Manchester, England, named Engels.

If readers were astonished at their Uncle Horace for bringing so alien a person as this Marx into their fold, they had only to remember that he had surprised them often before. In the ten years of its existence, his paper had espoused more varied causes and assembled around itself a more unconventional array of talents than any major daily had ever done before

(and, one may safely add, than any has done since). It had come out for free homesteading and labor unions at a time when these were drastic new ideas. It had also backed socialist community experiments, the graham bread cult, pacifism, vegetarianism, and Mrs. Bloomer's clothing reform. The utopian Albert Brisbane had preached in its pages the virtues of his North American Phalanx, a communal colony set up according to the principles of the Frenchman Charles Fourier. The formidable, rhapsodic Margaret Fuller, whom Nathaniel Hawthorne had once called "the Transcendental heifer," had preached feminism in it—and then moved right into Greeley's own married home. The paper's star performers ranged from Bayard Taylor, the romantic poet and world traveler whose profile made him look the part of an American Lord Byron, to George Ripley, the exuberant Unitarian minister who had broken away to found the cooperative retreat at Brook Farm where intellectuals carried on Socratic discourse and took in each other's washing.

Greeley himself was always inquiring and imaginative, and with the priceless possession of an independent popular newspaper at his command he stood at the center of the turbulence as a barometer, a bellwether, a broker of new notions and ideas. Nothing was quite alien to him in the assorted stirrings of that era—not even the Fox sisters of Rochester, who had attracted much attention with their clairvoyant "spirit-rappings," and whom he invited to his house for a séance along with the famed Swedish soprano, Jenny Lind, newly brought to this country as the protégée of his somewhat gamy yet still moralistic crony, Phineas T. Barnum.

For such a man as Greeley, then, not even Karl Marx was quite beyond the pale. What was meant by this new gospel of socialism, after all? Did it really involve total overthrow? One of the *Tribune*'s intellectual friends, Henry James senior, speaking at a time when his more famous sons, William and Henry junior, were still playing with building blocks, had put the case for socialism on a religious basis. Our present society, he had said, "affords no succor to the divine life in man." Yet every creature of God was entitled to ample physical as well as social subsistence—that is, the respect and brotherly affection of every other creature of God. Greeley, deeply devotional himself, had been moved by the force of the argument. At the same time he balked at the idea of an all-knowing new system that would paternally take care of everyone. The ancient conflict between freedom and order burned in his mind. Better go on listening to both sides, then, he thought.

Up to a point, the apostles of change had a good case, he said in the *Tribune.* "We . . . who stand for a comprehensive Reform in the social relations of mankind impeach the present Order as defective and radically vicious in the following particulars. . . . It does not secure opportunity to labor, nor to acquire industrial skill and efficiency to those who need it most. . . . It dooms the most indigent class to pay for whatever of comforts and necessaries they may enjoy . . . at a higher rate than is exacted of the more affluent classes . . . [and] for the physical evils it inflicts, Society has barely two palliatives—Private Alms-giving and the Poorhouse. . . ." Yet he did not want a class revolution, he insisted. He wanted to see co-operation and harmony. He looked forward to a reorganization of life amid the threatening weight of the factory system that would give each worker a share of the proceeds of the enterprise or else an opportunity to strike out on his own on free land from our national domain, where he could build his own enterprise.

Such ideas, far from seeming subversive, pulsed like wine through the veins of a young generation. One of those who had been swept up was a well-bred Harvard junior named Charles A. Dana. Young Dana, handsome, well-spoken, and idealistic, joined Ripley's colony when it was set up at Brook Farm and lived there for five years, milking the cows, teaching other intellectuals' children German and Greek, and waiting on tables to such distinguished visitors as Hawthorne, William Ellery Channing, Miss Fuller, and Greeley himself.

When Brook Farm burned down both Ripley and his young helper found berths on Greeley's ever-hospitable *Tribune*. The year 1848 broke—a time of real revolution abroad as against the pastoral make-believe of Brook Farm at home. Young Dana, fired by the reports the first packet steamers were bringing in, managed to get a leave of absence from the fourteen-dollar-a-week job he then held as Greeley's city editor to go to Europe and see the drama. He was in Paris at the height of the insurrection that overthrew the July Monarchy. Paris went to the barricades, and reporter Dana climbed them too. He saw blood flow in the rue de Rivoli.

From this scene Dana sped on to Germany for more hopeful signs. There, in Cologne, he called on editor Karl Marx, then functioning during a brief lifting of the police ban as editor of the grubby *Neue Rheinische Zeitung*.

Just what young Dana of the *Tribune* and Marx of the *Communist Manifesto* said to each other that midsummer day in Cologne is not of record. In later years, when he had graduated to become editor of the New York *Sun* in his own right and thereby a pillar of

Fragments of a Marx dispatch in the Tribune *for February 9, 1853, show how he combined news, research, and polemic.*

During the present momentary slackness in political affairs, the address of the Stafford House Assembly of Ladies to their sisters in America upon the subject of negro-slavery, and the "affectionate and Christian address of many thousands of the women of the United States of America to their sisters, the women of England," upon white slavery, have proved a god-send to the press. Not one of the British papers was ever struck by the circumstance that the Stafford House Assembly took place at the palace and under the Presidency of the Duchess of Sutherland, and yet the names of Stafford and Sutherland should have been sufficient to class the philanthropy of the British Aristocracy—a philanthropy which chooses its objects as far distant from home as possible, and rather on that than on this side of the ocean.

The history of the wealth of the Sutherland family is the history of the r...... and
....ness of Suther-
.an..., alias Marchioness of Stafford.

Let us first state that the ancestors of the Marchioness of Stafford were the "great men" of the most northern part of Scotland, of very near three-quarters of Sutherlandshire. This County is more extensive than many French *Departements* or small German Principalities. When the Countess of Sutherland inherited these estates, which she afterward brought to her husband, the Marquis of Stafford, afterward Duke of Sutherland, the population of them was already reduced to 15,000. My lady Countess resolved upon a radical economical reform, and determined upon transforming the whole tract of country into sheep-walks. From 1814 to 1820, these 15,000 inhabitants, about 3,000 families, were systematically expelled and exterminated. All their villages were demolished and burned down, and all their fields converted into pasturage. British soldiers were commanded for this execution, and came to blows with the natives. An old woman refusing to quit her hut, was burned in the flames of it. Thus my lady Countess appropriated to herself *seven hundred and ninety-four thousand acres of land*, which from time immemorial had belonged to the clan. In the exuberance of her generosity she allotted to the expelled natives about 6,000 acres—2 acres per family. These 6,000 acres had been laying waste until then, and brought no revenue to the proprietors. The Countess was generous enough to sell the acre at 2s. 6d. on an average, to the clan-men who for centuries past had shed their blood for her family. The whole of the unrightfully appropriated clan-land she divided into 29 large sheep farms, each of them inhabited by one single family, mostly English farm-laborers; and in 1821 the 15,000 Gaels had already been superseded by 131,000 sheep.

...tion ....ining .... een thrown
...e was ......cted in a se.
...ple.

The above Turkish reform by the Countess of Sutherland was justifiable, at least, from a Malthusian point of view. Other Scottish noblemen went further. Having superceded human beings by sheep, they superceded sheep by game, and the pasture grounds by forests. At the head of these was the Duke of Athol. "After the conquest, the Norman Kings afforested large portions of the soil of England, in much the same way as the landlords here are now doing with the Highlands." (R. Somer's Letters on the Highlands, 1848.)

As for a large number of the human beings expelled to make room for the game of the Duke of Athol, and the sheep of the Countess of Sutherland, where did they fly to, where did they find a home?

In the United States of North America.

The enemy of British Wages-Slavery has a right to condemn Negro-Slavery; a Duchess of Sutherland, a Duke of Athol, a Manchester Cotton-lord—never!   KARL MARX.

Everett's Tripartite ·

American society, Dana seems to have expunged all memory of that meeting from his mind. But it was there that the contact was made which led to Marx's ten-year connection with the *Tribune*. And if Dana remained reticent, another caller on Marx that same summer has left a vivid impression of what the Cologne radical was then like. This other visitor was Carl Schurz, then himself a fledgling fellow-revolutionist of the Rhineland, and destined—like Dana himself—to a distinguished public career in the United States. Marx that summer, Carl Schurz recalled, "was a somewhat thickset man, with his broad forehead, his very black hair and beard and his dark sparkling eyes. I have never seen a man whose bearing was so provoking and intolerable. To no opinion which differed from his, he accorded the honor of even a condescending consideration. Everyone who contradicted him he treated with abject contempt. . . . I remember most distinctly the cutting disdain with which he pronounced the word 'bourgeois.' "

Dana returned to the home office, aroused and enlarged by all he had seen abroad. Greeley, who had never been abroad himself, encouraged his bright young acquisition and made him managing editor. In this role, in 1851, he extended the *Tribune's* invitation to Marx, then living in penury and exile at 28 Dean Street, Soho. Would he begin with a series on the late revolution in Germany? Marx jumped at it as a lifesaver. No English newspaper had wanted him as a contributor. For one thing, although he spoke a thickly accented English, he could not write the language. Yet this could be overcome by his getting in his friend and fellow exile, Friedrich Engels, to translate for him. Engels, the highly cultivated scion of a prosperous German textile family, was busy managing his father's branch factory in Manchester and was always eager to assist.

Then Marx had a further thought. Why not have Engels write the whole series for him and thus leave him free to go on undisturbed with his studies for *Das Kapital*? So he wrote Engels imperiously, "You must, at this moment when I am entirely absorbed in political economy, come to my aid. Write a series of articles on Germany since 1848. Spirited and outspoken. These gentlemen [the *Tribune* editors] are very free and easy when it comes to foreign affairs." Soon acolyte Engels obliged, sending in his draft for Marx's signature. "Mes remerciements pour ton article," Marx acknowledged it, in that mixture of tongues he resorted to as a kind of exiled lingua franca; "Er . . . ist unverändert nach New York gesegelt. Du hast ganz den Ton für die *Tribune* getroffen." *

* "My thanks for your article. It . . . sailed off unchanged to New York. You have hit the tone for the *Tribune* precisely."

So, while Marx from his garret gave Engels the political line for his articles, saying he was too busy to do more than that, his faithful partner sat down after work at the factory to write what was required and then hurried downtown through Manchester's midnight fogs to put his copy on the late express to London, where Marx would see it and pass it on across the sea. It was a demanding life for Engels, as he sometimes pointed out. Once he minuted to Marx, "Busy the whole day at the office; supper from seven to eight; then right to work, and sending all I could get done off now at 11:30." Or "In spite of my greatest efforts, since I got your letter only this morning and it's now eleven P.M., I haven't yet finished the piece for Dana." Marx, for his part, cashed the monthly payment drafts coming in from the *Tribune*.

Still Marx's own life at that time was not one of ease. It resembled a nightmare. He was living and trying to do his thinking in a squalid two-room flat which he shared with his wife and as many as six children. Three died there while he went out begging from friends for food and medicine, and, in the case of one little girl whom the Marxes lost, the price of a coffin in which to bury her. When he finally did commence writing himself for Greeley in German in order to reduce the pressure on his friend, he sometimes found it impossible to go on. "My wife is sick," he complained to Engels one day, "little Jenny is sick, Lenchen [the family's factotum, also quartered in the same two rooms] has a sort of nerve fever. I couldn't and can't call the doctor, because I have no money for medicine. For eight to ten days I've fed the family on bread and potatoes, and it's doubtful whether I'll be able to chase up any today. . . . I haven't written anything for Dana because I didn't have a penny to go out and get newspapers to read."

Under such circumstances, the relationship to the *Tribune* of a man who was haughty and irascible to begin with, and stone-broke, bitter, and fearful of his family's very survival besides, promised to be stormy. Marx constantly importuned his New York employers for more linage, better treatment of his copy, and, above all, more pay. When this was not forthcoming, he vented his spleen in scribblings to Engels in which he variously described the *Tribune* as *Löschpapier* (that blotter) or *Das Lauseblatt* (that lousy rag), its editors as *Kerle* and *Burschen* (those guys, those bums), Dana as *Der Esel* (that ass) and Greeley himself as "*Dieser alte Esel* with the face angelic." The two German intellectuals consoled themselves by looking down their noses at the the mass-circulation Yankee daily for which they found themselves having to work. "One really needn't put one's self out for this rag," said Engels to Marx; "Barnum struts about life-size in its columns, and its English is appalling." And Marx in turn muttered to Engels, "It's disgusting to be condemned to regard it as good fortune to be taken into the company of such a rag. To pound and grind bones and cook up soup out of them like paupers in the workhouse—that's what the political work comes down to which we're condemned to do there."

Moreover, Marx disagreed with many of the *Tribune*'s policies—although he avoided an open break, fearful of losing his meal ticket. One particular anathema to him was the idea of a protective tariff. Yet Greeley, whose dallyings with socialism had never interfered with his enthusiasm for American business enterprise, felt that protectionism was just the thing. When he heard this, Marx erupted darkly to Engels, "Das alles ist very ominous."

Managing editor Dana had a difficult time with the impetuous pair in London. Most of the letters in which he answered Marx's multilingual torrent of demands and protests have been lost. But Dana was a born diplomat, shrewd, worldly, a trifle sardonic, and his responses were always smooth. He addressed Marx gracefully "in the name of our friendship," but avoided paying him the triple rate Marx had asked for, and eventually also cut down his space. Marx stormed but went on writing for the *Tribune,* which at least let him say what he wanted to say. "Mr. Marx has indeed opinions of his own, with some of which we are far from agreeing," an editorial note in the paper remarked; "but those who do not read his letters neglect one of the most instructive sources of information on the great questions of European politics."

For, in spite of all their letting off steam to one another about the "lousiness" of the *Yankeeblatt* the partners Marx and Engels finally settled down together to do an extraordinary journalistic job for it. In a day before the coming of the transatlantic cable, and when Europe's own overland telegraph lines were still too sparse and costly to carry more than fragmentary press reports, England was the world's great communications center by reason of its unrivaled sea traffic in every direction. Marx and Engels were keenly aware of this and set themselves up as a sort of central agency amassing world news and intelligence for their American client—with their own slant, of course. With Teutonic diligence they dredged up from diplomatic dispatches, statistical abstracts, government files, the British Museum, gossip, and newspapers in half a dozen languages gathered from Copenhagen to Calcutta, a mass of information on going topics such as had never reached an American newspaper before.

In 1853 the eyes of Europe turned apprehensively toward the growing crisis between the Western powers and Russia over the control of weak but strategic Turkey—a contest that soon led to the Crimean War. Marx and Engels provided their American readers with a background series that discussed the ethnic make-up of the area, reviewed its diplomatic history as far back as the treaty of 1393 between the Sublime Porte and Walachia, characterized all its chief personalities, and estimated down to battalion strengths the military forces and capabilities of the contenders. Some of this made for dry reading, but Marx had a way of breaking through into language of a vigor any American could understand. He poured vitriol on the Western rulers trying to maintain decadent Turkey as their tool:

"Now, when the shortsightedness of the ruling pygmies prides itself on having successfully freed Europe from the dangers of anarchy and revolution, up starts again the everlasting topic, 'What shall we do with Turkey?' Turkey is the living sore of European legitimacy. The impotency of legitimate, monarchial governments ever since the first French Revolution has resumed itself in the axiom, Keep up the *status quo.* . . . The *status quo* in Turkey! Why, you might as well try to keep up the present degree of putridity into which the carcass of a dead horse has passed at a given time, before the putridity is complete."

Equally, he turned on tsarist Russia, in whose "good will" toward Turkey the *Times* of London was at the moment voicing hopeful confidence. "The good will of Russia toward Turkey!" he snorted. "Peter I proposed to raise himself on the ruins of Turkey. . . . Czar Nicholas, more moderate, only demands the exclusive Protectorate of Turkey. Mankind will not forget that Russia was the *protector* of Poland, the *protector* of the Crimea, the *protector* of Courland, Georgia, Mingrelia, the Circassian and Caucasian tribes. And now Russia, the protector of Turkey!"

On this score there was trouble again between Marx and Greeley. Greeley, a perennial twister of the British lion's tail, was inclined to take sides with Russia's aspirations. Marx was violently against *all* imperial ambitions in Europe. "The devil take the *Tribune!*" he exploded to comrade Engels. "It has simply got to come out against Pan-slavism. If not, we may have to break with the little sheet." But he added quickly, "Yet that would be fatal."

When Marx turned around again and let fly at the British government and social system, he spoke a language more pleasing to Greeley and his American constituents. The foreign secretary, Lord Palmerston, was "that brilliant boggler and loquacious humbug." Lord John Russell was "that diminutive earth-man." Gladstone was "a phrase-mongering charlatan." And as for Queen Victoria's consort, Prince Albert, "He has devoted his time partly to fattening pigs, to inventing ridiculous hats for the army, to planning model lodging-houses of a peculiarly transparent and uncomfortable kind, to the Hyde Park exhibition, and to amateur soldiery. He has been considered amiable and harmless, in point of intellect below the general average of human beings, a prolific father, and an obsequious husband." By the time he wrote this, Karl Marx had clearly mastered English on his own and needed little further help from Engels.

But from under this coruscating surface there always emerged before the end of the article the same Marxian refrain. It was that of the inevitable approach of new and sweeping revolution. Marx saw it coming everywhere. One of his most scathing pieces, written with the atmosphere of a columnist's exclusive, was a detailed forecast of the cynical maneuvers which he said the five Great Powers were about to stage over the Middle East. "But," he wound up, "we must not forget that there is a sixth power in Europe, which at any given moment asserts its supremacy over the whole of the five so-called Great Powers, and makes them tremble, every one of them. That power is the Revolution. Long silent and retired, it is now again called to action. . . . From Manchester to Rome, from Paris to Warsaw to Perth, it is omnipresent, lifting up its head. . . ."

And so on. Eventually the *Tribune* began to weary of Marx's obiter dicta. For the next revolution in Europe showed no signs of coming. Instead of making for Marx's barricades, the masses seemed intent simply on pursuing their own business. In 1855 editor Greeley traveled to Europe, a somewhat incongruous figure in his Yankee whiskers and duster. But he refrained from calling upon his chief correspondent and revolutionary expert in London, Karl Marx. So the two men, moving like tall ships on contrary courses in the narrow seas of Europe, never met.

Perhaps Marx had laid on too thickly. Perhaps, while marshaling his massive batteries of facts and handing down his imperious conclusions, he had presumed too much on the hospitality of his readership. Or perhaps America, open-minded yet realistic and absorbed in the practicalities of its own fast-changing existence, had outgrown him. In any case he was not talking about unleashing the "divine life" in man, as the idealists around Greeley had done not so many years before. (Once a *Tribune* editor appended to a homily of Marx's that was run as an editorial a wind-up sentence beginning, "God grant that——" which at once aroused Marx's ire. He wasn't asking God to grant anything.) Marx was calling for revolutionary wars and barricades. A war did come—but not the one Marx had projected. It was our own.

In 1857, a year when American minds were intent on our imminent crisis over the extension of slavery, Dana wrote Marx circumspectly on Greeley's behalf to say that because of the current economic depression the *Tribune* found itself forced to reduce drastically all its foreign correspondence. "Diese Yankees sind doch verdammt lausige Kerle" (damned lousy bums), Marx burst out to Engels in his original German, charging that they now wanted to toss him aside like a squeezed lemon. But Dana, knowing Marx's financial situation, came through with an offer of outside help. He himself was editing on the side a compilation to be

called the *New American Cyclopaedia*. Wouldn't Marx like to do a number of short sketches on historic personalities for it, at two dollars per printed page? Marx had no alternative but to accept. So the twin revolutionists sat down, grumbling as ever, to deliver hackwork biographies beginning under letter *B* with Barclay, Bernadotte, Berthier, Blücher, Bourrienne . . .

A trickle of further letters from Marx and Engels to the *Tribune* did continue, and Greeley and Dana used them when they found inclination or space. But the spacious enthusiasm of the days that had prompted the first of them had died away. It had been smothered partly by the rush of American events and partly by the realization that Marx, for all his efforts to stake a claim in the *Tribune,* did not, after all, speak our language. Dana, ever the diplomat, and appreciative of what Marx (alias Engels) had contributed over the years, notified him when the war between North and South broke out that while all other foreign correspondence had been suspended because of the emergency, he himself could continue contributing—although on a still more reduced basis. Marx, increasingly dubious of his American outlet, wrote for a while longer, only to learn that Dana himself, after what was reported to have been a falling-out with Greeley, had left the staff of the *Tribune* to become assistant secretary of war. Not long afterward, Marx's own arrangement was canceled, too.

Now the frustrated team in London, who had so often reviled Dana as their immediate taskmaster, came around to the view that he, no less than they themselves, had been just the exploited wage slave of Greeley. "It's that old ass himself who is really responsible for everything," said Engels, as the curtain of their life with the *Tribune* rang down.

Marx was never again a correspondent for another newspaper. He had by now finished a great part of *Das Kapital,* for one thing, and henceforth went on to lead in organizing the Communist First International. Greeley, for his part, never once mentioned in his own memoirs the name of the most famous and controversial man who had ever worked for him.

Today all that remains of their episode together is a bundle of faded letters, a rash of multilingual expletives, and a file of published articles of whose authorship one can only rarely be quite sure. For Marx the collaboration was something less than a total success, for he never made Marxists of the subscribers to the New York *Tribune.* Did Greeley's *Tribune,* in turn, with its hospitality and willingness to give free run to new ideas, have any effect upon Marx?

Perhaps it was too much to expect that any outside influence (particularly when money was involved) would have any effect on that somber man, pursued by his own demon of the absolute. Still, although Marx and Greeley found they had little in common save sheer journalistic energy and a gift for rhetoric, there were occasions when what either one of them said could well be put into the mouth of the other. Such an instance occurred on the last day of 1853, when many of the readers of the *Tribune* were as absorbed with the issues of East and West, of freedom and organization, as their descendants are today:

"Western Europe is feeble . . . because her governments feel they are outgrown and no longer believed by their people. The nations are beyond their rulers. . . . But there is new wine working in the old bottles. With a worthier and more equal social state, with the abolition of caste and privilege, with free political constitutions, unfettered industry, and emancipated thought, the people of the West will rise again to power and unity of purpose, while the Russian Colossus itself will be shattered by the progress of the masses and the explosive force of ideas."

That passage was written by Karl Marx, not by Horace Greeley. You will not find it, though, in the official collected works of the father of Soviet communism.

SAMUEL SMILES: *The Gospel of Self-Help*

Asa Briggs

Asa Briggs is Provost of Worcester College, Oxford, and author of *The BBC, The First Fifty Years* (Oxford University Press, 1985).

Victorian Britain's prophet of honest toil was far from being the crudely complacent reactionary, as he has sometimes been caricatured.

SELF-HELP WAS ONE OF THE favourite mid-Victorian virtues. Relying on yourself was preferred morally – and economically – to depending on others. It was an expression of character even when it did not ensure – even, indeed, when it did not offer – a means of success. It also had social implications of a general kind. The progressive development of society ultimately depended, it was argued, not on collective action or on parliamentary legislation but on the prevalence of practices of self-help.

All these points .were made suc-

cinctly and eloquently, but none of them originally or exclusively, by Samuel Smiles whose *Self-Help* appeared in one of the golden years of mid-Victorian Britain, 1859, the year that also saw the publication of John Stuart Mill's *Essay on Liberty* and Charles Darwin's *The Origin of Species*. Mill examined the attractions of individuality as well as the restraints on individualism: Darwin explored struggle as well as evolution, or rather explained evolution in terms of struggle. Neither thinker escaped attack. Smiles by contrast was not looking for argument and counter-argument. He believed that he was expounding not something that was new or controversial but something that was old and profoundly true, a gospel, not a thesis; and that behind that gospel was a still more basic gospel, the gospel of work.

Smiles did not claim that all his contemporaries practised self-help. He rather extolled the virtues of self-help as part of an 'old fashioned' but 'wholesome' lesson in morality. It was more 'natural', he admitted, to be 'prodigal' than to be thrifty, more easy to be dependent than independent. What he was saying had been said by the wisest of men before him: it reflected 'experience, example and

foresight'. 'Heaven helps them who help themselves.'

As far as individuals were concerned, Smiles was anxious to insist on the value of perseverance, a favourite word of one of his heroes, George Stephenson. 'Nothing that is of real worth,' he insisted, 'can be achieved without courageous working. Man owes his growth chiefly to that active striving of the will, that encounter with difficulty, which he calls effort; and it is astonishing to find how often results apparently impracticable are then made possible.' As far as society was concerned, 'national progress was the sum of individual industry, energy and uprightness' as 'national decay' was of 'individual idleness, selfishness and vice. What we are accustomed to decry as great social evils will, for the most part, be found to be but the outgrowth of man's perverted life.' 'The spirit of self-help is the root of all genuine growth in the individual; and exhibited in the lives of many, it constitutes the true source of national vigour and strength. Help from without is often enfeebling in its effects, but help from within invariably invigorates. Whatever is done for men and classes to a certain extent takes away the stimulus and necessity of

First published in *History Today*, May 1987, pp. 37-43. Reproduced by kind permission of History Today, Ltd., 83-84 Berwick Street, London W1V 3PJ England.

doing for themselves; and where men are subjected to over-guidance and over-government, the inevitable tendency is to render them comparatively helpless.'

Smiles adopted the phrase *Self-Help*, which proved to be very difficult to translate into other languages, from a lecture by the American reformer and prophet, R.W. Emerson, delivered in 1841; and while Smiles' own book first appeared in 1859, its contents had first been delivered by Smiles in lectures to Leeds working men fourteen years before – one year, indeed, before the passing of the repeal of the corn laws. While the book belonged unmistakably to mid-Victorian Britain, the message, therefore, was an early-Victorian transatlantic message, delivered in years not of relative social harmony in Britain but of social conflict. The point is

of crucial importance in any discussion of Victorian values in the 1980s. Smiles emerged not from a conservative but from a radical background, the background of Chartism, and the Anti-Corn Law League. He was not encouraging Leeds working men to be quiescent or deferential but to be active and informed. Richard Cobden was one of his heroes. Another was the radical Joseph Hume, and both figured prominently in *Self-Help*. Smiles knew them both personally, and in a letter to Cobden in 1841 he had described the extension of the suffrage as 'the key to all great changes, whose object is to elevate the condition of the masses.'

Upward mobility — this 1861 cartoon shows a 'Lancashire working-man living rent free in his own home', the fruits of diligence and temperance.

Smiles' direct political involvement was limited, however, after the 1840s and he settled down during the next decade to the more complacent view, which he expressed in 1852, that 'as men grow older and wiser they find a little of good in everything ... they begin to find out that truth and patriotism are not confined to any particular cliques or parties or factions.' Indeed, he moved well to the right of Cobden, and by the late-Victorian years, when new political causes, radical or socialist of which he disapproved were being canvassed, what he had had to say had come to sound 'conservative', as it has done to late-twentieth-century defenders of 'Victorian values'.

Yet there is a difference in the response. Whereas late-Victorian rebels attacked Smiles for his cheerful economics, claiming – unfairly – that

he was interested only in individual advancement reflected in material success, late-twentieth-century defenders have praised him primarily for his hard economic realism. In particular, Sir Keith Joseph, himself writing from a Leeds vantage point, in the introduction to a new and abridged edition of *Self-Help* (1986), has set out to rehabilitate Smilesian trust in the *entrepreneur* and 'the virtues that make him what he is'. While describing *Self-Help* as 'deeply expressive of the spirit of its own times', he does not note that these were changing times and that modes of economic organisation and responses to 'entrepreneurship' were very different by 1904, the year when Smiles died, from what they had been when *Self-Help* was published.

Smiles was born not in Leeds but in Haddington, a few miles east of Edinburgh, seven years before the birth of Queen Victoria, and he took a medical degree from Edinburgh University. His first book was called *Physical Education: or the Nurture and Management of Children*, and was published in 1838, the year he moved to Leeds. There is an evident Scottish strain in his writing before and after, although curiously it is less apparent in *Physical Education* than in some of his other work. It was, after all, Robert Bruce who had had attributed to him the motto 'if at first you don't succeed, try, try, try again', and Calvin who had provided Scotsmen with a religion which made the most of austerity and vocation.

In more modern times Thomas Carlyle, born seventeen years before Smiles, had described life as 'a scene of toil, of effort, of appointed work', and had extolled 'the man who works' in the warmest language: 'welcome, thou art ours; our care shall be of thee'. The mill-owner economist, W.R. Greg, writing one year after the publication of *Self-Help*, praised Carlyle above all others for 'preaching upon the duty and dignity of work, with an eloquence which has often made the idle shake off their idleness and the frivolous feel ashamed of their frivolity. He has proclaimed, in tones that have stirred many hearts, that in toil, however humble, if honest and hearty, lies our true worth and felicity here below'.

Smiles himself took as one of his examples of perseverance in *Self-Help* Carlyle's prodigious effort to rewrite the first volume of his *French Revolution* after a maid had used the manuscript to light the kitchen and parlour fires: 'he had no draft, and was compelled to rake up from his memory facts, ideas and expressions, which had long been dismissed'. No one could have appreciated this experience more than Smiles who was a prodigious writer who followed up *Self-Help* with many volumes, including three related works *Character* (1871), *Thrift* (1875) and *Duty* (1880). He also produced a history of his publisher, John Murray and 'his friends' in 1891.

Self-Help was full of anecdotes. Essentially it was a case-book drawing its material, including some of its most apposite quotations, from personal biographies. 'Our great forefathers still live among us in the records of our lives', he claimed, again very much as Carlyle had always claimed. 'They still sit by us at table, and hold us by the hand'. There was more than a touch of Victorian hero worship here. Yet Smiles always broadened the range to include the humble as well as the great, extending the range as far as he possibly could in his *Life and Labour* (1887). Biographies offered demonstrations of 'what men can be, and what they can do' whatever their station. 'A book containing the life of a true man is full of precious seed. It is still a living voice'. And much as he made his own living out of books, Smiles maintained that living examples were far more potent as influences than examples on paper. His book *Thrift* took as its motto a phrase from Carlyle 'Not what I have, but what I do is my kingdom'. He might have chosen instead Emerson's motto, 'The importance of man as man ... is the highest truth'.

Smiles himself was a lively phrase-maker, interlacing his anecdotes, which by themselves were memorable and well set out, with short phrases that linger in the mind – 'he who never made a mistake never made a discovery'; 'the tortoise in the right road will beat a racer in the wrong'; 'the nation comes from the nursery'. Such phrases bind together the whole text of *Self-Help* which is far more readable – as it is pertinent – today than the verse of Martin

Tupper's *Proverbial Philosophy* (1838), the popularity of which (on both sides of the Atlantic) reached its peak during the 1850s. It is far more readable too than most of the many other Victorian books designed to inspire young men like the anonymous *Success in Life* (1852), the original idea of which had been suggested by 'an American publication', perhaps John Todd's *Hints Addressed to the Young Men of the United States* (1845), which included one chapter on 'industry and economy' and another on 'self-government and the heart'. Smiles himself acknowledged a debt to G.L. Craik's *Pursuit of Knowledge under Difficulties* (1831), published by Charles Knight who specialised in diffusing knowledge. Indeed, he had been so inspired by it, Smiles wrote, that he learnt some of its key passages by heart.

The transatlantic element in the self-help literature demands a study of differences as well as of influences. There were to be many American 'success' books aiming, as Smiles aimed, at large audiences, some of the first of which were influenced, as Smiles was, by the cult of phrenology. The later line of descent can be traced through books, which move from phrenology to popular psychology, like J.C. Ransom's *The Successful Man in his Manifold Relations with Life* (1887), A.E. Lyons' *The Self-Starter* (1924), Dale Carnegie's *How to Win Friends and Influence People* (1936), C.E. Poppleston's *Every Man a Winner* (1936) and Norman Vincent Peale's *The Power of Positive Thinking* (1955). Yet many of these authors are slick where Smiles was sturdy, and consoling where he was inspiring. Few would have had much sympathy either with Smiles' attack on 'smatter knowledge'. Such 'short-cuts', he explained, as learning French or Latin in 'twelve lessons' or 'without a master', were 'good for nothing'. The would-be learner was more to blame than the teacher, for he resembled 'the lady of fashion who engaged a master to teach her on condition that he did not plague her with verbs and particles'.

One American with whom Smiles has sometimes been compared is Horatio Alger (1832-99) after whom a twentieth-century American business award was named. In his own lifetime Alger's sales were spectacular, though his books took the form of stories rather than biographies or homilies. *Ragged Dick* was one title, *Upward and Onward* another. The *genre* has been well described as 'rags to riches stories', although the twentieth-century award was endowed more generally to honour a person who had 'climbed the ladder of success through toil and diligence and responsible applications of his talents to whatever tasks were his'.

There are as many myths about 'Holy Horatio' as Alger himself propounded. In fact, he allowed a far bigger place to luck (sponsors appearing by magic at the right time and place) than Smiles ever could have done, and he grossly simplified the nineteenth-century social context, particularly the city context, in which poor people found or failed to find their chances. As the late-nineteenth-century American institutional economist, Richard T. Ely, put it neatly, 'if you tell a single concrete workman on the Baltimore and Ohio Railroad that he may get to be president of the company, it is not demonstrable that you have told him what is not true, although it is within bounds to say that he is far more likely to be killed by a stroke of lightning.'

Smiles was less concerned with social 'mobility' than with mental and physical 'effort', but he, too, could be accused of living in a land of myth when he exclaimed that 'energy accomplishes more than genius'. It was a favourite mid-Victorian statement, however, which implied a contrast between what was happening then and what had happened before, and between what was happening in Britain and what was happening elsewhere. By stating it so simply Smiles actually did influence *entrepreneurs*, few of whom depended on great intellects or on deep and systematic study. William Lever, for example, fittingly born in 1851, was given a copy of *Self-Help* by his father on his sixteenth birthday, and treasured it so much that he in turn gave copies to young men he employed in his works at Port Sunlight. On the front page of one such copy the words are inscribed, 'It is impossible for me to say how much I owe to the fact that in my early youth I obtained a copy of Smiles' *Self-Help*.'

Andrew Carnegie (1835-1919)

would have made no such comment. Yet his own biography not only proclaimed many Smilesian virtues, but might well have provided the basis for an Alger true story. Carnegie was born in a tiny weaver's cottage at Dunfermline, and he had his first real break in life when he became a messenger boy in a Pittsburgh telegraph office at a salary of $2.50 a week. In 1901, when he had sold his steel business for $480 million, he became the richest man in the world. 'It's a God's mercy I was born a Scotsman,' he declared in a remark that might have appealed to Smiles, 'for I do not see how I could ever have been contented to be anything else.'

The testimonials Smiles himself received from readers of his books often came from people very differently placed from Lever or Carnegie. Thus, a working man in Exeter told him that his books had 'instructed and helped him greatly' and that he wished 'every working man would read them through and through and ponder them well'; a surgeon in Blackheath declared that *Self-Help* had given 'fresh energy and hopefulness to his career'; and an emigrant to New Zealand exclaimed that self-help had

'been the cause of an entire alteration in my life, and I thank God that I read it. I am now devoted to study and hard work, and I mean to rise, both as regards my moral and intellectual life. I only wish I could see the man who wrote the book and thank him from my heart'.

There was at least one late-Victorian socialist, a man who was himself capable of inspiring 'the millions', who was deeply impressed by Smiles. Robert Blatchford, pioneer of *Merrie England*, wrote an essay on *Self-Help* after Smiles' popularity had passed its peak in which he condemned fellow-socialists who spoke mockingly of Smiles as 'an arch-Philistine' and of his books as 'the apotheosis of respectability, gigmanity and selfish grab'. Blatchford himself considered Smiles 'a most charming and honest writer', and thought *Self-Help* 'one of the most delightful and invigorating books it has been my happy fortune to meet with.' He paid tribute to Smiles' indifference to worldly titles, honour and wealth, and declared that the perusal of *Self-Help* had often forced him 'to industry, for very shame'.

The prolific rationalist writer Grant Allen, a leading spokesman of the

A 'Punch' cartoon of 1858 attacking the adulteration of food — one of the areas where Smiles decidedly did not believe in the principle of *laissez-faire*.

late-Victorian revolt, took a very similar view. In a little book published in 1884 called *Biographies of Working Men* he asserted his debt to Smiles and made explicit what many of Smiles' critics then and since failed to see in Smiles' work. 'It is the object of this volume', Grant Allen began, 'to set forth the lives of working men, who through industry, perseverance and high principle, have raised themselves by their own exertions from humble beginnings. Raised themselves! Yes, but to what? Not merely, let us hope, to wealth and position, nor merely to worldly respect and high office, but to some conspicuous field of real usefulness to their fellow men.' Smiles made the same point in *Self-Help*. He would not have shared Allen's view, however, which brings out clearly the difference between the mood of the 1850s and the 1880s, that 'so long as our present social arrangements exist . . . the vast mass of men will necessarily remain workers to the last, [and] no attempt to raise individual working men above their own class into the professional or mercantile classes can ever greatly benefit the working classes as a whole'.

Nonetheless, on certain social matters, Smiles had often expressed radical views. Like many people trained as doctors he was deeply concerned with public health. As Mary Mack has pointed out, Jeremy Bentham had used medicine as a source of *analogy* for the understanding of morals and legislation, and Smiles, who as a young man met Edwin Chadwick and Dr Southwood Smith, Bentham's disciples, never believed that the environment should be left uncontrolled if it threatened the private health not only of the deprived but of people and power and influence. Smiles supported measures, too, to deal with the adulteration of food. Drawing a distinction between economic and social *laissez-faire* – and he was not alone in this – he was fully aware of the presence in mid-Victorian society not only of Adam Smith's beneficent invisible hand but of a 'terrible Nobody'. Indeed, Charles Dickens could not have written more forcefully than Smiles did:

When typhus or cholera breaks out, they tell us that Nobody is to blame. That terrible Nobody! How much he has

to answer for. More mischief is done by Nobody than by all the world besides. Nobody adulterates our food. Nobody poisons us with bad drink . . . Nobody leaves towns undrained. Nobody fills jails, penitentiaries, and convict stations. Nobody makes poachers, thieves, and drunkards. Nobody has a theory too – a dreadful theory. It is embodied in two words: laissez-faire – let alone. When people are poisoned with plaster of Paris mixed with flour, 'let alone' is the remedy . . . Let those who can, find out when they are cheated: *caveat emptor*. When people live in foul dwellings, let them alone, let wretchedness do its work; do not interfere with death.

Like many other believers in economic *laissez-faire* Smiles was prepared to use the machinery of the law to provide a framework for dealing with abuses:

Laws may do too much . . . but the abuse of a thing is no proper argument against its use in cases where its employment is urgently called for.

Throughout the whole of his life Smiles was far too active a Victorian to believe that *vis inertiae* was the same thing as *laissez-faire*. Nor was he ever tempted, as many Americans were, into the entanglements of social Darwinism. There is no reference to Herbert Spencer in his *Autobiography*, which appeared in 1905, one year after his death, and only one reference to Darwin. One of the lecturers he had heard at Edinburgh, he observed *en passant*, had already expounded very similar views 'or at all events had heralded his approach'.

There was another subject which fascinated Smiles and which he believed required very positive state intervention – national education. He had forcefully urged the need for a national system in Leeds in 1850, and he paid tribute in his *Autobiography* to W.E. Forster, MP for neighbouring Bradford, who 'by a rare union of tact, wisdom and commonsense, introduced and carried his measure [the 1870 Education Act] for the long-wished education of the English people. It embodied nearly all that the National Public School Association had so fruitlessly demanded years before.'

In pressing for nationally provided primary education in Leeds in 1850 and later, Smiles had been drawn into controversy with Edward Baines, editor of the *Leeds Mercury* and one of

the most vociferous advocates, then and in 1870, of education managed by voluntary agencies and not by the state. In the course of a continuing controversy Smiles had no doubts about his own position. There were no analogies between education and free trade in commodities, he pointed out:

The classes who the most require education are precisely those who do not seek it. It is amongst the utterly uneducated that the least demand exists. In the case of bread it is very different. The consumer wants it, knows he wants it, and will give every present consideration for it.

A further false analogy, he thought, was that between education and the freedom of the press:

Nobody proposes to establish newspapers for everybody, supported by the government, and the want of such a Press is not felt. But let it be shown that it is of as much importance to the interests of society that everybody should have a newspaper as that everybody should be educated, and then the analogy may be admitted . . . but not till then.

It was through his philosophy of education that Smiles blurred any divisions that others might have made between 'self-help' for the individual and 'mutual self-help' for the group. He always attached even more importance to adult – or continuing – education than to school education, necessary though the latter was. The process which started at school had to be followed through: 'the highest culture is not obtained from teacher when at school or college, so much as by our ever diligent self-education when we have become men.' Such education could be fostered in groups like the group of young working men he had addressed in Leeds. There were possibilities of other forms of 'mutual self-help' also, for example friendly societies. Indeed, in *Thrift* Smiles made as much as he could of the mutual insurance principle. He could never have been accused of neglecting 'welfare', provided that it did not lead to dependence.

The Smiles message was not merely a transatlantic one. It made its way round the world, sometimes to the most unlikely places. It was translated into Dutch and French, Danish and German, Arabic and Turkish, 'several of the native languages of India' (in the words of a happy publisher) and

The doctrine of 'honest toil' could have a radical cutting-edge, as in this 1858 'Punch' cartoon of the working man 'enlightening' the 'superior' (but idle) classes.

Japanese. Victorian values, it was implied, were universal values, and there was confidence in their power to change societies. The Japanese, in particular, treasured it, and many of them continue to treasure it. 'The English work forms an octavo of moderate size,' *The Times* wrote; 'in Japanese it is expanded into a book of fifteen hundred pages.' This was no handicap to its sale, for it seemed as useful as looms and steam engines. In Latin America the Mayor of Buenos Aires is said to have compared Smiles with Rousseau and to have added 'Alexander the Great slept with his Homer, Demosthenes and Thucydides, and every notable man of the times should have at hand the social gospel'.

The universalism was restricted, however, although it went with the universalism of steam power and railways, in particular. Smiles had become secretary of a a railway company in 1845 and he wrote *The Life of George Stephenson* two years before *Self-Help*. Nonetheless, he ended *Self-Help* with a chapter which introduced a word which was at least as difficult to translate from English into other languages as 'self-help' itself – the word 'gentleman'. Hippolyte Taine, convinced that the three syllables 'gentleman' summed up the whole history of English society, felt that the syllables expressed all the distinctive features of the English upper-class – a large private income, a considerable household of servants, habits of ease and luxury and good manners, but it also implied qualities of heart and character. Smiles, however, felt that:

> For Englishmen a real 'gentleman' is a truly noble man, a man worthy to command, a disinterested man of integrity, capable of exposing, even sacrificing himself for those he leads; not only a man of honour, but a conscientious man, in whom generous instincts have been confirmed by right thinking and who, acting righly by nature, acts even more rightly from good principles.

Taine's reference to Mrs Craik's novel *John Halifax, Gentleman* (1856) is a practical illustration of the extension of the old ideal of the gentleman in a new nineteenth-century society. He might have referred instead to the last pages of *Self-Help*, where Smiles chose a 'grand old name' to express the kind of character he most wanted to see in action. Smiles drew out the 'grand old name' of the gentleman from its upper-class context. It had no connection with riches and rank, he argued, but with moral worth.

The equipoise of society rested on such ideological balances as well as on the balance of interests. From the 1870s onwards, however, both kinds of balance broke down. Britain was never again the same.

FOR FURTHER READING:

Samuel Smiles, *Self-Help* (first edition 1853, Penguin Books with an introduction by Keith Joseph, 1986); Asa Briggs, *Victorian People* (Penguin Books, 1985); Grant Allen, *Biographies of Working men* (1884); J. Burnett, editor, *Useful Toil: Autobiographies of Working people from the 1820s-1920s* (Penguin Books, 1974); T. Travers, *Samuel Smiles and the Pursuit of Success in Victorian Britain* (Canadian Historical Association, 1971); M.D. Stephens and G.W. Roderick, *Samuel Smiles and Nineteenth-Century Self-Help in Education* (Nottingham Studies, 1983).

JOHN STUART MILL AND LIBERTY

The leading philosopher of mid-Victorian England, John Stuart Mill (1806–73), claimed an "ability and willingness to learn from everybody." This was not necessarily a celebrated man's ritual, if becoming, modesty. In Mill's mind, the ideas of earlier thinkers—e.g., John Locke, David Hume, Jeremy Bentham, his own father James Mill—were transformed over the years into classical liberalism, the idea that society is best served by maximum personal freedoms and minimal government. Recent scholarship, as Maurice Cranston relates, has provided new insight into the life of the philosopher who may have learned "from everybody," but was driven to heed some more than others.

Maurice Cranston

Maurice Cranston, 67, a former Wilson Center Guest Scholar, is professor of political science at the London School of Economics. Born in London, he was educated at St. Catherine's College and Oxford University. His books include John Stuart Mill *(1965),* Jean-Jacques, The Early Life and Work of Jean-Jacques Rousseau, 1712–54 *(1982), and* John Locke: A Biography *(1985).*

John Stuart Mill has held the attention of the reading public of the Western world longer than any other 19th-century philosopher, with the notable exception of Karl Marx.

Each man is known as theorist of one central idea. Marx is read by his admirers as a champion of equality. Mill is read for his words on liberty, words that have contributed much to the debates of our own time about the freedom of dissenters, minorities, and women. He was always controversial. William Gladstone, the great Liberal Party leader, disapproved of Mill's ideas, and refused to attend his funeral. Yet he called him "the Saint of Rationalism."

John Stuart Mill was born in his father's comfortable London home in 1806, a time when the Industrial Revolution was already beginning to transform England into a prospering urban nation with a rising middle class, whose leaders' concerns included how to govern and "improve" such a rapidly changing society. James Mill, a strict disciplinarian who had risen from humble origins to become a senior civil servant with the East India Company, was by then a noted historian, economist, and philosopher. He was an advocate of Jeremy Bentham's utilitarianism, which held that all issues of right and wrong could be settled by measuring the amount of pleasure or pain that might be caused by any private action or public policy.

James Mill did not send his eldest child to any school; he taught him at home following a strenuous plan of education devised by himself and Bentham to produce the perfect utilitarian. John learned both Greek and Latin before he was nine years old. Religion was excluded from his upbringing.

Mill's education was completed early—and early, too, appeared his oddly coexisting streaks of conformism and rigorous independence. At age 17, he was earning his living as a clerk in the India Office where his father worked. During that year he published his first article—in *The Westminster Review*, the leading English literary journal—and also made his debut as a radical reformer, spending two nights in jail for distributing pamphlets recommending contraceptive techniques as a solution to the problem of poverty in Britain.

At age 20—as he recalled in his *Autobiography*, published after his death in 1873—Mill suffered a depression, from which he recovered by reading poetry. Through Wordsworth and others he discovered romanticism, which challenged the rationalistic philosophy that had been so carefully inculcated in him. "I did not lose . . . sight," he wrote, of "that part of the truth which I had seen before." But "I thought that it had consequences which required to be corrected, by joining other kinds of cultivation with it."

Mill aimed at working out a new system of philosophy combining the virtues of rationalism with those of romanticism. But how to reconcile two schools of seemingly opposed thought? The rational solution, Mill decided, could only be to revise logic itself. Mill's chief contribution to this endeavor was his *System of Logic* (1843), which he began at age 24. That it took him 13 years to finish the work was closely related to Mill's less than rational personal life.

Mill was afflicted by a deep sense of loneliness. Once, at the age of 23, he wrote to a friend of his longing for a "perfect friendship." Soon after he started on his *Logic* essay, Mill met a handsome, intelligent, and imperious young woman named Harriet Taylor. He fell in love with her, and she with him. But Harriet happened to be married—to John Taylor, a prosperous wholesale druggist with a house in London and a country place. She was also the mother of two small children (soon to be joined by a third).

○

Even so, during the 19 years before the druggist's death in 1849 enabled them to marry, she and Mill kept constant company.

Alternately reckless and furtive, they behaved as if they were lovers, something they always denied. And yet it was a strangely guilt-ridden relationship. Harriet set up house on her own in rural Blackheath and traveled on the Continent with Mill. They remained, in Harriet's word, *Seelenfreunden* ("soul mates"), because, Mill said, they did not wish to hurt her husband. Mill seems not to have guessed that Mr. Taylor might be as much wounded by the appearance of adultery as by its reality. Nevertheless, Mill, in nervous anger, broke with both his friends and his relatives to lead a rather solitary life with Harriet at Blackheath.

Her hold over his thinking was considerable. If her situation with Mill was a "romantic" one, a triumph of love over convention, her views were not Wordsworthian at all. They were closer to those of the Enlightenment—rationalistic, utilitarian, and radical. Hence, paradoxically, she reinforced on Mill the influence of his father, and not that of the poets.

One example of her influence on Mill is his *Principles of Political Economy*, a long and not conspicuously original book, which debuted in 1848 when Mill was 42. It was originally dedicated to "Mrs. John Taylor," from whom, Mill wrote, he first grasped many of the book's ideas. After John Taylor's death, and their marriage nearly two years later in 1851, Mill took to describing each of his works as a "joint-production" with Harriet. He even spoke of his wife as "the inspirer, and in part the author, of all that is best in my writings." Mill's contemporaries took these tributes as polite hyperbole, but recent scholarship on his manuscripts confirms her larger role.

For instance, in the first edition of *Political Economy*, Mill accepted David Ricardo's theory of value, which focuses on the amount of labor invested in the manufacture of a product. Mill also accepted the Malthusian doctrine that any improvement in the condition of the poor will be negated by the growth of population (although Mill's remedy for overpopulation is not Thomas Malthus's "moral restraint," but contraceptive devices). And Mill endorsed Adam Smith's teaching against the state's intervention in the nation's economic life, arguing that England was already sufficiently burdened with taxes. Economic well-being, he said, required the spur of competition.

When, within a year, a second edition appeared, an essential part of the thesis was reversed. Harriet, who had been won over to the Left by the antimonarchical revolts that shook France and other Continental countries in 1848, pressed Mill to delete criticisms of socialism and communism. Thus, Mill first dismissed proposals for communal property ownership as "almost too chimerical to be reasoned with." In the new edition, these ideas became "the most valuable elements of human improvement now existing."

○

Harriet's influence is most significant in Mill's best-known work, *On Liberty*, published in 1859, not long after her death. It is not simply a defense of freedom in the liberal tradition of John Milton and John Locke; it outlines a conception that differs with their ideas, and, strikingly, with Mill's other writings.

For example, Mill described *On Liberty* as a "kind of philosophic textbook of a single truth." This truth was that "the sole end for which mankind are warranted, individually or collectively, in interfering with the liberty of action of any of their number, is self-protection." Elsewhere, Mill attacked the notion of building on a "single truth" in politics; he had criticized the French philosopher Auguste Comte for seeing only one point of view "when there are many others equally essential."

In a later work, *Utilitarianism* (1863), his best-known work on ethics, Mill saw liberty as a part of man's "social state," at once "so natural, so necessary, and so habitual to man, that [except at rare times] he never conceives himself otherwise than as a member of a body." In *On Liberty*, society is the enemy.

The essay is very much a plea for something that both Mill and Harriet felt strongly about: the freedom of the isolated person standing outside of and apart from the social body. Whereas earlier liberal

philosophers, such as John Locke, had depicted freedom as something to be secured against the constraints of governments or the state, Mill represents freedom as something to be secured primarily against the constraints of other people. Mill does not say much about political rulers; he dwells on the domination of the individual by unwritten laws, conventional ideas, social rules, and public opinion. "When society is itself the tyrant"—over the individuals it comprises—its tyranny is worse than "many kinds of political oppression." A need exists for protection against society's tendency to impose, "by other means than civil penalties, its own ideas and practices as rules of conduct on those who dissent from them."

○

We need to remember that Mill wrote *On Liberty* at a time and place when the constraints of the state were few and those of society were many, and, often, onerous. Victorian England was not the land of the despotic Stuart kings, where the liberty Locke pleaded for was mainly a right endangered by political interference. Mill's Victorian contemporaries were seldom oppressed by government, which was minimal (the 1851 census counted fewer than 75,000 public employees, compared with 932,000 in France in 1846). But nearly all individuals were constantly pressured by neighbors, employers, husbands, and fathers, who were dominated in turn by taboos and conventions governing a host of matters—courtship, dress, recreation, use of the Sabbath, and much else.

If Mill felt these constraints keenly, and Harriet even more so, he took care in presenting his case, so it should not seem to be the romantic protest of an alienated individual against a bourgeois environment. He argued as coldly and logically as possible.

There are, he suggested, three possibilities to consider when deciding if men should have freedom of opinion and expression. First, the opinion in question may be true, in which case it is plainly right that it should be published. Second, the opinion may be false; it would still be good for it to be published, because truth gains vigor from being challenged and vindicated. (A true belief that is never challenged becomes a dead maxim, which everyone repeats and nobody thinks about.) Third, the opinion may be partly true and partly false. Again Mill argued for expression, on the ground that the exercise of disentangling the false from the true would help to correct errors.

Since these exhaust the possibilities, Mill concluded, it must always be right to grant liberty of opinion and expression.

"If all mankind minus one were of one opinion, and only one person were of the contrary opinion," Mill wrote, "mankind would be no more justified in silencing that one person, than he, if he had the power, would be justified in silencing mankind." The "peculiar evil" of silencing one opinion is that it robs "the human race; posterity as well as the existing generation; those who dissent from the opinion still more than those who hold it."

Discussing freedom of action, Mill staked out even more dangerous ground, again under Harriet's sway. Mill rejected the Christian teaching that men are born in sin and that the self must be denied. He asserted his belief in the goodness—and the *potential* goodness—of man. While he conceded that there was sometimes a need for self-denial in putting public happiness before private happiness, Mill emphasized the value of self-expression. Far from accepting the doctrine of the depravity of man, he suggested that it is chiefly through the cultivation of their individuality that "human beings"—and it is to be noted that he uses that term rather than "men"—become "noble and beautiful object[s] of contemplation."

He pleaded for personality, variety, even eccentricity. "In this age the mere example of non-conformity, the mere refusal to bend the knee to custom, is itself a service." Eccentricity rises where "strength of character" abounds. "The amount of eccentricity in a society has generally been proportional to the amount of genius, mental vigour and moral courage which it contains."

○

Yet Mill was not advocating unbridled self-expression, or unlimited freedom. Indeed, he said at the beginning of *On Liberty* that his task was to set out exactly what the limits of freedom were. His conclusion: One man's right to liberty of action stops at the point where it might injure or curb the freedom of another man. "The only purpose for which power can be rightfully exercised over any member of a civilized community, against his will, is to prevent harm to others." Otherwise every adult should be allowed to do as he likes.

But supposing, the critic might ask, that what a man likes to do is wrong? Surely he should not then be allowed to do it? Surely the important thing is not that men should do what they want to do but what they *ought* to do? And might it not be the duty of society to help men do what they ought to do?

Mill did not shirk these questions. Take alcoholism, for instance. Britain's 19th-century prohibitionists viewed drunkenness as a social evil, which could be remedied by enforced abstinence. Mill denied that prohibition would uphold morality. If there was no temptation to overcome, he pleaded, there would be no virtue in overcoming temptation. Morality lies in choosing the better and rejecting the worse. No option, no morality. There would be no scope for character development in a society that closed its bars and brothels, making vice impossible. Mill did not deny that drink did harm. Yet his remedy was not to curb liberty, but to promote responsible behavior by spreading enlightenment.

It may be that Mill was too optimistic about the power of enlightenment to educate people, too confident about the capacity of men to better themselves morally. And yet, one must not overstate his optimism. His concern for freedom for self-improvement was essentially a concern for those individuals who *chose* to improve themselves. He did not think that the majority had yet developed that capacity. This was why the majority was, in his eyes, the chief enemy of the individual's liberty.

Mill was a liberal, but not a democrat.

Of all tyrannies, he dreaded most the "tyranny of the majority." When Mill thought of freedom, he had in mind the rights of minorities—for example, Irish Catholics, West Indian blacks, and, above all, the minority that was a numerical majority, women. In two tracts, *The Enfranchisement of Women* (1851) and *The Subjection of Women* (1869), he made a remarkable contribution to the literature of feminism, though neither essay had much impact until years later.

Harriet surely inspired these writings. But what is singular about them is that they do not demand, in the manner of most feminist writing, equality for women. Rather, Mill argues for the *liberty* of women, which is linked with the liberty of men. He does not urge that women should be freed from the domination of men, but that women as well as men should be freed from the rule of custom, habit, and tradition, which holds both sexes in bondage.

○

"Women's rights" are claimed—for instance, the right to own property or to vote in parliamentary elections. Yet these are not claimed as natural rights or ends in themselves, but as elements of a wider program of human emancipation, in which women's interests are seen as identical to men's. In *Considerations On Representative Government* (1861), Mill rejected the idea of "Mr. [John] Bright and his school of democrats" that a vote was any man's or woman's right. A vote, Mill argued, was a trust. It should be exercised only by responsible people, male or female. Mill recommended that educated persons be allowed plural votes, to give their voice the added weight it deserved. He suggested that proportional representation be introduced into parliamentary elections, not because it was more democratic, but to provide better for the representation of minorities.

Mill believed that the day would come when the demand for universal suffrage would prove irresistible. The answer, he thought, would be to reform the tax system so that "every grown person in the community" should become a taxpayer. He did not want a system of voting "like that of New York," which enabled people who paid no taxes to vote for levies on people who did.*

Mill also urged preparation for universal suffrage via immediate universal education. His belief in the saving powers of enlightenment led him to favor the enlargement of the state's powers to counteract the pressures of society. He agreed that the state had the right to interfere with the freedom of the family in forcing children to go to school. Since children are excluded from the class of people for whom

freedom is demanded in *On Liberty*, his proposal for compulsory education (which began, at the primary level, in 1880) is not, in itself, inconsistent with his principles. But his plea for the control of marriage and childbearing cannot escape that criticism. He asks not only for laws that would "forbid marriage unless the parties can show that they have the means for supporting a family," he also invites society to step in where the laws are ineffective, so that an improvident marriage shall become a subject of social stigma.

○

It was precisely because Mill set such a high value on intellectual and general culture that he mistrusted those who lacked it. He scorned the proletariat. The English working classes, he wrote, "are in conduct the most disorderly, debauched, and unruly, and least respectable and trustworthy of any nation whatsoever." He was, therefore, anxious to ensure that universal suffrage did not raise the status of the people in any more than a nominal sense. "The people ought to be the masters," he wrote, "but they are masters who must employ servants more skilful than themselves." He even proposed that institutions be set up to ensure a "standing opposition to the will of the majority."

Mill detested the idea of the nation being ruled by nobles or by the rich. But he did favor rule by another elite—professional administrators, civil servants, and bureaucrats like himself and his colleagues at the India Office, who were responsible for governing millions on the subcontinent.

"There is a radical difference," he wrote, "between controlling the business of government and actually doing it." He wanted the controlling to be done by Parliament and a representative body of taxpayers, and the actual governing to be done by specialists, with a "commission of legislation" (also composed of specialists) to draft measures on which Parliament would be invited to vote.

Ordinary people "do not need political rights in order that they may govern, but in order that they may not be misgoverned."

When Harriet died in 1858, at Avignon, France, Mill wrote to Louis Blanc, the French socialist, that England had lost its "greatest mind." Mill's grief was intense, but short-lived. His health, frail throughout his years with Harriet, improved. During their seven years of marriage, he had published little. He emerged from his long seclusion, during which he had earned the reputation of a misanthrope, to become a popular figure in London intellectual society.

In 1865, at age 59, Mill was invited to stand for Parliament as a Liberal Party candidate in London's Westminster district. He said he would do so if it was understood that his only object in the House of Commons would be to promote the ideas expressed in his writings and that no further pledges were demanded of him.

As a campaigner, Mill did not promise to be a crowd-pleaser. At one of his election meetings, the novelist Thomas Hardy—a distant relation of Harriet's—described him standing "bareheaded," with "his vast pale brow, so thin-skinned as to show the blue veins, sloped back like a stretching upland," conveying "to the observer a curious sense of perilous exposure."

○

Yet Mill had blunt-spoken charm. Once he held a meeting for working people—who had no vote, but, Mill thought, possessed as much right as the middle classes to see and hear their representative. Mill's foes exhumed all the harsh words he had ever written about the proletariat. A man carrying a placard saying that the lower classes, "though mostly habitual liars, are ashamed of lying," asked Mill if he had written those words. Said Mill: "I did." After a pause, the workers cheered. Their leader told Mill that they appreciated his candor. Mill soon found he had more power to sway such a crowd than any other Liberal M.P. except William Gladstone.

In his *Autobiography*, Mill recalls the time when a Tory government sent police to break up a meeting of workingmen in Hyde Park. The men, says Mill, "showed a determination to make another attempt at meeting in the Park, to which many of them would probably have come armed; the Government made military preparations to resist the attempt, and something very serious seemed impending." Mill decided to address the workers' meeting. "I told them that a proceeding which would certainly produce a collision with the military could only be justifiable on two conditions; if the position of affairs had

---

*Various qualifications (e.g., property ownership, taxpayer status) kept British voter rolls low during the 19th century. Mill, as a Liberal M.P., tried but failed to amend the Reform Bill of 1867 to allow women to vote in national elections. In 1918, Parliament enfranchised all men over age 21 and women over 30 who could (or had husbands who could) vote in local elections. Women were finally welcomed at the polls on the same terms as men only in 1928—nine years after U.S. women got the vote, 16 years before French women did.

3. INDUSTRY AND IDEOLOGY

become such that a revolution was desirable, and if they thought themselves able to accomplish one. To this argument, after considerable discussion, they at last yielded."

In Parliament, Mill upheld workers' right of assembly and backed working-class candidates. In general, Mill argued for progressive causes in the Commons. He tried to save the lives of some Irish nationalists condemned for fomenting rebellion. He led a campaign against Governor Edward Eyre of Jamaica, who had arrested and hanged more than 30 black rebels. He fought for prostitutes' civil liberties, imperiled by a Contagious Diseases Act, and gave speeches (invariably to a derisive audience) in favor of women's suffrage.

But Mill was not always progressive. He distanced himself from the men he called "philanthropists" on, for instance, the abolition of capital punishment. In 1868, he spoke in the Commons for retention of the death penalty for murder, with his arguments drawn from his utilitarian theory of morals.

The threat of death, he said, was uniquely powerful as a deterrent, more likely than any other form of punishment to diminish the number of murders. Since the general goal of public policy should be to minimize pain, such deterrence should be paramount. Second, Mill argued that a quick death on the gallows was less painful in fact than a lingering death in prison (even though the fear of such a death had a greater power to deter criminals); execution was thus less cruel than life imprisonment. Mill did not imagine that even the "philanthropists" would be so foolish as to advocate any punishment for murder less severe than a life sentence without parole.

Mill's support for capital punishment was popular, but some of his other views were too advanced for even Westminster's enlightened 19th-century bourgeoisie. His support for contraception and divorce, his association with union leaders, and above all his feminism, cost him re-election in 1868. When he lost his Commons seat, he went to Avignon; there, near the cemetery where Harriet was buried, he bought a house, which he furnished with items from the hotel room in which she had died.

Five years later, at age 66, Mill died at Avignon.

Before he left London, Mill had become a close friend of a fellow parliamentarian, Viscount Amberley, who shared his ideas and continued to champion them. Shortly before he died, Mill became the agnostic's equivalent of a godfather to the Amberleys' infant son. Said Lady Amberley: "There is no one in whose steps I would rather see a boy of mine following." The child's name was Bertrand Russell.

Sarah Bernhardt's Paris

Christopher Hibbert

CHRISTOPHER HIBBERT is a prize-winning British author of more than 30 books of history, military history and biography. They include *The Days of the French Revolution; The Great Mutiny: India 1857; Versailles; The Court of St. James's; The House of the Medici; Disraeli and His World;* and biographies of Charles I, George IV and Edward VII.

In the summer of 1862 an astonishingly thin young girl with a pale face, frizzy reddish hair, intense blue eyes and a prominent nose stood on the corner of the Rue Duphet and the Rue St. Honore in Paris looking at the yellow playbills which were pasted up to advertise forthcoming productions at the Theatre Francais. *Iphigenie by Jean Racine,* one of these playbills announced, *For the Debut of Mademoiselle Sarah Bernhardt.* "I have no idea how long I stood there, fascinated by the letters of my name," she recorded years later. "But I remember that it seemed to me as though every person who stopped to read the poster looked at me afterwards."

Sarah Bernhardt was then just eighteen. Her mother, a beautiful woman of Jewish Dutch descent, had once been a milliner and was now a highly successful courtesan with an apartment in the Rue St. Honore where, so it was said, attractive women of her calling could command a hundred thousand francs a month and enjoy the use of two carriages and the services of a footman and a chef. Certainly Julie Bernhardt lived well, and in her comfortable apartment received a succession of generous friends, protectors and lovers, bankers and noblemen, musicians and writers. They included the Italian composer Gioacchino Rossini, who had settled in Paris

some years before, Alexandre Dumas, the prodigal, exuberant author of *The Three Musketeers,* who believed that in fiction as in life the two most important ingredients were *"l'action et l'amour,"* and Charles Auguste-Louis-Joseph, Duc de Morny, the half-brother of the Emperor Napoleon III whose *coup d'etat* he had helped to engineer.

Napoleon III had been born in Paris in 1808, the third son of a younger brother of Napoleon I. Adventurer and idealist—though with his waxed moustache and half-closed eyes, looking, as Theophile Gautier said, "more like a ringmaster who has been sacked for getting drunk"—he believed himself to be a man of destiny, bound to follow his star. After the overthrow of the Orleans monarchy in 1848 he was elected Prince President of the Second Republic, and four years later, following the *coup d'etat* by which he forcibly dissolved the *Assemblee Nationale Legislative,* he was proclaimed Emperor. Since then, with the help of Baron Haussmann, Prefet de la Seine, he had been transforming Paris, intent not only upon freeing the fine monuments of the past from the jumble of buildings that enclosed them on every side, and upon creating a modern dazzling *ville lumiere* with wide, gaslit boulevards and magnificent perspectives, but also upon ensuring that it became a capital city which artillery could overawe with clear fields of fire against revolutionary mobs.

Under Haussmann's ruthless direction pavements were torn up and narrow streets demolished; grandiose apartment blocks took the place of huddled houses whose poor occupants were forced out into the suburbs. Five hundred miles of water mains were laid, over 200 miles of sewers; more than 30,000 gas lamps replaced the an-

cient lanterns; railway stations were constructed close to the heart of the city. Imposing new thoroughfares were driven through the gardens of the Luxembourg Palace; the Boulevard de Sebastopol made its way through a populous district beside the cast-iron and glass food markets known as Les Halles; the Boulevard Haussmann pushed east from the Place de l'Etoile; the Boulevards Saint-Germain and St. Michel and the Rue de Rennes appeared on the Left Bank. The Ile de la Cite was transformed and its greatest pride, Notre-Dame, restored under the direction of Eugene-Emmanuel Viollet-le-Duc. The Tuileries and the Cour Carree were joined by a new gallery along a lengthened Rue de Rivoli. The Bois de Boulogne was laid out with artificial lakes and carriage drives. In 1861 the foundation stone of a vast opera house, which was to occupy almost three acres, was laid to the north of the Boulevard des Italiens; and here, after fourteen years' work, Charles Garnier's extravagant edifice, decorated with 33 varieties of marble and the works of 73 sculptors, was opened at last, a fitting tribute to the pomp and opulent display of the Second Empire.

In this prosperous and rapidly changing city of 1,825,000 people, the cosmopolitan capital of the world, the working day of the poor began as those more fortunate were going to bed after a night of pleasure. Before dawn *chiffonniers* appeared with lanterns and forks and with baskets on their backs to poke through the piles of rubbish which had been thrown out into the streets, searching for rags and bones, bottles and jars, hoping to find, and sometimes finding, an article more valuable before the rubbish wagons trundled along to cart the mounds away. And then, as the sun came up, bootblacks came out with scissors as well as brushes for they were as expert at clipping poodles as they were at polishing shoes; women who sold sweetmeats in the streets prepared their trays of cakes and chocolates, while soup and coffee vendors took up their places on the Pont Notre-Dame; *marchands de coco,* relics of the time of King Louis Philippe, wearing cocked hats and little bells, chopped up lemons and sticks of licorice to flavor the water they carried on their backs in highly polished ornamental tanks to offer for sale in goblets to thirsty passers-by; mechanics greased the wheels of the roundabouts in the Champs Elysees where gardeners watered the exotic flowers; and waiters scattered damp sand under the tables of cafes where clerks and laborers called for coffee and croisettes, brandy plums, absinthe or cheap Orleans wine as they streamed down on their way to work from the heights of Montmartre and La Chapelle, smoking clay pipes, toolbags slung on their backs and loaves of bread under their arms—masons in white jackets, locksmiths in blue overalls, tilers in blouses and small round caps, painters in long smocks swinging their pots, bricklayers with hods on their shoulders, chimney-sweepers harnessed to their barrows of soot.

After their *petit dejeuner* visitors from the country and foreign tourists emerged from their hotels, from the Hotel de Helder; the Hotel Louvre in the Place du Palais Royal which the enterprising Pereire brothers, Emile and Isaac, had built for the Paris Exhibition of 1855; from the even larger Grand Hotel on the Boulevard des Capucines which, with its 750 rooms was the largest in Europe; and from the Ambassade, the Ritz, and the Bristol which, patronized by the Prince of Wales who stayed there, ineffectively incognito, as the Duke of Lancaster, was to become the most fashionable of all.

The doors of the shops now opened, of the smaller, smarter boutiques whose prices varied in accordance with the apparent wealth or gullibility of their customers; of Denton's bookshop in the Palais-Royal where 6,000 copies of the Goncourt brothers' *La Lorette* had been sold in a single week in 1853; and of those recent phenomena, the large department stores, the Maison du Bon Marche, which

had been founded by Norman Boucicaut in 1852, Chaucard's Louvre in the Rue de Rivoli and Jaluzot's Au Printemps on the Boulevard Haussmann. Their shopping done, mothers and nurses took their children and charges out to play with hoops and balls and wooden horses on wheels by the sparkling fountains in the gardens of the Tuileries, wearing billowing, brilliantly colored and intricately embroidered crinolines and flowered hats, while men walked past on their way to the Jockey Club, the Club de L'Union or Le Cercle Agricole, resplendent in shining silk hats, long, narrow-waisted coats, elaborate cravats and tight trousers with buttons down the seams.

By midday the boulevards were crowded with horse-drawn *imperiale* omnibuses, with phaetons and *voitures a laquais,* cockaded coachmen and footmen sitting on the boxes. Smaller equipages, fiacres, traps, landaus and tandems rattled down the Champs Elysees towards the Bois de Boulogne to parade around the lakes and along the Allee des Poteaux. Soon the green iron chairs beneath the striped awnings of the cafes and restaurants were occupied; and familiar faces could be seen at the Cafe de Cardinal on the corner of the Rue Richelieu, at Tortoni's on the Boulevard des Italiens, next door to the Restaurant de la Maison Doree, at the Cafe de Paris which was the favorite haunt of Eugene Sue, Heinrich Heine and Balzac, and at the Moulin Rouge, a smart restaurant on the Champs Elysees where "at the bottom of the garden, at all the windows on every floor, in the lighted depths of private rooms, just as in boxes at the theater, women's heads could be seen nodding left and right to former companions of their nights." In the evenings, as guests set out for fancy dress balls and private dinner parties and the cafe-concerts and the theaters began to fill, crowds collected outside the Theatre Francais to watch the fashionable and famous go into the House of Moliere.

H ere it was that Sarah Bernhardt had decided to become an actress. She had been taken by her mother and three of her mother's friends—Regis Lavolie, a rich banker, Dumas

and the Duc de Morny—to see a performance of Racine's *Britannicus*. She had found it so moving that she had burst into tears and then into sobs so loud that her mother blushed scarlet in embarrassment, other members of the audience had turned round calling *"Sh! Sh!"* and Lavolie had stalked out of the box in disgust, slamming the door behind him.

On their return to Julie Bernhardt's apartment, Sarah had been sent to bed in disgrace. But Dumas had kindly gone up with her and, kissing her at her door, had whispered in her ear, "Good night, little star." Her chance of being a star had come in 1862 with her performance of *Iphigenie*. She had worked hard for the opportunity. With the influential help of the Duc de Morny, she had been granted an audition at the Conservatoire; then, having attended the classes there with enthusiastic assiduity, she had been taken on as a *pensionnaire* by the Comedie Francaise.

Overcome by stage fright, she gabbled her words throughout the first act, and although she recovered her confidence later on, neither audience nor critics were favorably impressed. Her subsequent performances were equally disappointing, and it was widely felt that the Comedie-Francaise had been ill-advised to take her on in the first place. There was little regret when, after breaking her parasol over the head of the stage doorkeeper for some imagined slight and punching an elderly actress in the face during a violent quarrel, she was told to resign from the company. At least she could comfort herself with the thought that she had made a name for herself. Caricatures and stories about her appeared in the newspapers; and her mother's friend, Lavolie, had little difficulty in persuading the directors of the Gymnase, a theater which specialized in popular comedies, to give the now notorious young actress another chance. She did not flourish at the Gymnase either, though, and after one particularly disastrous performance, which reduced her to thoughts of suicide, she decided to follow Dumas' advice and go abroad for a time. According to her own account she went to Spain. But, since her own accounts were always flavored by a reckless indifference to truth, she may well have gone no further than Brussels. Certainly she returned to Paris pregnant by a Belgian aristocrat, the paternity of whose child she ascribed at various times to Leon Gambetta, Victor Hugo, General Boulanger and even to the infant Duke of Clarence who was, in fact, born a fortnight before his alleged progeny.

Within a few weeks of Maurice Bernhardt's birth, his mother went back to work, this time at the Porte-Saint-Martin, a theater renowned for its melodramas and *vaudevilles feeriques*. Here yet again she proved a disappointment. And it was not until—once more with the help of one of her mother's friends—she signed a contract at the Odeon, a national theater on the Left Bank near the Jardin du Luxembourg, that she made her mark at last. Here, in the leading female role in a revival of Dumas' *Kean,* she enjoyed her first unalloyed success. Thereafter triumph followed triumph. Her name on the playbills was sure to fill the theater. She became the darling of the Left Bank. After her portrayal of the minstrel boy Zanetto in Francois Coppee's *Le Passant* in 1868, the Emperor's cousin, Princess Mathilde, arranged for a command performance at the Tuileries where she so impressed the Emperor himself that he gave her a splendid brooch blazing with diamonds. She moved into a large apartment in the Rue Auber; and here, in an untidy clutter of furniture and ornaments, over which turtles with gold-plated shells crawled to escape from barking dogs, she received an assortment of friends and lovers even more varied and distinguished than those who had paid court to her mother.

She entertained Leon Gambetta, then a young barrister and leading member of the political opposition, who was one day to become President of the Chamber of Deputies. She welcomed Princess Mathilde's brother, Prince Napoleon, like his sister a patron of literature and the arts, and a patron, too, of Cora Pearl, the saucy, irresistible English courtesan who was known to have presented herself to her admirers wearing nothing but a sprig of parsley. Sarah Bernhardt also welcomed Theophile Gautier, *"le bon Theo,"* whose praise of her art had done much to further her career. And, with particular pleasure, she opened her arms to Gautier's friend, George Sand, who, many years before, had

left her husband, Baron Dudevant, to lead an independent, unconventional life in Paris, writing novels, wearing trousers, smoking incessantly, nursing Alfred de Musset through an illness before deserting him for his doctor, then going to live with Chopin. She was in her mid-sixties now, but working as hard as ever: Sarah Bernhardt appeared in two of her plays and grew to admire and to love her.

Both Gautier and George Sand were members of that coterie of writers and artists who, during these final years of the Second Empire, met regularly at Magny's, the restaurant in the Rue Contrescarpe-Dauphine which was run by Modeste Magny, an exceptionally gifted restaurateur from the Marne. George Sand had been one of his earliest customers, preferring his restaurant to the Pinson in the Rue de l'Ancienne-Comedie which she had previously patronized, despite the row made next door to Magny's by the performers and spectators at Aublin's *Les Folies Dauphine,* a *boui-boui* or music-hall known more familiarly as *Le Beuglant* because of the bellowing sounds that burst from its windows.

George Sand had not, however, been present at the inauguration of the dining club at Magny's on November 22, 1862. On this Saturday evening among those present had been the once lively but now rather morose lithographer and caricaturist Gavarni, whose sketches of Parisian life had been one of the most notable features in the satirical paper, *Le Charivari;* Gavarni's friends and future biographers, the two inseparable brothers, Edmond and Jules de Goncourt, novelists, social historians, diarists and men of letters, who spoke alternately, the one elaborating, complementing and developing the remarks of the other; and the great critic, Sainte-Beuve, an ugly, fat little man with a black skull-cap on his bald head, now nearing the end of his life but seeming to enjoy it as much as in those earlier days when he had been the lover of Victor Hugo's wife and had dined in a private room every Saturday night at Magny's with other women friends. On later occasions these four had been joined by Gustave Flaubert, the robust though syphilitic author of *Madame*

Bovary and *Salammbo*; by the philogist and historian, Ernest Renan whose influential and controversial *Vie de Jesus* cost him the professorship of Hebrew at the College de France; the towering, bearded Ivan Turgenev, out of favor with the rulers of his native Russia; and Hippolyte Taine, critic and philosopher, whose *Histoire de la litterature anglaise* had appeared in three volumes in 1862.

They dined in one of the seven private rooms on the first floor, served by the head waiter, Charles Labran, who was to remain at Magny's until his master's death. And, as the Goncourts wrote in their journal after their first dinner there, they enjoyed "an exquisite meal, perfect in every respect, a meal such as [they] had thought impossible to obtain in a Paris restaurant." The *specialites de la maison* were *tournedos Rossini, chateaubriand, petites marmites, puree Magny* and *becasses a la Charles,* all of which the proprietor had contrived himself. Also exquisitely cooked at Magny's were *pieds de mouton a la poulette,* and *ecrevisses a la Bordelaise* which, as one customer said, "once you had begun eating there was no reason to stop, and you didn't stop either, unless there was a revolution or an earthquake."

With such dishes Magny gained for himself a special commendation in Adolphe Joanne's guide to the restaurants of Paris which, dividing them all into six categories, considered only a few worthy of being listed in the first class. Apart from Magny's and Philippe's in the Rue Montorqueil, the knowledgeable *bon viveur* recommended Brebant's, haunt of the racing people from Longchamps and Chantilly; Vefour's for Rhenish carp, baked and stuffed and surrounded by soft roe; Ledoyen's for salmon with a green sauce the secret of which was unknown to other establishments; Aux Trois Freres Provencaux for cod with garlic; the Cafe Riche for *sole aux crevettes*; the Maison Doree for fillet steak, braised with tomatoes and mushrooms and served with "a veritable gravy of truffles"; and Bignon's for *barbue au vin rouge* and *filet Richelieu.* But though there were so few restaurants which Joanne could recommend without reserve, he calculated that there were 4,000 pot-houses which were "frequented only by workmen and coachmen." And even in these cheaper places the food was generally good and the service excellent, for in a city where prosperity had created an apparently insatiable demand for pleasure, those in search of it had learned to be discriminating.

"Civility appears to be the motive power of his life," an English visitor wrote of the Parisian waiter. "That wonderful fleetness with which he dashes through the cafe into the open air, and threads his way through rows of lounging customers at the green tables, carrying on the tops of his four fingers and thumb an immense pile of cups, liqueur glasses, bottles of iced water, and lumps of sugar . . . appears to be the noble effort of a chivalrous nature. Ask him for a light and he produces lucifers from any pocket. Although people are calling him or hissing to him in various directions, he finds time to light two or three lucifers and even to hold them till the fumes of the sulphur have passed away before he presents them to you . . . He is free with you; he has a light retort for any attempted joke; but he is never familiar—never rude . . . The reader who wishes to study the Parisian waiter in perfection, should choose a fine summer's night, and take his seat outside the rotunda in the Palais Royal about eight o'clock, in the midst of about 300 people, served by about eight waiters, who caper, loaded with crockery and newspapers with an activity that any Harlequin might envy."

There were numerous cafes in the Palais Royal, mostly expensive and respectable. But for those who preferred less decorous establishments there were even more of these elsewhere. Paris, indeed, was a very *embarras de richesse* of cafes, cafe-concerts, taverns, *bouillons, cremeries, brasseries, pensions bourgeoises, assommoirs* and *estaminets* as well as brothels, *cabinets particuliers* and licentious dance-halls. One on the best known brothels was Farcy's where, in the drawing-room, sprawling on red velvet divans around the floral-papered walls, the girls smiled and cooed and asked for drinks. One of the most expensive *cabinets particuliers* was the Grand Seize, an exotic private room at the Cafe Anglais hung with red wall-paper and gold hieroglyphics, furnished with gilt chairs and a crimson sofa, where Sarah Bernhardt was herself to be entertained by the Prince of

Wales. And one of the most lively and wanton dance-halls was Mabille's in the Allee des Veuves where an orchestra of 50 played in a Chinese pavilion surrounded by artificial palm trees with gas globes hanging from the leaves; where, as a guidebook warned, "the limits of propriety [were] frequently passed"; and where parlor-maids, *grisettes* and milliners could find men willing to pay them twenty francs for a night of pleasure, more than they could otherwise earn in a month.

In the summer of 1870 the carefree frivolity of the Second Empire came suddenly to a close. Napoleon III declared war on Prussia, and a few weeks later his army was crushingly defeated at Sedan. The confidence of the Parisians, who had never believed in the remotest possibility of such a catastrophe, was shattered overnight.

"Who can describe the consternation written on every face," wrote Edmond de Goncourt as his fellow citizens pondered on the consequences of the fall of the imperial government, "the sound of aimless steps pacing the streets at random, the anxious conversations of shopkeepers and *concierges* on their doorsteps, the crowds collecting at street-corners, the siege of the newspaper kiosks, the triple line of readers gathering around every gas-lamp."

At news of the German army's approach, preparations for the expected siege of Paris gathered momentum. Mines were laid, woods chopped down, road blocks thrown up, road and river approaches obstructed, monuments protected by sandbags and boarding; and the capital's extensive defensive system of bastions, walls, moats and forts—which Adolphe Thiers had had constructed in 1840 but which had subsequently been neglected—was hastily restored and strengthened. Railway stations were converted into balloon factories or cannon-foundries, theaters into hospitals; couturiers' workshops began to make military uniforms, the Louvre to turn out armaments. Regular troops, marines and sailors marched into the city; conscripts and volunteers paraded through the streets; thousands of heavy guns were dragged out to the forest, while herds of cattle and sheep

were driven into the Bois de Boulogne.

In the excitement of all this activity the morale of the Parisians rose. On September 13, a few days before the last mail-train left the city and the one remaining telegraph line to the west was cut, a review of the defenders was held by General Louis-Jules Trochu, president of the newly formed Government of National Defense, who galloped onto the scene to the rattle of drums and to shouts of *"Vive la France! Vive la Republique! Vive Trochu!"* Tens of thousands of soldiers lined the boulevards from the Place de la Bastille to the Arc de Triomphe. The National Guard, some in frock-coats, others in workmen's smocks, marched past to the strains of the *Marseillaise,* their rifles decorated with flowers and ribbons, children holding their fathers' hands.

Poets declaimed their verses; journalists issued proclamations; politicians harangued the crowds; priests preached sermons. Adelaide de Montgolfier, daughter of the great balloonist, watched the *Neptune*, the first postal balloon to leave Paris, soar into the sky above the Place Saint-Pierre in Montmartre, shouts of *"Vive la Republique!"* ringing in her ears, proud to think that her "dear father's invention [was] now proving of such great value to his country."

Enthusiasm was not matched, though, by achievement. Outside the city the French troops proved no match for the German invaders. Dejected and dispirited soldiers returned disconsolately from the front to the streets of Paris where already long queues were to be seen outside the butchers' shops as early as two o'clock in the morning and the restaurants started to serve beef that looked suspiciously like horse flesh. Looking for scapegoats, the Parisians turned on foreigners, particularly on the English residents who were believed to share their Queen's sympathetic attitude towards Germany: *Les Nouvelles* proposed that the best way to settle the question as to whether the British were spies or not was to shoot the lot of them. "Anyone who did not speak French with purity was arrested," commented Trochu's aide-de-camp, Maurice d'Herisson. "Englishmen, Americans, Swedes, Spaniards and Alsatians were arrested alike. A similar fate befell all those who, either in dress or manner, betrayed anything unusual. Stammerers were arrested because they tried to speak too quickly; dumb people because they did not speak at all; and the deaf because they did not seem to understand what was said to them. The sewermen who emerged from the sewers were arrested because they spoke Piedmontese.''

The people turned, too, on Trochu and his government whom they accused of not facing the crisis with sufficient determination. Demonstrations were held in the Place de la Concorde; marches made to the Hotel de Ville; demands presented for a *levee en masse* and a *sortie en masse,* the election of a Municipal Commune, the formation of a corps of Amazons, the manufacture of ''guns, more guns and still more guns.'' At the end of October news reached the capital that Marshal Bazaine had surrendered Metz to the enemy and that Le Bourget, a village north of Paris which had been captured by the Prussians, had been retaken by them. There were also rumors that Leon Gambetta, who, with a basket of homing pigeons, had left Paris by balloon at the beginning of the month to join the elderly members of the Delegation of Tours, was inclining to their view that surrender was inevitable.

Incensed by all this, a crowd of about 15,000 demonstrators advanced on the Hotel de Ville, shouting ''No armistice!'' and ''The Commune forever!'' Several hundred of them burst inside the building, demanding the resignation of all the members of the Government of National Defense and calling out the names of men whom they wished to replace them. Their leaders—with Gustave Flourens, a revolutionary member of the National Guard, well to the fore—climbed onto the baize-covered table of the council-chamber and strode along it, trampling on papers and notebooks, knocking over inkstands and sandboxes, crushing pens and pencils, their voices lost in the clangor of shouts, drums and trumpets, while General Trochu calmly smoked his cigar.

Trochu's apparent indifference to these agitators was justified: an energetic colleague, Ernest Picard, called upon the more constructive leaders of the National Guard for help, and a bourgeois battalion marched to the Government's rescue. While Flourens went into hiding, Parisians were asked to answer the following question in a plebiscite: ''Does the population of Paris wish to maintain the powers of the Government of National Defense? *Oui ou Non*?'' Overwhelmingly the answer was yes.

So Trochu continued in office; his forces remained on the defensive; and Paris grew more and more to resemble a beleaguered city. Many shops put up their shutters, having nothing to sell; others filled their windows with telescopes, knives, revolvers and brandy-flasks. Fashionable clothes were no longer conspicuous on the boulevards: men wore makeshift uniforms, women their oldest dresses or nurses' aprons.

As Henry Labouchere, Paris correspondent of the London *Daily News,* recorded on November 15, Paris' mood now veered wildly ''from the lowest depths of despair to the wildest confidence. Yesterday afternoon a pigeon arrived covered with blood, bearing on his tail a despatch from Gambetta, announcing that the Prussians had been driven out of Orleans . . . The despatch was read at the Mairies to large crowds, and in the cafes by enthusiasts who got up on the tables. I was in a shop when a person came in with it. Shopkeepers, assistants and customers immediately performed a war dance round a stove.''

This festive mood was short-lived. People were soon complaining again about the National Guard, who performed very confidently on parade but showed little inclination to fight the enemy, and about General Trochu who, so one junior officer said, had associated so much with lawyers that he had become to resemble one himself: ''He has dipped his pen in his scabbard and his sword in his inkstand, and when he finally attempts to draw the sword, he'll unsheath a penholder.'' Hopes were raised at the end of November by rumors of a great sortie involving 150,000 men who were to cross the Marne and occupy the enemy's positions at Champigny. But these hopes were dashed when the crowds, which had gathered at Pont d'Austerlitz and along the Avenue du Trone, learned that the sortie had ended in tragic failure. Hard upon this reverse came news of the defeat of the Army of the Loire and the recapture of Orleans. Less than a fortnight later the spirits of the people were revived again by an optimistic message from Gambetta published in the *Journal Officiel,* only to be dampened soon afterwards by the failure of another sortie.

In common with most other theaters and many hotels, the Odeon was converted into a hospital. Assuming the responsibility for organizing it, Sarah Bernhardt rushed from one admirer to another, asking for supplies, obtaining brandy from Baron Rothschild, chocolate from Meunier, sardines from the rich grocer, Felix Potin, outside whose store in the Boulevard de Strasbourg long queues stood throughout the night. Acting as nurse as well as storekeeper, she dressed wounds, assisted at operations, carried food to the helpless and brandy to the dying; and as the weeks passed and the supplies of food grew ever more depleted, often went without meals herself so that the patients might be fed.

By the end of the year the shortage of food in Paris had become acute. Beef and mutton, at first severely rationed, now disappeared from the shops altogether. Cab-horses and race-horses were sold by the butchers instead, then cats, rats and dogs. Eels and gudgeons from the Seine fetched their weight in silver.

''People talk of nothing but what is eaten, can be eaten, or is there to be eaten [wrote Edmond de Goncourt]. Conversation has come down to this:

'' 'You know, a fresh egg costs twenty-five sous.'

'' 'It appears there's a fellow who buys up all the candles he can find, adds some coloring, and produces that fat which sells at such a price.'

'' 'Mind you don't buy any coconut butter. It stinks a house out for three days at least.'

'' 'I've had some dog chops, and found them really very tasty: they look just like mutton chops.'

'' 'Who was it who told me he had eaten some kangaroo?' ''

As well as kangaroo, the director of the zoo sold all manner of animals for slaughter—buffaloes and zebras, reindeer and camels, yaks and elephants. But these animals were soon consumed. And ''failing meat,'' one commentator observed, "you cannot fall back on vegetables: a little turnip costs eight sous and you have to pay seven francs for a pound of onions. Nobody talks about butter any more, and every other sort of fat except candle-fat and axle-grease has disappeared too. As for the two staple items of the diet of the poor—potatoes and cheese— cheese is just a memory, and you have to have friends in high places to obtain potatoes at twenty francs a bushel. The greater part of Paris is living on coffee, wine and bread." And even bread, a hard black substance made principally of bran, rice and starch, was scarce.

Hunger was not the only privation. By the end of the year the temperature had fallen to twelve degrees below zero. While sentries froze to death, orders were given for the felling of six square miles of trees in the Bois de Boulogne and the Bois de Vincennes and along the city's boulevards. But the people could not wait: fences, trellises, benches and telegraph poles were cut up as well and dragged away to their homes.

To cold and hunger and the attendant sickness and disease was added the horror of bombardment. At first it was only the forts that were shelled. But at the beginning of January 1871, shells began also to burst in the city itself, mainly on the poorer houses on the Left Bank where the people bore the cannonade with stoic courage. "On every doorstep, women and children stand, half frightened, half inquisitive," wrote Edmond de Goncourt, "watching the medical orderlies going by, dressed in white smocks with red crosses on their arms and carrying stretchers, mattresses and pillows."

Before long most people grew quite accustomed to the bombing. Children, hearing an explosion, would say, "That was a shell," and then calmly continue with their game. And street urchins on seeing a well dressed person walk by, so Henry Labouchere observed, would cry out, "Flat! Flat! A shell—a shell—*a plat ventre!* Down on your faces!" "The man, gorgeous in fur, falls flat on the ground—perhaps in the gutter—and the Parisian urchin rejoices with exceeding great joy."

Despite all the hardships, Labouchere continued, the Parisians

behaved with remarkable resignation. They criticized Trochu and the government endlessly, denouncing their mistakes and blunders; but, they made "no complaint about their miseries," accepting them "with an unpretending fortitude which no people in the world could surpass." By the end of January, however, it was clear that resistance could not much longer be maintained. Men and women were falling down dead in food queues; the death rate rose to almost 4,500 a week, many of these being children. "At every step," one survivor wrote, "you met an undertaker carrying a little deal coffin."

Edmond de Goncourt was struck by the deathly silence that had fallen over the city. You could no longer hear Paris living, he noted in his journal. Every face looked liked like that of a sick person or convalescent. You saw "nothing but thin, pallid features, faces as pale and yellow as horse-flesh." One day a prostitute, splashing along behind him in the Rue Saint-Nicholas, called out pathetically, "Monsieur, will you come up to my room, for a piece of bread?"

On January 23, Jules Favre, the Foreign Minister, left Paris for the German headquarters at Versailles to open negotiations for surrender. "A tall, thin, stooping, miserable-looking lawyer," as his secretary described him, "with his wrinkled frock-coat and his white hair falling over his collar," he seemed no match for Count Bismarck, the robust, broad-chested Iron Chancellor, who received Favre in the tight, white tunic and yellow-banded cap of the White Cuirassiers. Yet Favre's apparent weakness, real dignity and "good old French manners" worked to his advantage. "It is very difficult for me to be as hard with him as I have to be," Bismarck told his wife. "The rascals know this, and consequently push him forward." The terms imposed upon them were, therefore, not as hard as the French had feared they might be. But they were nevertheless obliged to agree to the German army's ceremonial march into the capital. So, on Wednesday, March 1, German troops escorted by blaring bands and by cavalry with drawn swords, paraded through the Arc de Triomphe and down the Champs Elysees.

Parisians, their houses shuttered and their shops closed, were now in a bitter mood, harboring resentment not only against the Germans but also against the Government and the generals who, they felt, had failed them, as well as against the rich who, during the siege, had been able to pay for the food and warmth denied to others and who, now that it was over, had left for the country. There was resentment, too, against the provinces which, having escaped most of the horrors of the war, chose to elect a predominantly royalist assembly. In protest a *Federation Republicaine de la Garde Nationale* was formed; and insurgents established the Commune of Paris.

Civil war was now inevitable. On the orders of Adolphe Thiers, soon to be President of the Third Republic, an army of regulars was collected at Versailles under General MacMahon and marched into Paris. The subsequent slaughter was fearful. Prisoners taken by the Versailles forces were shot out of hand; in retaliation the Commune seized hostages, including the Archbishop of Paris and the Presiding Judge of the Court of Appeals, and executed them. In the Rue Haxo scores of other hostages, among them several priests, were shot by a frenzied crowd of men and women. Street battles raged and the pavements ran with blood; numerous public buildings were destroyed. The Palais des Tuileries and the Hotel de Ville, the Palais Royal and the Louvre, the Ministry of Finance and the Prefecture de Police were all set on fire. By the time the last defenders of the Commune had been shot down in the Pere Lachaise cemetery nearly 20,000 people, men, women and children, had lost their lives—more than the total number who had perished in the whole of France throughout the six years of the Revolution of 1789-95.

During the days of the Commune Bernhardt had left Paris to escape from the vindictive Prefect of Police whom she had much offended in the past by contemptuously returning to him a play he had written which she had said was "unworthy to touch let alone to read." But as soon as the troubles were over she returned to her apartment over which she splashed bottles full of her favorite scent to disperse the smell of smoke from the still smoldering buildings on every side. Victor Hugo had also returned from exile in Guernsey to what he himself described as "an indescribable welcome" from fellow republicans who elected him a senator. Although he was now in his seventies his career as poet, novelist and dramatist was far from over; but it was in a play which he had written over 30 years before, *Ruy Blas,* that Bernhardt, as the Queen of Spain, was to achieve the greatest triumph she had yet enjoyed. After the first night Hugo knelt before her to kiss her hand; cheering crowds filled the Rue Vaugirard; and a band of admiring young men unharnessed the horses of her carriage to drag it back themselves to her apartment, excitedly shouting "Make way for our Sarah!"

A few weeks later she was invited to return to the Theatre Francais. And here, in *Britannicus,* in Voltaire's *Zaire,* above all in Racine's *Phedre,* which some critics thought she played even more movingly than Rachel, she established herself as the most powerful dramatic actress of her time, mesmerizing her audiences, as Arthur Symons thought, "awakening the senses and sending the intelligence to sleep," interpreting her parts instinctively rather that intellectually with a kind of hypnotic fervor, and speaking in a voice in which, as Lytton Strachey said, "there was more than gold, there was thunder and lightning, there was heaven and hell."

As well as a great actress, Bernhardt also become known as a most outlandishly eccentric showman about whom stories—many invented, others that were not, yet seemed so—filled column after column in newspapers and magazines. Her apartment in the Rue de Rome and the house she later built on the corner of the Rue Fortury and the Avenue de Villiers, were furnished and decorated in the most bizarre manner, with a satin-lined resewood coffin in which she sometimes slept and a canopied fur-strewn divan prominent amidst the medley of ill-matched chairs, tables, cupboards, carpets, a stuffed vulture, a leering skeleton and works of art of extraordinarily uneven quality. Visitors were likely to be accosted by an alarming variety of strange animals, wild cats, hawks, a baby tigress, a puma that ate Dumas *fils'* straw boater and a boa constrictor that devoured its owner's cushions.

They were also likely to meet many of the most famous and notorious people in Paris, from actors and actresses such as the lovable comedian Constant Coquelin whose creation of *Cyrano de Bergerac* was to become legendary, Sophie Croizette in whose company Bernhardt used to stuff herself with cakes and chocolates in Chiboust's *patisserie,* and the alluring Jean Mounet-Sully, to exotic aesthetes like Robert de Montesquiou and Oscar Wilde, the composer Gounod, Ferndinand de Lesseps and Louis Pasteur. She would hold court on her divan, Persian hangings and the leaves of jungle plants framing her intense, pale, quizzically seductive face, a vast Russian wolfhound sprawled by the fur hem of a dress raised slightly to reveal a pretty, provocative white-stockinged ankle. It was in this pose that one of her numerous lovers, the painter Georges Clairin, portrayed her in a picture which was the principle talking-point of the Academy's 1876 exhibition in the Salon d'Apollon in the Louvre.

Those interested more in art than in iconography, however, were discussing another exhibition that year, the second held by the so-called Impressionists. The growing dissatisfaction of these artists with academic teaching had been brought to a head in 1863 when an exhibition of works rejected by the Salon, including Manet's *Dejeuner sur l'herbe,* was ridiculed by traditionalists. Four of them, Renoir, Sisley, Bazille and Monet were fellow-students at the studio of Marc Charles Gabriel Gleyre. They remained friends after leaving Gleyre's studio and used to meet regularly at the Cafe de la Nouvelle-Athenes in Montmartre, where they were often joined by Pisarro, Cezanne, Degas, Manet and Berthe Morisot. In 1873, after works by several of these artists were turned away by the Salon, they decided to hold an exhibition of their own; and the next year they did so in the studio of Nadar, the aeronaut, caricaturist and photographer. One of the pictures shown was Manet's *Impression, soleil levant* which led a mocking journalist from *Le Charivari* to deride the whole movement as Impressionism, a term which the artists themselves accepted as applying to them all. For, although their school was never a homogeneous one with a jointly recognized purpose, they did share a common belief that painting and its techniques should not be restricted in the way that the Salon seemed to prescribe. "One does not paint a landscape, a seascape, a figure," Manet declared in a summary of the Impressionists's view: "one paints the impression of one hour of the day in a landscape, in a seascape, upon a figure." The Impressionists' exhibition of 1876 was followed by six others in which Caillebotte, Forain and the American exile, Mary Cassatt, also showed their work.

But none of them aroused any interest in Sarah Bernhardt. She far preferred the traditional style of Georges Clairin and the sweetly Romantic pictures of her Lesbian friend, Louise Abbema; and in her own watercolors and facile sculptures, which she occasionally exhibited at the Salon, she displayed no sign of willingness to depart from the accepted Academy style. Discerning critics did not take her work seriously, agreeing with Rodin—whose masterpiece of 1877, *The Age of Bronze,* was condemned by Academicians as scandalous—that it was nothing but "old-fashioned tripe." Bernhardt, however, had one powerful apologist, a moody art critic, the first of whose great cycle of twenty *naturaliste* novels, *Les Rougon-Macquart,* had just been published. This was Emile Zola.

The Paris which Zola described in some of these novels was a far cry from the fashionable restaurants of the Boulevard des Italiens. It was a Paris where life was hard and the working day long, the Paris of the poor as depicted by Honore Daumier, a sad contrast to that of the elegant dandy as sketched by Constantin Guys. Here, in those mean streets northwest of the Gare du Nord, streets of crumbling, leaking tenement buildings and lodging-houses with rotting, rain-sodden shutters, scraggy hens scratched for worms between the pavements; colored streams of water poured from dye-works; butchers in bloodstained aprons stood before the doors of slaughter-houses;

men dragged beds and mattresses to pawnshops from which they emerged to get drunk in wine shops, to eat six-sous meals in *bistingos* or to take home paper bags of chipped potatoes or cans of mussels; and, as the factory bells summoned their husbands to work, women carried their dirty clothes to the wash-house where, in steamy air, smelling of sweat and soda and bleach, they banged shirts and trousers against their washboards, their red arms bare to the shoulders, their skirts caught up to reveal darned stockings and heavy laced boots, shouting to each other above the din. This is the world of *L'Assommoir,* of Coupeau, the roofer, and Gervaise, the laundry-woman, and of their daughter, Nana, whose career Zola later unfolded in his great novel of1880.

The year before *Nana* was published Bernhardt left Paris for the first of those foreign tours which were to make her as celebrated abroad as she was at home. She returned from America in 1881 at the age of 36 to find Zola the most discussed and widely read author in France. She also found herself far from popular with her fellow Parisians who were resentful of her having abandoned their theaters for more lucrative appearances overseas and who were assured by various hostile journalists that she was becoming a prima donna of the most selfish, pretentious and avaricious kind. Her electrifying recitation of the *Marseillaise* at the end of a gala performance of the Opera on the glorious 14th of July, however, followed by a magnificent performance in Victorien Sardou's *Fedora*—whom she portrayed, in Maurice Baring's words, with "such tigerish passion and feline seduction which, whether it be good or bad art, nobody has been able to match since"—restored her to her former preeminence. She followed her Fedora with other equally brilliant performances—as Marguerite Gauthier in Dumas *fils' La Dame aux camelias,* as the Empress in Sardou's even more melodramatic *Theodora,* and as the heroine of Sardou's *Tosca.*

There were failures, too, though, and her private life was unhappy. Her sister, whom she loved dearly and had helped to bring up, died a drug addict. The Greek diplomat and would-be actor, the arrogant, selfish, compul-

sively satyric Aristide Damala, whom she found sexually enchanting and married, also became a morphine and cocaine addict, shamelessly injecting himself through his trouser leg in front of her friends, and further humiliating her by spending the money she gave him on other women before dying at the age of 34. Her former friend and colleague, Marie Colombier, of whom Manet painted a delightful portrait, revenged herself upon her for a professional slight by writing an obscene and libelous book, *The Memoirs of Sarah Barnum,* which induced Bernhardt to burst upon the author in her apartment, brandishing a dagger in one hand and a riding crop in the other, committing a violent assault which furnished journalists and caricaturists with irresistible copy. Finally, Bernhardt's beloved son, as costly an expense as her husband, quarrelled bitterly with his mother over the Dreyfus case and took himself off with his wife and daughter to the South of France where he remained for over a year, refusing to communicate with her.

Captain Alfred Dreyfus, a Jewish officer of unsullied reputation, was court-martialled in December 1894, found guilty of having passed military secrets to the German Embassy, and sentenced to life imprisonment on Devil's Island. It later appeared that the German's informant was not Dreyfus but another officer, Major Esterhazy. But the War Office suppressed this damaging discovery; and, when Esterhazy was himself court-martialled, he was acquitted. The resultant uproar divided France into rival factions of furiously antagonistic *Dreyfusards* and *anti-Dreyfusards.* Sarah Bernhardt was as violent a champion of Dreyfus as her son was a denigrator of the "Jewish traitor." It is said that it was she who approached her friend Zola and persuaded him to write the celebrated letter, *J'Accuse,* to the President, denouncing the Army's disgraceful behavior. Certainly she proclaimed her sympathies loudly and publicly; professed her horror when Dreyfus, despite all the evidence, was found guilty after a fresh trial; and rejoiced when at last he was pardoned.

The quarrels over the Dreyfus affair were still raging when Bernhardt appeared as the Duc de Reichstadt in Edmond Rostand's *L'Aiglon* which

night after night filled the large theater in the Place Chatelet that she had recently taken over at the age of 55 on a 25-year lease, restored and redecorated at immense expense, and renamed the Theatre Sarah Bernhardt. The play opened in March 1900 and was still running to packed houses in the summer when the Great Exhibition of that year filled Paris with visitors from all over the world.

This Exhibiton was one of several which Paris had seen in Sarah Bernhardt's lifetime. The first had been in 1855 when a huge Palais de l'Industrie had been built beside the Champs Elysees and when Gustave Courbet had defiantly held a private exhibition of his work, entitled *Le Realisme,* immediately opposite the Palais des Beaux Arts where the more respectable paintings of Delacroix, Ingres, Vernet and Winterhalter had been shown. The next had been in 1867 when, in an immense brown and gold palace covering 40 acres on the Champ de Mars, the pictures of Jean Francois Millet had been displayed together with numerous marvels of modern science.

"A day at the Exhibition seems a mere hour," wrote Ludovic Halevy, who with Henri Meilhac wrote the libretto for Offenbach's *La Grande-Duchesse de Gerolstein* in which Hortense Schneider appeared at Varietes during the Exhibition's course. "How many things there are to see! . . . There are two miles or so of cafes and restaurants . . . You can eat and drink in every language . .'. And the park round the palace, the houses from every land, the factories for glass-blowing and diamond-cutting, the bakery, the machine for making hats, and the machine for making shoes, and the machine for making soap . . . They make everything, these damned machines. I looked everywhere for the machines that turned out plays and novels. They are the only ones that are missing. They will be there at the next Exhibition."

The next Exhibition, the Universal Exhibition, had been held in 1878 to celebrate Paris' quick recovery from the horrors of the Commune. Another Palais de l'Industrie had appeared on the Champ de Mars, and Davioud's ornate palace on the Trocadero; and electric light had illuminated the Avenue de l'Opera. Eleven years later, another Universal Exhibition was held on the anniversary of the Revolution. And in that year visitors to Paris had their first sight of what was to become one of Paris' most familiar landmarks, the 300-meters-high iron tower constructed to the designs of Gustave Eiffel. And then in 1900 this new Universal Exhibition attracted over 50,000,000 visitors who visited the fine art shows in the new cast-iron halls by the Pont Alexandre III, who went for rides on the vast great wheel, and admired the immense metal bouquet glittering with electric lights near the Ecole Militaire.

Paris was now a modern city. Horse-drawn vehicles still trotted down the busy streets, but motor cars and electric trams were also to be seen, and the underground metropolitan railway was spreading fast beneath the pavements. *Haute couture* had become a large and thriving industry, enormously expanded since the days when the rich, following the example of the beautiful Empress Eugenie, had gone to the rooms in the Rue de la Paix where the Englishman, Charles Frederick Worth, held sway as the acknowledged arbiter of fashion. Now the firm founded by the banker Isadore Paquin and his wife alone employed nearly 3,000 people. Yet, for all the city's change and growth, its traditional pleasures remained unaltered. The essence of that Paris, to which King Edward VII made his famous and triumphant state visit in 1903, was the same as it had been when he was first captivated by its charm half a century earlier. The cafes of Montmartre, where Paul Verlaine had sat in slippered feet drinking hard until his death in 1896, were little different from those the Goncourts had known a generation before; the performers at the Moulin Rouge,

where La Goulue, plump and lascivious, and the pale, thin-legged Jane Avril kicked out their legs in the cancan, were as lively and exciting as Rigolette and Mogador and those other polka dancers at the Mabille in the days of Bernhardt's childhood. The brothels of the Rue des Moulins and Rue d'Amboise, where the ugly, crippled Comte de Toulouse-Lautrec sat closely observing the naked women through his pince-nez and portraying them with realistic sincerity, were much the same as those that Baudelaire had known at the time of the Second Empire.

When Toulouse-Lautrec died in 1901, Bernhardt was approaching her 57th birthday. But age meant nothing to her. She dismissed all thoughts of retirement, putting on play after play, some successful, others not, choosing them for the roles they offered her genius. In 1904 she was still "highly triumphant over time," in the words of Max Beerbohm, who was a professed "lover of Sarah's imcomparable art," though he had derided her Hamlet which had made him wonder if she would next play Othello opposite the booming voiced Mounet-Sully as Desdemona. So little regard did Bernhardt pay to her age, in fact, that when she was 65 she took the leading role in Emile Moreau's *Proces de Jeanne d'Arc* in which she turned with serene confidence to the audience, when the Grand Inquisitor asked Joan her age, to answer in her still beautifully clear, silvery voice, *"Dix-neuf ans"* (19). Night after night the audience broke into rapturous applause.

Not long after the finish of this play's run the Great War broke out. Bernhardt announced her intention of remaining in Paris as she had done in 1870; but she was persuaded to leave by Clemenceau himself who told her that, as she was likely to be on a list of possible hostages, the Government did not want to be responsible for her safety.

She asked to be taken to the station by way of the Champs Elysees which she feared she might never see again. And as she drove into it she was amazed to come upon long lines of taxis, nose to tail and packed with soldiers, stretching as far as the eye could reach. These were the famous *Taxis de la Marne*, rushing troops to the front to reinforce the French 5th and 6th Armies which were making what was to prove a successful counterattack against the German forces on the River Marne.

Bernhardt had left Paris with her right leg in a plaster cast. She had injured it some time before, and by the time she reached the villa in the Bay of Arcachon where she was to stay, gangrene had set in. In February 1915 the leg was amputated in a hospital in Bordeaux. Yet even this did not destroy her determination to continue on the stage. By the end of the year she was back in Paris, appearing in Eugene Moraud's patriotic piece *Les Cathedrales,* balancing on one leg as she supported herself on the arm of a chair. She protested that she would carry on thus until she died, having herself strapped to the scenery if necessary. "Madame," she said to Queen Mary during a visit to England, "I shall die on the stage. It is my battlefield."

The prediction was almost fulfilled. On the night of a dress rehearsal of a play in which she was to appear with her old friend Lucien Guitry, his son Sacha and his daughter-in-law, Yvonne Printemps, she collapsed in a coma. Some weeks later, on May 26, 1923, her doctor opened a window of her house in the Boulevard Pereire and announced to the crowds below, "Messieurs, Madame Bernhardt is dead."

"Bernhardt is dead" one Parisian said, passing on the sad news to another. "How dark it seems all of a sudden."

Modernism and Total War: The Twentieth Century

At the end of the nineteenth century, there were high hopes for the future of Western civilization. Popular novelists foresaw air travel, television, visual telephones, sound recordings, interplanetary travel, and even the construction of a new continent in the Pacific. Technology would liberate those living in the twentieth century from most of their burdens, or so the futurists of the day argued. There were skeptics, of course: Mark Twain punctured the pious hypocrisies of fellow Occidentals who presumed that their Christianity and their technology demonstrated their superiority over the benighted heathens of the non-Western world. And a few observers questioned whether humankind would be any happier, even with all the material benefits the future offered.

Even before this glittering future could be realized, turn-of-the-century artists and thinkers brought forth an alternative vision of far greater originality. They set in motion a period of unprecedented cultural innovation and artistic experimentation, out of which emerged modern music, modern theater, modern literature, modern art, and modern architecture. (These developments are covered in "How the Modern World Began.") Never before had there been so many cultural manifestos: Fauvism, Cubism, Futurism, and other avant-garde movements declared themselves. In philosophy it was the age of pragmatism, positivism, and Bergsonism. On another intellectual frontier, Alfred Binet, Pavlov, and Freud reformulated the premises of psychology. Advanced work in experimental science concentrated on rays, radioactivity, and the atom, setting the stage for Einstein's abstract but unsettling theories.

Thus, in the years before the Great War, the West was able to point to unrivaled accomplishments. Aristocrats and the middle class were confident of the future because they were eminently satisfied with the present. Their general sense of well-being was captured by Osbert Sitwell in his autobiography:

Never has Europe been so prosperous and so gay. Never had the world gone so well for all classes of the community. . . . I remember from my childhood, what must have been a common experience with members of my generation, reading the Bible, and books of Greek, Roman, and English history, and reflecting how wonderful it was to think that, with the growth of commerce and civilization, mass captivities and executions were things of the rabid past, and that never again would man be liable to persecution for his political or religious opinions. This belief, inculcated in the majority, led to an infinite sweetness in the air we breathed.

In light of subsequent events, all of this seems a great illusion. Millions of lives were lost in the Great War, which demonstrated the destructive force of Europe's vaunted technology (as Edmund Stillman observes in "Sarajevo: The End of Innocence"). The war dashed the hopes of an entire generation and contributed to revolution in Russia, the collapse of the international economy, and the emergence of totalitarian dictatorships. It finally played itself out in a second, even more devastating, conflict. The impact of Europe's second great war is conveyed in "1945" and "The War Europe Lost." "When the Red Storm Broke" provides an unusual perspective on the Russian Revolution, while "The Big Picture of the Great Depression" surveys the economic upheaval between the wars. So-called totalitarian systems are treated in "The Nazi State: Machine or Morass?"

Looking Ahead: Challenge Questions

How did the certainties of the nineteenth century give way to the relativism of the twentieth century? What role did the new discoveries in physics and psychology play in this transformation?

How were women affected by the social and intellectual changes of the period?

What sparked the political chain reaction that produced two world wars?

What were the consequences of the two major wars of this century? Who were the real winners and losers?

What were the causes and consequences of the Great Depression?

Was the "cold war" between Russia and the United States caused by the unique geopolitical circumstances of the immediate postwar period, or was it the inevitable consequence of irreconcilable differences between two fundamentally antithetical systems?

How the Modern World Began

PETER GAY

When did our minds become "our" minds? Our fears of overpopulation, of race riots, of wasted resources, of extinction through nuclear war, are recent in origin, at least in their acute form. But the minds that furnished our minds reach farther back: practically all the ideas that determine our vocabulary, direct our taste, dominate our lives, were generated or revived in the years between 1890 and 1914.

That quarter century was the seedbed of our way of thinking and feeling, of responding to poetry and music, to novels and buildings. The masters of the modern literary movement in the 1920's and 1930's—William Butler Yeats, T. S. Eliot, D. H. Lawrence, James Joyce, Marcel Proust, Thomas Mann—had all begun to write before 1914, and some had already published important work. The expressionist play, poem, and novel, which we tend to associate with the early 1920's, were flourishing by 1910. Experimental painting—neoimpressionism, expressionism, cubism, futurism, abstraction—all predate World War I: Kandinsky made his famous discovery of nonobjective art, one of the decisive revolutions in the modern mind, some time in the year 1910. Philosophical movements like logical positivism, pragmatism, and phenomenology emerged before the war. The International style in architecture, which became the avant-garde style in the 1920's and 1930's in the buildings of Gropius and Mies van der Rohe, was developed in a series of buildings and designs between about 1907 and 1914; the functionalism of Frank Lloyd Wright was mature by 1911, when two books on his houses brought him European fame.

In music, the sonorities of Wagner, though kept alive by Mahler and Strauss, found determined challengers. "We ought to have our own music," Eric Satie said to Claude Debussy, "if possible without sauerkraut." By 1908, music without sauerkraut was a reality: Schönberg, Berg, and Webern had broken through to atonalism. The dominant questions of modern physics—relativity, atomic structure, and quantum theory—were first asked well before the war by Albert Einstein, Ernest Rutherford, and Max Planck. It was in this period, too, that Emile Durkheim and Max Weber wrote the classics of sociology, bringing into focus such modern concerns as charisma, bureaucratization, the disenchantment of a world without religion, and, above all, the personal dilemmas of anomie and alienation.

We are the children of that quarter century, 1890 to 1914, crowded as it was with men of genius, with startling new ways of seeing the world, and with radical innovations in literary and artistic techniques. One of the participants in that heady time, Virginia Woolf, recorded its impress in her inimitable manner: "In or about December 1910," she said not long after the war, "human character changed."

But what of World War I? How do we leap across *that* abyss? For if there is agreement on any event in recent history, it is that that war was the end of an epoch, a knife wound from which there was no recovery. "The war," Wyndham Lewis wrote in 1937, "is such a tremendous landmark that locally it imposes itself upon our computations of time like the birth of Christ. We say 'pre-war' and 'post-war' rather as we say B.C. or A.D." Many, recalling or reconstructing that vanished world, mourned it as a lost paradise. As John Maynard Keynes wrote in 1919:

What an extraordinary episode in the economic progress of man that age was which came to an end in August 1914! The greater part of the population, it is true, worked hard and lived at a low standard of comfort, yet were, to all appearances, reasonably contented with this lot. But escape was possible, for any man of capacity or character at all exceeding the average, into the middle and upper classes, for whom life offered, at a low cost and with the least trouble, conveniences, comforts, and amenities beyond the compass of the richest and most powerful monarchs of other ages. The inhabitant of London could order by telephone, sipping

"How the Modern World Began," by Peter Gay, *Horizon,* Spring 1973. Reprinted with the permission of the author.

his morning tea in bed, the various products of the whole earth, in such quantity as he might see fit, and reasonably expect their early delivery upon his doorstep. . . . He could secure forthwith, if he wished it, cheap and comfortable means of transit to any country or climate without passport or other formality, could despatch his servant to the neighbouring office of a bank for such supply of the precious metals as might seem convenient, and could then proceed abroad to foreign quarters, without knowledge of their religion, language, or customs, bearing coined wealth upon his person, and would consider himself greatly aggrieved and much surprised at the least interference. But, most important of all, he regarded this state of affairs as normal, certain, and permanent, except in the direction of further improvement, and any deviation from it as aberrant, scandalous, and avoidable. The projects and politics of militarism and imperialism, of racial and cultural rivalries, of monopolies, restrictions, and exclusion, which were to play the serpent to this paradise, were little more than the amusements of his daily newspaper, and appeared to exercise almost no influence at all on the ordinary course of social and economic life, the internationalisation of which was nearly complete in practice.

Yet there were skeptics, observers who acknowledged Keynes's facts but placed the accents quite differently; they were inclined to see militarism, imperialism, racial rivalries, and the rest, not as amusements, but as insidious and growing menaces. Kandinsky glumly contemplated what he thought to be the spiritual emptiness of the age. In 1926 G. Lowes Dickinson called the decade from 1904 to 1914 "the international anarchy." And V. S. Pritchett, remembering the "Sunday processions of unemployed marching with their banners," has testified: "When I read books of nostalgia about Edwardian times, I find I remember nothing but the English meanness."

Such doubts emerged very early. On August 10, 1914, when the war was a week old, Henry James wrote an anguished letter to a friend. "Black and hideous to me is the tragedy that gathers, and I'm sick beyond cure to have

lived on to see it," he wrote. "You and I, the ornaments of our generation, should have been spared this wreck of our belief that through the long years we had seen civilization grow and the worst become impossible. The tide that bore us along was then all the while moving to *this* as its grand Niagara— yet what a blessing we didn't know it. It seems to me to *undo* everything, everything that was ours, in the most horrible retroactive way . . ." All the past, he added later, "with this hideous card all the while up its sleeve, seems now a long treachery, an unthinkable humbug."

These conflicting testimonies only deepen the paradox. If the period before the war was sick, a Heartbreak House near collapse, then how could it have produced such magnificent ideas and works of art? And if it was essentially healthy, how did its ideas and its art persist across that gulf, the war?

The first step toward an answer is to take a second look. There was nothing sick about modern artists rebelling against the stuffiness of the academy and the dictatorship of the respectable: their rebellion was vigorous and, though apt to be frantic, more often cheerful than despairing. There is nothing sad about the exuberant color of the fauves, or the inventive experiments of the cubists, or the deftly sketched nudes of the *Brücke* fraternity. However limited its artistic merits, the very term "art nouveau" is significant. It was called *Jugendstil* in Germany, where youth was almost a cult. The young were a favorite subject, and avid consumers, of the new in literature and art. In their manifestoes and their letters, the painters of the *Brücke* group— Kirchner, Schmidt-Rottluff, Heckel— praised their own work for its strength, its originality and, above all, its youthfulness. When Gabriele Münter came to Munich in 1901 and found the *Jugendstil* in aggressive combat with the "old naturalism," she hailed this as "a great time of artistic renewal." And

Leonard Woolf, remembering these same years in his own country, thought of "this period of our early manhood" as "an age of revolution. We found ourselves living in the springtime of a conscious revolt against the social, political, religious, moral, intellectual, and artistic institutions, beliefs, and standards of our fathers and grandfathers. We felt ourselves to be the second generation in this exciting movement of men and ideas. The battle, which was against what for short one may call Victorianism, had not yet been won, and what was so exciting was our feeling that we ourselves were part of the revolution, that victory or defeat depended to some small extent upon what we did, said, or wrote."

Later generations of the young were to turn to communism, fascism, or defeatism because they had "grown up under the shadow of defeat in the past and the menace of defeat in the future." But Leonard Woolf's generation, around 1900, was weighed down by no "shadow of past defeat; the omens were all favourable. . . . We were in the van of the builders of a new society which should be free, rational, civilised, pursuing truth and beauty. It was all tremendously exhilarating." Writers and painters borrowed freely from scientists and philosophers. Freud began to make an indelible impression on experimental novelists and surrealist artists; discoveries in physics were a stimulus to the neoimpressionists, an inspiration to the cubists, and a problem for Kandinsky. The city and the machine, two symbols (or symptoms) of modern civilization, aroused the most divergent responses. For every D. H. Lawrence, who disliked the city, there was a T. S. Eliot to record its ambiguous fascination; for every proponent of arts and crafts, there was a philosopher, or a painter, in love with the machine. And success did not necessarily spoil the avant-garde: artists like Monet continued to paint masterpieces even after they were recognized. The great innovators of the age were by no means doomed to permanent neglect, poverty, and alienation; many of them found that their experiments brought them private pleasure and public recognition.

With these qualifications in mind, we can approach the years between 1890 and 1914 a little more closely. The first thing that strikes us is that they were a rule-breaking time. This is not to say that the age that preceded this one had no rule breakers, nor is it to say that there were no areas in social life in which discipline did not stiffen; as manufacturers and organized workers came to understand the new industrial age, their conduct became more purposeful and organized. But in general the 1890's and the years leading up to the First World War were a time of loosening bonds.

The nineteenth century, beginning with the defeat of Napoleon, had been essentially a rule-making age. The period had its rebels, its romantics, and even its revolutionaries; but while they succeeded in the bookstalls, in the drawing rooms, and on the stage, they failed in the cabinets, in the universities, and in the streets. The figure most characteristic of the years between 1815 and 1890 was probably Metternich, the man who devoted his life to containing the energies of innovation. His best-known successors—Disraeli, Bismarck, Thiers —shared Metternich's aims, though they varied his methods; their policies were efforts at a modern conservatism, attempts to solve, mitigate, or, failing that, paper over, social problems, while preserving as much of the past as possible. Middle-class gentility, the target of so much scorn, was simply another aspect of this search for order, of the need to control dangerous, irrational forces. Novelists, Henry James complained, distrusted "any but the most guarded treatment of the great relation between men and women, the constant world-renewal." "Love-making"—it is James's word—was quite simply left out. There were, he said, "many sources of interest neglected—whole categories of manners, whole corpuscular classes

and provinces, museums of character and condition, unvisited; while it is on the other hand mistakenly taken for granted that safety lies in all the loose and thin material that keeps reappearing in forms at once ready-made and sadly worse for wear."

Typically, James, though circumlocutory, is penetrating; what was at work in Biedermeier, or Victorianism, was not a deliberate policy of suppression but a search for safety. Liberal ideas, like nationalism, were pressed into service by the old order. The French and Industrial revolutions, the population explosion, the increase in migration, the growth of cities—these were demons to be stuffed back into the bottle.

Then, around 1890, the bottle exploded. Dissent itself was hardly new. For many years Bohemians and dandies had derided the bourgeoisie, lofty litterateurs had battled the philistines, revolutionaries had published inflammatory tracts or comprehensive treatises. The abuse with which the avantgarde belabored established society went back to Flaubert and before him to the romantics. For a dizzying moment in 1848, radicals had disturbed the even flow of time. But they had been defeated, and, by and large, forgotten.

Their time came, often posthumously, in the last decade of the nineteenth century. The year 1890 is a useful dividing line; Bismarck was dismissed in March, and with him went the last check on the ambitious policies he had initiated but kept under control. In 1890, in *Axël,* Villiers de l'Isle-Adam flung his defiance into the face of the bourgeoisie: "Living?" says one doomed protagonist to the other, "living? The servants will do that for us." In 1890, too, Ibsen published *Hedda Gabler,* and in the following year, George Bernard Shaw had to defend him against a hysterical chorus of disapproval. The epithets Shaw cites eloquently testify that Ibsen had of-

fended established society to its very bones. Otherwise, why did reviewers reach for expressions suggestive of the anal and sexual function? Ibsen's *Ghosts* was "an open drain; a loathsome sore unbandaged; a dirty act done publicly.... Candid foulness; crapulous stuff.... nastiness and malodorousness laid on thickly as with a trowel." And those who enjoyed Ibsen's plays were nearly all "nasty minded people who find the discussion of nasty subjects to their taste in exact proportion to their nastiness." They were "the sexless.... The unwomanly woman, the unsexed females.... Effeminate men and male women."

It was in this charged atmosphere that Stefan George published his first book, and the German drama, amid general scandal, broke away from the well-made play and safe naturalism. Frank Wedekind published his drama *Frühlings Erwachen* in 1891; candidly sympathetically, almost lyrically, it dealt with the sexual awakening of puberty, including homoeroticism. In England, the great combat between art and life, long in the air, was launched in the same year, with Oscar Wilde's *Picture of Dorian Gray* and the bitter debate that followed it.

In addition to producing its own revolutionaries, the decade of the 1890's drew energy from the neglected and despised past. The avant-garde, more than other men, chose their ancestors, and nothing perhaps is more instructive about them than the ancestors they chose. The 1890's revived Baudelaire, whom Huysmans, the pioneer, had hailed as a master as early as 1884: Baudelaire, as T. S. Eliot was to observe in the 1920's, "had something to do with the 'nineties.' " The 1890's brought recognition, at least among young painters, to Van Gogh, who committed suicide in 1890. And the 1890's discovered Nietzsche, who lost his reason in 1889 and then sank into helpless silence.

Politics were stirring with the same excitement. The dismissal of Bismarck launched the German empire into international complications from which there was to be no return, and brought an end to Germany's antisocialist legislation. In the following year the newly legal Social Democratic Party drafted its fateful Erfurt program, which committed it to revolution precisely when it was moving toward parliamentary tactics. In England strikes and intelligent agitation produced a novel phenomenon, the "new unionism," which enlisted many thousands of unskilled laborers under the trade union banner.

These memorable names and dates, pregnant with the future, do not add up to unbroken triumphs for the innovators. The Establishment was by no means ready to yield up what it had so laboriously amassed; victories for the moderns were often followed by defeats, and in some areas there was continuous disaster. Two spectacular trials of the 1890's go far to demonstrate the tenacity of the old order under fire. The Dreyfus case almost shattered the Third Republic—that precarious bargain with modernity. And the Wilde case almost ruined the avant-garde in England; if a select band remained loyal to the fallen king of wit, the general public took the taming of Wilde, in 1895, as an invitation to act out long-inhibited aggressions and to exact revenge upon those who had trampled on its pieties. It was as though by brutalizing the hapless Wilde respectable England could bring under control sensual impulses at once fascinating and threatening.

"The Book World," Ford Madox Ford remarked of the period preceding the trial, "was then electric. Books were everywhere . . . It was good to be a writer in England. And it is to be remembered that, as far as that particular body was concerned, the rewards were earned. They were skillful and earnest writers. They were an immense improvement on their predecessors. They were genuine men of letters. . . . But all that went with the trial of Wilde." Oscar Wilde "brought down the *Yellow*

Book group and most of the other lyrists of a London that for its year or two had been a nest of singing birds. . . . Poets died or fled to other climes . . . prosateurs were fished out of the Seine or reformed and the great public said: 'Thank heavens, we need not read any more poetry!' "

Despite these setbacks, the period between 1890 and 1914 was one of immense fertility. There was an intense desire to push back frontiers, to dig down to fundamentals, and to capture truth behind cant. The ideals and methods of the innovators, as I have said, varied enormously. The futurist painters who made a fetish of movement and the machine were in a minority; secularists like Gropius and Marinetti were outnumbered by mystics like Yeats, Marc, Mondrian, and Klee. In 1910, in his preface to the prospectus for the second exhibition of the *Neue Künstlervereinigung,* Kandinsky sought to resolve the "conflict between spirit and matter," which, he wrote, afflicted "tormented souls"; he wanted to "speak of mystery in terms of mystery," while others sought lucidity above all. Statesmen, too, acknowledged inner confusion. In May, 1891, Lord Salisbury, then prime minister, attempted to explain how it had come to pass that Great Britain had acquired a vast new empire in defiance of its traditional morals and practices. "I do not exactly know the cause of this sudden revolution," he confessed. "But there it is."

What unity the time possesses, then, lies in a certain concentration, a self-awareness. The earlier rejections of Baudelaire, Kierkegaard, Marx, Nietzsche, and Dostoevsky seem emblematic of decades vital enough to produce such prophets, and yet secure enough to scorn them. Now their time had come. "The real forms of things," the Belgian architect Henry van de Velde recalled, "were covered over. In that period the revolt against

the falsification of forms and against the past was a moral revolt."

It was a time when the philosophy of the English idealists, still dominant, displeased young rebels as the kind of bargain with error that decent men seemed willing to strike. Santayana and Dewey were starting to call for "reformation in philosophy"; Wittgenstein was beginning the ruminations that would lead to the most radical critique of language and of philosophy itself. With all due respect, the rebels could not swallow philosophers like Francis Bradley, who, Bertrand Russell wrote, "keep a shadow of religion, too little for comfort, but quite enough to ruin their systems intellectually." The day not only produced brilliant scapegraces, like Maynard Keynes and Lytton Strachey, but secular saints as well: when Russell met G. E. Moore, then a freshman at Cambridge, he found him "beautiful and slim, with a look almost of inspiration, and with an intellect as deeply passionate as Spinoza's. He had a kind of exquisite purity. I have never but once succeeded in making him tell a lie, and that was by a subterfuge. 'Moore,' I said, 'do you *always* speak the truth?' 'No,' he replied. I believe this to be the only lie he has ever told."

The sciences of man and society registered the same impatience with compromise, the same exhilarated sense of a new age at hand. The "present day," T. S. Eliot noted shortly after the end of the war, "began, in a sense, with Tylor and a few German anthropologists; since then we have acquired sociology and social psychology, we have watched the clinics of Ribot and Janet, we have read books from Vienna and heard a discourse of Bergson; a philosophy arose at Cambridge; social emancipation crawled abroad; our historical knowledge has of course increased; and we have a curious Freudian-social-mystical-rationalistic-higher-critical interpretation of the Classics and what used to be called the Scriptures." However ungracious Eliot's tone, it was a great age for sociology and psychology, both sciences devoted to the search for reality behind appearances.

The first volume of Sir James Frazer's *Golden Bough* appeared in 1890—that date again!—and while his work soon showed serious deficiencies, his collector's passion brought together materials from which all religion might be judged—not polemically, but scientifically. Thorstein Veblen's first and still most famous book, *The Theory of the Leisure Class,* published in 1899, laid bare the predatory captains of industry as barbaric chieftains and pronounced the utility of uselessness with an irony so irresistible that his serious anthropological intentions were quite overshadowed. Max Weber, Robert Michels, and Graham Wallas analyzed social conduct down to the irrational roots of behavior. In his *Human Nature in Politics,* Wallas expressed hope for a quantitative science of politics and added that the inquiry into society typical of the age was not a revolt against, but a higher form of, positivism.

This judgment finds support in Emile Durkheim's work, which falls entirely within this period. In his last major book, *The Elementary Forms of the Religious Life,* published in 1912, Durkheim insisted, over and over again, that sociology is a science, a "positive science," whose task, like that of all sciences, is explanation. Subjective speculations are without value; the sociologist must offer testable hypotheses which the candid adoption of determinism will help him to formulate. The student of "social facts" must, in a word, free himself from primitive methods and preconceptions and resort to the laborious methods of the natural sciences. "This alone will dispel the darkness of men's ignorance."

Among the scientists of man it was Freud who pushed the scientific search for the hidden dimension to its logical conclusion—the unconscious. Freud thought himself a conquistador, a modern of moderns, destined to uncover mysteries of the mind that shame had hitherto kept inaccessible. The unconscious itself was the boldest of his conquests, infantile sexuality the most disturbing content of that unconscious, and his claim that man's mental and behavioral furniture—his moral ideas, sexual tastes, facial tics, slips of the pen—cohere as a single world, the most immediate scientific gain. Freud's excavations were extraordinarily painful to the men of his time and after; they first ignored and then denounced him, and finally tried to disarm him by trivializing his radical conclusions. And as painful as his conclusions were to his culture, they were even more painful to Freud himself. He wrung his first masterpiece, *The Interpretation of Dreams,* from himself with great reluctance, and used his private traumas and dreams as evidence only because he found them indispensable. He wrote that in one of his dreams he recognized "the self-analysis which I was performing, as it were, by publishing my present book on dreams, I actually found so painful that I postponed the printing of the completed manuscript for more than a year." The book, he wrote, was "a piece of my self-analysis, my reaction to my father's death—that is, to the most important event, the most poignant loss, in a man's life."

It would be easy to go on listing rebels intent on redrawing the map of knowledge and assaulting respectability: sexual reformers, political playwrights, innovating architects, experimental painters and sculptors. Man's very sense of truth was changing. Chekhov, with his distaste for fine writing and artificial plots, best embodies this change. "Literature," he insisted, "is called artistic when it depicts life as it actually is. Its aim is absolute and honest truth." Among Chekhov's allies was James Joyce, attempting, as he did, to free literature from lying "parables." Oscar Wilde, subversive as he was, sim-ply reversed the signs of moral approval and disapproval. Far more subversive than Wilde were respectable social scientists like Durkheim, who defined a crime as a "normal" social activity forbidden by law, or a respectable physician like Freud, who refused to draw hard and fast lines between healthy and neurotic conduct, or to differentiate between normal and perverted sexuality.

I want to add to this partial roster only one group, the English war poets. These poets were single-mindedly intent on expressing the truth. Wilfred Owen spoke for a generation in the much-cited preface he wrote to his poems: "All a poet can do today is warn. That is why the true Poets must be truthful." This search for truthfulness was complicated by the poets' problematic relation to their public; but it was eased by the glaring defects of popular poetry. The solution might be elusive, but the target was highly visible, and immensely vulnerable. As T. S. Eliot remembered: "The situation of poetry in 1909 or 1910 was stagnant to a degree difficult for any young poet of today to imagine." Bad poetry sold well; it secured general approval and favorable reviews. And bad poetry was *bad.* Consider Alfred Austin's "Why England is Conservative":

Because of our dear Mother, the fair Past,
On whom twin Hope and Memory safely lean,
And from whose fostering wisdom none shall wean
Their love and faith, while love and faith shall last:
Mother of happy homes and Empire vast,
Of hamlets meek, and many a proud demesne,
Blue spires of cottage smoke 'mong woodlands green,
And comely altars where no stone is cast.
And shall we barter these for gaping Throne,
Dismantled towers, mean plots without a tree,
A herd of hinds too equal to be free. . . .

Austin, England's poet laureate, also wrote sacrifice poems like "Who would not die for England!" a refrain he called "this great thought." Such martial vigor, of course, was part of a muscular craze, part Social Darwinism, part boredom, part innocent nostalgia, that nfected much of society before 1914—and even after: Laurence Binyon could, n his *The Fourth of August,* hail the war as an ennobling deliverance:

The cares we hugged drop out of vision;
Our hearts with deeper thoughts dilate.
We step from days of sour division
Into the grandeur of our fate.

Walter Raleigh, the literary historian, was one of many to cheer the boys on. "The air is better to breathe in than it has been for years. I'm glad I lived to see it, and sick that I'm not in it." As late as November, 1915, Siegfried Sassoon showed Robert Graves some patriotic lines he had written. "This was before Siegfried had been in the trenches," Graves comments. "I told him, in my old-soldier manner, that he would soon change his style." And so, of course, he did.

From this perspective, a war hawk like Theodore Roosevelt emerges as by no means an isolated figure. "We must have war," he told a friend about the time of the Spanish-American War. "The old people had years fighting in the Civil War. The younger ones have had none, so must have it now." In England, what Arnold Bennett contemptuously called "the sea-and-slaughter school" kept up the barrage. In 1912 Ezra Pound predicted that the poetry of the next decade would probably "move against poppy-cock," and would "be harder and saner" with its "force" springing from "its truth"; his prediction seemed like wishful thinking even after the war began to claim its vic-

tims. For Sir Henry Newbolt, war had long been the continuation of sport by other means:

The sand of the desert is sodden red,—
    Red with the wreck of a square that broke;—
The Gatling's jammed and the Colonel dead,
    And the regiment blind with dust and smoke.
The river of death has brimmed its banks,
    And England's far, and Honour a name,
But the voice of a schoolboy rallies the ranks:
    "Play up! Play up! and play the game!"

It was as though in direct answer to this hearty invocation of upper-middle-class stress on sport that Wilfred Owen wrote his *Disabled:*

One time he liked a blood-smear down his leg,
After the matches, carried shoulder-high.
It was after football, when he'd drunk a peg,
He thought he'd better join.—He wonders why.
Someone had said he'd look a god in kilts,
That's why; and may be, too, to please his Meg;
Aye, that was it, to please the giddy jilts
He asked to join. He didn't have to beg;
Smiling they wrote his lie; aged nineteen
    years. . . .
Some cheered him home, but not as crowds
    cheer Goal.
Only a solemn man who brought him fruits
Thanked him; and then inquired about his soul.

Now, he will spend a few sick years in Institutes,
And do what things the rules consider wise,
And take whatever pity they may dole.
To-night he noticed how the women's eyes
Passed from him to the strong men that
    were whole.
How cold and late it is! Why don't they come
And put him into bed? Why don't they come?

War was hell, and this war more hellish than most. Instead of ending the need to find and tell the truth, the war made the need more desperate than ever.

In quoting Owen, I have stepped beyond the period between 1890 and 1914. This was deliberate, for I want to

suggest that the war was not merely an abyss, but a bridge as well. Doubtless, for all who participated in it directly or witnessed it from afar, World War I was a searing experience. It invaded Proust's *Remembrance of Things Past,* then still in progress; it transformed Thomas Mann's politics from cultural conservatism to a sympathetic interest in democracy; it gave poets like T. S. Eliot new grounds for despair and provided artists like George Grosz with new subjects for satire. By decimating the emerging elite of the West, the war brought grief too deep to heal and hatreds too powerful to soothe. It caused political, economic, and social upheavals of unprecedented scope, and simultaneously killed the very youth that might have coped with them.

But at the same time—and this is less well known than the terrible truths just mentioned—the war was a kind of encapsulated crisis. While, after November, 1918, nothing seemed the same, much in fact returned to an earlier condition. Harding was not the only spokesman for normalcy. Expressionists remained expressionists; Picasso remained Picasso. Proust's style did not change. Shaken but determined, painters and novelists went back to work. That is why, understandable though his anguish may be, Henry James was wrong to dismiss the years before the war as a gigantic fraud. They were a dazzling time. We have not yet exhausted the ideas and techniques of that time. It made us what we are today.

SARAJEVO

The End of Innocence

After fifty years of explanations, it is still difficult to see why a political murder in a remote corner of the Balkans should have set off a war that changed the world forever

Edmund Stillman

A few minutes before eleven o'clock in the morning, Sunday, June 28, 1914, on the river embankment in Sarajevo, Gavrilo Princip shot the archduke Franz Ferdinand and brought a world crashing down.

After fifty years and so much pain, Sarajevo is worth a pilgrimage, but to go there is a disappointing and somehow unsettling experience: this dusty Balkan city, in its bowl of dark and barren hills, is an unlikely setting for grand tragedy. Blood and suffering are endemic to the Balkans, but Sarajevo is so mean and poor. Why should an age have died *here*? Why did the double murder of an undistinguished archduke and his morganatic wife touch off a world war, when so many graver pretexts had somehow been accommodated—or ignored—in the preceding quarter-century? It was an act that no one clearly remembers today; indeed, its details were forgotten by the time the war it engendered was six months old. Nowadays, even in Sarajevo, few pilgrims search out the place where Princip stood that morning. Nearby, on the river embankment, only a dingy little museum commemorates the lives and passions of the seven tubercular boys (of whom Princip was only one) who plotted one small blow for freedom, but who brought on a universal catastrophe. Within the museum are faded photographs, a few pitiable relics of the conspirators, a fly-specked visitors' book. A single shabby attendant guards the memorials to a political passion that seems, well, naïve to our more cynical age. "Here, in this historic place," the modest inscription runs, "Gavrilo Princip was the initiator of liberty, on the day of Saint Vitus, the 28th of June, 1914." That is all, and few visitors to present-day Yugoslavia stop to read it.

There is so much that goes unanswered, even though the facts of the case are so well known: how the failing Hapsburgs, impelled by an unlucky taste for adventure, had seized Bosnia and Herzegovina from the Turks and aggravated the racial imbalance of the Austro-Hungarian Empire; how the southern Slavs within the Empire felt themselves oppressed and increasingly demanded freedom; how the ambitious little hill kingdom of Serbia saw a chance to establish a South-Slavic hegemony over the Balkans; and how Czarist Russia. itself near ruin, plotted with its client Serbia to turn the Austro-Hungarian southern flank. But there is so much more that needs to be taken into account: how Franz Ferdinand, the aged emperor Franz Josef's nephew, became his heir by default (Crown Prince Rudolf had committed suicide at Mayerling; Uncle Maximilian, Napoleon III's pawn, had been executed in Mexico; Franz Ferdinand's father, a pilgrim to the Holy Land, had died—most improbably—from drinking the waters of the Jordan); how the new heir—stiff, autocratic, and unapproachable, but implausibly wed in irenic middle-class marriage to the not-quite-acceptable Sophie Chotek—sensed the danger to the Empire and proposed a policy that would have given his future Slav subjects most of what they demanded; how the Serbian nationalists were driven to panic. and how the secret society of jingoes known as "The Black Hand" plotted Franz Ferdinand's death; how seven boys were recruited to do the deed, and how one of them. Gavrilo Princip, on the morning of June 28, 1914. shot Franz Ferdinand and his Sophie dead.

But why the mindlessness of the war that followed, the blundering diplomacies and reckless plans that made disaster inevitable once hostilities broke out? It is all so grotesque: great and shattering consequences without proportionate causes. When the inferno of 1914–18 ended at last, the broken survivors asked themselves the same question, seeking to comprehend the terrible thing that had happened. To have endured the inferno without a justifying reason—to be forced to admit that a war of such terror and scope had been only a blind, insouciant madness—was intolerable; it was easier to think of it as an unworthy or a wrongful cause than as a ghastly, titanic joke on history. After the event Winston Churchill wrote: "But there was a strange temper in the air. Unsatisfied by material prosperity the nations turned restlessly towards strife internal or external. . . . Almost one might think the world wished to suffer." Yet if this opinion had been widely accepted, it would have been a judgment on human nature too terrible to endure. And so a new mythology of the war grew up—a postwar mythology of materialist cynicism almost as contrived as the wartime propaganda fictions of the "Beast of Berlin" or the wholesale slaughter of Belgian nuns. It embraced the myths of the munitions manufacturers who had plotted a war they were, in fact, helpless to control; of Machiavellian, imperialist diplomacies; of an ever-spiraling arms race, when in fact the naval race between England and Germany had, if anything, somewhat abated by 1914. But no single cause, or combination of such causes, will explain the First World War. Neither the Germans, the Austrians, the Russians, the French, the Italians, nor the British went to war to fulfill a grand ambition—to conquer Europe, or the world, or to promote an ideology. They did not even seek economic dominion through war. The somber truth is that Western civilization, for a hundred years without a major war and absorbed in a social and technological revolution—progress, in short—turned on itself in a paroxysm of slaughter.

On both sides the actual war aims, so far as they were articulated at all, were distressingly small. Merely to humiliate Serbia and to "avenge" a man whose death few particularly regretted, the Austro-Hungarian Empire began a war which cost it seven million casualties and destroyed its fabric; to prevent a senile Austria-Hungary from gaining a precarious (and inevitably short-lived) advantage in the poverty-stricken western Balkans, imperial Russia lost more than nine million men—killed, wounded, or taken prisoner. To support an ally, and to avoid the public humiliation and anxiety of canceling a mobilization order once issued, Germany lost almost two million dead, Alsace-Lorraine, a third of Poland, and its growing sphere of influence in Central Europe and the Middle East. England, to keep its word to Belgium, committed eight million men to the struggle, and lost nearly one million dead. France, to counter its German enemy and to avenge the peace treaty it had accepted in 1870, endured losses of 15 per cent of its population and initiated a process of political decline from which it may not yet have emerged.

This was the price of World War I. Two shots were fired in Sarajevo, and for more than four years thereafter half the world bled. At least ten million soldiers were killed, and twenty million were wounded or made prisoners. But the real legacy of the war was something less tangible—a quality of despair, a chaos, and a drift toward political barbarism that is with us to this day. We have not recovered yet.

In the summer of 1914 the armies marched out to Armageddon in their frogged tunics, red Zouave trousers, and gilded helmets. Five months later they were crouching in the mud, louse-ridden, half-starved, frozen, and bewildered by the enormity of it all. "Lost in the midst of two million madmen," the Frenchman Céline was to write of the war, "all of them heroes, at large and armed to the teeth! . . . sniping, plotting, flying, kneeling, digging, taking cover, wheeling, detonating, shut in on earth as in an asylum cell; intending to wreck everything in it, Germany, France, the whole world, every breathing thing; destroying, more ferocious than a pack of mad dogs and adoring their own madness (which no dog does), a hundred, a thousand times fiercer than a thousand dogs and so infinitely more vicious! . . . Clearly it seemed to me that I had embarked on a crusade that was nothing short of an apocalypse."

The savagery of the war and the incompetence of the military commanders quickly became a commonplace. The generals proved wholly unprepared for quick-firing artillery, machine guns, field entrenchments, railroad and motor transport, and the existence of a continuous front in place of the isolated battlefield of earlier centuries. They were helpless in the face of a combat too vast, too impersonal, too technical, and too deadly to comprehend. Quite aside from their intellectual shortcomings, one is struck by the poverty of their emotional response. Kill and kill was their motto. No one in command was daunted by the bloodletting, it seems. No more imaginative battle tactic could be devised than to push strength against strength—attacking at the enemy's strongest point on the theory that one side's superior *élan* would ultimately yield up victory. Verdun in 1916 cost the French some 350,000 men and the Germans nearly as many; the German penetration was five miles, gained in a little more than three months. The Somme cost the Allies more than 600,000 casualties, the Germans almost half a million; the offensive gained a sector thirty miles wide and a maximum of seven deep in four and a half months.

That it was an insane waste of lives the combatants realized early, but no one knew what to do. The waste of honor, love, courage, and selfless devotion was the cruelest of all: at the first Battle of Ypres, in the opening days of the war, the young German schoolboy volunteers "came on like men possessed," a British historian records. They were sent in against picked battalions of British regulars who shot them to pieces on the slopes of Ypres with the trained rifle fire for which they were famous. The incident has gone down in German history as the *Kindermord von Ypern*—"the Slaughter of the Innocents at Ypres." No other phrase will do.

It was a strange world that died that summer of 1914. For ninety-nine years there had been peace in Europe: apart from the Crimean War, only eighteen months of all that time—according to Karl Polanyi—had been spent in desultory and petty European wars. Men apparently believed that peace was man's normal condition—and on those occasions when peace was momentarily broken, war was expected to be comprehensible and salutary, an ultimately useful Darwinian selection of the fittest to lead. To us, after the profuse horrors of mustard gas, trench warfare, Buchenwald, the Blitz, Coventry, and Hiroshima, to name only a few, this is incomprehensible naïveté. But that we have been disillusioned and have awaked to our condition is due to the events of 1914–18.

In the nineteenth century the belief in progress—automatic progress—went deep. The American anthropologist Lewis Morgan had sounded a note of self-confident hope for the entire age when he said, in 1877, "Democracy in government, brotherhood in society, equality in rights and privileges, and universal education, foreshadow the next higher plane of society to which experience, intelligence and knowledge are steadily tending." The emphasis here was on *steadily*: nothing could stop the onward march of mankind.

And the progress was very real. The age that died in 1914 was a brilliant one—so extravagant in its intellectual and aesthetic endowments that we who have come after can hardly believe in its reality. It was a comfortable age—for a considerable minority, at least—but it was more than a matter of Sunday walks in the Wienerwald, or country-house living, or a good five-cent cigar. It was an imposing age in the sciences, in the arts, even in forms of government. Men had done much and had risen high in the hundred years that came to an end that summer. From Napoleon's downfall in 1815 to the outbreak of war in 1914, the trend had been up.

"As happy as God in France," even the Germans used to say. For France these were the years of the *belle époque*, when all the world's artists came there to learn: Picasso and Juan Gris from Spain, Chagall and Archipenko from Russia, Piet Mondrian from the Netherlands, Brancusi from Romania, Man Ray and Max Weber from America, Modigliani from Italy. All made up the "School of Paris," a name which meant nothing but that in this Paris of the *avant-guerre* the world of the arts was at home.

"Paris drank the talents of the world," wrote the poet-impresario of those years, Guillaume Apollinaire. Debussy, Ravel, and Stravinsky composed music there. Nijinsky and Diaghilev were raising the modern ballet to new heights of brilliance and creativity. The year 1913 was, as Roger Shattuck puts it in *The Banquet Years*, the *annus mirabilis* of French literature: Proust's *Du Côté de chez Swann*, Alain-Fournier's *Le Grand Meaulnes*, Apollinaire's *Alcools*, Roger Martin du Gard's *Jean Barois*, Valéry Larbaud's *A. O. Barnabooth*, Péguy's *L'Argent*, Barrès's *La Colline inspirée*, and Colette's *L'Entrave* and *L'Envers du music-hall* appeared that year. "It is almost as if the war *had* to come in order to put an end to an extravaganza that could not have been sustained at this level." That was Paris.

Vienna was another great mongrel city that, like Paris, drank up talent—in this case the talents of a congeries of Austrians, Magyars, Czechs, Slovaks, Poles, Slovenes, Croats, Serbs, Jews, Turks, Transylvanians, and Gypsies. On Sunday mornings gentlemen strolled in the Prater ogling the cocottes; they rode the giant red Ferris wheel and looked out over the palaces and parks of the city; or they spent the morning at the coffeehouse, arguing pointlessly and interminably. It was a pleasure-loving city, but an intellectual one, too. The names of the men who walked Vienna's streets up to the eve of the war are stunning in their brilliance: Gustav Mahler, Sigmund Freud, Sandor Ferenczi, Ernst Mach, Béla Bartók, Rainer Maria Rilke, Franz Kafka, Robert Musil, Arthur Schnitzler, Hugo von Hofmannsthal, Richard Strauss, Stefan Zweig—these hardly begin to exhaust the list. (There were more sinister names, too. Adolf Hitler lived in Vienna between 1909 and 1913, an out-of-work, shabby *Bettgeher*—a daytime renter of other people's beds—absorbing the virulent anti-Semitism that charged the Viennese social atmosphere; so did Leon Trotsky, who spent his evenings listening contemptuously to the wranglings of the Social Democratic politicians at the Café Central.)

England was still gilded by the afterglow of the Edwardian Age: the British Empire straddled the earth, controlling more than a quarter of the surface of the globe. If the realities of trade had begun to shift, and if British industry and British naval supremacy were faced with a growing challenge from the United States and Hohenzollern Germany, the vast British overseas investments tended to hide the fact. England had its intellectual brilliance, too: these were the years of Hardy, Kipling, Shaw, Wells, the young D. H. Lawrence and the young Wyndham Lewis, Arnold Bennett, Gilbert Murray, A. E. Housman, H. H. Munro (Saki)—who would die in the war—and many others, like Rupert Brooke, Robert Graves, Siegfried Sassoon, and Wilfred Owen, who were as yet hardly known.

As for the Kaiser's Germany, it is melancholy to reflect that if Wilhelm II himself, that summer in 1914, had only waited —five years, ten years, or twenty—Germany might have had it all. But Wilhelm was shrewd, treacherous, and hysterical, a chronic bully whose mother had never loved him. His habitual style of discourse was the neurotic bluster of a small man who has had the bad luck to be called upon to stomp about in a giant's boots. Wilhelm II lived all his life in the shadow of "the Great Emperor," his grandfather Wilhelm I, who had created a united Greater Germany with the help of his brilliant chancellor, Prince Otto von Bismarck; he wanted to make the world stand in awe of him, but he did not know, precisely, how to go about it.

If only he could have been patient: Austria-Hungary was really a German satellite; the Balkans and the Middle East looked to Berlin; Germany's industrial hegemony on the continent was secure, and might soon have knocked Britain from her commanding place in the world's trade. By 1914, fourteen Germans had won Nobel Prizes in the sciences (by contrast, their nearest competitors, the French, had won only nine).

But the lesson is something more than a chapbook homily on patience. Wilhelm's personal anxiety merely expressed in microcosm the larger German anxiety about the nation's place in the world. Something strange lay beneath the stolid prosperity of the Hohenzollern Age—a surfeit with peace, a lust for violence, a belief in death, an ominous mystique of war. "Without war the world would quickly sink into materialism," the elder Von Moltke, chief of the German General Staff, had proclaimed in 1880; and he, his nephew the younger Von Moltke, and the caste of Prussian militarists they represented could presumably save the world from that tawdry fate. But this belief in war was not a monopoly of the Right: even Thomas Mann, spokesman of German humanism, could ask, in 1914, "Is not war a purification, a liberation, an enormous hope?" adding complacently, "Is not peace an element in civil corruption?"

There had been peace in the world for too long. From Berlin, in the spring of 1914, Colonel House wrote to Woodrow Wilson: "The whole of Germany is charged with electricity. Everybody's nerves are tense. It only requires a spark to set the whole thing off." People were saying: "Better a horrible ending than a horror without end." In expressing this spirit of violence and disorientation, Germany was merely precocious. It expressed a universal European malaise.

The malaise was evident everywhere—in the new cults of political violence; in the new philosophies of men like Freud, Nietzsche, and Pareto, who stressed the unconscious and the irrational, and who exposed the lying pretensions of middle-class values and conventions; and in the sense of doom that permeated the avant-garde arts of the prewar years. Typical of this spirit of rebellion was the manifesto set forth in 1910 by the Italian Futurist painters: it declared that "all forms of imitation should be held in contempt and that all forms of originality glorified; that we should rebel against the tyranny of the words 'harmony' and 'good taste' . . . ; that

a clean sweep be made of all stale and threadbare subject matter in order to express the vortex of modern life—a life of steel, pride, fever, and speed . . ."

In England and France, as in Germany and Italy, the darker strain was there. When the war came, a glad Rupert Brooke intoned:

Now God be thanked Who has matched us with His hour.

A fever was over Paris as the spring of 1914 slipped into summer. Charles Péguy—Dreyfusard, Socialist, man of good will and reason, to his intellectual generation "the pure man"—had caught this other darker spirit as well. That spring he had written:

Heureux ceux qui sont morts dans les grandes batailles . . .
Happy are those who have died in great battles,
Lying on the ground before the face of God . . .

By September of that year he himself was dead.

No doubt we shall never understand it completely. What is absolutely clear about the outbreak of the First World War is that it was catastrophic: the hecatombs of dead, the appalling material waste, the destruction, and the pain of those four years tell us that. In our hearts we know that since that bootless, reckless, bloody adventure nothing has really come right again in the world. Democracy in government, brotherhood in society, equality in rights and privileges, universal education—all those evidences of "the next higher plane of society" to which experience, intelligence, and knowledge seemed to be steadily tending—gave way to mass conscription and the central direction of war, the anonymity of the trenches, the calculated propaganda lie: in short, between 1914 and 1918 Europe evolved many of the brutal features of the modern totalitarian state. And twenty-one years after the last shot was fired in the First World War, a second war came: a war of even greater brutality, moral degradation, and purposeful evil, but one where the issues at last matched the scale on which men had, a quarter-century earlier, blindly chosen to fight. Here was a deadly justice. That such a war should be fought at all was the direct outcome of the spiritual wasteland that the first war engendered.

Woodrow Wilson, greeting the Armistice, was able to proclaim to his fellow Americans that "everything" for which his countrymen had fought had been accomplished. He could assert that it was America's "fortunate duty to assist by example, by sober, friendly counsel, and by material aid in the establishment of a just democracy throughout the world."

But today we know that the poet Robert Graves more truly expressed the spirit of the nightmare from which the world awakened in 1918 when he wrote, "The news [of the Armistice] sent me out walking alone along the dyke above the marshes of Rhuddlan . . . cursing and sobbing and thinking of the dead."

WHEN THE RED STORM BROKE

To a Russia in revolution, America sent rival groups of amateur diplomats. The calamitous results of their indecision still afflict us

WILLIAM HARLAN HALE

In the early days of November, 1917, a wiry, abbreviated man bearing on his face the expression of a determined ferret and in his pocket an important commission from President Woodrow Wilson, stopped off in London at the Savoy Hotel, then noisy with officers on leave from the western front and a banjo band straight from Dixie. He soon heard disconcerting news. "Vague word of a strange new Russian disturbance called Bolshevik" (so he was to recall in his memoirs) had begun to permeate London. "Petrograd became silent. Accounts from points outside Russia were murky and contradictory. The American Embassy was no better informed than others."

Among the least informed was the traveler himself, which was somewhat ironic, since he was momentarily on his way direct to Petrograd as a supposed expert on information, propaganda, and counterintelligence. The October Revolution was fought and won before Edgar Sisson, the special Petrograd representative of President Wilson's wartime Committee on Public Information, ever got wind of it.

Sisson, a minor and now forgotten actor who briefly blundered onto center stage in an erupting world, is interesting historically only as a symbol. He stands, so to speak, for the shortcomings of American diplomacy at one catastrophic moment. And further, he represents what could be called the Great Russo-American Reversal of 1917–18, which brought to an end our century-old friendly relations with a czarist empire remote from our interests but hitherto benevolent to our own republican growth. When social upheaval toppled the Autocrat of all the Russias in early 1917, the United States believed that the old relations would continue as before, but the events of late 1917 doomed these simple hopes. When Red Russia threatened to leave the war against the Kaiser's Germany just after we had gotten into it, and next threatened to substitute for that war of nations a war of classes—to be fomented even inside America as well—the sudden reversal reached its climax. A few shattering months led to a total breakdown of communications between Russia and America, to the point where the two hitherto cordial peoples and governments on opposite sides of the globe grew so riddled with mutual fears and suspicion as to become all but incomprehensible to one another. From this situation, as everyone knows, we have never really recovered; the few intervals of *rapprochement* over the years have all turned out to be **false dawns, and we still live under the sign of that darkness which descended between the two contrasting world powers in the bitter winter of 1917–18.**

Did it have to happen—or happen as it did? His-

torians keep sifting the evidence, each through his own sieve. All agree that revolutionary Russia provided the challenge; what remains at issue is the shrewdness, the imagination, and the wisdom of America's response. In its upheaval, the far-off empire that we had so long looked upon as the legendary haven of the ikon and the muzhik suddenly swung into America's ken with a spectacle of total disorder and social threat. The shock was great, and a surprised and inexperienced America responded to it with its own spectacle of confusion and disorder, presented first of all right on the ground of Petrograd.

For it was there, even before the guns went off and snows and machine-gun nests clogged the wintry streets, that our troubles with the new Russia began. The United States, a newcomer to great-power politics, had been content to choose, as the great majority of its emissaries, rank amateurs—in the form of deserving campaign contributors, political pensioners, and an occasional hungry intellectual seeking a paid-for existence overseas. When Russia erupted in such a violent and confusing way, we did not greatly change our manner of selecting diplomats; we simply sent more of them. The result was that America descended upon Petrograd with such a cloud of assorted trouble-shooters, visiting firemen, adventurers, and idealists as had never before been seen in the relations between civilized states—each of them independent of the next, and all of them amateur. Therewith began a new stage of American diplomacy under threat of crisis—that of mass deployment abroad designed to conceal by sheer numbers underlying cross-purposes and indecision at home.

President Franklin D. Roosevelt, in the succeeding generation, was to prove himself a past master of this tactic of sending out multiple and often mutually contradictory emissaries, and then letting the pieces fall where they might; but President Wilson, fresh in the exercise of American world power, was the pioneer. Perhaps never before had one nation dispatched to another in times of the latter's travail such a mixed company of the unskilled and innocent, with so little knowledge and preparation for what lay ahead. Nor had so many American diplomats ever gone forth with such lack of concerted purpose. Ridden with rivalries and cross-purposes that added to the general misunderstandings now arising between the United States and Russia, these multiple envoys were no match for the monolithic Lenin and Trotsky, who knew precisely what they wanted; and the end result of a winter's tortuous efforts in Petrograd was the breakdown of relations that had existed between the two countries for over a century.

The "strange new disturbance" of which Sisson wrote, referring to the Bolsheviks, had been making itself felt for quite some time before his arrival there,

and with increasing virulence for fully seven months— in fact, ever since the Czar's war-battered regime had collapsed in March, 1917, and given way to a Provisional government of republican reformists. But it had not as yet penetrated the consciousness of faraway Washington. Indeed, practically all America, then just entering upon its crusade against the Kaiser's autocratic Germany, had hailed the Czar's abdication as the removal of an autocratic incubus on our own side, and—upon receiving confident advice from our Embassy in Russia—had fully believed through the summer and into the fall of 1917 that such enlightened new leaders as Prince Lvov and Alexander Kerensky would democratize Russian institutions, rebuild fighting morale, and make of their nation a worthy partner of ours in a common cause. This was the dream; and here was one of its carriers, Sisson, chosen for his mission because of his stature as one of America's most astute journalists (editor of the *Cosmopolitan Magazine* and, before that, managing editor of *Collier's*), passing through London with little inkling of what had been occurring under the surface farther east and none at all as to where this was now about to lead.

On November 25, after making his way across a U-boat-infested North Sea and a wintry Scandinavia, he reached the Russian capital's Finland Station. There he found, as he bounced in his sleigh over the icy hummocks of the Liteiny Prospekt and turned down the Furshtatskaya to the American Embassy, a city of dim-lit streets, tight-shuttered windows, and long-coated, muffled figures with rifles warming themselves before wood fires at the intersections. These were no policemen of a friendly, Provisional Kerensky; these were the Red Guards of the Petrograd Soviet of V. I. Lenin, who had arrived at the Finland Station too (but half a year earlier than Sisson) and who, while the bemused American editor was traveling, had seized the capital and then all Russia as well. Almost overnight Kerensky had been toppled by the Bolshevik Revolution of October, 1917 (November, by the Western calendar). Russia's ill-used armies were melting away, as the slogan "Peace, Bread, and Land" resounded through their ranks; banks, businesses, church properties, great estates were being seized. Moreover, the very day after Sisson arrived in Petrograd, bearing vague and now antiquated general instructions which he summed up as meaning "To be helpful to Russia in any practical way that might develop" and "To place before Russians the American viewpoint on the waging . . . of the war," Lenin's Commissar for Foreign Affairs, Leon Trotsky, formally appealed to the German high command for an armistice.

When Sisson took up quarters in the Embassy building—a low, sprawling monstrosity in a once-fashionable street, whose imitation-classical friezes, swollen balus-

trades, misbegotten balconies, and squashed-down man-
sard roof embodied the worst taste of the recent Romanov past—he found it stuffed to the rafters with a
small army of assorted Americans as confused and at
loose ends as he, and, moreover, at loggerheads with
one another.

There were four other key and contrasting men at
the core of the American official colony in Petrograd:
the Ambassador, David R. Francis, an elderly St.
Louis grain dealer and Democratic politician; William
Boyce Thompson, a multimillionaire copper magnate,
promoter, and flamboyant high-liver, who headed the
American Red Cross Commission to Russia; Thompson's deputy, Raymond Robins, a fiery Chicago social
reformer and Progressive party orator with Indian
blood in his veins, who had made a fortune in the
Alaska gold rush; and Brigadier General William V.
Judson, military attaché—the only one of them who
had had any previous experience of Russia or even of
foreign service, having witnessed the Russo-Japanese
War as a military observer. Of these, Ambassador Francis should have been, by virtue of his position, the
dominant and controlling personality. That he was not
—that he became in fact the very opposite—was due
partly to his own shortcomings and partly to the Washington approach to appointments abroad that was both
frivolous and chaotic.

In times past America had sent to Russia both some
very good envoys and some very bad ones, the range
extending all the way from the masterly John Quincy
Adams and the scholarly Andrew D. White to the alco-
holic John Randolph, the notoriously corrupt Simon
Cameron, and that boisterous showman from border
Kentucky, Cassius M. Clay, who in President Lincoln's
day liked to sport his pearl-handled bowie knife at the
Czar's court. In this ill-assorted gallery, David R. Francis was not as outrageous as some who had preceded
him; he was simply quaint and totally miscast for his
job. A mayor of St. Louis back in the rough-and-tumble
1880's, and then governor of Missouri, he looked like
a period piece out of those days, with his white mane,
high stand-up collar, and thick gold watch chain; his
tastes ran to long evenings of poker, and during the
ten days that shook the world, he sometimes seemed
to be concerned chiefly with maintaining his supply
of bourbon and cigars. In the delicious portrait George
F. Kennan paints of him in *Russia Leaves the War*,
the author suspects that the legend of Francis' "portable cuspidor, with its clanking, foot-operated lid may
have been apocryphal," but recounts the Ambassador's
custom of accompanying his diplomatic dinners with
records played on a squeaky gramophone behind a
screen, with his Negro butler and confidant "inter-
rupting the service at table from time to time to crank
it," all to the astonishment of the guests.

Elderly as he was, the amiable grain dealer sent out
by the Calvinist Woodrow Wilson was not too old to
indulge his tastes in another direction—which resulted
in one of the more grotesque indiscretions in the chron-
icles of American diplomacy. While the eyes of the
world were focused apprehensively on the progress of
Lenin's uprising, cables hurried between Washington
and Petrograd on the subject of the American ambassador's relationship with a certain Mme. Matilda de
Cram. This handsome lady had sought out Francis'
acquaintance aboard ship while he was on his way
without his family to his post, and subsequently became a constant visitor of his at the Embassy. It was
understood that she was giving him French lessons.
All might have been well, in the worldly environment
of continental diplomacy, save that Mme. de Cram, the
wife of a Russian officer, was strongly suspected by
Russian authorities of being a German agent. She was
also on the secret suspect list of the Inter-Allied Passport Agency. General Judson, who was particularly
concerned about her proximity to coded messages and
code books when in the Ambassador's private presence,
finally confronted Francis with the stories going round
about her—only to be told to mind his own business.
Then someone at the Embassy directly informed the
State Department, which took the extraordinary step
of requesting Francis to discontinue his relationship
with Mme. de Cram. To this Francis replied crustily
that the lady in question hadn't visited him for quite
some time. A second exchange took place; then the
department, realizing that to remove Francis, a deserving Democrat, might produce a scandal, sent
him a mollifying cable welcoming his information
that Mme. de Cram's visits had ceased. End of episode
—and whether she was in fact what she was suspected
of being has never been substantiated.

While these intramural exchanges were going on,
Lenin and Trotsky had entered upon somewhat
more significant ones with the German high command
at Brest-Litovsk. It was midwinter; they sought a separate peace and were about to dissolve the multiparty
Constituent Assembly at Petrograd in order to establish a complete Bolshevik dictatorship over Russia.
The Ambassador, however, who had rarely ventured
out of his Embassy during the explosive days of November, made no personal contact with either of the
new Russian chiefs. In this he was acting on instructions from Washington on December 6 to refrain from
such contact—instructions which, however, were in effect just Francis talking to Francis, since they had been
drafted in response to his own cabled advice, the burden of which over many months had been that he saw
no point in talking with the Bolsheviks. They were
a minority agitational group, he explained, and evidently not here to stay.

As time off from poker and Mme. de Cram allowed,
Francis had kept informing the President and Secre-

tary of State Robert Lansing of his satisfaction with the way matters in Russia were proceeding under Kerensky. Thus on May 31, 1917: "Kerensky is still continuing his inspection of the front, and is met everywhere with the greatest enthusiasm." "Enthusiasm," however, had been hardly the right word with which to describe the state of mind of Russia's sullen conscripts, then on the verge of throwing down their guns. Meanwhile the Ambassador's private, conservative predilections had run much deeper; soon after Kerensky took power in March of 1917, Francis had written one of his chief deputies, Consul General Maddin Summers at Moscow (a Foreign Service professional who held high prestige in Francis' eyes because of his marriage into a highly connected czarist family), "I am much pleased to hear that the President of the [new] Ministry, [Prince] Lvov, is a first cousin of your mother-in-law and that other members of the Ministry are connected with your family. . . . I have been of the opinion that it would be unwise to attempt to establish a republican form of government in Russia just now, but if such men as these are put at the helm, it is possible they may be able to steer through the breakers . . ."

It seems never to have occurred to President Wilson that an envoy of such predilections might become a drawback in exploding Russia, and that he should be replaced. Instead, vaguely uneasy, Wilson had begun in the spring of 1917 to send out numbers of other missions, commissions, and individuals to strengthen Francis' and America's hand there—although none of these was responsible to the chief missionary on the ground.

Would Kerensky's Russia keep fighting the Germans? Wilson, whose lack of knowledge of that far country was as conspicuous as his command of political processes at home, had dispatched in May a nine-man fact-finding and good-will committee headed by the venerable Republican ex-Secretary of State, Elihu Root. Mr. Root's mandate was simply to display to troubled Russia America's "sympathy and interest," and he was hardly an ideal choice: he had confessed before setting out that he expected to be "awfully bored" there, and after a month-long round of receptions and banquets with Provisional ministers, during which he and his fellow committeemen disdained contact with the emerging Left, he returned home to deliver a bland report saying that Russia was out of danger and could be relied on. Almost simultaneously, another American delegation descended upon Russia— also without invitation: a task force of eminent American railroad men, arriving to lend advice on how to strengthen the deposed Czar's floundering transportation system. The prospect of American dollar aid was invigorating to Kerensky's officials, but the presence of so many Americans at once was rather crushing to their working hours and protocol. What next?

Next came the Red Cross Commission—and a group of men with more unusual designs under the cross of Geneva had never set foot from one nation into another. William Boyce Thompson, the squat, thickset victor of many a stock-market raid and Montana mining scheme, was one of many Americans anxious in that spring of 1917 to get into the war. As his biographer, Hermann Hagedorn, recalls:

His friends were already deep in [it] as field-marshals and ambassadors. Baruch, on the Council for National Defense, was wielding dictatorial power in the economic field. . . . Henry P. Davison [a partner of the House of Morgan], as head of the American Red Cross, was dramatizing the code of the Samaritan on an almost mythical scale. Thompson no longer found promotions and stock operations stimulating enough for his imagination. . . . The overthrow of the Czar startled and thrilled him. Russia would be the decisive factor in the war, he said. If Russia could be held firm, Germany would be defeated. If the Russian front broke—. . .

So Thompson approached his friend Davison, then projecting a Red Cross relief mission to Russia, to propose that he himself go along on it—not, indeed, simply to help supervise the distribution of foodstuffs and blankets, but to enlarge its scope immensely, its goal to be nothing less than to shore up the Provisional regime. Thompson, whose means were as spacious as his dreams, offered to pay all costs of the mission himself! The proposal was dazzling, and no one seems quite to have sensed the implications of letting a private relief body mix in with high politics abroad. The President, casting about for at least some way of influencing the course of affairs in Russia, gave the scheme his blessing, and before midsummer a party of some twenty experts, all decked out for the occasion in military uniforms and sporting assimilated military titles, was on its way across the Pacific to Vladivostok.

Kerensky's people had let it be known that they did not see the need of an American Red Cross mission: their own hospitals and food supplies were adequate, thank you. Ambassador Francis also opposed it, fearing (quite rightly, as it turned out) that it would trespass on his own domain. Yet the caravan came on. Before its departure, though, Davison startled Thompson—now "Colonel" Thompson—by including on the roster a Chicago Progressive friend of Theodore Roosevelt. Having refused to let the ex-President lead an infantry division in France, the Administration was trying to appease him.

"What! Raymond Robins, that uplifter, that Roosevelt shouter!" exploded Thompson on learning of the appointment. "What the hell is he doing on this mission?"

With Robins, there entered upon the stage a figure

who was to prove the one brilliant, although short-lived, star in a cast of many-colored American principals in Russia. For principals they all were, each man regarding himself the direct representative of the President by virtue of blessing or laying-on of hands, and thus responsible first to the White House, second to his own conscience and beliefs, and to the ambassador on the spot not at all—a situation that President Wilson did nothing to resolve. The ebullient Thompson, setting himself up in high style in Petrograd and taking over the imperial box at the Opera, reported directly to Washington and did not even show the unhappy Francis his cables; thus, when Thompson donated a million rubles' worth of his own money to the moderate Social-Revolutionary party, Ambassador Francis learned of this startling American involvement only through the newspapers. Nor did General Judson, busily maneuvering in the revolutionary murk at the head of his own independent military mission, confide in the Ambassador; while Edgar Sisson too, a small man inflated by a sense of sovereign responsibility, was to write proudly of *his* mission to Petrograd, "I was not sent to work under [Francis], and was independent of him, in powers and in funds."

In this chaos of unco-ordinated equals, the municipal reformer from Chicago was to stand out by the sheer intensity of his personality as America's strongest man on the scene. Although submerged in memory today, Raymond Robins was in 1917 a famous figure in the liberal camp at home. His physical presence itself was commanding: broad-shouldered, deep-chested, square-jawed, with intense, searching eyes and a rasping, emotional voice that could carry away whole convention halls of reformers. He had been the Progressive party's keynoter in 1916 and had run for the Senate. Yet there was something else in him, too—a suggestion of mystical exaltation that thrilled some followers and left others thinking him slightly unbalanced.

A "rough and ready evangelist," Sisson called him, and something of his passionate reformist spirit now communicated itself to Russia's far-left revolutionaries. They were not used to this: their own followers had been reared rigidly according to the gospel of St. Marx. Yet they were all still young in exercise of power, and not yet so calloused by it as to denounce every non-Marxist reformer as an enemy; and so, responding to the warmth and virility of Robins' presence, they saw in him a bridge—perhaps the only bridge—between their erupting Russia and the capitalist West. And Robins, whose experience was also limited but whose sympathies were broad, responded in kind. As his British friend and opposite number as London's special agent in Russia, R. H. Bruce Lockhart, was to remark,

[Robins] was an Indian chief with a Bible for his tomahawk. . . . Yet, in spite of his sympathies for the underdog, he was a worshipper of great men . . . Strangely enough, Lenin was amused by the hero-worship, and of all foreigners Robins was the only man whom Lenin was always willing to see and who ever succeeded in imposing his personality on the unemotional Bolshevik leader.

So it happened that while David Francis remained closeted in the Furshtatskaya over cards, American initiative in dealing with the new rulers of Russia passed into the hands of this assimilated lieutenant colonel of the Red Cross.

All during the autumn of 1917, the unlikely combination of Thompson and Robins had worked together to succor the weakening Kerensky regime with money, foodstuffs, and propaganda placed in judiciously subsidized newspapers. But in mid-October Robins read the handwriting on Russia's wall and called for a change in our own response. The Provisional regime was doomed amid the rising cry of "Peace, Bread, and Land," he argued, unless Kerensky at once proceeded to distribute land to the peasants and launch other major social reforms. It should be America's new policy to exert pressure on all Russian moderates to move in this direction, he went on, if the Bolsheviks were not to take over at any moment and pull Russia out of the war altogether. Also, Robins thought it might be a good idea at least to talk with these Bolshevik chieftains, size them up, and discover whether we could influence them at all.

Then in October-November, the second and greater revolutionary storm in Russia broke out—just as Robins had predicted it would. The multimillionaire Thompson, finding himself in full agreement with his deputy's analysis, sped home to Washington to try to swing the Administration onto a new policy tack—only to find himself coolly rebuffed by Wilson, who was still reading David Francis' bland cables and who now refused to let himself be jolted. Meanwhile, in Petrograd, the headstrong Colonel Robins had taken it upon himself to approach Trotsky personally—and Lenin too.

In order to reach Trotsky, the Foreign Commissar of a regime the United States declined to recognize, Robins needed an intermediary. Soon he found one in the person of Alexander Gumberg, a squat, mournful-looking, shrewd Jewish Russo-American who had emigrated to the Bronx to become manager there of the Russian-language Socialist weekly, *Novy Mir*, to which Trotsky had contributed during his own American exile. Now returned to his old country to be close to his Socialist friends in action, Gumberg became Robins' personal aide—and threw open the Bolshevik leader's doors to him.

When Robins drove to the Smolny Institute in mid-November for his first meeting with Trotsky, he was still convinced, as were most of the other Americans in Petrograd, that the Commissar was in effect a German agent, bent on creating total upheaval in the Allied camp and on delivering a shattered Russia into the hands of Hindenburg and Ludendorff. When he came away, he had reversed his opinion. Trostky, he later said, with the emotionalism typical of him, was indeed a ". . . son of a bitch, but the greatest Jew since Jesus Christ. If the German General Staff bought Trotsky, they bought a lemon."

"I won Trotsky," Robins recalled, "by putting my case absolutely on the square. By not hiding anything." He told Trotsky that he was there because he wanted to deal with those in power, that he wanted to maintain Red Cross activities in Russia, that he wanted to keep Russia in the war, and that he wanted to know plainly whether the Bolsheviks' sympathies were on the side of Germany or not. Trotsky, evidently astonished by this forthright approach, convinced his visitor that he was as anxious as Robins himself to keep vital war supplies out of the hands of the oncoming German legions, and on the spot worked out an arrangement with him to safeguard some essential stocks.

Soon after, though, Trotsky began commuting between the Smolny and the wintry waste of occupied Brest-Litovsk, in search of a separate peace with Germany—negotiations that, in Allied eyes, were an infamous betrayal. Could anything be salvaged from the wreckage? Robins still hoped so. It was now January, 1918, and there was no time to lose. At any moment the Germans, if sure of victory on their eastern front, might begin mounting a fresh onslaught in the west.

"We have started peace negotiations with the Germans," Trotsky told Robins flatly. "We have asked the Allies to join us in starting peace negotiations for the whole world, on a democratic basis—no forcible annexations, no punitive indemnities, and a full acceptance of the principle of the self-determination of all peoples. The Allies have refused to accept our invitation. We still hope, of course, to compel them."

The Progressive gazed at the Commissar. "How?"

"By stirring up comrades in France and in England and in America to upset the policy of their governments by asserting their own revolutionary socialist will. . . . Germany will want a peace with annexations. *But we have these raw materials.* Germany needs them. If we can keep them away from Germany we have an argument in reserve, a big argument, perhaps a winning argument."

"I begin to see," said Robins.

The long-haired, bespectacled revolutionist ground on. "I want to keep them away, but you know our difficulties at the front. The front is in chaos. Send your officers, American officers, Allied officers, any officers you please. I will give them full authority to enforce the embargo against goods into Germany all along our whole front."

Which was it, then: were these new Russian masters sworn enemies of ours or still, despite all differences, potential allies against German domination? Gen-

eral Judson, after quiet talks on his own at the Smolny, agreed with Robins: by recognizing them and showing them sympathy, we could keep Russia in the war and influence it in victory. (Back home, Thompson was saying to anyone who would listen, "Let's make them *our* Bolsheviks.") Ambassador Francis, on the other hand, after one brief moment of illumination in which he too agreed that we might do well to recognize the new rulers in order to revive Russia's role in the war, returned to regarding them as foes beyond the pale; and in late December he encouraged his consul general at Moscow, the aristocratically connected Maddin Summers, to send an emissary to make contact with the counterrevolutionary White Russians gathering in the northern provinces—a move sure to bring about further enmity once the Soviets learned of it.

Very briefly, at the end of the year, a pale sun of possible Russo-American reconciliation rose over the wintry Neva. The Germans' territorial demands on Russia proved so outrageous that negotiations at Brest-Litovsk came near breaking down. On December 31, agog with excitement at the thought that Bolshevik Russia might yet resume the fight against Germany, Robins rushed to the Smolny to confront Trotsky. Then Trotsky asked him point-blank: What support could America give to Soviet Russia if it turned down the Germans' terms and thus re-entered the war? This, until the events of World War II, was perhaps the most formidable question asked of America in a crucial time —and Trotsky had to ask it of a man whom Francis described as a "wild Indian," and who could of course give him no authoritative answer.

One answer from the very summit did come, though, stimulated in part by another man on the spot: Edgar Sisson. Aware with Robins of the parlous state of American relations with Russia, Sisson on January 3 cabled his chief at the Committee on Public Information in Washington, George Creel, to propose that the President issue a statement on American war aims as against those of Germany, with particular reference to the latter's as revealed at Brest-Litovsk, "to . . . open up our opportunities for publicity and helpfulness" in Russia.

Just how directly the Sisson message influenced President Wilson remains a matter of dispute. Five days later, however, there emerged from the White House the famous statement known to history as the "Fourteen Points," calling for many of the same principles in international settlement that Trotsky had aired to Robins. Sisson described its reception in Petrograd:

This time Lenin was back and we [*i.e.,* Sisson, Robins, and Gumberg, with a copy of the translation in hand] were able to get direct to him. It did not take one minute to convince him that the full message should go to Trotsky [who was then again at Brest-Litovsk] by direct wire. He grabbed the copy and sprinted for the telegraph office himself. . . . It was the first time either Robins or myself had met Lenin

. . . Lenin, in appearance, might be the *bourgeois* mayor of a French town—short, sparsely bearded, a bronze man in hair and whiskers, small, shrewd eyes, round of face, smiling and genial when he desires to be. And this time he did. But he is the Wildest of the Wild Men of Russia . . . He welcomed the message . . . but he did not let us forget for a moment that he regarded it as coming not from a fellow thinker but from a just and tolerant class opponent.

Yet, while Wilson's Fourteen Points declaration momentarily re-inspirited the Bolsheviks in their idea of resistance, it was not followed up by any move of American recognition or aid, and thus did not affect the grim negotiations for Russian surrender and dismemberment now being resumed at Brest-Litovsk. (The Bolsheviks, for their part, had done their perverse best to reduce any chances of such aid by appropriating two million rubles for the use of their agents to foment world revolution—and publicizing this fact.) Trotsky, who reviled both the Germans and the Allies and who had no effective forces in hand to fight either, save through the deployment of ideas and slogans, hit upon the startling formula in the snows of Brest-Litovsk, "No peace and no war"—meaning that Russia was taking itself entirely out of the international community, refusing to fight, negotiate, or settle. Observers throughout the world were nonplused—none more so than our own in Russia. Sisson, falling out with Robins, said he was sure now that Lenin and Trotsky were playing Germany's game, and he managed to acquire a stack of secret papers that in his opinion proved it. Robins, on the other hand, kept hoping that as Germany heightened its demands and backed them up with a march on Petrograd, a new fighting spirit among the Russians could yet be kindled—if only we recognized and aided their new chieftains. But his military ally, General Judson, had in the meantime been called home and shelved for "interfering" too much; and Ambassador Francis observed the final day of January, 1918, by breaking out a new stock of bourbon.

The Kaiser's hordes approached the capital, meeting no resistance. The Allied embassies burned their papers and fled to Vologda, a mud-ridden junction town on the railroad line to Archangel. On March 5 Robins had an extraordinary meeting with Lenin and Trotsky, then wavering between surrender and renewed resistance, and the three together drafted an inquiry to the United States government asking what kind of aid might be forthcoming if the Soviets refused to ratify the Brest-Litovsk treaty and resumed fighting. Nine days later Lenin confronted Robins again, just before entering the chamber of his All-Russian Congress of Workmen's, Soldiers', and Peasants' Deputies for the debate on the treaty. "Have you heard from your Government?" he asked.

"No, I've not heard yet."

"Has Lockhart heard from London?"

"Not yet," said Robins, and added, "Couldn't you prolong the debate?"

"The debate must take its course."

Two days later, a final confrontation at the Congress: once more Lenin asked Robins whether a reply had come from Washington. There had been none. Lenin turned away: "I shall now speak for the peace. It will be ratified."

Events thus moved quickly to their denouement. The Soviets ratified. Allied troops landed at Murmansk to protect war materials shipped there in aid of Russia from the West, and then to support White Russians against the regime. In America the sentiment for like armed intervention grew: the Bolsheviks, first dismissed as dim and distant agitators, now took on the image of world-wide ogres in cahoots with the Hun. Francis, an ambassador without an embassy to perform, bestirred himself enough to order that any contacts with the Soviets by General Judson's remaining aides cease. In May, Robins was recalled; Secretary of State Lansing cut him off brusquely, and the President refused to see him. Sisson, for his part, had already slipped quietly out of Russia with his cache of documents purporting to show that Lenin and Trotsky were in the pay of Germany, and these were to be published amid great excitement under the seal of the United States—though many experts, like Lockhart, later held them to be forgeries. In July, Francis himself packed up and left Vologda, thereby ending an American representation in Russia maintained ever since John Quincy Adams had arrived 109 years before; and in July, President Wilson agreed to American armed intervention on Russian soil (*see* "Where Ignorant Armies Clashed by Night," in the December, 1958, AMERICAN HERITAGE).

What had been undone on both sides was never fully to be repaired. As to the actors themselves, Robins, a lost soul, haunted the halls of Congress for a few years, trying to bring about recognition of the Soviets as a means of influencing them, and then dropped from sight. Sisson lived on to become a wizened minor propagandist in the Second World War, still buttonholing people to convince them of the authenticity of his documents. Francis, back in St. Louis with his gramophone, wrote a long book defending all he had done in Petrograd; Gumberg, a Socialist with a sure instinct for adaptation, became a highly paid executive in Wall Street; Trotsky, as everyone knows, met his end under the blow of an axe in Mexico City.

THE BIG PICTURE OF THE GREAT DEPRESSION

The crisis swept over France and Germany and Britain alike— and they all nearly foundered. Now more than ever, it is important to remember it didn't just happen here.

John A. Garraty

John A. Garraty is Chairman of the Department of History at Columbia University. His most recent book is The Great Depression.

Back in 1955 John Kenneth Galbraith called the Great Depression of the 1930s "the most momentous economic occurrence in the history of the United States," and thirty-odd years later that judgment, recorded in Galbraith's best seller, *The Great Crash*, still holds. Since then there have been more recessions, some quite severe, but nothing like what happened in the thirties. As dozens of economists and historians have shown, we now know, in theory, how to deal with violent cyclical downturns. We have learned what we should do to manipulate what Lester V. Chandler of Atlanta University has called "the determinants that influence the behavior of employment, output, and prices."

Yet fears of another terrible collapse persist, even among the experts. And the higher the stock market soars, the greater the underlying fear. In *The Great Crash* Galbraith spoke of "fissures" that "might open at . . . unexpected places," and Chandler warned of some sort of "political deadlock" that might prevent the government from doing the things that would revive a faltering economy.

These fears are not without foundation. The American economy is complex and influenced by forces beyond the control of economists or politicians. More and more, economists are becoming aware of what historians have always known: that they can do a good job of explaining why the economy is the way it is and how it got to be that way, but that knowing exactly what to do to make it behave in any particular way in the future is another matter entirely.

The Great Depression of the 1930s was a worldwide phenomenon, great not only in the sense of "severe," but also in the sense of "scope." While there were differences in its impact and in the way it was dealt with from one country to another, the course of events nearly every-

where ran something like this: By 1925 most countries had recovered from the economic disruptions caused by the Great War of 1914–18. There followed a few years of rapid growth, but in 1929 and 1930 the prosperity ended. Then came a precipitous plunge that lasted until early 1933. This dark period was followed by a gradual, if spotty, recovery. The revival, however, was aborted by the steep recession of 1937–38. It took a still more cataclysmic event, the outbreak of World War II, to end the Great Depression. All this is well known.

The effects of the Great Depression on the economy of the United States, and the attitudes of Americans toward both the Depression and the politics of their government, did not differ in fundamental ways from the situation elsewhere. This, too, scarcely needs saying.

However, there has been a tendency among historians of the Depression, except when dealing with specific international events, such as the London Economic Conference, and with foreign relations generally, to concentrate their attentions on developments in a single country or region. The result has been to make the policies of particular nations and particular interest groups seem both more unique and, for good or ill, more effective than they were.

It is true, to begin with, that neither President Calvin Coolidge nor President Herbert Hoover anticipated the Depression. In campaigning for the Presidency in 1928, Hoover stressed the good times, which, he assured the voters, would continue if he was handling the reins of government. After the election, in his last annual message to Congress, Coolidge remarked that "the country can regard the present with satisfaction and anticipate the future with optimism." When the bottom fell out of the American economy some months later, statements such as these came back to haunt Hoover and his party, and many historians have chortled over his discomfiture.

However, the leaders of virtually all the industrial nations were as far off the mark in their prognostications as Hoover and Coolidge were. When the German Social Democrats rode a "wave of prosperity" to power in June 1928, Hermann Müller, the new chancellor, assured the Reichstag that the Fatherland was in a "firm and unshakable" condition.

Great Britain had been plagued by high unemployment and lagging economic growth in the late 1920s, but in July 1929 Prime Minister Ramsay MacDonald scoffed at the possibility of a slump. And as late as December 1929, the French Premier, André Tardieu, announced what he described as a "politics of prosperity." Fewer than a thousand people were out of work in France, and the Treasury was full to overflowing. The government planned to spend five billion francs over the next five years on a "national retooling" of agriculture, industry, commerce, health care, and education. Statesmen of many other nations made similar comments in 1928 and 1929.

Hoover has been subject to much criticism for the way in which he tried to put the blame for the Depression on the shoulders of others. In his memoirs he offered an elaborate explanation, complete with footnote references to the work of many economists and other experts. "The Depression was not started in the United States," he insisted. The "primary cause" was the World War. In four-fifths of what he called the "econom-

The typical French economist of the period was like a "doctor, stuffed with theories, who has never seen a sick person."

German desperation is reflected in a grim 1932 election poster captioned "Our Last Hope."

ically sensitive" nations of the world, including such remote areas as Bolivia, Bulgaria, and Australia, the downturn was noticeable long before 1929, a time when the United States was enjoying a period of great prosperity.

Hoover blamed America's post-1929 troubles on an "orgy of stock speculation" resulting from the cheap-money policies adopted by the "mediocrities" who made up the majority of the Federal Reserve Board in a futile effort to support the value of the British pound and other European currencies. Hoover called Benjamin Strong, the governor of the Federal Reserve Bank of New York, a "mental annex of Europe," because the Fed had kept American interest rates low to discourage foreign investors.

According to Hoover, he had warned of the danger, but neither the Fed nor his predecessor, Calvin Coolidge (whom he detested), had taken his advice. Coolidge's announcement at the end of his term that stocks were "cheap at current prices" was, Hoover believed, particularly unfortunate, since it undermined

his efforts to check the speculative mania on Wall Street after his inauguration.

But Hoover could not use this argument to explain the decline that occurred in the United States in 1930, 1931, and 1932, when he was running the country. Instead he blamed the decline on foreign countries. European statesmen "did not have the courage to meet the real issues." Their rivalries and their heavy spending on arms and "frantic public works programs to meet unemployment" led to unbalanced budgets and inflation that "tore their systems asunder." These unsound policies led to the collapse of the German banking system in 1931, which transformed what would have been no more than a minor economic downturn into the Great Depression. "The hurricane that swept our shores," wrote Hoover, was of European origin.

These squirmings to avoid taking any responsibility for the Depression do Hoover no credit. But he was certainly not alone among statesmen of the time in doing so. Prime Minister MacDonald, a socialist, blamed capitalism for the debacle. "We are not on trial," he said in 1930, "it is the system under which we live. It has broken down, not only on this little island . . . it has broken down everywhere as it was bound to break down." The Germans argued that the Depression was political in origin. The harsh terms imposed on them by the Versailles Treaty, and especially the reparations payments that, they claimed, sapped the economic vitality of their country, had caused it. One conservative German economist blamed the World War naval blockade for his country's troubles in the 1930s. In the nineteenth century "the English merchant fleet helped build up the world economy," he said. During the war "the British navy helped to destroy it."

When in its early stages the Depression appeared to be sparing France, French leaders took full credit for this happy circumstance. "France is a garden," they explained. But when the slump became serious in 1932, they accused Great Britain of causing it by going off the gold standard and adopting other irresponsible monetary policies, and the United States of "exporting unemployment" by substituting machines for workers. "Mechanization," a French economist explained in 1932, "is an essential element in the worsening of the depression."

Commentators in most countries, including the United States, tended to see the Wall Street crash of October 1929 as the cause of the Depression, placing a rather large burden of explanation on a single, local event. But in a sense the Depression was like syphilis, which before its nature was understood was referred to in England as the French pox, as the Spanish disease in France, the Italian sickness in Spain, and so on.

When the nations began to suffer the effects of the Depression, most of the steps they took in trying to deal with it were either inadequate or counterproductive. Hoover's signing of the Hawley-Smoot protective tariff further shriveled an already shrinking international trade. The measure has been universally deplored by historians, who point with evident relish to the fact that more than a thousand economists had urged the President to veto the bill. The measure was no doubt a mistake because it caused a further shrinking of economic activity, but blaming Hoover for the result ignores the policies of other countries, to say nothing of the uselessness of much of what the leading economists of the day were suggesting about how to end the Depression. Even Great Britain, a nation particularly dependent on international trade, adopted the protective imperial preference system, worked out with the dominions at Ottawa in 1932. Many Latin American countries, desperately short of foreign exchange because of the slumping prices of the raw materials they exported, tried to make do with home manufactures and protected these fledgling industries with tariffs. In Europe, country after country passed laws aimed at reducing their imports of wheat and other foreign food products.

And while the Hawley-Smoot tariff was unfortunate, if Hoover had followed all the advice of the experts who had urged him to veto it, he would surely have been pushing the American economy from the frying pan into the fire, because most of their recommendations are now seen to have been wrongheaded. Opposition to protective tariffs, almost universal among conservative economists since the time of Adam Smith and Ricardo, was no sign of prescience, then as now. In their *Monetary History of the United States*, Milton Friedman and Anna Jacobson Schwartz characterize the financial proposals of the economists of the 1930s as "hardly distinguished by the correctness or profundity of understanding of the economic forces at work." A leading French economic historian, Alfred Sauvy, compares the typical French economist of the period to a "doctor, stuffed with theories, who has never seen a sick person." An Australian historian characterizes the policies of that country as "deeply influenced by shibboleths."

The most nearly universal example of a wrongheaded policy during the Depression was the effort that nations made to balance their annual budgets. Hoover was no exception; Albert Romasco has counted no fewer than twenty-one public statements stressing the need to balance the federal budget that the President made in a four-month period. As late as February 1933, after his defeat in the 1932 election, Hoover sent a desperate handwritten letter to President-elect Roosevelt pleading with him to announce that "there will be no tampering or inflation of the currency [and] that the budget will be unquestionably balanced even if further taxation is necessary."

But Hoover had plenty of company in urging fiscal restraint. Roosevelt was unmoved by Hoover's letter, but his feelings about budget balancing were not very different. In 1928 William Trufant Foster and Waddill Catchings published a book, *The Road to Plenty*, which attracted considerable attention. Roosevelt read it. After coming across the sentence "When business begins to look rotten, more public spending," he wrote in the margin: "Too good to be true —you can't get something for nothing." One of Roosevelt's first actions as President was to call for a tax increase. According to his biographer Frank Freidel, fiscal conservatism was a "first priority" in Roosevelt's early efforts to end the Depression.

Budget balancing was an obsession with a great majority of the political leaders of the thirties, regardless of country, party, or social philosophy. In 1930 Ramsay MacDonald's new socialist government was under pressure to undertake an expensive public works program aimed at reducing Great Britain's chronic unemployment. Instead the government raised taxes by £47 million in an effort to balance the budget. The conservative Heinrich Brüning recalled in his memoirs that when he became chancellor of Germany in 1932, he promised President Hindenburg "that as long as I had his trust, I would at any price make the government finances safe."

France had fewer financial worries in the early stages of the Depression than most nations. Its 1930 budget was designed to show a small surplus. But revenues did not live up to expectations, and a deficit resulted. The same thing happened in 1931 and again in 1932, but French leaders from every point on the political spectrum remained devoted to "sound" government finance. "I love the working class," Premier Pierre Laval told the National Assembly during the debate on the 1932 budget. Hoots from the left benches greeted this remark, but Laval went on: "I have seen the ravages of unemployment. . . . The government will never refuse to go as far as the resources of the country will permit [to help]. But do not ask it to commit acts that risk to compromise the balance of the budget." In 1933, when France began to feel the full effects of the Depression, Premier Joseph Paul-Boncour, who described himself as a socialist though he did not belong to the Socialist party, called for rigid economies and a tax increase. "What good is it to talk, what good to draw up plans," he said, "if one ends with a budget deficit?"

Leaders in countries large and small, in Asia, the Americas, and Europe, echoed these sentiments. A Japanese finance minister warned in 1930 that "increased government spending" would "weaken the financial soundness of the government." Prime Minister William Lyon Mackenzie King of Canada, a man who was so parsimonious that he cut new pencils into three pieces and used them until they were tiny stubs, believed that "governments should live within their means." When King's successor, R. B. Bennett, took office in 1931, he urged spending cuts and higher taxes in order to get rid of a budget deficit of more than eighty million dollars. "When it came to . . . 'unbalancing' the budget," Bennett's biographer explains, "he was as the rock of Gibraltar."

The Brazilian dictator Getúlio Vargas is reported to have had a "high respect for a balanced budget." When a journalist asked Jaime Carner, one of a succession of like-minded Spanish finance ministers in the early 1930s, to describe his priorities, Carner replied that he had three: "a balanced budget, a balanced budget, and a balanced budget." A recent historian of Czechoslovakia reports that the statesmen of the Depression era in that country displayed an "irrational fear of the inflationary nature of a budget deficit."

These examples could be extended almost without limit. The point is not that Hoover was correct in his views of proper government finance; obviously he was not. But describing his position without considering its context distorts its significance. Furthermore, the intentions of the politicians rarely corresponded to what actually happened. Deficits were the rule through the Depression years because government revenues continually fell below expectations and unavoidable expenditures rose. Even if most budgets had been in balance, the additional sums extracted from the public probably would not have had a decisive effect on any country's economy. Government spending did not have the impact on economic activity that has been the case since World War II. The historian Mark Leff has recently reminded us, for example, that the payroll tax enacted to finance the new American Social Security system in 1935 "yielded as much each month as the notorious income tax provisions of Roosevelt's 1935 Wealth Tax did in a year."

It is equally revealing to look at other aspects of the New Deal from a broad perspective. Franklin Roosevelt's Brain Trust was novel only in that so many of these advisers were academic types. Many earlier Presidents made use of informal groups of advisers—Theodore Roosevelt's Tennis Cabinet and Andrew Jackson's Kitchen Cabinet come to mind. There is no doubt that political leaders in many nations were made acutely aware of their ignorance by the Depression, and in their bafflement they

found that turning to experts was both psychologically and politically beneficial. Sometimes the experts' advice actually did some good. Sweden was blessed during the interwar era with a number of articulate, first-rate economists. The Swedish government, a recent scholar writes, was "ready to listen to the advice of [these] economists," with the result that by 1935 Sweden was deliberately practicing deficit spending, and unemployment was down nearly to pre-Depression levels.

Throughout the period British prime ministers made frequent calls on the expertise of economists such as Ralph Hawtrey, A. C. Pigou, and, of course, John Maynard Keynes. In 1930 Ramsay MacDonald, who was particularly fond of using experts to do his thinking for him, appointed a committee of five top-flight economists to investigate the causes of the Depression and "indicate the conditions of recovery." (The group came up with a number of attractive suggestions, but avoided the touchy subject of how to finance them.) The next year MacDonald charged another committee with the task of suggesting "all possible reductions of national Expenditure" in a futile effort to avoid going off the gold standard. Even in France, where political leaders tended to deny that the world depression was affecting their nation's economy and where most economists still adhered to laissez-faire principles, French premiers called from time to time on experts "to search," Sauvy explains, "for the causes of the financial difficulties of the country and propose remedies."

Many specific New Deal policies were new only in America. In 1933 the United States was far behind most industrial nations in social welfare. Unemployment insurance, a major New Deal reform when enacted in 1935, was established in Great Britain in 1911 and

in Germany shortly after World War I, well before the Depression struck. The creation of the New Deal Civilian Conservation Corps and the Civil Works Administration in 1933, and later of the Works Progress Administration and Public Works Administration, only made up for the absence of a national public welfare system before 1936.

The New Deal National Recovery Administration also paralleled earlier developments. The relation of its industrywide codes of "fair" business practices to the American trade-association movement of the 1920s and to such early Depression proposals as the plan advanced by Gerard Swope of General Electric in 1931 are well known. (The Swope Plan provided that in each industry "production and consumption should be coordinated . . . preferably by the joint participation and joint administration of management and employees" under the general supervision of the Federal Trade Commission, a system quite similar to NRA, as Roosevelt himself admitted.)

That capital and labor should join together to promote efficiency and harmony, and that companies making the same products should consult in order to fix prices and allocate output and thus put a stop to cutthroat competition, all under the watchful eye of the government, were central concepts of Italian fascist corporatism in the 1920s and of the less formal but more effective German system of cartels in that period. The Nazis organized German industry along similar but more thoroughly regimented lines at about the same time as the NRA system was being set up in America. Great Britain also employed this tactic in the 1930s, albeit on a smaller scale. The British government allowed coal companies to limit and allocate production and to fix prices, and it encouraged similar practices by steel and textile manufacturers. The only major industrial power that did not adopt such a policy before the passage of the National Industrial Recovery Act was France. Later, in 1935, the Chamber of Deputies passed a measure that permitted competing companies to enter into "accords" with one another "in time of crisis." The measure would have allowed them to adjust, or put in order, the relations between production and consumption, which is essentially what NRA was supposed to make possible. This *projet Marchandeau* died in the French Senate, but some industries were encouraged to cooperate for this end by special decree.

But the area in which American historians of the Depression have been most myopic is New Deal agricultural policy. The extent to which the Agricultural Adjustment Act of 1933 evolved from the McNary-Haugen scheme of the Coolidge era and the Agricultural Marketing Act of the Hoover years has been universally conceded. Beyond these roots, however, historians have not bothered to dig. The stress on the originality of the AAA program has been close to universal. Arthur Schlesinger, Jr., put it clearly and directly when he wrote in his book *Coming of the New Deal* that "probably never in American history has so much social and legal inventiveness gone into a single legislative measure."

Schlesinger and the other historians who expressed this opinion have faithfully reflected statements made by the people most closely associated with the AAA at the time of its passage. Secretary of Agriculture Henry A. Wallace said that the law was "as new in the field of social relations as the first gasoline engine was new in the field of mechanics." President Roosevelt told Congress in submitting the bill that it was a new and untried idea.

In fact, Wallace and Roosevelt were exaggerating the originality of New Deal policy. The AAA did mark a break with the past for the United States. Paying farmers not to grow crops was unprecedented. Yet this tactic merely reflected the constitutional restrictions of the American political system; Congress did not have the power to fix prices or limit production directly. The strategy of subsidizing farmers and compelling them to reduce output in order to bring supplies down to the level of current demand for their products was far from original.

As early as 1906 Brazil had supported the prices paid its coffee growers by buying up surpluses in years of bountiful

harvests and holding the coffee off the market. In the 1920s France had tried to help its beet farmers and wine makers by requiring that gasoline sold in France contain a percentage of alcohol distilled from French beets and grapes. More important in its effect on the United States, Great Britain had attempted in the 1920s to bolster the flagging fortunes of rubber planters in Britain's Asiatic colonies by restricting production and placing quotas on rubber exports. This Stevenson Plan, referred to in the American press as "the British monopoly," aroused the wrath of then Secretary of Commerce Herbert Hoover. It also caused Henry Ford and Harvey Firestone, whose factories consumed huge amounts of imported rubber, to commission their mutual friend Thomas A. Edison to find a latex-producing plant that could be grown commercially in the United States. (Edison tested more than ten thousand specimens and finally settled on goldenrod. Ford then bought a large tract in Georgia to grow the stuff, although it never became profitable to do so.)

After the Great Depression began, growers of staple crops in every corner of the globe adopted schemes designed to reduce output and raise prices. In 1930 British and Dutch tea growers in the Far East made an agreement to cut back on their production of cheaper varieties of tea. British and Dutch rubber planters declared a "tapping holiday" in that same year, and in 1931 Cuba, Java, and six other countries that exported significant amounts of cane sugar agreed to limit production and accept export quotas. Brazil began burning millions of pounds of coffee in 1931, a tactic that foreshadowed the "emergency" policy of the AAA administrators who ordered the plowing under of cotton and the "murder" (so called by critics) of baby pigs in 1933.

Far from being an innovation, the AAA was actually typical—one of many programs put into effect in countries all over the world in the depths of the Depression to deal with the desperate plight of farmers. The year 1933 saw the triumph nearly everywhere of a simple supply-and-demand kind of thinking that the French called "economic Malthusianism," the belief that the only way to raise prices was to bring output down to the level of current consumption. In Febru-

ary 1933, Indian, Ceylonese, and East Indian tea growers agreed to limit exports and prohibit new plantings for five years. A central committee of planters assigned and administered quotas limiting the exportation of tea. Dutch, British, French, and Siamese rubber growers adopted similar regulations for their product. In April 1933 representatives of nearly all the countries of Europe met in London with representatives of the major wheat-exporting nations, of which the United States, of course, was one of the largest. The gathering produced an International Wheat Agreement designed to cut production in hopes of causing the price of wheat to rise to a point where it would be profitable for farmers, yet still "reasonable" for consumers.

In addition to these international agreements, dozens of countries acted unilaterally in 1933 with the same goals in mind. Argentina adopted exchange controls, put a cap on imports, and regulated domestic production of wheat and cattle. The government purchased most of the 1933 wheat crop at a fixed price, then dumped the wheat abroad for whatever it could get. A Danish law of 1933 provided for government purchase and destruction of large numbers of low-quality cattle, the cost to be recovered through a slaughterhouse tax on all cattle butchered in Denmark. Declining demand caused by British restrictions on importation of Danish bacon led the Danish government to issue a specified number of "pig cards" to producers. Pigs sent to market with such cards brought one price, those without cards a lower one. The Dutch enacted similar restrictions on production of pork, beef, and dairy products.

Switzerland reduced milk production and limited the importation of feed grains in 1933, and Great Britain set up marketing boards that guaranteed dairymen a minimum price for milk. Sweden subsidized homegrown wheat and rye, and paid a bounty to exporters of butter. In 1933 France strengthened the regulations protecting growers of grapes and established a minimum price for domestic wheat. After Hitler came to power, the production, distribution, and sale of all foodstuffs was regulated. Every link from farmer to consumer was controlled.

Looking at the situation more broadly, the growers of staple crops for export were trying to push up prices

141

by reducing supplies, ignoring the fact that higher prices were likely to reduce demand still further. At the same time, the agricultural policies of the European industrial nations were making a bad situation worse. By reducing imports (and in some cases increasing domestic output) they were injuring the major food-producing countries and simultaneously adding to the costs of their own consumers.

It was, the British historian Sidney Pollard has written, "a world of rising tariffs, international commodity schemes, bilateral trade agreements and managed currencies." The United States was as much a part of Pollard's world as any other country.

One further example of the need to see American Depression policies in their world context is revealing. It involves the recession of 1937–38 and President Roosevelt's supposed responsibility for it. In early 1937 the American economy seemed finally to be emerging from the Depression. Unemployment remained high, but most economic indicators were improving. Industrial production had exceeded 1929 levels. A group of New Dealers who met at the home of the Federal Reserve Board chairman Marriner Eccles in October 1936 were so confident that the Depression was ending that their talk turned to how to avoid future Depressions. The general public was equally optimistic. "When Americans speak of the depression," the French novelist Jules Romains wrote after a visit to this country at that time, "they always use the past tense."

At this point Roosevelt, egged on by his conservative secretary of the treasury, Henry Morgenthau, warned the public in a radio speech that "the dangers of 1929 are again becoming possible." He ordered a steep cut in public works expenditures, and instructed the members of his cabinet to trim a total of $300 million from their departmental budgets. The President promised to balance the federal budget, and in fact brought the 1937 deficit down to a mere $358 million, as compared with a deficit of $3.6 billion in 1936. This reduction in federal spending, combined with the Federal Reserve's decision to push up interest rates and the coincidental reduction of consumer spending occasioned by the first collection of Social Security payroll taxes, brought the economic recovery to a halt and plunged the nation into a steep recession. The leading historian of the subject, K. D. Roose, called the recession a downturn "without parallel in American economic history."

Roosevelt had never been happy with deficits, and he was not much of an economist, but he was far from being alone in thinking that the time had come to apply the brakes to the economy. Economists who were far more knowledgeable than he saw the situation exactly as he did. Prices were still below 1929 levels in most countries, but they were rising rapidly. Using 1929 levels as an index, during 1937 prices jumped from 83 to 96 in Great Britain, from 80 to 93 in Italy, from 87 to 98 in Sweden, and from 80 to 86 in the United States.

These increases caused the grinding deflation of the years since 1929 to be forgotten. Fear of inflation resurfaced. The economist John Maynard Keynes had discounted the risks of inflation throughout the Depression. Inflation was a positive social good, he argued, a painless way to "disinherit" established wealth. But by January 1937 Keynes had become convinced that the British economy was beginning to overheat. He was so concerned that he published a series of articles in the *Times* of London on "How to Avoid a Slump." It might soon be necessary to "retard certain types of investment," Keynes warned. There was even a "risk of what might fairly be called inflation," he added. The next month the British government's Committee on Economic Information issued a report suggesting a tax increase and the postponement of "road improvements, railway electrification, slum clearance," and other public works projects "which are not of an urgent character."

During this same period the Federal Reserve Board chairman Marriner Eccles, long a believer in the need to stimulate the economy, warned Roosevelt that "there is grave danger that the recovery movement will get out of hand, excessive rises in prices . . . will occur, excessive growth of profits and a boom in the stock market will arise, and the cost of living will mount rapidly. If such conditions are permitted to develop, another drastic slump will be inevitable."

It did not take much of this kind of talk to convince President Roosevelt. When Roosevelt's actions triggered the downturn, he reversed himself again, asking Congress for budget-busting increases in federal spending. The pattern elsewhere was similar. In the United States the money was spent on unemployment relief and more public works; in the major European countries the stimulus chiefly resulted from greatly increased expenditures on armaments. In 1939 World War II broke out, and the Great Depression came to a final end.

When viewed in isolation, the policies of the United States government during the periods when economic conditions were worsening seem to have been at best ineffective, at worst counterproductive. Those put into effect while conditions were getting better appear to have been at least partly responsible for the improvement. This helps to explain why the Hoover administration has looked so bad and the New Dealers, if not always good, at least less bad.

When seen in broader perspective, however, credit and blame are not so easily assigned. The heroes then appear less heroic, the villains less dastardly, the geniuses less brilliant. The Great Depression possessed some of the qualities of a hurricane; the best those in charge of the ship of state could manage was to ride it out without foundering.

Economists and politicians certainly know more about how the world economy functions than their predecessors did half a century ago. But the world economy today is far more complex and subject to many more uncontrollable forces than was then the case. A great depression like *the* Great Depression is highly unlikely. But a different great depression? Galbraith ended *The Great Crash* with this cynical pronouncement: "Now, as throughout history, financial capacity and political perspicacity are inversely correlated." That may be an overstatement. But then again, maybe not.

Munich at Fifty

Williamson Murray

WILLIAMSON MURRAY, a new contributor, teaches European, military, and diplomatic history at Ohio State, and is the author of *The Change in the European Balance of Power 1938-1939* and *Luftwaffe*. Mr. Murray wishes to thank MacGregor Knox for help in the preparation of this article.

IT IS now fifty years since Adolf Hitler, Neville Chamberlain, Edouard Daladier, and Benito Mussolini met at Munich in September 1938 to strip Czechoslovakia of its territory and its defenses. The rationales for British and French policy ran the gamut from strategic *raison d'état,* to a basic rejection of the use of force in the international arena, to abject fear. The results were catastrophic. The British and the French came close to losing everything to a Nazi tyranny that would, in Winston Churchill's memorable phrase, have brought "a new Dark Age made more sinister, and perhaps more protracted, by the lights of perverted science." But as is often the case, historians have obscured such moments when the world has turned in new and darker directions. Perhaps it is unavoidable; we all turn our faces from darkness.

To the people who taught me history in the 1960's Munich represented one of those hinges on which history had turned; Munich, of course, had determined their lives over the seven years that followed, and considerably for the worse. Current historiography, however, suggests that Munich was only a symptom of larger trends in the world, presaging the collapse of British and French empires and the rise of American and Soviet hegemony (at least for a short period). Munich, so the argument runs, came out of a desperate effort by the British to prevent a world war that, whether won or lost, would mean the end of empire. If so, the British failed to grasp that there is a difference between winning a war and losing one's empire and losing a war and losing one's national existence. The alternatives in 1938 were that stark.

Nevertheless, whatever revisionists may write, Munich today still best symbolizes the blighted fruit of a decade of appeasement and surrender.

What most surprises me, as a military and diplomatic historian, about the wreckage of those years is the speed with which the Germans in the 1920's convinced themselves and the Anglo-American world that poor little Germany, pummeled by its neighbors and everyone else, had made peace in November 1918 on the basis of Wilson's Fourteen Points and then, tricked by sanctimonious Americans and vicious Frenchmen, awoke to find itself accused by the Treaty of Versailles of having started the war. In fact, given what we now know of their behavior before the war and their actions during it—not to mention their plans for the postwar world—the Germans got off lightly indeed in 1919.

But that was not how the Germans saw it, and they persuaded a remarkably gullible Anglo-American public and academic world that "war guilt" might be strewn generously among any number of actors: wicked merchants of death, misguided statesmen overwhelmed by events, idiotic general staffs, corrupt big businessmen. All became fashionable culprits for the war's origin, and together they gave powerful reinforcement to the tenets of modern pacifism: that anything was preferable to war, and that in any case military force and strategic issues no longer counted in international affairs. To British appeasers, whose hearts and minds were laden with the suffering and losses of World War I, it was clear that reasonable men must conclude that there had been no winners in the Great War, only losers.

The Germans, unfortunately, were neither so "reasonable" nor so averse to war. Even before Hitler came to power, they were busily engaged in kicking over the traces; after January 30, 1933 things went to hell in a hand-basket. Rearmament began in February 1933, full-scale conscription and creation of an air force followed in 1935, remilitarization of the Rhineland the year after that. But after all, said European liberals, were not the Germans only playing in their own back yard?

Then in March 1938 came the *Anschluss*, the union with Austria. In Vienna's streets tens of thousands of Waldheims cheered themselves hoarse at being absorbed into the German state. The response of the Western powers was silence. At a Cabinet meeting held as German tanks rolled across the Austro-German frontier, Prime Minister Chamberlain admitted that such unsavory activity shocked and distressed the world as "a typical illustration" of the kind of "power politics" that unfortunately made international appeasement somewhat more difficult. Alexander Cadogan, Permanent Secretary in the Foreign Office, noted in early April: "Thank goodness Austria's out of the way. . . . I can't work up much moral indignation until Hitler interferes with other nationalities."

CZECHOSLOVAKIA was next on Hitler's agenda. By June 1938 he had determined to smash this child of Versailles in the coming fall, ostensibly because of Czech mistreatment of the German minorities inhabiting the Sudeten border regions in which, not irrelevantly, reposed the Czech military defenses. One of the ironies of the 1938 crisis lay in the fact that in terms of minority rights, one nationality being mistreated by another—the very cause so fervently supported by today's consensus—justice lay solidly with the Germans. With the collapse of Austria-Hungary in 1918, the German-populated districts of Bohemia had petitioned the peace conference at Versailles to join the new Republican Reich. Though the affected districts were overwhelmingly in favor of union with Germany, such an aggrandizement of German political and economic power was simply unacceptable to sensible Frenchmen and Britons in 1919. It would add territory to defeated Germany and give the Germans a hammer lock on Czechoslovakia and its economic power.

By the 1930's, however, the British, like the Bourbons, had "forgotten everything and learned nothing." It had now become fashionable to argue that Britain must right the wrongs done to Germany and "appease" the German state. The British ambassador to Berlin, Neville Henderson, typified such attitudes. In his endless dispatches to London he argued that most Germans, including Hitler, were reasonable people who wished only to join the European community on terms of equality. In April 1938 Henderson wrote his boss, the British Foreign Secretary, Lord Halifax:

What is defeatism? Is it to say that war sooner or later between Great Britain and Germany is inevitable? Or is it to say that peace can only be preserved if Germany is allowed to become one of the satisfied angels? I believe the latter; she may never be satisfied but that is a risk we have got to face. I do not mean, when one talks of satisfying Germany, giving her a free hand, but I do mean *basing one's policy toward her on moral grounds and not allowing oneself to be influenced by considerations about the balance of power* or even the Versailles treaty. We cannot win the battle for the rule of right versus might unless and until our moral position is unassailable. I feel this strongly about the Sudeten question. [Emphasis added]

Barely three weeks later His Majesty's Ambassador to Berlin commented again to Halifax:

Yet even when I try to imagine that that which I feel in my heart to be inevitable and evolutional is neither, and when I think in terms of British interests only, regardless of right or wrong, I still feel that however repugnant, dangerous, and troublesome the result may be . . . the truest British interest is to come down on the side of the highest moral principle. And the only lastingly right moral principle is self-determination. The British Empire is built upon it [*sic*] and we cannot deny it without incalculable prejudice to *something which is of infinitely greater importance to the world than apprehensions of the German menace*. [Emphasis added]

Finally, for our purposes (the list of wonderfully perverse Henderson quotations could be extended indefinitely), in the summer of 1938 the ambassador in Berlin told Halifax:

Personally I just sit and pray for one thing, namely, that Lord Runciman [who had been sent to conciliate the Czechs and Sudeten Germans] will live up to the role of impartial British liberal statesman. I cannot believe that he will allow himself to be influenced by ancient history *or even arguments about strategic frontier and economy* in preference to high moral principles. The great and courageous game which you and the Prime Minister are playing will be lost in my humble opinion if he [Runciman] does not come on this side of the higher principles [i.e., give the game away to the Germans] for which in fact the British Empire really stands. [Emphasis added]

THE question remains: did such attitudes reflect the general consensus within the Chamberlain government? Alas, to a large extent they did. Shortly after becoming Prime Minister, Chamberlain commented to Ivan Maisky, Soviet ambassador to London: "If only we could sit down at a table with the Germans and run through all their complaints and claims with a pencil, this would greatly relieve all tension." Lord Halifax, the Foreign Secretary, wondered aloud in a Cabinet meeting in summer 1938 whether it would be

worthwhile to draft an appeal to the contending sides in Spain to stop the wars. Such an appeal would, of course, be based on grounds of humanity, Christianity, the peace of the world, and so forth. He feared that it would not be likely to succeed, but it would strengthen the moral position of His Majesty's government and might put them in a position to take helpful action later on.

But the true indicator of the Prime Minister's attitudes came in his actions. Assuming the leadership of Britain's defense and foreign policies in May 1937, Chamberlain reined in British rearmament (which was only then getting under way). His argument was that too much emphasis on armaments would ruin the economy and drive Britain into bankruptcy. Instead, Britain must husband its resources for humanitarian expenditures.

Whatever the merits of the case for the impact of military spending on the civilian economy and welfare appropriations, there is a worse fate than national economic difficulties. It is called national defeat, something that had not been experienced in the Anglo-Saxon world since 1066 (if one excepts the American South in 1865—a precedent that, unfortunately, has had little impact on our historiography save in terms of romantic nonsense).

For Chamberlain, then, the foreign-policy agenda was simple: limit military spending (in Britain and, if possible, elsewhere), employ appeasement as a device to reduce international tension, and get on with the serious business of social reform in the British Isles.

Reinforcing Chamberlain's desire to appease Germany was not only a best-case analysis of Nazi foreign policy but a set of worst-case military appreciations done by the British Chiefs of Staff. Thus the British government's military advisers underlined the weaknesses of the Anglo-French strategic situation. Yet there was no crash effort at major rearmament. Rather, the British government aimed at a settlement with the Germans.

The problem was that Hitler did not want a settlement; he wanted a limited war with Czechoslovakia, a war in which he could pay back the Czechs for their impudence in ruling Germans since 1919 and their impertinent political attacks on the German ruling race in Hapsburg days. In June 1938 the German military began, in resolute, efficient, and competent fashion, the planning necessary for it to attack the Czechs in late September.

As those German preparations became steadily more obvious, Halifax speculated that Hitler's behavior stemmed from one of two explanations. Either the Fuehrer was mad and actively seeking war, or else, as Henderson had so tirelessly depicted him, he was a moderate surrounded by extremists whose military preparations, at least in Hitler's own eyes, were essentially defensive in nature.

Chamberlain, convinced that the latter explanation was the correct one, tried everything—from informal contacts, to his ambassador, to an "impartial mediator" (Lord Runciman)—only to meet with impassive silence from Berlin. But once embarked on appeasement he was not to be deflected from his course. By September, therefore, as German military preparations ominously rolled toward their conclusion, he decided to fly to Germany for a meeting with Hitler.

Before leaving Britain, he announced to the Cabinet that should Hitler demand a plebiscite in German-populated areas of Czechoslovakia, the West would have to accede. For, he said, "It would be difficult for the democratic countries to go to war to prevent the Sudeten Germans from saying what form of government they wanted." In conclusion he announced to his assembled ministers that the Czechs might be rather unwilling to give up their strategic frontiers; consequently, Britain would have to join in guaranteeing the integrity of a new, pared-down Czech state. Britain would, in short, guarantee the security of what its diplomacy was rendering indefensible.

CHAMBERLAIN'S visit to Berchtesgaden lived up to expectations. The Fuehrer wrung his hands and wept at the injustices of history and the unfairness of leaving Sudeten Germans under the ruthless heel of Czech oppression. He presented a picture of angry, rock-throwing Sudeten German youths seeking their rightful "national" and racial identity; and, of course, he delighted in recounting the various atrocities the Czech police and army had perpetrated on the innocent German minority.

After all this, Chamberlain returned to London, more than ever convinced that Czechoslovakia must surrender the Sudetenland to avoid a European war; he now had to persuade the Cabinet, and the French and the Czechs as well. That was no easy task, since the Cabinet doubted German trustworthiness, the French put up a good show of opposition, and the Czechs despaired at what signaled the end of national independence. But when the diplomatic dust had settled, the ducks had lined up.

Amazingly, no British diplomats or military advisers over the spring and summer of 1938 bothered to ask the essential strategic questions. What would be the consequences if the Western powers abandoned Czechoslovakia to the Third Reich with all its military equipment, one of the great armament factories of Europe (the Skoda Works, which in May 1945 would still be grinding out military equipment for the Wehrmacht), and its great financial and economic reserves (enough to keep the German war economy afloat over the summer and fall of 1939)? Would the strategic situation improve if the German army had another year to train? How would the fall of Czechoslovakia affect the strategic balance in Eastern Europe? These questions simply failed to appear in either the military or political considerations. As the historian Lewis Namier once pointed out about the British diplomatic documents:

In the 1,250 large pages of the British pre-Munich documents, the question of Europe's political and strategic configuration after Czechoslovakia had been obliterated is nowhere dealt with: amazing mental reticence. . . . On the British side a blind wall is raised against the future by those vocal in the documents. All they know is that war must be averted.

Halifax even admitted on September 8 to his colleagues in the Cabinet that until the preceding day he had not known that the main Czech fortifications lay within the Sudeten German districts. Not until September 16 did Oliver Stanley, president of the Board of Trade (a Cabinet position), ask what the military balance might look like if Germany absorbed Czechoslovakia without a fight. The question provoked some scrambling to determine an answer, but no substantive analysis appeared.

In any event, it was too late in the game for inquiries on these basic strategic issues. Churchill, to be sure, had been providing such analyses, but to those in power he was an obnoxious troglodyte, tiresome in his constant refrain that Britain must prepare for war, and outmoded in his insistence that the balance of power and strategic frontiers still mattered. (In the House of Commons during the preceding spring someone had called out "How much is enough?" during a Churchill speech on air defense. The future Prime Minister replied that the question reminded him of a man who had received a telegram from Brazil informing him of the death of his mother-in-law and requesting instructions. "Embalm, cremate, bury at sea," the man had wired back, "take no chances." Whatever the sharpness of Churchill's wit, the point remains that the British government consciously and deliberately took chances with national defense in the hope that the Germans would behave.)

Having persuaded the French to run away from their ally and the Czechs to roll over and die, Chamberlain flew a second time to Germany to meet Hitler at Godesberg and serve up the Sudetenland. Hitler, who was after war pure and simple, tried to kill the negotiations. But still Chamberlain would not be deflected. Back from Godesberg he told the Cabinet that

in his view Herr Hitler had certain standards. Herr Hitler had a narrow mind and was violently prejudiced on certain subjects; but he would not deliberately deceive a man whom he

respected and with whom he had been in negotiation. . . . When Hitler announced that he meant to do something it was certain that he would do it.

Despite considerable restiveness in the country and even within the Cabinet, the Prime Minister yet again went to Germany (this time to Munich) within the week to finish his work. Before his departure he provided the British public a statement (later to become notorious) of his fundamental beliefs in the foreign-policy arena:

How horrible, fantastic, incredible it is that we should be digging trenches and trying on gas masks here, because of a quarrel in a far away country between people of whom we know nothing! It seems still more impossible that a quarrel which has already been settled in principle should be the subject of a war. . . . However much we may sympathize with a small nation confronted by a big and powerful neighbor we cannot in all circumstances undertake to involve the whole British Empire in war simply on her account. If we have to fight it must be on larger issues than that. I am myself a man of peace to the depths of my soul. Armed conflict between nations is a nightmare to me.

And there at Munich, in company with the French Premier, Daladier, the sinister and pompous Italian dictator, Mussolini, and the Fuehrer himself, Chamberlain helped slice up the Czech republic past redemption. (Not that the Czechs were democratic sweethearts: they had indeed given the German minority short shrift and their treatment of minorities was reasonable only by the standards of Eastern Europe.) The Russians were not a factor, not just because Chamberlain and Daladier were anti-Communist, but because Stalin was too busy killing his officer corps and party elite to play a diplomatic role at this point. Even so, the British gave away nothing less than the strategic balance of Europe. Czechoslovakia may have been, as Chamberlain complained, a small nation "far away . . . of whom we know nothing," but it was nevertheless a nation whose geographic position held the key to the Danube basin and whose economic resources provided a vital bridge for German rearmament and for the Wehrmacht.

It is worth enumerating what the Western powers surrendered at Munich. The Czech army went out the window: Czech tanks would equip three of the ten German Panzer divisions that invaded France in May 1940, while four Waffen SS divisions, plus a further four of the army's infantry divisions, would possess Czech equipment. The remainder of the materiel acquired when they occupied rump Czechoslovakia in March 1939 the Germans sold to the Rumanians for oil and to the Yugoslavs and Hungarians for other raw materials. As important as all this was the fact that Czech industrial resources, raw materials, and financial strength played a major role in keeping the German war economy afloat to the end of 1939.

Moreover, the Germans were now in a position to dominate Eastern Europe diplomatically, economically, and strategically.

For a short time in the 1960's and 1970's it became popular among historians to argue that Chamberlain had saved Britain from a devastating German air attack; German air-force records have made nonsense of such claims. As late as August 1938 half of the Luftwaffe's aircraft were out of commission, good for expensive static displays but not much else. A senior staff officer of the German Second Air Force, when informed that its units would have to attack Britain, noted in August 1938 that his command had the ability to inflict only "pinpricks" on the British Isles.

The Germans, then, did not possess the force structure, the munitions, or the training for a sustained attack on Britain in 1938. If war had broken out then, it would have been less costly and less destructive than the war that broke out in September 1939.

YET on Chamberlain's return to London, the multitudes cheered when, from the balcony of the Prime Minister's residence, he breathlessly announced: "My good friends, this is the second time in our history that there has come back from Germany to Downing Street peace with honor." As Britons serenaded Chamberlain, only a few saw the gathering darkness. Churchill, of course, caught the full significance of Munich. The government, he remarked in a letter, had the choice between war and shame; it had chosen shame, it would get war. And before a sullen and frequently indignant House he declared:

All is over. Silent, mournful, abandoned, broken Czechoslovakia recedes into the darkness. . . . Every position has been successively undermined and abandoned on specious and plausible excuses.

I do not grudge our loyal, brave people, who were ready to do their duty no matter what the cost, who never flinched under the strain of last week, the natural, spontaneous outburst of joy and relief when they learned that the hard ordeal would no longer be required of them at the moment; but they should know the truth. . . . They should know that we have sustained a defeat without a war, the consequences of which will travel far with us along our road, when the whole equilibrium of Europe has been deranged, and that the terrible words have for the time being been pronounced against the Western democracies: "Thou art weighed in the balance and found wanting." And do not suppose that this is the end. This is only the beginning of the reckoning. This is only the first sip, the first foretaste of a bitter cup. . . .

Hitler's attitude toward the results of Munich was one of disbelief. As he told the Hungarian ambassador in January 1939:

Amazing things had been achieved. "Do you think," he asked, "that I myself would have

thought it possible half a year ago that Czechoslovakia would be served up to me, so to speak by her friends? I did not believe that England and France would go to war, but I was convinced that Czechoslovakia would have to be destroyed by war. The way that everything has happened is historically unique. We can offer each other heartfelt congratulations."

Munich was not the end of appeasement. The British government would shrug off the November 1938 "Crystal Night" pogrom, in which the windows of synagogues and Jewish-owned stores were smashed all over Germany, with worries that *any* British action might lead to a break with the Germans or that *any* British support for Germany's Jews might lead to an increase in anti-Semitism in Great Britain.

Despite its "triumph" at Munich, however, the Chamberlain government found itself under considerable pressure from two separate directions in the House. The first was from those who expected some concrete result from the Munich conference in terms of what was left of Czechoslovakia. The Germans obviously had no intention of guaranteeing the settlement; that meant a unilateral British guarantee. (How seriously the British government regarded this guarantee is suggested retroactively by a Labor question put in 1973 to the Foreign Secretary, a man who had formerly been Chamberlain's parliamentary private secretary, asking whether an undertaking the British were then thinking of making to the Israelis was the same as the one Chamberlain had given to the Czechs in October 1938. "No, this time it is meant," replied Lord Douglas-Home.)

The other pressure on the government came from a general sense even among Chamberlain's supporters that Britain's defense required more than the government's half-hearted and belated efforts. The government answered during the Munich debate that it had already embarked on a "great program of rearmament" when in fact it had no intention of changing its approach to rearmament. While German rearmament proceeded in nonstop fashion, the crew that had made Munich possible did nothing for the army, authorized construction of only twenty escort vessels and twelve minesweepers, dredged a few harbors, and reluctantly extended the contract dates for Spitfire and Hurricane production, thereby increasing the number of aircraft on order but not acting to make more of them available in the immediate future. (The production run of both aircraft had just begun.) In short, until March 1939, when the Germans removed the remaining ambiguities in most European minds, the British government talked rearmament, did little else, and got the worst of both worlds.

WELL, what does all this ancient history mean? A generation ago (1961), it suggested to those who had suffered through the consequences of Munich (and lived) that we should "pay any price, bear any burden" in the defense of liberty. That attitude disappeared rapidly in the late 1960's in the wreckage of American policy in Vietnam. Still unresolved, Vietnam lies like some great shadow over our consciousness, darkening and obscuring the increasingly foggy landscape. But through the fog we can detect a resurgence of the illusions of Munich.

Thus we receive a constant bombardment from the print and television media slanted toward the easy, soft assumptions of appeasement, steadily wearing on our collective consciousness. In one recent issue of the New York *Times* (March 27, 1988) alone, an article on the op-ed page by a leading American historian managed to denounce the Reagan administration's "*vengeful* [*sic*] military actions in Lebanon, Libya and Grenada"; to announce that the American government in the 1930's showed *great* prudence in not intervening in the Spanish Civil War, the Japanese war on China, and "the Italian bombardment of Ethiopia"[*sic*]; and finally, with great pride of scholarship, to praise Thomas Jefferson's bizarre rules of engagement against the Tripoli pirates (soon modified by the realities of the world).

If this exercise in foolishness (by no less weighty a figure than Henry Steele Commager) were not enough, the *Times*'s own Karl E. Meyer managed on the same day to write nonexistent history on the editorial page in a signed piece entitled "The Mirage of Secure Borders"—a piece that made light of the territorial concerns of Israeli leaders. Bismarck, according to Meyer, was not able, by keeping the provinces of Alsace-Lorraine, to protect Germany from the vicious French enthusiasm for revenge (this, obviously, is why *Germany* invaded *France* in 1914). The French attempted to protect themselves from a renewed German effort to bring order to the West by building the Maginot Line in the 1920's, which, Meyer assures us, the Wehrmacht sliced through like a knife through butter (actually, they went around it through the Ardennes). And finally, in his effort to destroy history, Meyer brings us back to Munich. The parallel drawn by Henry Kissinger between the Czech situation in 1938 and Israel's today would, writes Meyer,

be more persuasive if any Arab neighbor could be compared to Nazi Germany. In fact Israel is the regional superpower, and its military edge is greater now that Egypt is no longer a likely adversary [*sic*] and the Sinai no longer a security problem [*sic*]. What truly doomed Czechoslovakia was its isolation, and its abandonment by France and Britain. Does Mr. Kissinger really think that Prague would have prevailed over Hitler if only it had secure frontiers?

Within the week, the New York *Times* would carry the words from a poem by a prominent "moderate" in the PLO. Mahmoud Darwish ends his wonderfully "reasonable" argument with these lines to the Israelis:

Get out of our land
our continent, our sea
our wheat, our salt, our sore
our everything, and get out
of the memory of memories.

But of course, he doesn't mean those words literally. And those rock-throwing youths who shout "this is our country and the Jews are our dogs," only want a little slice of Israeli territory for their homeland. Like us, they are only after "peace."

ON THE 50th anniversary of Munich, then, we have some serious thinking to do. But it will certainly not occur in the academic world: no conferences, no international meetings of scholars funded by foundations, no collection of articles to discuss the "meaning" of Munich. Why not? Perhaps the lessons might be too inimical to the fundamental tenets and beliefs of our world, too disturbing to our sense of how that world works. Perhaps silence is preferable precisely because the spirit of appeasement *is* alive and well. It stalks the nation crying that all men are reasonable (except ourselves), that the world's irrationality and anger are the result of our own actions, and that there is nothing worth fighting for. If we go on in this spirit, the only question will be not if we shall surrender our larger responsibilities in the world, but when.

THE NAZI STATE:
Machine or Morass?

Michael Geyer

The vices which despotism engenders are precisely those which equality fosters. These two things mutually and perniciously complete and assist each other. Equality places men side by side, unconnected by any common tie; despotism raises barriers to keep them asunder: the former predisposes them not to consider their fellow-creatures, the latter makes general indifference a sort of virtue. Despotism then, which is at all times dangerous, is most particularly to be feared in democratic ages.
Alex de Tocqueville, *Democracy in America* (vol. II, chapter iv)

UNFETTERED COMPETITION IS ONE OF the least understood features of the National Socialist regime, although it is one of the most discussed. Political historians have long debunked the myth of the National Socialist state as a totalitarian and rationally organised modern Leviathan. More recently, historians have been fascinated by the rampant competition, even chaos, of Nazi institutions. At the same time, social historians have come to regard as a major aspect of the National Socialist regime not the ideological infiltration of Nazi doctrine among the German people as though it were a new catechism, but the increasing pressures of competitive behaviour among social groups and individuals

Competing interests as much as ideology fuelled the functioning of the Third Reich, augmented by forced labour and the plunder of Occupied Europe.

that reshaped private and public life, within the family no less than on the shop floor.

National Socialism replaced the hard driving, entrepreneurial, 'economic man' – with a new breed of *compradores* who craftily exploited the chances of improvement and upward mobility provided by an expanding Third Reich. Their main pursuits were not economic or productive but 'political', using the powers of domination and subjugation that were provided by the state – starting with the repression of trade unions and the seizure of their property and the exclusion of Jews from public life and continuing in the wars of plunder and extortion which reached their zenith in the war against the Soviet Union.

All this has been fairly well described, but little understood. Historians, like most people, prefer to keep state and society, men and women, production and destruction neatly apart, and have very distinct ideas about what should and should not be considered modern. German and English historians both stop short of the notion of a state's institutions as the main arena of competition, although their reasons differ. The Germans imagine a well-organised and smooth-functioning state machine in which institutions not only fit together but, by functioning so well, also further the common good. English historians on the other hand, come from a tradition that views the state or, more generally, the political sphere as an arena where a ruling class constitutes itself by establishing its claims to dominate through the consent of the subordinated classes.

Whichever way we approach it, the sprawling Nazi state with its many and diffuse institutions was different. Very clearly it became the site of pervasive competition between individuals and institutions for control over this power to dominate others; in turn this became the pre-requisite

From *History Today*, January 1986, pp. 35-39. Reproduced by kind permission of History Today, Ltd., 83-84 Berwick Street, London W1V 3PJ England.

for the wealth and the status of an institution. This competition increased in leaps and bounds with Nazi conquest. Those institutions and individuals who had the licence to plunder – and all too often the right to kill as well – ruled supreme. The SS and its sprawling empire under Himmler was the prime example of this kind of activity. This is what makes the Nazi regime so extraordinary and, at the same time, so difficult to understand. The Nazi state and the emerging Nazi society were not centred around production and maintaining its conditions, but around the ability to prey on other people and whole societies, much as industry preys on nature.

The consequence of this slash-and-burn approach to state activities was the collapse of the rule of law and of the rationality of bureaucratically organised domination. At the same time, the sphere of the state and the number of those who were employed by the state directly or indirectly expanded dramatically. This expansion, it should be noted, occurred in tandem with the intensification of terror and domination, beginning in 1933. At the zenith of the Second World War, in 1941, a state system had emerged in which literally hundreds of institutions were engaged in the project of dominating the defeated and occupied countries.

We are only slowly beginning to uncover the cumulative impact of these institutions, which fought each other tooth and nail. While we have a good sense of the plunder by the big machines' – the SS, the military, and industry – we still need to uncover the little privileges of 'Germans' over other 'races'. Thus we know a great deal about forced labour in Germany, but we know next to nothing about the behaviour of, for example, the administrators in the East – or about the increasingly inter-ethnic master-servant relations in the German countryside during the war. By the same token, a great deal is known about the 'Aryanisation' of industry and trade, but what happened to all the Jewish offices and houses, and to the property of Jewish families in Germany and Europe, say in Hamburg, Krakow, or Vienna? We really do not know.

However, a recent study on Passau has shown that even in the staunchly Catholic backwoods of Germany where Nazism never took a firm hold, the Third Reich could unleash a creed which broke through the old solidarities of the community and destroyed tolerance among people. Of all its vices, the ability of the National Socialist regime to separate and set human beings against one another in competition over plunder was the worst.

By destroying bonds of solidarity, by fostering the egotism of both individuals and institutions, and by applauding as strong and healthy those 'who have no sympathy for any but themselves' (de Tocqueville), the National Socialist regime proceeded to create a state and a society which 'placed men side by side, unconnected by any common ties' (de Tocqueville). This competition did not centre around production or markets, but around terror and force, the capacity to impose one's will on others by means or physical coercion.

War was the natural extension of this violent system, and war in the National Socialist context took on a very special meaning. It has been appropriately called a *Weltanschauungskrieg*, an ideological war. This kind of war happened not only to be Hitler's main and ultimate goal; it was also the centrepiece of the reconstruction of German society and the German state around domination. Ideological war was the product neither of old-fashioned interest-politics nor of atavistic sentiments. Rather it was fought in order to create and maintain a state and a society in which German individuals and institutions could share in the domination of others.

If we consider war, and ideological war at that, as the focus of the National Socialist state, this may shed some light on the initial observation about the chaotic and competitive nature of Nazi rule.

It is true that the business of governing in the Third Reich was transformed into competitive interaction between powerholders and their institutions. There was no coherent system of government. Every institution carved out its own niche in an increasingly vicious struggle for influence and resources. Looking at the endless squabbles between them, it might indeed be surmised that the Nazi state was chaotic.

Even worse, the sharp division between state, economy, and societ became lost under the impact of th competition. Industrial groups gaine quasi-state authority and the differ ence between private and publi ownership (one may think of th Hermann Goering Werke or of th holdings of German files in th occupied countries), became blurred By the same token, the SS combine state institutions like the police wit party institutions like the SD informa tion service under one roof. Thus, National Socialist state emerged tha lacked a coherent centre an expanded beyond traditional bound aries to encompass parts of societ and the economy.

Yet, as competitive as this system National Socialist politics and a blurred the line between state, soc ety, and economy were, this entit did not lack direction. To step bac from the infighting and look at th system as a whole is to discover tha the momentum of competition led i the direction of war. Many attribut this to Hitler personally, but this vie is too simplistic an explanation for modern despotic regime. Hitler's sta ture in the Third Reich did indeed ris and he was increasingly able impose his 'goals', but his rise predominance was a result rathe than a precondition of the pervasiv struggles over power, influence, an resources. A state system, built o plunder, could not but move in th direction of war – or it had to b thoroughly rebuilt.

However, we cannot leave it ther for National Socialist (and Hitler' politics were not exhausted in follov ing an institutional drive towarc war. They wanted war and strov towards it. War was the means reconstruct German society and th German state on the basis of co quest, subjugation, and annihilatio War was the goal of a process of soci reconstruction that began with raci purification as the core of *Wiede wehrhaftmachung* (military prepare ness) and was supposed to reach climax with the anticipated domin tion of the Germans over other 'race This was the ideological programm It was guided by the promise of don nation for every German as part of new 'master race' in a racist empir While the big 'machines' fought it o among themselves, the Nazi leade hip, and especially Hitler, never lost their populist touch. Both trajectories pointed towards war, and a racist war at that.

Competition over domination formed the material practice of the Third Reich. As de Tocqueville put it, 'a despot easily forgives his subjects for not loving him, provided they do not love each other'. The latter – love, trust, solidarity – indeed were in short supply among the Germans, and solidarity with the dominated became treason. Equality for all Germans in a new *Volksgemeinschaft*; freedom as participation in domination; egotism in the interest of the 'common good' – these were the ideological essentials of the Nazi state, which did not require that everyone become a Nazi as long as the National Socialist leadership could convince Germans of the benefits of racist rule.

Ideological politics were thus the promise of participation in the domination of others for one's own and the common German benefit. It was thus a peculiarly perverted system of participation; for while the Germans were not allowed to govern themselves, they were encouraged to dominate others. This was the National Socialist 'social contract' on which the state, with its competitive and predatory institutions, rested.

It is easy to be confused by the convenient 'mix-up' between Nazi propaganda and Nazi ideology. However, National Socialist ideology consisted neither of the bad political habits of the 'masses' nor the dreams produced in Dr Goebbels' celluloid factories. The special quality of National Socialist ideology consisted in its increasing concreteness with the approach and the conduct of war. Its very core, racist domination and annihilation, was its least debated and propagandised aspect, but it comprised the essence and the practice of politics in the Third Reich.

The National Socialist state system of competitive centres of power and a racist 'social contract' did not emerge overnight and it always remained tenuous, dependent both on the state's ability to reconcile the political interests of the institutional centres of power and the ability to create a new social contract through war. The National Socialist state was not the inevitable outcome of the seizure of power; nor did the Third Reich simply follow a path mapped out by Hitler. Rather, the conditions for ideological war and for the foundation of a new social contract were established in a series of struggles. There is, in other words, no linear progression in National Socialist rule, but a series of contested choices that made the Nazi state.

Conflicts over priorities were built into the coalition government that came to power in 1933. Least important in this coalition were the few conservative-bourgeois politicians who were quickly ousted or sidestepped. What counted was the power of industry and the military on the one hand, and of society mobilised in the National Socialist movement on the other. Not the parties which were quickly co-opted, but the autonomous powerblocks of industry and the military were the initial counterweights, but also the partners of the National Socialists. National Socialist leaders depended on industry in combatting unemployment and on the military to wage war, just as the latter depended on the National Socialist capacity to mobilise (and terrorise) people. As a result of the Nazi takeover, the powers of industry and the military expanded dramatically during 1933. But all attempts to fuse the National Socialist movement with the interests of industry and the military – as was tried in 1933 with the SA and the *Wehrmacht* and with the *Mittelstand* and industry – were frustrated, and failed. Both the attempt to bring together middle-class and industrial politics in the formation of a new corporate economy and the attempt to fuse para-military mobilisation with rearmament in a new hybrid military came to naught.

In fact the two sides came to a head-on collision in 1934 which the para-military and middle-class ideologies in the National Socialist movement lost. The *Reichswehr* became the dominant military force against and over the storm troopers just as industry pushed back *Mittelstand* demands. While the former demanded the subordination of the whole nation under the yoke of rearmament, the latter strove for efficiency and managerial control over the workforce. Both aims were as total in their scope as those of the National Socialists. They wanted to reorganise society in their own right to assure the smooth functioning of production and destruction. Even if the military and industry never fully succeeded, this constituted a most threatening challenge for the National Socialist leadership. In effect, they had to negate their past and the interests of their most dedicated followers in order to maintain their alliance with the military and industry on whom they depended in their short-term struggle against unemployment and their long-term objectives of waging war. The National Socialist leadership entered a most critical phase – and yet it survived and emerged stronger than before.

Nazi leaders all acted differently in this situation. The opportunistic Goering seized the first opportunity to join industry and the military as a third force through the Four Year Plan, although he and the Plan remained unwelcome among the tycoons of the Ruhr. Nevertheless, Goering established his own powerbase, centred around a military-industrial complex that linked the airforce with aeroplane manufacturers and chemical (especially synthetic petrol) industries, mainly IG Farben. Himmler concentrated on building his own apparatus of domination, which was the first in the Third Reich that lived entirely off the domination of others. In a series of crafty manoeuvres against his own National Socialist comrades (Roehm, Goering, Goebbels) and against state bureaucracies, he not only centralised policing, but also reforged the whole complex of 'domestic security' into a proselytising centre for ideological politics. Himmler's powerblock thus not only contained the political police, the Gestapo, but also the Race and Settlement Office which championed the reconstruction of German society along racist lines. It also developed its own 'resource' base by exploiting the victims of the Third Reich (concentration camp labour) and by seizing and controlling the property of those who were expelled from Germany. However, the survival of the Nazi leadership as a whole, and of Hitler in particular, was due to other factors.

Hitler's ideological base had always been somewhere else, and it was the clever preservation of this base by Goebbels which propelled Hitler to the centre of the stage without his having to make the decisions that industry and the military expected him to make. He was never a good mediator in the competition between his own leaders and between the institutions of the state and, from what is known, he did not care to perform well in this particular field. However, Hitler always retained his close ties with a German society which adored him despite the blunders of his entourage. While the party lost in credibility, Hitler's star rose thanks to the ceaseless propaganda campaigns of Goebbels. These bonds of loyalty and adoration that linked Hitler to society proved to be exceedingly important. While Hitler and the National Socialist regime did not fare very well in guiding the competition within the Nazi state, they continued to guarantee the conditions of production and destruction both internally and externally. In this capacity of establishing and maintaining a social contract, Hitler was desperately needed. The organisation of society for war or, for that matter, for production, could not have taken place without a growing Hitler myth without Hitler's 'peace' initiatives or, without the dose of terror against those who did not opt for the emerging community of the Third Reich.

Had the Third Reich been an ordinary despotic regime, nothing further would have happened. The myth would have given way to disappointment and the dynamism of the regime would have petered out. There was the possibility of this kind of development all along, despite Goebbels efforts. Yet at the first possible chance the National Socialist leadership proved that it was not an ordinary regime and that it was not ready to leave the social contract to propaganda and goodwill.

This chance arose in 1937-38 for complex reasons. Both the military and industry had over-extended, while neither of them had reached their goal. The military was still unable to fight a war, and industry continued to fear for profitability. They were in a genuine impasse, in which one side had to give. The military wanted more rearmament, industry a course of stability and profitability, and both were ready to pass the costs on to society. Hitler resisted this choice by pursuing a third, his own course. He drove towards a quick, even premature war – and not just any war, but ideological war. He used the impasse of 1937-38 to give the

National Socialist social contract a substantive base through wars of exploitation and domination. He revived the quest for *Volksgemeinschaft* and *Lebensraum*. In 1938 the Nazi leadership succeeded in establishing the primacy of ideological politics. This was a most important change, for it shaped the quality of the wars to be fought. They were not simply fought in order to consolidate and to placate interests. They were fought as social wars in order to facilitate the reconstruction of German society.

This kind of war reached its apogee with the war against the Soviet Union in 1941. For that war linked the key aspects of ideological rule: exterminism and genocide and the reconstruction of German society as the superior 'race' over the subjugated peoples and nations came together in the planning and the implementation of 'Operation Barbarossa'. This campaign was ideology transformed into political, social, and military practice. In summer 1941, when the Soviet Union seemed to be defeated, a vision emerged of a German society, a National Socialist state, and a prosperous industry preying on subordinated peoples and resources, being protected by the SS against the resistance from within and by the *Wehrmacht* against the dangers from without. In 1941-42 the high watermark of the establishment of a racist social contract was reached. It is only appropriate that exactly at this point the preparations for a 'final solution', the annihilation of the Jewish people in occupied Europe, took shape.

However, this vision was destroyed in the very same winter by the tenacity of the Red Army. The ending of *Blitzkrieg* initiated a last phase in the development of a Nazi state. By 1941 the pendulum had begun to swing back to a more instrumental and functional organisation of society in the interests of production and destruction, while ideological politics were cramped into the annihilation campaign against Jews that escalated to its heights in 1941-42. Speer, and with him a corporate solution for the mobilisation of resources, gained the upper hand as far as the Germans were concerned. However, the main costs of the re-emergence of corporate power within the Nazi state and the reassertion of the imperatives of production in total war were still not paid

by the Germans, but by forced labour, plunder, and starvation in occupied countries. This was and is Speer' legacy.

Underneath the pressures of wa production organised in Speer' Ministry, alternatives were debatec which proved to be more palatable i Germany and to the Germans. Man (like the future Minister of Economi Affairs and Chancellor Ludwi; Ehrhard, but, intriguingly also the S! leader Ohlendorf who never gave uj the vision of the reconstruction o German society) retained their dislik for Speer's corporatism with its ques for a clean and functional organisatior of society in subordination to bij industry. After all hopes for domina tion vanished in 1943, they began tc debate alternative ways of mapping out a social contract – no longer on the basis of violence, but built around new economic policies. They aimed a achieving, in due course, higl employment and a high standard o living as well as the creation of European 'co-prosperity sphere', tha is a zone of influence in which Ger many would predominate, though not by force and violence, but due tc its economic strength. They envis aged a new social contract, based no on the domination of others, but on share in consumption in a revitalisec and prospering European economy Thus the basis for post-war recon struction was laid during the war ir response to the failure of the Nationa Socialist state to establish a new anc racist German order through war However, the National Socialist state could not be reformed from withir as some of the proponents of *Volks-kapitalismus* had thought. Th National Socialist regime had to be destroyed before a new social contrac could be negotiated.

FOR FURTHER READING:
The pertinent literature and debates on the Third Reich can be found in John Hiden an John Fauquharson, *Explaining Hitler's Germany Historians and the Third Reich* (Croom Helm 1983) and in Ian Kershaw, *The Nazi Dictatorship Problems and Perspectives in Interpretation* (Edward Arnold, 1985). Michael Geyer, 'Th State in National Socialist Germany', in Charles Bright and Susan Harding, eds., *State Making and Social Movements. Essays in History anc Theory* (University of Michigan Press, 1984) Recent discussions of state theory are found ir Bob Jessop, *Theories of the State* (New Yorl University Press, 1983) and Martin Carnoy, *Th State and Political Theory* (Princeton University Press, 1984).

REMEMBERING MUSSOLINI

Charles F. Delzell

Charles F. Delzell, 68, is professor of history at Vanderbilt University. Born in Klamath Falls, Oregon, he received a B.S. from the University of Oregon (1941) and an M.A. (1943) and a Ph.D. (1951) from Stanford University. He is the author of Mussolini's Enemies: The Italian Anti-Fascist Resistance *(1961),* Italy in Modern Times *(1964), and* Italy in the 20th Century *(1980).*

After meeting Benito Mussolini in Rome in 1927, Winston Churchill, then a Conservative member of Parliament, said that had he been an Italian, he would have "wholeheartedly" supported the Fascist leader's "triumphant struggle against the bestial appetites and passions of Leninism." In 1940, however, when he was prime minister of an embattled Britain, Churchill called the *Duce* a "jackal," and blamed this "one man alone" for dragging Italy into World War II and disaster.

There have been few, if any, dictators of the Right or Left in our century whose rise to power owed more to the myopia of democratic statesmen and plain citizens. Mussolini's fall from power was as dramatic as his ascent, and the Fascist era merits our reflections today.

Many younger Americans may think of Mussolini only as actor Jack Oakie portrayed him in Charlie Chaplin's classic 1940 film, *The Great Dictator*: a rotund, strutting clown, who struck pompous poses from his Roman balcony and tried to upstage Adolf Hitler when they first met, in Venice in 1934.

Yet the caricature should not blind us to history. Perhaps the most sobering aspect of Benito Mussolini's career was how much applause he once enjoyed from highly respected intellectuals, journalists, and politicians, abroad and at home. Exasperated by Italy's fragile, fractious parliamentary democracy, worried about increasing popular unrest, and fearful of the Socialists' rising popularity, statesmen such as the Liberal Party leader Giovanni Giolitti and King Victor Emmanuel III welcomed Mussolini's advent to power in 1922. And the King supported him during most of the 21 years that the *Duce* ruled in Rome.

Mussolini's strong-man appeal—and that of the Fascism he espoused—grew out of the postwar disorder and economic hardship which reigned in Italy and much of Europe. It also stemmed in some measure from the fact that during the late 19th and early 20th centuries, Italy had been governed by squabbling legislators. By 1883, the year Mussolini was born, the various kingdoms and duchies on the Italian peninsula had only recently been unified under Victor Emmanuel II, King of Sardinia-Piedmont. "The patriotism of the Italians," as the 19th-century Neapolitan historian Luigi Blanch has observed, "is the love of a single town, not of a country; it is the feeling of a tribe, not of a nation."

Indeed, Italy was heir to long-embedded regional differences; these were aggravated by poor transportation and great disparities in education, wealth, and class. During the early 20th century, the church was powerful almost everywhere. And every corner of the country had its own traditions, customs, and dialect. The north-south contrasts were striking: At the turn of the century, for example, there were no primary schools in the south; in fact, nearly 80 percent of all southerners were illiterate. Many peasants lived in a kind of Third World poverty, subject to drought, malaria, and the vagaries of absentee landlords.

The nation was politically fragmented too. In rural Italy, especially in the central "Red" Romagna region where Mussolini was born, anarchist-socialist ideas had spread rapidly. By the 1890s, a Marxist brand of socialism won favor among workers in northern Italy's new "industrial triangle." By 1919 Italy's Socialist Party—"revolutionary" and "revisionist" factions—held more seats than any other single party (though still not a majority) in the Parliament, thanks to the introduction of universal manhood suffrage and proportional representation. The Roman Catholic Church, meanwhile, was at odds not only with the Socialists but also with the kingdom of Italy itself. The kingdom had annexed the papal states of Rome and central Italy between 1861 and 1870, prompting Pope Pius IX to proclaim himself a "prisoner of the Vatican."

In the eyes of his early Fascist supporters, Benito Mussolini was the man who was restoring order and establishing national unity.

His origins were no more auspicious than Hitler's or Stalin's. He was born on July 29, 1883, into a poor but politically active household. His father, Alessandro Mussolini, was a blacksmith and an anarchist-socialist who helped organize a local group of the Socialist International, and who read aloud parts of *Das Kapital* to his family. Benito's mother, Rosa, was a pious Catholic schoolteacher who insisted that the family speak high Italian, rather than the Romagna dialect. Benito lived with his parents and a younger brother and sister in two rooms on the second floor of a small, shabby building outside of Predappio, about 50 miles southeast of Bologna. Two pictures hung on a wall in the parents' bedroom: one of the Virgin Mary and one of the Italian nationalist and anticlerical agitator Giuseppe Garibaldi. The parents named their eldest son not after a saint but after Benito Juarez, the Mexican revolutionary who had helped overthrow Santa Anna's dictatorship in 1855.

In his youth, Benito was moody at home and a bully at the Catholic boarding school he attended in nearby Faenza. Indeed, he was expelled after stabbing a fellow student with a knife and assaulting a priest who tried to discipline him. Benito was, nevertheless, an academic achiever; in 1901 he got his diploma from another school, in Forlimpopoli, and later became a part-time school teacher. At age 19, Mussolini left Italy for Switzerland ("that republic of sausages"), partly to avoid compulsory military service. "I was a bohemian in those days," he later wrote. "I made my own rules and I did not keep even them."

Changing Tunes

At first, Mussolini lived a vagabond's life in Switzerland—moving from town to town, doing odd jobs to survive, sometimes sleeping in public lavatories and parks. But the young man's interest soon turned to politics. In 1903 Mussolini took up residence in Bern; he began contributing articles to socialist journals, organized a strike of masons, and fought a (harmless) pistol duel with a fellow socialist.

After wandering through Switzerland, France, and Germany, Mussolini returned to Italy to do his military service. In 1909 he decided to move to Italian-speaking Trento in Austria-Hungary. There he edited a weekly socialist newspaper, *L'Avvenire del Lavoratore* ("The Workers' Future"). Later, in Forlì, Italy, he edited another socialist weekly, *La Lotta di Classe* ("The Class Struggle"), and translated Pyotr Kropotkin's *Great French Revolution*. By 1910, displaying a natural talent, he was one of Italy's best-known socialist journalist-polemicists. That year he also began to live with Rachele Guidi, the 17-year-old daughter of a widow with whom Benito's father had lived after the death of his wife. Their civil marriage would not take place until 1915.

Mussolini's early commitment to socialism, or to any other *ism*, should not be taken too seriously, despite his passionate rhetoric. Mussolini would repeatedly demonstrate his willingness to change his political stance whenever it advanced his prospects. As a young man he read the works of Niccolò Machiavelli, Friedrich Nietzsche, Georges Sorel, and others. But he was mostly interested in ideas that he could appropriate for his own use. Like other Italian socialists, Mussolini at first con-

From *The Wilson Quarterly*, Spring 1988, pp. 118-135. Copyright © 1988 by The Woodrow Wilson International Center for Scholars.

demned World War I as an "imperialist war." His country's involvement, he said, would constitute an "unpardonable crime." But after France's amazing survival at the Marne in September 1914, he reversed his position. In *Avanti!*, the Socialist Party newspaper that he then edited in Milan, he urged that Italy enter the conflict on the side of Britain and France. The Socialists promptly expelled him as a traitor.

Fasci di Combattimento

Now a maverick "national" socialist, Mussolini quickly founded his own newspaper in Milan, *Il Popolo d'Italia* ("The People of Italy"). The paper was financed, in part, by local industrialists. Slogans on the paper's masthead read: "Whoever has steel has bread" (from the French revolutionary Auguste Blanqui) and "The Revolution is an idea which has found bayonets!" (from Napoleon). When the government declared war on Austria-Hungary in May 1915, Mussolini hailed the event as "Italy's baptism as a great power" and "a culminating point in world history."

Mussolini's own role in the conflict—he was drafted in August 1915 and served in the Alps—would provide him with a lode of (mostly imaginary) stories about his heroics in combat. Never involved in any major battles, the young sergeant was injured on February 22, 1917, when a mortar accidentally exploded in his trench, spraying his backside with 44 pieces of shrapnel. After recovering, Mussolini returned to *Il Popolo*, where he pounded out fiery editorials in favor of the war effort and against bolshevism. He considered Lenin a "man of straw" and observed that "only a Tartar and Mongolian people could fall for such a program as his."

As time went on, Mussolini became increasingly nationalistic. Insisting upon Italy's "great imperial destiny," he demanded the annexation of the Austro-Hungarian territories where Italian was spoken, such as the port of Trieste, the Italian Tyrol, and most of Dalmatia. With strong business support, Mussolini changed the subtitle of *Il Popolo d'Italia* from "a socialist newspaper" to "the newspaper of combatants and producers." And in a speech in Rome in February 1918, Mussolini declared that Italy needed "a man who is ferocious and energetic enough to make a clean sweep, with the courage to punish without hesitation, particularly when the culprits are in high places."

Although Italy emerged as a victor in World War I, the conflict had wreaked havoc on Italian society. Some 650,000 soldiers had perished. Returning veterans swelled the ranks of the unemployed; nearly two million Italians found themselves out of work by the end of 1919. A wave of industrial strikes broke out in the north. Some workers, stirred by the news of the Bolshevik Revolution in Russia, urged a "dictatorship of the proletariat" for Italy. Meanwhile, in Rome, one feeble Liberal Party coalition government after another tried vainly to restore stability.

With the Great War at an end, and the fear of bolshevism widespread, Mussolini cast about for a new nationalist cause to lead. On March 23, 1919, he founded Italy's Fascist movement in a businessmen's club off Milan's Piazza San Sepolcro. His *Fasci di Combattimento* ("Fighting Fasces") took their name from the bundle of rods with protruding axe-blades that had been the symbol of authority and discipline in ancient Rome. About 120 people were present at the Milan meeting, including veterans of the *arditi*, a group of wartime shock troops. "We, the survivors who have returned," Mussolini wrote, "demand the right of governing Italy." The Fascists chose as their uniform the same black shirt Romagna laborers had favored.

Though Mussolini's Fascist movement was always anti-Marxist, anti-Liberal, and virulently nationalistic, it would endorse (and quickly drop) many causes. At first Mussolini called for a republic and universal suffrage, and criticized the Roman Catholic Church. Later, he would endorse the monarchy, render elections meaningless, and cozy up to the church. The Fascist movement attracted unemployed youths, frightened members of the bourgeoisie, industrialists, landowners, and, especially, war veterans who believed that Italy, at the 1919 Paris peace conference, had not gained all of the territories she was due.

"When I came back from the war," Italo Balbo, a noted Fascist, would later recall, "I, like so many others, hated politics and politicians, who, it seemed to me, had betrayed the hopes of the fighting men and had inflicted on Italy a shameful peace . . . Struggle, fight to return the country to Giolitti who had bartered every ideal? No. Better [to] deny everything, destroy everything in order to build everything up again from the bottom."

Cudgels and Castor Oil

The Fascist movement's ability to straddle, however awkwardly, Italy's conventional political divisions between Right and Left proved to be one of its greatest initial strengths. During the "Fascism of the First Hour," Mussolini's program did not differ much from that of the Socialists, except that the Fascists had favored Italy's wartime role and still praised it. But when the Fascist movement failed to elect even one of its candidates to Parliament in the November 1919 election, Mussolini decided to shift to the Right.

To win more support from Catholics, he muted his anticlerical rhetoric and said that Rome should subsidize churches and religious schools. The Liberal government's decision to withdraw troops from Albania, which they had occupied since 1914, Mussolini said, represented a "disgusting exhibition of national cowardice." Above all, Mussolini intensified his anti-Socialist rhetoric and berated the Liberal government for "doing nothing" when, in September 1920, metal workers in the north forcibly occupied the factories and set up Soviet-style workers' councils. The Fascists, Mussolini promised, would restore "law and order."

Mussolini's message won over many employers, who believed that the Fascists could keep militant labor at bay. Bands of Fascist thugs, known as *squadristi*, launched "punitive expeditions" against Socialist and Catholic leagues of laborers and farmworkers. They beat some members with cudgels and forced castor oil down their throats. By official count, the Fascists destroyed 120 labor union offices and murdered 243 persons between January and May of 1921.

The ruling Liberals were happy to look the other way. Local police officers even supplied the Blackshirt militias with weapons. And when Prime Minister Giovanni Giolitti called for new elections, to take place on May 15, 1921, he proposed to the Fascists that, following the election, they should join his constitutional bloc in Parliament. This time, Mussolini's Fascist Party would win 35 seats.

By 1922, Mussolini was impatient to seize power in what seemed more and more like a political vacuum. In October of that year, the Fascist Party held a congress in Naples, where Mussolini and his colleagues drew up plans for a "March on Rome." Under the plan, Fascist militias would lead the march while Mussolini prudently remained close to the Swiss border in case the attempted coup d'état failed. "Either we are allowed to govern," Mussolini warned in a speech to the Fascist militiamen, "or we will seize power by marching on Rome" to "take by the throat the miserable political class that governs us."

Taking Power

The weak coalition government led by Luigi Facta knew that Mussolini was planning a coup, but at first the prime minister did not take the Fascists' intentions seriously. "I believe that the prospect of a March on Rome has faded away," Facta told the King. Nor were all of the Socialists eager to confront the Fascist threat. Indeed, some radical Marxists hoped that Mussolini's "reactionary buffoonery" would destroy both the Socialists and the Liberals, thus preparing the way for a genuine Communist revolution. For their part, the Liberals worried most about the Socialists, because of their anticapitalist ideology. Indeed, Liberals and Socialists were "as anxious to scuttle each other," as historian Denis Mack Smith has observed, "as to prevent a Fascist revolution."

The Fascists initiated the "March on Rome" on the night of October 27–28, 1922. The militias began taking over telephone exchanges and government offices. Luigi Facta wanted the King to declare a state of siege, but in the end no showdown occurred. Unconvinced that the army could or would defend Rome from the Fascists, or that the Liberals could provide effective leadership, Victor Emmanuel refused to sign a formal decree declaring a state of emergency. Instead, he telegraphed Mussolini, asking him to come to Rome to form a new government.

Boarding a train in Milan, Mussolini informed the stationmaster that he wanted to depart "exactly on time [because] from now on everything must function perfectly"—thereby giving rise to the myth that he made Italy's trains run on time. Upon his arrival in Rome, the *Duce* proceeded at once to the Palazzo del Quirinale. Still wearing a black shirt, he told the 53-year-old monarch (who had expected him to appear in formal dress): "I have come from the battlefield."

Thus, on October 31, 1922, at age 39, Mussolini became the youngest prime minister in Italy's short parliamentary history. With the Fascists holding only 35 seats in the 510-member Chamber of Deputies, he headed a cabinet of "national concentration" composed mostly of Liberals, socialist Democrats, and Catholic *Popolari*. In his first speech to the deputies, who gave him an overwhelming vote of confidence, he boasted: "I could have transformed this drab hall into a bivouac for my squads . . . I could have formed a government exclusively of Fascists, but I chose not to, at least not for the present."

Despite the *Duce*'s threats, many veteran politicians in Rome thought that, in time, they could co-opt Mussolini. Even Giovanni Giolitti and Antonio Salandra, the two senior members of the Liberal Party establishment, favored Mussolini's ascension to power. Luigi Albertini, the editor of Milan's *Corriere della Sera* voiced his delight that Fascism had, above all, "saved Italy from the danger of Socialism."

Others were pleased that, finally, Italy enjoyed strong leadership, of whatever kind. "The heart of Fascism is the love of Italy," observed the Liberal senator and philosopher Benedetto Croce in January 1924. "Fascism is overcoming the traditional indifference of Italians to politics . . . and I value so highly the cure which Italy is undergoing from it that I rather hope the patient will not get up too soon from his bed and risk some grave relapse."

In Britain, France, and the United States, many conservatives also gave their blessings. The *New York Tribune* remarked that "the Fascisti movement is—in essentials—a reaction against degeneration through socialistic internationalism. It is rough in its methods, but the aims which it professes are tonic." Even the *New York Times* suggested that Mussolini's coup was of a "peculiar and relatively harmless type."

The Matteotti Crisis

Now at the center of power, Mussolini increasingly became a solitary figure. During his first five years in office, the *Duce* lived alone in a small rented apartment; his wife Rachele remained in Milan, where she cared for their five children. He lived austerely, dined on vegetarian meals, and, partly to avoid irritating a gastric ulcer, eschewed alcohol and tobacco. (He once bragged of his "utter contempt for the lure of money.") An inveterate womanizer, Mussolini evinced little genuine affection for the opposite sex, or for people in general. "I have no friends," he once admitted to the German publicist Emil Ludwig, "first of all because of my temperament; secondly because of my views of human beings. That is why I avoid both intimacy and discussion."

Mussolini managed to project a more congenial image to the outside world. He contrived frequent "photo opportunities," posing at the controls of an airplane, grinning behind the wheel of a sports car, or taming a lion cub in its cage at the zoo. Many Americans saw him as an Italian Teddy Roosevelt—a stout-hearted advocate of the strenuous life.

But "image" was not enough. Eager to put more Fascists in Parliament, Mussolini called for an election, to take place on April 6, 1924. During the campaign and voting, the *squadristi* engaged in widespread intimidation. "When it is a matter of the Fatherland or of Fascism," Mussolini said on January 28, 1924, "we are ready to kill and die."

In the election, the Fascists claimed to have won 64.9 percent of the votes. But on May 30, Giacomo Matteotti, the widely respected leader of the Unitary Socialist Party, courageously stood up in Parliament to read a list of incidents in which Blackshirts had threatened voters and tampered with the ballot boxes. Fascist deputies, now in the majority, taunted him, yelling "Hireling!", "Traitor!", "Demagogue!" Ten days later, Fascist toughs who were closely linked to Mussolini's press office kidnapped Matteotti near his home in Rome, stabbed him, and then half buried his corpse in a grove outside the capital.

The assassination precipitated the most serious crisis of Mussolini's early days in power. Many Italians, after all, believed that Mussolini had at least incited, if not ordered, the murder. The anti-Fascist opposition—Socialists, Catholic *Popolari*, Republicans, and Constitutional Democrats—boycotted the Parliament, forming the "Aventine Secession." It was time for the King, they believed, to dismiss Mussolini and call for new elections.

But the ever-timid King, who was weary of the governments of the past, refused to intervene. Nor did the Vatican support the oppositionists. Pope Pius XI himself warned Italians against "cooperation with evil" (i.e. the Socialists) for "whatever reason of public welfare."

In a fit of wishful thinking, many foreign commentators did not blame Mussolini for the murder. They preferred to cite certain "gangster elements" among the Fascists. "The Matteotti incident," lamented

the *New York Times* "is of a kind that may kill a movement by depriving it at one stroke of its moral content."

In Rome, Mussolini taunted his hapless, divided opponents during a speech to Parliament:

> But after all, gentlemen, what butterflies are we looking for under the arch of Titus? Well, I declare here before this assembly, before the Italian people, that I assume, I alone, the political, moral, historical responsibility for everything that has happened . . . .

By failing to oust Mussolini during the Matteotti crisis, his foes effectively entrenched the *Duce* as Italy's all-powerful leader.

On January 3, 1925, Mussolini launched a counter-offensive, announcing in an impassioned half-hour speech to Parliament that "force" was the "only solution" to the threat of disorder. Under a series of "exceptional decrees," Mussolini censored the press and outlawed all opposition parties, including the Socialists and Liberals. He replaced labor unions with Fascist syndicates. His Special Tribunal for the Defense of the State sentenced thousands of opposition activists (especially Communists and anarchists) either to long prison terms or to internal exile in the south. Youngsters were recruited by Fascist youth organizations—a future model for Germany's Hitler Youth—which stressed indoctrination and discipline, and exhorted them to "Believe! Obey! Fight!"

All the while, Mussolini continued to garner praise abroad. "Mussolini's dictatorship," observed the *Washington Post* in August 1926, "evidently appeals to the Italian people. They needed a leader, and having found him they gladly confer power upon him."

Giving Italy Back to God

Mussolini called his regime the Totalitarian State: "Everything in the State, Nothing outside the State, Nothing Against the State!" But his "totalitarianism," harsh and noisy as it often was, was far less brutal than that of Stalin's Russia or Hitler's Germany—partly because the King retained control of the Italian Army and the right to dismiss the prime minister. Not until 1938 did the regime begin to discriminate against the nation's roughly 40,000 Jews; many would lose their jobs in government and academia. But Mussolini did not seek a "final solution" to Italy's "Jewish problem"—as the Germans did after they occupied northern Italy in September 1943.

On the economic front, Mussolini's "Corporative State" tried to foster "class conciliation." The regime set up parallel Fascist syndicates of employers and workers in various sectors of the economy. Labor courts settled disputes under a system of compulsory arbitration.

In 1933, the regime established the Institute for Industrial Reconstruction (IRI) as a holding company to shore up failing industries. State-subsidized (or "parastate") industrial organizations would soon furnish about 17 percent of all goods and services. To stimulate the economy, Mussolini built roads, sports stadiums, and government buildings. The government launched numerous programs for mothers and children and developed a land reclamation scheme, which was responsible for draining the Pontine Marshes near Rome. Mussolini initiated a much-publicized "battle for grain"; newsreel cameramen filmed him pitching straw, bare from the waist up. Perhaps most significantly, the *Duce* began an ill-fated effort to rebuild the nation's army, navy, and air force.

Despite Mussolini's promise to restore "the Augustan Empire," he generally failed to push Italy's backward economy forward. The regime's cartels sometimes hindered economic advance by discouraging innovation and modernization. The *Duce* demoralized workers by cutting wages, raising taxes, and banning strikes and other forms of protest. Even as the government took over industries and prepared for war, unemployment remained high. Fully half of those who did work were employed in agriculture. Italian families, meanwhile, were spending 50 percent of their incomes on food.

Mussolini, however, sought (and gained) amicable relations with the Catholic church by signing the Lateran Pacts with the Vatican in February 1929. The pacts created the State of Vatican City, within which the Pope would be sovereign. They established Roman Catholicism as Italy's state religion, bestowing on it extensive privileges and immunities. The *Duce*'s star soared throughout the Catholic world; devout Italian peasants flocked to church to pray for the man who had "given back God to Italy and Italy to God." Ignoring the suppression of civil liberties, Pope

4. MODERNISM AND TOTAL WAR

Pius XI referred to Mussolini as "a man whom Providence has caused to meet us" and sprinkled him with holy water.

Grabbing Ethiopia

By the late 1920s, the *Duce* had solidified support for his regime, both in Rome and abroad. Soon after entering the White House in 1933, Franklin D. Roosevelt wrote that he was "deeply impressed" by this "admirable Italian gentleman," who seemed intent upon "restoring Italy and seeking to prevent general European trouble."

Indeed, until the mid-1930s, Mussolini stayed (for the most part) out of foreign ventures. But great nations, Mussolini believed, could not be content with achievements at home. "For Fascism," as he wrote in the *Enciclopedia Italiana* in 1932, "the growth of empire . . . is an essential manifestation of vitality, and its opposite a sign of decadence. Peoples which are rising, or rising again after a period of decadence, are always imperialist: any renunciation is a sign of decay and death."

Mussolini would become increasingly obsessed with foreign conquests after January 1933, when Adolf Hitler became chancellor of Germany and soon won dictatorial powers. Although Mussolini and Hitler, as fellow Fascists, admired each other, their alliance would be marked by periodic fits of jealousy on the *Duce*'s part. Hitler, as biographer Joachim C. Fest has written, "aroused in Mussolini an inferiority complex for which he thereafter tried to compensate more and more by posturings, imperial actions, or the invoking of a vanished past."

Mussolini's first major "imperial action" would occur in Africa. The *Duce* had long coveted Emperor Haile Selassie's Ethiopia, which an Italian army had failed to conquer in 1896. On the morning of October 2, 1935, as 100,000 troops began moving across the Eritrea-Ethiopia border, Mussolini announced that "A great hour in the history of our country has struck . . . forty million Italians, a sworn community, will not let themselves be robbed of their place in the sun!"

Paralyzed by economic depression and public antiwar sentiment, Britain's Prime Minister Stanley Baldwin refused to intervene, despite the inherent threat to British colonies in Africa. The League of Nations denounced the Fascist aggression. However, lacking any coherent leadership or U.S. support, the League stopped short of closing the Suez Canal or imposing an oil embargo on Italy. Either action, Mussolini said later, would have inflicted "an inconceivable disaster."

The barefooted Ethiopian levies were no match for Italy's Savoia bombers and mustard gas. The *Duce*'s pilot son, Vittorio, told journalists in Africa that the Ethiopian soldiers, when hit from the air, "exploded like red roses." Addis Ababa fell in May 1936. With this victory, Mussolini reached the pinnacle of his popularity at home. Speaking to an enormous crowd from his Palazzo Venezia balcony, the *Duce* declared that his "triumph over 50 nations" meant the "reappearance of the Empire upon the fated hills of Rome." Signs everywhere proclaimed *Il Duce ha sempre ragione* ("The leader is always right").

Emboldened by his Ethiopian success, Mussolini began to intervene elsewhere. He dispatched aircraft and some 70,000 "volunteers" to help Generalissimo Francisco Franco's Falangist insurgents in the Spanish Civil War. He pulled Italy out of the League of Nations and decided to line up with Hitler's Germany, which had already quit the League. Thus, in June 1936, Mussolini's 33-year-old foreign minister and son-in-law, Count Galeazzo Ciano, negotiated the Rome-Berlin Axis, which was expanded into a full-fledged military alliance, the "Pact of Steel," in May 1939. Both countries also established links with Japan through the Anti-Comintern Pact. The *Duce* now belonged to what he called the "most formidable political and military combination that has ever existed."

Humiliations in the Desert

Mussolini's military forces, however, could not be described as formidable. Lacking coal, iron, oil, and sufficient heavy industry, Italy's economy could not support a major war effort. The *Duce*, who spoke of "eight million bayonets," proved a better propagandist than military planner. On the eve of World War II, the Italian Army owned 1.3 million outdated rifles and even fewer bayonets; its tanks and artillery were obsolete. By June 1940, the Italian Navy boasted fast battleships and Western Europe's largest fleet of submarines. But it sadly lacked radar, echo-sounding equipment, and other new technologies. And Mussolini's admirals and generals were better known for their political loyalty than for professional competence.

When Hitler quickly annexed Austria in March 1938, and Czechoslovakia in March 1939, Mussolini complained to Count Ciano: "The Italians will laugh at me. Every time Hitler occupies a country, he sends me a message." The *Duce*, ignoring Catholic sensibilities, ordered the invasion of Albania on Good Friday, April 7, 1939, bringing that backward Adriatic country into his empire.

When Germany invaded Poland on September 1, 1939, thereby launching World War II, Mussolini knew that Italy was not ready to fight. He initially adopted a position of "non-belligerency." The list of needed war supplies that the *Duce* requested from Berlin, noted Count Ciano, "is long enough to kill a bull." But as Hitler's Blitzkrieg brought Denmark, Norway, the Low Countries, and France to their knees in 1940, Mussolini decided he had little to lose, and perhaps some spoils to gain.

On June 10, 1940, without consulting either his cabinet or the Fascist Grand Council, Mussolini declared war on both France and Britain. In joining the conflict, Mussolini inadvertently let Hitler become the master of Italy's fate.

The Italian people soon felt the pain. The battlefield performance of Mussolini's armed forces reflected the homefront's lack of zeal. One debacle after another ensued. Under Field Marshal Rodolfo Graziani, Italy's much-touted armored brigades in Libya attacked the British in Egypt, hoping to capture the Suez Canal. But in the seesaw battles across the desert, as well as in naval engagements in the Mediterranean, the outnumbered British inflicted repeated humiliations on the Italians, who had to beg the Germans for help. By the end of 1941, the British had also shorn Mussolini of Italian Eritrea and Somalia, as well as Ethiopia, reinstating Haile Selassie as emperor.

The King Says Good-bye

Italy's invasion of Greece, launched from Albania on October 28, 1940, did not fare much better. Saying he was "tired of acting as Hitler's tail-light," Mussolini launched the attack without notifying Berlin. The war against the Greeks, the *Duce* predicted, would be little more than a "military promenade." But the Italians were bogged down in the mountains for months, until Hitler's spring 1941 invasion of the Balkans rescued Mussolini's lackluster legions. And Italy's participation in Germany's 1941 invasion of the Soviet Union yielded few triumphs. Mussolini dispatched three infantry divisions and one cavalry division. At least half of the 240,000 Italian soldiers sent to the Eastern front never returned.

For Italy, the beginning of the end came on December 7, 1941, when the Japanese bombed Pearl Harbor, bringing the United States into the war against the Axis powers. Although Mussolini seemed delighted to be fighting "a country of Negroes and Jews," he knew that his regime was now in deep trouble.

Across the Mediterranean, in November 1942, General Dwight Eisenhower put Allied forces ashore in Morocco and Algeria. He began a push to meet Field Marshal Bernard Montgomery's British Eighth Army, which had already broken through Axis defenses at el-Alamein. The German *Afrika Korps* fought a tough delaying action. But when the North Africa campaign ended in May 1943, some 200,000 Italians had been taken prisoner; few had fought the Allies with much enthusiasm.

New bases in North Africa enabled Allied airmen to step up the bombing of Italian cities and rail centers, which left the nation's already hard-pressed economy in tatters. Tardily, the regime rationed food supplies and restricted the consumption of gas and coal. Despite wage and price controls, inflation soared, and a black market flourished. Ordinary Italians began to demonstrate their disaffection. In early 1943, public employees in Turin and Fiat workers in Milan went on strike. "In Italy," Mussolini would later write, "the moral repercussions of the American landing in Algiers were immediate and profound. Every enemy of Fascism promptly reared his ugly head . . . ."

By the time the Allies invaded Sicily on July 10, 1943, even those Italian politicians who had long enjoyed privileges and perquisites were fed up; plots were being hatched in Rome to oust Mussolini and turn over political power to King Victor Emmanuel. All this came to a head on the night of July 24–25, when the Fascist Grand Council met at the Palazzo Venezia to decide Mussolini's fate. Some Fascist councillors criticized the shaken dictator to his face for being too indecisive; others berated him for not ridding the government of incompetents. Nothing was working, they said, and the Germans in Italy, coping with Anglo-American advances, regarded their sagging ally with contempt.

In a two-hour monologue, the *Duce* tried to defend himself, saying that "this is the moment to tighten the reins and to assume the necessary responsibility. I shall have no difficulty in replacing men, in turning the screw, in bringing forces to bear not yet engaged." But the Council adopted a resolution, which had been supported by Count Ciano, calling upon the King to take over the leadership of the nation.

The next afternoon, Mussolini went to the King's villa, hoping to bluff his way through the crisis. But the King had decided, at last, to separate himself from the Fascist regime. He quickly informed Mussolini that he had decided to set up a royal military government under the 71-year-old Army Marshal, Pietro Badoglio. "Then everything is finished," the *Duce* murmured. As the ex-dictator left the Villa Savoia, a *Carabiniere* officer motioned him into an ambulance, pretending this was necessary to avoid "a hostile crowd."

Mussolini was taken to a police barracks, unaware that he was under arrest. At 10:45 a government spokesman announced over the radio the formation of the new regime by the King and Badoglio. Jubilant crowds rushed into the streets to celebrate. But they were dismayed by Badoglio's statement that "the war continues"—a statement made to ward off German retaliation.

Rescuing the Duce

Marshal Badoglio placed the former *Duce* under guard. Later, he was transferred to a ski resort atop Gran Sasso, the tallest peak in central Italy. He remained there for almost a fortnight, while the new regime secretly negotiated an armistice with the Allies. The armistice was announced on September 8—even as American and British troops landed against stiff German resistance at Salerno, near Naples.

Thereafter, events moved swiftly.

Anticipating Italy's about-face, Hitler had dispatched strong *Wehrmacht* reinforcements across the Alps; the Germans were able quickly to disarm and intern the badly confused Italian troops. Fearing capture, the King and Badoglio fled Rome before dawn on September 9 to join the Allied forces in the south. Six weeks later the Badoglio government, now installed in Bríndisi, declared war on Germany.

On September 12, 1943, Captain Otto Skorzeny, leading 90 German commandos in eight gliders and a small plane, landed outside the mountaintop hotel on Gran Sasso where the sickly *Duce* was still being kept. Skorzeny's men brushed aside the Italian guards, and took Mussolini to Munich, where Hitler met him. Henceforth, the *Duce* would be one of Hitler's lackeys, a "brutal friendship" as Mussolini put it.

The *Führer* ordered Mussolini to head up the new pro-Nazi Italian Social Republic (RSI) at Salò, in German-occupied northern Italy. The Italian Fascists would help the Nazis deport, and later exterminate, over 8,000 Jews. From Munich, Mussolini appealed by radio to his "faithful Blackshirts" to renew Axis solidarity, and purge the "royalist betrayers" of the regime.

But few Italians willingly backed the "Salò Republic." Instead, most hoped for a swift Allied victory. A determined minority even joined the partisans—the armed anti-German and anti-Fascist resistance—in northern Italy. But Mussolini did manage to punish the "traitors of July 25." In Verona, a special Fascist tribunal put on trial Mussolini's son-in-law, Count Ciano, and others in his party who had voted for "the elimination of its *Duce*." Rejecting the pleas of his daughter Edda, Mussolini decreed that Ciano and his co-conspirators be shot to death, and so they were, on January 11, 1944.

At last, in April 1945, the grinding Allied offensive, having reached northern Italy, overwhelmed the Germans, whose homeland was already collapsing under attack from East and West. At this point, Mussolini tried to save himself by negotiating with anti-Fascist resistance leaders in Milan. But when he learned that they insisted on an "unconditional surrender," he fled with several dozen companions to Lake Como, where he was joined by his mistress, Clara Petacci. From there, they planned an escape to Switzerland.

Per Necessità Familiale

Unable to cross the border, Mussolini and his band decided to join a German truck convoy that was retreating toward Switzerland through the Italian Alps. But Italian partisans halted the convoy near Dongo. Ever the actor, Mussolini donned a German corporal's overcoat, a swastika-marked helmet, and dark glasses, and climbed into one of the trucks. But the partisans identified Mussolini, arrested him and his companions, and let the Germans proceed unmolested.

The next day, Walter Audisio, a Communist resistance chief from Milan, arrived, claiming he had orders to execute the *Duce* and 15 other Fascist fugitives. He summarily shot Mussolini and his mistress at the village of Giulino di Mezzegra on April 28. Their corpses were taken to Milan and strung up by the heels in Piazzale Loreto, where an infuriated mob repeatedly kicked and spat on the swinging cadavers.

Looking back on Mussolini's career, it might be said that he changed Italy more than he changed the Italians. Indeed, the *Duce* left behind a network of paved roads, reclamation projects, and a vast centralized bureaucracy. The IRI holding company and other para-state corporations that Mussolini founded still exist today; they account for the most inefficient 20 percent of the nation's economy.

But Mussolini convinced few Italians for long that Fascism was the wave of the future. To be sure, many had supported the *Duce* enthusiastically, especially from the time his regime signed the concordat with the Pope (1929) through the easy conquest of Ethiopia (1936). And a small neo-Fascist party, the *Movimento Sociale Italiano* (MSI), still wins roughly five percent of the popular vote in national elections today.

Most Italians quietly turned their backs on Mussolini once it became clear that he had engaged the nation in costly ventures that could not succeed. (More than 400,000 Italians lost their lives in World War II.) During the *Duce*'s foolish expeditions against the Greeks, the British, and the Soviets, many Italians considered themselves to be "half-Fascists," who had taken out their Fascist Party membership cards only *per necessità familiale* (for the good of the family).

On June 2, 1946, the first time that Italians got a chance to vote in a postwar election, they chose to oust the monarchy. They could not forgive King Victor Emmanuel for inviting Mussolini to take power, and for supporting the *Duce*'s imperial ambitions—even if they forgave themselves. The voters elected a constituent assembly, which drafted a new constitution for the republic, providing for a prime minister, a bicameral parliament, and a system of 20 regional governments.

Mussolini and his ideology proved influential beyond Italy's borders. As the world's first and perhaps most popular Fascist leader, he provided the model for other aspiring authoritarian rulers in Europe and Latin America, who, for a time, would make fascism seem an attractive alternative to socialism, communism, or anarchy.

In Germany, Adolf Hitler called Mussolini's 1922 March on Rome "one of the turning points of history." The mere idea that such a march could be attempted, he said, "gave [Germany's National Socialists] an impetus." When Nazis did their outstretched arm salutes, or when Spanish Falangists cried "Franco! Franco! Franco!", they were mimicking their counterparts in Italy. Juan Perón, Argentina's president (1946-1955), echoed the sentiments of many another ambitious Latin strongman when he called Mussolini "the greatest man of our century."

Just before Mussolini came to power, Italians, like citizens of several troubled European societies after World War I, faced a choice—either muddling through disorder and economic disarray under often inept, yet essentially benevolent democratic regimes, or falling in line behind a decisive but brutal dictatorship. Italians chose the latter. They embraced the strong man's notions of a grand New Age. But Mussolini's intoxicating vision of Italy as a great power, they eventually discovered, was a disastrous delusion.

The Fascist era serves to remind Italians and others of something important: that national well-being may not come from charismatic leadership, revolutionary zeal, or military might. Indeed, Italy's peculiar greatness today may lie in its citizens' tolerance of regional and economic differences, in their ability to cope with the inefficiencies of democratic government, in their pragmatic acceptance of human foibles—and, most of all, in their appreciation of the rich texture of everyday life.

1945

RYSZARD KAPUŚCIŃSKI

Ryszard Kapuściński, the Polish journalist and writer, is the author most recently of Shah of Shahs *(Harcourt Brace Jovanovich). Born in 1932, he now lives in Warsaw. This essay was translated by Klara Glowczewski.*

TODAY, when I go back in memory to those years, I realize, not without a certain surprise, that I remember better the beginning rather than the end of the war. The beginning is clearly fixed for me in time and place. I can easily recreate its image because it has retained all its coloring and emotional intensity. It begins with my suddenly noticing one day, in the clear azure sky of the end of summer (and the sky in September 1939 was marvelously blue, without a single cloud), somewhere very, very high up, 12 glimmering silver points. The entire bright, lofty dome of sky is filled with a hollow, monotonous hum, of a kind I've never heard before. I'm seven years old, I'm standing in a meadow, and staring at the points barely, barely moving across the sky.

Suddenly, nearby, at the edge of the forest, there's a tremendous roar. I hear bombs exploding with an infernal racket. (That these are bombs I will learn later, for at this moment I still don't know that there is such a thing as a bomb, the very concept is foreign to me, a child from the sticks who doesn't yet know about the radio or the movies, doesn't know how to read or write, and also hasn't heard of war and lethal weapons.) I see gigantic fountains of earth spraying upward. I want to run

toward this extraordinary spectacle; it astounds and fascinates me. I have no war experiences yet and cannot relate into a single chain of causes and effects these glistening silver airplanes, the roar of the bombs, the plumes of earth flying up to the height of trees, and my imminent death. So I start to run toward the forest, in the direction of the falling and exploding bombs. But a hand grabs me from behind and throws me to the ground. Stay down, I hear my mother's trembling voice, don't move. And I remember that my mother, pressing me to her, is saying something that I don't yet know exists, whose meaning I don't understand, and about which I want to ask her: *that way is death.*

It's night and I'm sleepy, but I'm not allowed to sleep. We have to leave, run away. Where to, I don't know; but I do understand that flight has suddenly become some kind of higher necessity, some new form of life, because everyone is running away. All highways, roads, even country paths, are jammed with wagons, carts, and bicycles, with bundles, suitcases, bags, buckets, with terrified, helplessly wandering people. Some are running away to the east, others to the west, north, south; they run in all directions, circle, fall from exhaustion, sleep for a moment, then, summoning the rest of their strength, begin anew their aimless journey. I must hold my younger sister firmly by the hand. We mustn't get lost, my mother warns; but even without her telling me, I sense that the world has suddenly become dangerous, foreign, and evil, that one must be on one's guard.

I'm walking with my sister beside a wagon. It's a simple ladder wagon, lined with hay, and high up on the hay, on a cotton sheet, lies my grandfather. He cannot move; he is paralyzed. When an air raid begins, the entire patiently trudging and now suddenly panicked throng dives into ditches, burrows into bushes, drops down into the potato fields. Only the wagon on which my grandfather lies remains on the deserted road. He sees the airplanes flying at him, sees them violently dip and take aim at the abandoned wagon, sees the fire of the weapons aboard, hears the roar of the engines passing over his head. When the planes disappear we return to the wagon and my mother wipes my grandfather's perspiring face. Sometimes there are air raids several times a day. After each one, perspiration pours from my grandfather's gaunt, tired face.

WE'RE entering an increasingly gloomy landscape. There's smoke on the horizon. We pass by deserted villages, solitary, burned-out houses. We pass battlefields strewn with abandoned war equipment, bombarded railway stations, overturned cars. It smells of gun powder, and of burning, decomposing meat. Carcasses of horses are everywhere. The horse—a large, defenseless animal—doesn't know how to hide; during a bombardment it stands motionless, waiting for death. There are dead horses at every step, right in the road, by the side in the ditch, further away in the field. They're lying with their legs up in the air, taunting the

From *The New Republic*, January 27, 1986, pp. 39-42. Reprinted by permission of The New Republic, © 1986, The New Republic, Inc.

world with their hooves. I don't see any dead people, for these are buried quickly; only horses, everywhere—black, bay, piebald, chestnut, as if this were not a people's war but a war of horses, as if it were they who waged among themselves a fight to the death, as if they were its only victims.

A hard, freezing winter comes. If people are badly off, they feel more keenly the chill of the environment, the cold is more piercing. For those who live in normal conditions, winter is but another season, a waiting for the spring, but for the poor and the unfortunate, it is a disaster, a catastrophe. And that first winter of the war was truly severe. In our apartment the stoves are cold, and a white, hoary frost covers the walls. There's nothing with which to heat the oven; we cannot buy fuel, and we cannot risk stealing it. For the theft of coal—death; for the theft of wood—death. Human life is now worth next to nothing: a lump of coal, a bit of wood.

WE HAVE nothing to eat. My mother stands for hours at the window; I can see her fixed stare. One can see people staring out into the street from many windows, as if they were counting on something, waiting for something. I roam around the backyards with a gang of boys; it's something between play and searching for something to eat. Sometimes the smell of cooking will come wafting through a door. Then one of my friends, Waldek, sticks his nose into the crack and hurriedly, feverishly, inhales the smell, stroking his stomach as if he were sitting at a richly laden table.

One day we hear that they'll be giving out candy in a store near the marketplace. Immediately we make a line—a long queue of cold and hungry children. It's afternoon, dusk is approaching. We stand in the frost all evening, all night, and the following day. We stand huddled together, hugging one another for warmth. Finally they open the store. But instead of candy each of us receives an empty metal container that once held some fruit drops (what happened to the candy, who took it, I don't know). Weak, numb from the cold, yet at this moment happy, I carry my booty home. It's valuable, because on the inside wall of the can there remains a residue of sugar. My mother heats some water and pours it into the

can. We have a hot, sweet drink: our only nourishment in several days.

Then we're on the road again, traveling from Polesie, from our town Pińsk, west, because there, my mother says, in a village near Warsaw, is our father. He was on the front, was captured, escaped, and is now teaching in a small country school. Today, when we who during the war were children reminisce about that time and say "father," or "mother," we forget, because of the gravity of those words, that our mothers were young women and our fathers young men, that they desired each other very much, missed each other very much, wanted to be with each other. My mother, too, was a young woman then, so she sold everything she had in the house, rented a wagon, and we set out in search of my father. We found him by accident. As we were passing through a village called Sieraków, my mother suddenly cried out to a man crossing the street: Dziudek! It was my father.

From that day on we lived together in a tiny room without light or water. When it grew dark we went to sleep, for there wasn't even a candle. Hunger followed us here from Pińsk. I was constantly looking for something to eat, a crust of bread, a carrot, anything. One day my father, having no other choice, said in class: children, anyone who wants to come to school tomorrow must bring one potato. He didn't know how to trade, didn't know how to do business, he had no salary, so he realized he had only this one option. Some children brought a half, even a quarter. A whole potato was a great treasure.

NEAR MY village is a forest, and in this forest, near a settlement called Palmira, is a clearing. SS men carry out executions there. At first they shoot only at night, and we are awakened by hollow-sounding machine-gun volleys, repeated at even intervals. Later they also do it in daytime. They bring the condemned in covered, dark green trucks, and at the end of the convoy in an open truck rides the firing squad. Those from the squad are always in long coats, as if a long belted coat were an indispensable prop of the murder ritual. When a convoy passes, we, a group of country children, watch, hidden among the roadside bushes. In a moment, behind the cover of trees, something we are forbidden to look at will begin to happen. I can feel my flesh

tingling, can feel myself trembling all over. With bated breath we wait for the volleys of gunfire. There they are. Then we hear individual shots. After a time the convoy returns to Warsaw. At the end, in the open truck, ride the SS men from the firing squad, smoking cigarettes and talking.

At night the partisans come. I can see their faces, pressed to the glass, as they appear suddenly at the window. I look at them as they sit at the table, always moved by the same thought: they can die today, they are as if marked by death. Of course we could all perish, but they boldly embrace that possibility, meet it face-on. They came once, as always, at night. It was autumn and raining. They spoke in whispers with my mother. (I hadn't seen my father in a month and wouldn't until the end of the war; he had gone into hiding.) We had to get dressed quickly and leave. There was a roundup in the area, and entire villages were being deported to the camps. We were to go to Warsaw, to a designated hideout. It was my first time in a big city, the first time I saw a trolley car, tall, multistoried buildings, rows of large stores. How we later found ourselves in the country again, I don't remember. It was some new village, on the other side of the Vistula. I remember only walking again next to a wagon and hearing the sand of a warm, country road sifting through the wheels' wooden spokes.

THROUGHOUT the entire war I dream of a pair of shoes. *To have shoes.* But how to get them? What did I have to do to have shoes? In the summer I walk barefoot and the soles of my feet are tough as leather. At the beginning of the war my father made me some shoes out of felt, but he's not a shoemaker and they look ill-shaped; besides, I've grown, and they're already too tight. I dream of strong, massive shoes with taps, shoes that make a loud, distinct sound as they strike the pavement. The fashion then was for boots. They were a symbol of masculinity, of strength. I could stare for hours at a pair of good-looking boots. I liked the luster of the leather, I liked to listen to its crunch. But it wasn't just a matter of the beauty of a good pair of shoes, or of comfort. A good strong shoe was a symbol of prestige and power, a symbol of rule. A poor, torn shoe was a sign of degradation, the mark of a man stripped of all dignity, condemned to a subhuman existence. Having a good pair of shoes meant being strong, or simply *being*. But in those years all my dream shoes, which I encountered in the streets and roads, passed me by indifferently. I was left (thinking that I would remain thus forever) in my heavy wooden clogs covered with black tarpaulin, to which I tried, unsuccessfully, with the help of some greasy stuff, to impart a bit of luster.

In 1944 I became an altar boy. My priest was the chaplain of a field hospital. Rows of camouflaged tents stood hidden in a pine forest on the left bank of the Vistula. During the Warsaw uprising, and then later, when the January offensive began, there was feverish, exhausting activity here. From the front, which thundered and smoked nearby, arrived speeding ambulances bringing the wounded, who were often unconscious, piled up in haste and confusion one on top of the other, as if they were sacks of grain (only sacks dripping blood). The orderlies, themselves already half-dead with exhaustion, took out the wounded and laid them on the grass. Then, with a rubber hose, they sprayed them with a strong jet of cold water. Whichever of the wounded began to show signs of life they carried into the tent that housed the operating room. (In front of it, right on the ground, there was each day a fresh heap of amputated arms and legs.) Whoever did not move again they carried to an enormous grave at the back of the hospital. It was there, over that boundless tomb, that I stood for hours on end beside the priest, holding his breviary and aspersorium. I repeated after him the prayer for the dead. "Amen," hundreds of times a day, "Amen," in haste, for somewhere nearby, beyond the forest, the machine of death was working overtime. Until finally, one day, it grew empty and quiet. The rush of ambulances ceased, the tents disappeared (the hospital moved west), and in the forest only crosses remained.

And after? Now, as I write these pages for a book about my war years (a book I'll probably never write), I'm thinking about how its final pages would look, its end, its epilogue. What would it say about the end of the great war? Nothing, I think. I mean nothing definitive, nothing that would close the subject once and for all. Because in a certain but essential sense the war did not end for me in 1945, or even soon

thereafter. In many ways something of it endures even today, because for those who live through it, war never, finally, ends. There is an African belief that someone really dies only when the last of those who knew and remembered him die, that someone (or something) ceases to exist when all bearers of memory leave this world. Something like this also happens with war.

Those who live through a war never free themselves from it. It remains within them like some sort of mental hump, a painful growth which even that excellent surgeon, time, will be unable to remove. Listen to a gathering of survivors, around a table, in the evening. It doesn't matter what they start out talking about. There can be a thousand beginnings, but there will be one end: remembering the war. These people, even in changed, peacetime circumstances, think in terms of its images, superimpose them on every new reality, with which they can no longer fully identify because that reality is of the present and they are possessed by the past, the constant returning to what they lived through and how they managed to live through it. Their thinking is an obsessively repeated retrospection.

BUT what does it mean to think in wartime images? It means seeing everything as existing in a state of extreme tension, as breathing cruelty and dread. For wartime reality is a world of extreme, Manichaean reduction, which erases all intermediate hues, gentle, warm, and limits everything to a sharp, aggressive counterpoint, to black and white, to the primordial struggle of two forces—good and evil. Nothing else on the battlefield! Only the good, in other words, us, and the bad, meaning everything that stands in our way, which appears to us, and which we lump into the sinister category of evil. The wartime image is saturated with the atmosphere of force, a physical, material, crackling, smoking, frequently erupting force, constantly attacking someone, brutally expressed in every gesture, in the sound of every footstep striking the pavement, of a rifle butt striking a skull. Force is the only criterion of value: only the strong counts, his reason, his shout, his fist—because conflict is resolved not through compromise, but by destroying the opponent. All this takes place in a climate of intensified emotion, exaltation, fury, passion, in which we feel constantly stunned, deafened, and—

above all—threatened. We move about in a world full of hateful glances and clenched jaws, full of gestures and voices that terrify.

I thought for a long time that was the only world, that was how it looked, how life looked. For the war years coincided with my childhood and then with the start of maturity, of first understanding, of the birth of consciousness. It seemed to me that war, not peace, was the natural state, even the only state, the only form of existence; that roundups and executions, lies and shouts, contempt and hatred, were part of the natural and immemorial order of things, the content of life, the essence of being. So when the guns suddenly fell silent, when the roar of exploding bombs died away and suddenly there was quiet, I was astonished by it. I didn't know what it meant, what it was. I think that a grown-up, hearing this quiet, could say: hell is over. Finally peace has returned. But I did not remember what peace was. I was too young for that; when the war ended hell was all I knew.

THE YEARS passed, yet the war constantly reminded us of its presence. I lived in a city reduced to ashes, I climbed mountains of rubble, roved through a labyrinth of ruins. The school to which I went had no floors, no windows, no doors; everything had gone up in flames. We had no books, no notebooks. I still had no shoes. War as affliction, as want, as hardship, went on. I still had no home. The return home from the front is the most keenly felt symbol of war's end. *Tutti a casa!* But I could not go home, because what had been my home was now abroad, in another country. Once, after class, we were playing soccer in a nearby field. One of my friends, chasing the ball, ventured into some bushes. There was a terrible bang; we were thrown to the ground. He died from a mine that had been left there. War was still laying traps for us, it refused to surrender. Its victims hobbled along the streets leaning on wooden crutches, waved empty arm sleeves in the wind. Those who survived it, it tormented by night, reminding them of itself in bad dreams.

But war continued for us above all because of the fact that for five years it had shaped our young characters, our psyche, our mentality. It had tried to deform and ruin us, setting the worst examples, compelling us to ignominious behavior, letting loose the basest emotions. "War," wrote in those years the Polish philosopher Boleslaw Miciński, "warps not only the souls of those who try to oppose the invader." Yes, to come out of the war meant to cleanse oneself internally, and above all to cleanse oneself of hatred. But how many really tried? And how many were successful? It was a process, in any event, exhausting and long, which could not take place overnight; the wounds from that conflagration, the psychological and moral wounds, were truly deep.

When there's talk of 1945 . . . I'm irritated by the phrase one often hears in reference to it: the joy of victory. What joy? So many people died. Millions of bodies were buried. Thousands lost arms and legs, lost sight and hearing, lost sanity. Each death is a misfortune. No, the end of every war is sad: yes, we survived, but at what a cost! War is proof that man, as a thinking and feeling being, failed the test, let himself down, was defeated.

When there's talk of 1945 . . . some-time in the summer of that very year, my aunt, who through some miracle survived the Warsaw uprising, brought out to us in the country her son Andrzej, born during the uprising. Today he is a 40-year-old man. When I look at him I think—how long ago all that was! How many generations have already been born who have no idea what war is! But those who survived should bear witness. Bear witness in the name of those who fell by their side, and often in their place. Bear witness about what the camps were, the extermination of the Jews, the destruction of Warsaw and Wroclaw. Is this easy? No. We who survived know how difficult it is to convey the truth about it to those for whom, happily, it is an unfamiliar experience. We know how language fails us, words fail us; how all that, at bottom, cannot be conveyed; how often we feel helpless. (Once someone said to me in Chicago: "They took him to Auschwitz? But why did he agree? Why didn't he get a lawyer?")

Still, despite these difficulties and limitations, of which we must be aware, we should speak. Because talking about all that does not divide but unites, allows us to establish threads of understanding, threads of community. The dead admonish us. They transmitted something important to us, and we must be responsible. To the degree that we are able, we should oppose everything that could again give rise to war, to crime, to catastrophe. Because we who have survived war know how it begins, whence it comes. We know that it comes not only from bombs and rockets. We know that it comes also, perhaps above all, from fanaticism and from pride, from stupidity and from contempt, from ignorance and from hatred. That it feeds on all that, that on that and from that it grows.

When there's talk of 1945 . . . I think of those who were no longer there.

When there's talk of 1945 . . .

Wild passions have gone to sleep
And rash acts;
Love of God, love of man,
Quietly revives in us.
—J.W. Goethe, *Faust*

If only. If only.

The War Europe Lost

Ronald Steel

September 1939. For a few a searing memory. For most a dim recollection or a date in a history book. The Luftwaffe spreading death and destruction from the air, Hitler's Panzer divisions slicing through a hapless Poland. Britain and France, having refused a year earlier to help a defensible country, Czechoslovakia, come to the aid of an indefensible one. World War II is under way.

Forty years have passed, and yet the event has not been put into perspective. We are still uncertain as to what it means. Young Germans, not even born when the war began, are only now learning the truths that their elders preferred not to think about, learning of the Holocaust from a commercial television program. The evil that was once unspeakable has now become historic and, judging from the current spate of books and films about Hitler, dramatically entertaining.

Unlike World War I, which was fought entirely in Europe and whose consequences were largely confined there, the second war was truly a world war, one that undermined the authority of the vanquished European states and broke their imperial hold on the colonial world. In this sense the consequences of the war were at least as great, perhaps greater, outside Europe as within. A world centered on Europe and defined in terms of it—the "Near East," the "Far East," the "New World"—shifted in perspective as Europe's hold on its colonies and clients was broken.

The demise, or at least the precipitous decline, of Europe itself as a power center and arbiter of the world's destiny was an event few could have predicted. Hitler's attempt to unify the continent in a Pax Germanica had cataclysmic consequences. It made Europe the instrument of the two victorious flanking powers, America and Russia, and destroyed the political and moral authority of the European state system. Europe, having been the predatory power, became the quarry, the object of others' diplomacy rather than the prime mover. One of the great unintended effects— and surely one of the most ironic—of World War II was to end the hegemony of Europe in the very act of trying to assert it.

Europe may rise again as a political power. But it will be in very different form. And such revival can find its impetus only in an attempt to regain what has so incontestably been lost—lost not only to America and Russia, but, as hardly needs to be underlined, to colonial areas Europe once held in thrall. This condition has become so accepted that few anymore think it remarkable that the value of the pound sterling should be dependent on Arab deposits in British banks.

Although Europe indeed lost much as a result of World War II, it gained a great deal—perhaps even more on balance. It gained liberation from its own colonies; liberation from the costly and often bloody pursuit of empire; liberation from the deadly rivalries of a state system perpetually out of balance because a unified Germany was simply too big and too powerful to contain. One of the few happy results of the war was the division of Germany, a division that solved the problem, temporarily at least, of how it would be possible to create a European balance Germany would neither dominate nor try to overturn. This development, most Germans would agree, has been as desirable for them as for their neighbors. It has provided an answer to the dilemma first posed a century ago when Bismarck created a Reich under Prussian dominance. What was achieved by the sword in 1870 was undone by the sword in 1945.

Thus it can be said that the result of World War II, unintended though it may have been, was to save Europe from itself. Europe, as a political entity, lost the war it had brought on itself. America and Russia expanded to a global scale in quest of a balance that was no longer possible to maintain within Europe itself. The successor powers, America and Russia, not only gained control over Europe, but to protect their newfound role also developed a vested interest in the continued division of Europe. A divided Europe is of no harm to either superpower. A unified Europe, either allied to one of them or standing between them, represents an enormous and potentially threatening change in the world political balance.

Thus, looking back from the perspective of 40 years, we can see World War II not only as a human tragedy, as all wars are, but as a political lesson. The war itself resulted from the attempt to resolve the German question. This problem had been left hanging ever since the Treaty of Versailles 20 years earlier, in 1919. World War I, for all its carnage, resolved nothing. It neither gave Germany the mastery of Europe, as the Kaiser and his generals hoped, nor removed Germany's power to seek that mastery once again. It could be argued that, if the United States had not entered the European war in 1917, the Allies would have been obliged to agree to a compromise peace giving Germany hegemony over Eastern Europe. Such a compromise in turn probably would have allowed Kerensky's parliamentary regime to have survived in Russia and avoided the conditions within Germany that allowed Hitler to come to power in 1933.

A concern with the European power balance is what brought the United States into the Second World War, as into the first one. That concern was twofold, although we tend to forget the second part. It was, first, that Europe not fall under the control of an aggressive power hostile to the United States; and, second, that Europe not be dominated by *any* single power. The reason for the second concern is simply that a unified Europe with a single political will inevitably would have needs and ambitions different from, and even hostile to, those of the United States.

The sadistic brutality and maniacal racial practices of Nazi Germany gave a moral patina, so far as Britain and America were concerned, to what was essentially a dynastic conflict. The United States, like Britain, was not drawn into World War II because it found Nazi evil insupportable. Had Hitler confined his genocide within the German frontiers fixed at Versailles, the democratic nations would have done no more to stop him than they did to stop his latter-day admirer, Idi Amin. Rather it was his attempt to overturn the European balance by force, to gain control of the continent, that brought Britain and France, and ultimately the United States and Russia, into belated alliance against him.

Thus it is worth remembering that the last European war, whose 40th anniversary we note this fall, was not about freedom versus slavery, but about more mundane considerations of the balance of power. The character of the Nazi regime, appalling and inhuman though it was, was not the question at issue. The question was whether that regime should be allowed to impose its authority by force of arms upon all of Europe. When that objective moved from the abstract to the verge of attainment, the United States set up the conditions by which it was drawn into the European war.

It is well to remember anniversaries like the current one, but there is danger in overdrawing or misunderstanding their significance. World War II is not the cold war. Soviet Russia is not Nazi Germany. Angola is not republican Spain. History does not repeat itself. The person who overlearns its "lessons" is condemned to relive its chastisements. Conditions change, and so do alliances. If, as Palmerston said, nations have no allies, only interests, the definition of those interests changes with time and circumstance.

What happened on the plains of Poland 40 years ago represented the last attempt to resolve the German problem within a strictly European context. It was a "world" war only as a result of its unintended consequences. That situation cannot recur because Europe has lost the mastery of its fate—precisely as a result of that war for the mastery of Europe. The slogans of World War II—"appeasement," "isolation," "neutrality"—are of no more value today than that war's antiquated tanks and Flying Fortresses.

THINKING BACK ON MAY 68

Diana Johnstone

F RANCE IS commemorating the twentieth anniversary of May 68 with a certain nostalgia and pride. However it may be interpreted, the massive French revolt of May 1968 quickly became the symbol of an era. The "events," featuring an ephemeral revolution at the Sorbonne and the biggest general strike in French history, marked the last time that Paris could claim to be the center of the world.

That position was usurped from countless other places where far more dramatic events were happening, first of all from Vietnam. In that year of the Tet offensive, it was the Vietnamese being torn from their grass hiding places by flames and bayonets that fired revolt all over the world.

In 1967, French leftists organized Vietnam committees whose activities prepared the ground for May 68. The Trotskyists drew in well-known intellectuals on the national and even international level, while the Maoists concentrated

on neighborhood organizing. The extreme right "Occident" mounted physical attacks, and the leftists prepared to fight back. Incidents concerning Vietnam led to the overkill police repression that inflamed the Latin Quarter in the early days of May. Ironically, a key reason the French government clamped down so excessively on the pro-Vietnam activists may well have been to prove Paris' fitness as a neutral and orderly capital for the peace talks that were opening there between the Americans and the Vietnamese.

The issue of the Vietnam War was uniquely ambiguous and complex in France. In the United States, students and other citizens who protested against the war were clearly protesting against their own government. West German students protested against their own government's complicity in "genocide" against the Vietnamese. This was also true to a lesser extent in other allied countries.

But France was a special case. President Charles de Gaulle had recently taken France out of NATO and, in a

From *Zeta Magazine*, May 1988, pp. 4-9. Copyright © 1988 by The Institute for Social and Cultural Communications, part of The Institute for Social and Cultural Change, Inc., Boston, MA.

resounding speech in Phnom Penh, clearly marked his distance from the American war. After defying the far right in order to make peace in Algeria, de Gaulle granted at least nominal independence to most of the rest of France's colonial possessions in Africa and embarked on a policy of friendly relations with the Third World. Unlike other Western leaders, de Gaulle was not particularly hostile to the movement in support of Vietnam, as long as its targets were the Americans or even the French Communist Party (PCF), criticized for being too lukewarm in its support of Third World revolution.

Domestic political complexity was compounded by the presence of a diehard colonialist far right which, whatever satisfaction it might derive from watching the Americans lose a war the French could not win, nevertheless hated Charles de Gaulle above all for throwing away the French Empire.

The revolt broke out on May 3 after police entered the sanctuary of the Sorbonne and arrested leftist leaders. In the streets, police charged. Some ran for cover. Some fought back. After several days of violent skirmishs between growing groups of students and baton-wielding security policy (CRS..."CRS SS!"), on May 10 the entire Latin Quarter was besieged in the "night of the barricades." All night, students around the Pantheon calmly built barricades, passing the paving stones from hand to hand with the same gestures seen in the 16-millimeter films shown by Vietnam committees, of Vietnamese peasant women rebuilding bombed dikes.

The next day, the streets were cluttered with debris from the police charge. The Latin Quarter was occupied by rows of armed CRS and students who had been apolitical a few days before wandered in a new landscape, transformed into an oppressed people with an occupation army to overthrow.

Paris was nearly the last student population in the world to get into the spirit of the times. But such was the mystique of Paris, capital of revolution, that it was only when students in Milan or Berlin heard of the Paris events that they thought something truly momentous was happening. Many set out on pilgrimage for Paris heedless of transport strikes and gasoline shortages, to join the revolution in the Sorbonne.

TWENTY YEARS later, May 68 seems to have left fewer traces in France than in those other countries where it was seen as a beacon. There are many reasons for this, some to be found in the complex and ambiguous political situation of Gaullist France at that time. The very suddenness and size of the explosion caused problems (1) of interpretation and (2) of countermeasures. France has a history of heavy lids alternately clamped down and blown off by social explosions. Once again, the French state wielded the carrots of reform and the stick of police brutality to normalize society before the rebels could work out what it was they wanted.

To a certain extent, no explanation was needed. Students of the sixties had not yet been enslaved by fear of unemployment and felt free to care about the world for its own sake, to express indignation at the brutality of power with a freshness hard to recall after the moral ravages of the seventies "me" generation and the greedy eighties meanness of Reaganism.

But French students suddenly found themselves leading a revolt bigger than Che Guevara's, yet with much less obvious reason d'etre. The spectacle of a world in upheaval was momentarily shifted from the sweaty tangle of the jungles of Vietnam to a more familiar stage, in a city where the living is easy and the graceful facades are steeped in historic and literary memories. When it came to acting out revolution, Paris students had the advantage of a national tradition—May 68 was no orphan, but part o the line running from 1789 to 1830 to 1848, and above all through the Paris Commune of 1871. "The Student Commune" was the title of philosopher Edgar Morin's glowing essay opening the most widely noted of the shelf-load of books that appeared in shops more quickly than the streets could be repaved: *La Breche.*

May 68 fell into a political context where it was instantly interpreted and utilized for particularly French purposes.

CONTRARY TO the media images, street battles were marginal to the feeling of May 68, which was definitely "make love not war." The casualties were light and nobody resorted to firearms. The chief of Paris Police at the time, Maurice Grimaud, credits himself and Alain Krivine, the Trotskyist leader whose organization's service d'ordre still protects left-wing demonstrations from far right attacks, for keeping the war dance within certain bounds.

I was living at the time in the Marais section of Paris, whose gentrification (sponsored by de Gaulle's Minister of

Culture, Andre Malraux) was still in the planning stages. The Marais was something of a Maoist stronghold. The Vietnam Comites de Base were out in the markets every Sunday morning, with dazibao and photographs of the war, selling earnest tracts on people's war. The Maoist leadership in the elite Ecole Normale Superieure located in the rue d'Ulm had stayed clear of the student revolt and even regarded it as a bourgeois plot—an attitude shared by many of their arch adversaries in the PCF, where the suspicion still smolders that May 68 was a CIA plot to bring down de Gaulle and install a more pro-American government. (According to Maurice Grimaud, this suspicion was shared by the French government, which publicly accused East Germany but privately suspected the CIA of subsidizing the Trotskyists to weaken the pro-Moscow PCF.)

The Maoists stayed far from the street battles so cherished by international news photo agencies. In the Marais, their Vietnam Committees rapidly turned into Action Committees making the revolution in community workplaces. In cultural workplaces like schools and libraries, employees everywhere were going on strike, reorganizing their own work, which often needed it. This was by far the most interesting development of the May movement, the practical basis for the seventies faith in *autogestion*, or self-management, but totally out of the internal spotlight focused on policemen's clubs and burning cars. The Maoists' proudest achievement in the Marais was to get parents and teachers at the local nursery school to dismiss the "racist" director and admit a dozen North African children who had been excluded.

Sociology Defeats Politics

TWO SORTS of tension existed in the Paris student milieu leading up to May 68: a political tension carried by the Trotskyist or pro-Chinese dissident offshoots from the PCF's student union where a Stalinist backlash had driven out the "pro-Italian" (influenced by the Italian Communist Party) leadership in the wake of Khrushchev's fall; and a social tension stemming from the disorientation of students in a University unable to adapt from its old elitism to the influx of masses from the middle class. These tensions were entangled, notably in incidents at Nanterre starring sociologist Alain Touraine's notoriously impertinent student, Daniel Cohn-Bendit—incidents that led to the police occupation of the Sorbonne and random clubbing of passers-by that touched off the incredible May escalation.

Still, one can venture to say that without the spark provided by CRS billy-clubs, those tensions might have remained marginal or simply a matter of routine grumbling. When thousands of Latin Quarter students found themselves on the morning after the night of the barricades enlisting in "The Revolution," the vast majority were literally rebels without a cause—yet. One simple lesson struck everyone: the lesson of sudden, total change: revolution can happen.

Political groups and sociologists were immediately on the scene to explain to the rebels what they were rebelling about, and political and sociological explanations have vied with each other ever since. At a distance of twenty years, one can say that from the start, the sociological explanation benefited from endorsement by prestigious intellectuals and the most respected journals, and that it has easily won acceptance as the major factor. More than that, sociology in

DANIEL COHN BENDIT IN COURTYARD OF THE SORBONNE

general has won out over politics in the twenty years since May 68, to the point where political behavior risks becoming a minor category of sociological observation. France since May 68 has seen a drastic decline of political thinking, other than the very specialized sort practiced by the small (and brilliant) professional political class.

The sociological explanation has triumphed largely as a result of the inadaptability of the contending political explanations. Alain Touraine calls May 68 "new wine in old bottles." Karl Marx, he recalls, was very hard on the Paris Commune. The Communards used the exalted language of the 1789 Revolution, unaware that the future was with the labor movement, which they rejected. In May 68, the students, not realizing that they themselves were the new agent for social change, insisted on bringing out the workers, who were much weaker than they were, and who "used the language of the previous century."

Touraine's old student Daniel Cohn-Bendit agrees that May was "a mix between the last revolution of the nineteenth century and a completely new movement which raised the problems of the end of the twentieth."

It is certainly true that the revolutionary projects championed by the contending Leninist vanguard groups, of which Krivine's Communist Revolutionary League and the short-lived Maoist Gauche Proletarienne were the most influential, were remarkably anachronistic and unsuited to a contemporary advanced industrial society. But it is also true, as Edgar Morin wrote in his article on "The Student Commune," that "workerism, far from dividing the movement as one might have thought, provided the ideology enabling it to self-justify its cultural struggle (for a university open to the people) and its political struggle (for a people's state)."

"Workerism" was unifying insofar as it expressed an essential generosity of the sixties revolt, the students' demand for equality not only for themselves but, even more, for others. The sociologists who consider this a mistake are only partly right. It is right that the student revolutionaries, awed by the presumed revolutionary role of the working class, often had trouble realizing who they were and what their own social power could be. But their failure to think only of their own interests, if sociologically a mistake, was politically correct.

WORKERS ON STRIKE AT THE RENAULT FACTORY

IN A few days, the student revolt touched off the biggest strikes in French history. Some nine million employees went on strike, shutting down the country and bringing the seemingly solid regime of General de Gaulle to the brink of collapse. These heady happenings suggested to the participants that purely spontaneous individual self-assertion might miraculously merge in a unanimity called Revolution.

While the Communist-led General Confederation of Labor (CGT) worked with the government on an agreement to get the workers back on the job before they could be further contaminated, the fact of the massive strikes rekindled the French students' interest in their own working class as a potential "revolutionary subject." For prior to May, it was understood from the vantage point of Francois Maspero's well-furnished bookstore La Joie de Lire in the rue Saint Severin that the contemporary front lines of the world revolution were in the imperialist periphery, in Vietnam or Latin America, and certainly not in France.

Cobblestones to Modernize France

BARRICADES ARE a Paris revolutionary tradition. The act of piling up paving stones reawakened historic memories, and, confirmed by the massive strikes, revived the old notion of France as the revolutionary country par excellence.

Yet even as it attracted the attention of the world, the May movement looked inward, turning its back on the Third World in its effort to unfold revolution according to national patterns. This was the start of the loss of interest in the Third World that soon ruined Maspero (along with "revolutionary" shop-lifting supposed to punish the publisher for "exploiting" the subjects he published books about, unlike all those other publishers only interested in making money). It is significant that La Joie de Lire was sold to Nouvelles Fron-

tieres, a budget travel agency. The sixties trips to Algeria, Cuba, China, and even California in search of revolutionary models gave way to vacations in warm climates, period.

But in May 68, as Edgar Morin observed, an "osmosis" occurred between the "existential libertarian exigency" of some and the "planetary politicization" of the others. The world seemed to be coming together politically when it was in fact falling apart. The seventies were, of course, marked by the total fragmentation of leftist movements in all the developed countries, but this was most destructive in France because of the peculiarly French rejection of pragmatism and demand for an overall political project or ideology as context for even the slightest action.

According to the sociological explanation, French society had lagged behind its own economic development, and May 68 was a sort of cultural revolution led by the younger generation to catch up.

Yet one of the peculiarities of the French May revolt, noted by foreign contemporaries, was the absence of the cultural, or counter cultural-aspects prevalent in other Western countries. The emblematic figure of Daniel Cohn-Bendit can be deceptive: thrown out of France he continued his revolt in the more congenial Frankfurt scene. If it took May 68 to "modernize" France, oddly the French left itself was not modernized, as is attested to by the shallowness of the peace, ecology, and women's movements. However the French left is more "modern" than it was before in a way dear to the hearts of most sociological analysts: it has a much smaller and weaker Communist Party.

The hatred of French intellectuals for the French Communist Party has been an obsession overflowing political categories. Hatred for the PCF comes from right, left, and center. A specialist in the matter, Cornelius Castoriadis, writing under the name of Jean-Marc Coudray in *La Breche,* ex-

AT THE MEDICAL FACULTY "THE GREAT DISRUPTION"

plained why: the PCF is "*neither* reformist *nor* revolutionary." The PCF's revolutionary language provides long-range hopes for its apparatus, consoles the working class, and gets in the way of modern social democratic reforms.

"Prisoner of its past, the Stalinist bureaucratic apparatus is incapable, in France as almost everywhere, of turning the corner that would allow it in theory to play a new role. Not, certainly, a revolutionary role, but the role of the great modern reformist bureaucracy needed for the functioning of French capitalism, which has been recommended to it for years by volunteer advisors, knowledgeable sociologists, and subtle technicians," Castoriadis wrote.

In 1968, both Maoist revolutionaries and budding technocrats saw the youth revolt as a blessed historic opportunity to snatch the working class from the clutches of the PCF. The PCF needed to be destroyed in order "to make the revolution" or conversely to modernize French capitalism. Mortal hatred for the PCF was an often unspoken but crucial element unifying the most politicized of May 68 leaders, even if they disagreed on almost everything else.

There was, after all, a basic difference between those who wanted to take over leadership of the working class and those who rejoiced to see a new "revolutionary subject," or at least a new social category, replacing the working class as the key to historic change.

The second interpretation was suggested in the title of the widely-read book *La Breche*. An historic "breach" or "breakthrough" had opened up. Castoriadis was ecstatic: "whatever comes next, May 68 has opened a new period in universal history."

This extravagant appraisal of the significance of May 68

was by no means unusual. The exaltation of May's spontaneity by established intellectuals like Castoriadis, who in many respects are themselves anything but spontaneous, was a way of celebrating the relegation of the PCF and its bureaucracy to the ashcan of history. Castoriadis perceived an explosion of creativity, "brilliant, effective and poetic slogans surged from the anonymous crowd," teachers were astonished to discover that they knew nothing and their students knew everything. "In a few days, twenty-year olds achieved political understanding and wisdom honest revolutionaries haven't yet reached after thirty years of militant activity." Did this stupefying miracle really take place? It was hailed in any case: for, if innocent youth could rise from its tabula rasa and make the revolution, there was obviously no need for a structured organization like the Communist Party.

There was immense joy among intellectuals at discovering a new revolutionary subject close to themselves. Castoriadis announced that in modern societies youth is a *category* more important than the working class, which has become a dead weight on revolution.

But could spontaneous youth actually make the revolution? Even as he was extolling the glorious "explosion," Castoriadis pointed to its limits. "If the revolution is nothing *but* an explosion of a few days or weeks, the established order (know it or not, like it or not) can accommodate itself very well. Even more, contrary to its belief, it has a profound need for it. Historically, it is the revolution that permits the world of reaction to survive by transforming itself, by adapting," he observed. The outcome could be "new forms of oppression better adapted to today's conditions."

These words unfortunately proved more prophetic for post-May 68 France than Castoriadis' recommendations on how to organize the revolution: "In the conditions of the modern world, getting rid of dominant and exploiting classes requires not only the abolition of private ownership of the means of production, but also the elimination of the division between those who give orders and those who carry them out as social strata. Consequently, the movement combats that division everywhere it finds it, and does not accept it inside the movement itself. For the same reason, it combats hierarchy in all its forms."

THE TROUBLE with this advice is that, taken to extremes, it tends to turn the movement in on itself, destructively. When it comes to combatting "hierarchy" and "authority" wherever they are found, it soon emerges that they are most easily found close to home: in the university, at school, in the left itself. In places far enough down the ladder to be close at hand. The real powers running the world were not seriously disturbed by all this turmoil and this combat was not always carried out with discernment.

After May 68, Raymond Aron's former assistant Andre Glucksmann became the theoretician of a "Grassroots Committee for the Abolition of Wage-Earning and the Destruction of the University." Abolishing wage-earning was a bit too much even for geniuses destined to become "new philosophers." But as for destroying the university, they could get to work right where they were, at the faculty of Vincennes, the experimental campus that admitted working class students without diplomas and allowed leftist professors to teach what they wanted. Glucksmann and company did not destroy "the bourgeois university and the power of

the bourgeoisie," but their disruptions did contribute to destroying the faculty of Vincennes.

A few seasons later, Glucksmann discovered the Gulag and Pol Pot and began to sound like somebody raving about Raymond Aron's lessons on totalitarianism in the midst of a feverish nightmare. When last heard of, he was defending the necessity of a nuclear arms buildup.

A recent monumental two-volume work by Herve Hamon and Patrick Rotman, *Generation* (published by Seuil), traces the personal histories of a number of the main actors of the period from the mid-sixties to the mid-seventies. Some worked, suffered, and even died for their revolutionary ideal. In Guatemala in 1968, Michele Firk shot herself through the head as the police were battering down her door. Of the success stories, the most spectacular is former Maoist Serge July, who eventually turned the newspaper he was assigned to run by the *Gauche Proletarienne* into the fashionably successful daily *Liberation*. July told Hamon and Rotman that 1968 was a "change of planet." France went from a "culturally rural society to an urban society—with the barricade as the symbol between them separating two worlds."

If July has done well, those who were on the other side of the barricades in May 68 have done even better. Alain Madelin and Gerard Longuet, in 1968 leaders of the far right organization Occident whose attacks on supporters of the Vietnamese cause heated the atmosphere of the Latin Quarter shortly before police violence sparked the May events, became cabinet ministers in 1986 in the government of Jacques Chirac.

MAY 68 attained none of its proclaimed goals. There was no revolution, and the reforms—as of the University—served mainly to contain the ferment by isolating leftists in

playgrounds like the faculty at Vincennes, to be harassed by their more revolutionary colleagues. A few years later, authority was reasserted. Today, the university in France is arguably worse than ever.

Hierarchies are so firmly in place that the left's greatest aspiration is to re-elect its patriarch, Francois Mitterrand.

Serge July epitomizes the successful few who are consoled for these failures by the spectacular entrance on stage of the new class nicknamed "young urban professionals." The revolt against the most immediate authorities—father, mother, teacher, trade union—has given the individualistic educated middle class more elbow room to pursue its personal pleasures, interests, and careers. This liberation has not been accompanied by any sustained interest in the more distant power structures that continue to dominate the world, and that Marxism at its best attempted to understand and combat.

But not everybody is consoled.

Two years ago, a report by the French Planning Commission entitled *Faire Gagner la France* raised the question: "Is France going to implode?" The report, directed by Henri Guillaume, warned of the trend toward a "dual society" with a growing cleavage between a middle class and an "excluded" class. The suicide rate among 15 to 25-year-olds has doubled in 20 years. The happiness and progress brought by technological advance are not for everyone.

French society, the report noted, has made a specialty of "unexpected explosions." Government planners warned that an accumulation of negative factors such as loss of purchasing power, of jobs, of status, might provoke "a sort of May 68 in reverse," an explosion of special interests demanding a return to secure pre-68 values.

The lid is back on. But will it stay put?

Conclusion:
The Human Prospect

From the perspective of the 1980s, the West contemplates the year 2000 and the turn of another century. This time the prospects for disillusionment seem slight, for there is little optimism, unfounded or otherwise, about the current condition or future prospects of Western civilization. Indeed, with the development of nuclear weapons and intercontinental missiles, we are forced to consider the possibility that our civilization might destroy itself in an instant. Of course, like our ancestors a century ago, we can point to continued progress, particularly in science and technology. But, unlike our ancestors, we are attuned to the potential for the unforeseen disruptions and disasters that can accompany such innovation.

Our ambivalence about technology is paralleled by our growing recognition that we can no longer depend upon an unlimited upward spiral of economic growth. In the course of this century other dreams have eluded us, including the hope that we could create a just and equal society through drastic and rapid social reorganization. Most of the great revolutionary promises of the age have not been kept. Nor do we continue to believe very fervently that the elimination of repressive social and moral taboos will produce an era of freedom and self-realization. By now virtually all areas of human conduct have been demystified (and trivialized), but confusion rather than liberation seems to be the immediate result. Finally, modernism, that great artistic and intellectual movement of the century's early years, has exhausted itself. For decades, as one commentator observes, the avant-garde had "pushed back frontiers of form, structure, and tonality until there was no structure left to topple."

These developments are marked by an uncommon degree of self-consciousness in our culture. Seldom in any era have people been so concerned about the future of civilization and the prospects for humanity. The articles in this concluding section convey some current concerns, including the nature and causes of war, the fragility of democracy, prospects for reform in the Soviet Union, America's slippage as a world power, and the future of the cold war.

Looking Ahead: Challenge Questions

Are we witnessing, if not the end of our civilization, the end of the modern era? If so, what kind of future can we expect?

Are those who predict the decline of the West unduly pessimistic?

Based on current theories about the causes of war, what are the prospects for another major war?

Would the end of the cold war be an unmixed blessing?

Unit 5

Is Gorbo another Louis XVI?

PARISTROIKA

DAVID A. BELL

David A Bell is a doctoral candidate in history at Princeton.

FOR THE second most powerful nation in the world, '87 and '88 were extraordinary years. A series of reforms ended some of the autocratic government's worst abuses. A reform-minded leadership experimented with plans for the liberalization of a calcified and corrupt state. The press flourished, and with each day the limits on what could be published were pushed outward. A young and attractive ruler seemed to articulate popular hopes. Yet the population's material situation remained poor, and notoriously stubborn entrenched elites held on to their privileges with increasing desperation. Attention focused on the convocation of a representative body that had not met for a very long time . . .

This may sound like a description of the year 1987-88 and Gorbachev's U.S.S.R., but for a historian, what comes to mind is 1787-88 and the France of Louis XVI. It is often forgotten today, but in the period that preceded the French Revolution, the royal government carried out reforms as shocking and exhilarating as those now taking place in the Soviet Union. These reforms, however, failed to prevent the impending upheaval, and may even have hastened it. As Tocqueville observed, the drama of 1789 began not when things were at their worst, but when things were finally starting to improve—as things may now start to improve under Gorbachev.

King Louis XVI was not a particularly charismatic or competent leader. Nonetheless, under his rule France experimented with a series of provincial assemblies, the greatest concession to democracy ever made by the absolute monarchy. In 1787-88 it abolished the venerable institution of judicial torture, and granted defendants in criminal trials the right to attorneys. It also gave official toleration to Protestants, who had within living memory been the target of massacre and deportation. In those years the young and popular king seemed to side with the people against an intransigent nobility. And by the summer of 1788 official censorship had collapsed and effective freedom of the press came into being, complete with raucous criticism of the existing order.

This was the bright side of Louis's reign. Yet his government made frustratingly little progress against France's mammoth social and economic problems. The most immediate of these was the state's massive debt, incurred in large part through military spending. The country's financial apparatus functioned less as a collector than as a sieve for money, and needed radical reform. The nobility obstinately refused to abandon its own considerable financial privileges. And, ominously, a catastrophic harvest in 1788 sent the price of bread skyrocketing and unleashed the familiar specter of famine. In retrospect it hardly seems surprising that revolution soon broke out.

Of course, Louis XVI and his ministers thought they could control the reform process. They did not see a contradiction between rapid political liberalization and slow structural change. Seeing the nobility as the main obstacle to such change, they believed that the pressure of newly liberated public opinion would help overcome noble resistance. For this reason, the crown subsidized pamphleteers who peddled its line, and Marie Antoinette, in other contexts the epitome of aristocratic haughtiness, declared herself "the queen of the Third Estate." However, the strategy soon backfired. Independent public opinion, initially supportive of Louis XVI, soon forced the king and

From *The New Republic*, July 11, 1988, pp. 21, 24. Reprinted by permission of The New Republic, © 1988, The New Republic, Inc.

the nobility back into each other's embrace, and eventually destroyed both.

Now consider the situation in the Soviet Union. One week a new political party forms in Moscow. The next, Lenin himself comes in for criticism, despite Gorbachev's protestations of following Lenin's true line. Bukharin, Kamenev, and Zinoviev are rehabilitated, and since textbooks have failed to keep up with *glasnost*, the state cancels high school history exams. The Tatars, brutally exiled from their Crimean home under Stalin, are allowed to start returning. The Orthodox Church is given unprecedented freedom and publicity. Eduard Shevardnadze meets in New York with the prime minister of Israel. Andrei Sakharov gives a quasi-official news conference. A protest march for more *glasnost* proceeds in Moscow under the gaze of Western reporters without police interference. In short, taboos are collapsing like dominoes. Yet at the same time the new regime has brought about little improvement either in the population's material condition or in the efficiency of the unwieldy economic system.

Needless to say, Gorbachev too hopes to control the reform process. He seems to believe that public opinion, given a voice for the first time in Soviet history, will help him prod a recalcitrant party and bureaucracy into motion. Indeed, he and his supporters seem almost cocky about this strategy. As one Soviet official said recently about the relaxation of religious controls: "Since the power belongs completely to us, I think we are capable of pointing this track in whatever direction is to our interest." To be sure, the Soviet state exercises a sort of social control that Louis XVI could not have begun to imagine. And Gorbachev is far more able and shrewd than the hapless French king. But he has already underestimated the power and unpredictability of his newly articulated public opinion. Take Armenia and Azerbaijan. If Gorbachev had simply crushed nationalist rumblings there, he would have alienated public opinion and lost crucial support for other aspects of his program. Louis XVI faced similar dilemmas.

So what is in store for the U.S.S.R.? Obviously any historical comparison with revolutionary France has severe limits. Even in 1917, when the Russian revolutionaries consciously compared themselves to the great figures of 1789-99, history failed to follow a proven script. It would be absurd to cast the upcoming Communist Party conference as a Soviet Estates General. But the parallels do suggest three general points.

First, Gorbachev's motivations for *glasnost* and *perestroika*—the question of whether he is a "true Leninist," for instance—may ultimately prove of little importance. Historians have argued about Louis XVI's sincerity in 1787-88, yet agree that it mattered far less than the events Louis helped bring on. Even if Gorbachev were a Machiavellian master of disinformation, plotting every *Pravda* letter to the editor in order to lull Western suspicions, *glasnost* would still have the same consequences.

Second, the greatest opposition to Gorbachev may ultimately come not from the "conservative" Party hierarchy, but from those now calling for further and faster reform. In France an entrenched and ambitious aristocracy long posed the greatest apparent threat to Louis XVI. Yet it was very little time before a new force, calling itself "the nation," emerged and took control of the state, even though in 1788 it possessed no political structure and no military strength. The crown possessed an enormous police apparatus, but the collapse of royal authorities made the police a useless weapon.

Finally, by opening the existing order to criticism and by giving legitimacy to public opinion, Gorbachev may well have destroyed the Soviet state's own last vestiges of legitimacy. Tocqueville noted that when Louis XVI called upon his subjects to air their grievances, the individual complaints collectively formed nothing less than a call for the abolition of the entire regime. By the time the Estates General convened in 1789 many Frenchmen saw little logic or reason in their national institutions, and were eager to wipe the slate clean. Today a whiff of that revolutionary spirit is present in the recent call by Moscow political clubs for a new constitution.

So though we are not likely to see Muscovites storming the Lubyanka anytime soon, we may well see considerable turmoil in the Soviet Union. The French monarchy had survived civil war, invasion, famine, and plague. In the end, what it could not survive was *glasnost*.

Decline—Not Necessarily Fall—Of The American Empire

Paul Kennedy
Special to *The Washington Post*

Born and educated in England, Paul Kennedy is Dilworth Professor of History at Yale. He is the author of "The Rise and Fall of the Great Powers: Economic Change and Military Conflict from 1500 to 2000.

The world is coming to the end of another century, and its No. 1 power is faltering. Forty years earlier, it was in a class of its own in manufacturing output, per capita productivity, high-technology goods and average personal income. Now, with the country's overall growth rate lagging behind that of its chief rivals, that is no longer the case.

At the same time, the social problems of its educational system, the eroding infrastructure, all call for a vast allocation of resources. So, too, do its armed services, which are grappling with a dreadful spiral in the cost of weaponry, and have numerous theaters of war to prepare to fight in.

So many military commitments overseas have been assumed in more favorable times that, with the global economic and strategical balances changing so rapidly, it is doubtful whether the country could fulfill one-half of its treaty obligations in the event of a large-scale war. Being No. 1 remains a source of pride, but it also has its disadvantages, especially in a period of relative decline.

Most readers will take the remarks above as a description of America's current predicament. In fact, it could also be a fair description of an earlier power, Great Britain, which a century ago found itself in very similar circumstances: its economic and industrial ascendancy being eroded, its preeminent position in various parts of the world coming under challenge, its military obligations being far in excess of its capacity to fulfill them all.

And in just the same way as thoughtful American politicians do today, late-Victorian statesmen worried about inner-city poverty, inadequate educational facilities, the erosion of manufacturing jobs, "unfair" foreign competition, and the constant press of demands for more spending on health care, social services and defense.

In the mid-19th century, Britain's industrial and strategical position had been secured. But by 1903, in the words of the Colonial Secretary, Joseph Chamberlain, it resembled a "weary Titan," staggering under the orb of its own fate. In the opinion of certain members of the Prussian General Staff, the future would probably see what they termed "the war of the British Succession"—that is, a struggle to carve up the empire which Britain could no longer control.

And yet the British Empire survived for much longer than those gloomy turn-of-the-century forecasts. It emerged victorious, albeit at heavy cost, from the two great wars of this century. Its empire did not suffer a devastating blow, like the fall of Rome or the sack of Constantinople. It was dismantled more gently, and transferred into a Commonwealth.

Britain's overseas obligations were ceded, at least in the less vital regions, to others who took over the burdens and privileges of power. And while it was no longer able to preserve or recover its predominant position of former times, it did ensure that its relative decline was both reasonably smooth and gradual.

Is there something in this story for America today? It needs to be said immediately that there are enormous differences between Britain and the United States, simply because of their respective size, population and natural resources.

Thus, the argument here is not that

global trends are relegating this country to second- or third-class status. In 50 years, America still ought to be a major player in world politics. It is with the British example in mind, therefore, that one poses the question: How can the United States' own relative decline be made to occur just as smoothly and slowly as possible?

In the sphere of preserving economic competitiveness, for example, it is clear that the British record was a mixed one. While its share of world manufacturing was virtually bound to decline, did that decline have to be so swift? Probably not.

Dozens of studies of Britain's eclipse as "the workshop of the world" have pointed to the low esteem held for manufacturing and commerce (as opposed to the law, or merchant banking) by the educated classes, to the inability to sell in foreign markets, to the limited technical training of the workforce, and, in particular, to the comparatively low rates of investment in new manufacturing plant and in civilian research and development.

Since this latter element is probably the most important indicator of an economy's long-term future, it is worth wondering whether the contemporary American economy is devoting a sufficient share of its resources towards non-military R & D in order to remain competitive with such countries as Japan and West Germany. If the answer is "no," as I suspect it is, the British example should pose a grim warning.

The British had an altogether better record than recent American administrations in budgetary policy and in handling their balance of payments. A strong Treasury department, resting firmly upon pre-Keynesian economic assumptions, insisted that central government revenues and expenditures always be balanced. In fact, in most years there was a slight surplus, which could be used to reduce the National Debt, the total of which was decreased in each peacetime year.

Borrowing from the money markets to cover government deficits was thus restricted to wartime, and widely regarded as one of the great "reserve engines" of British national strength, giving it an advantage over rivals whose credit-worthiness was much shakier. The government's fiscal rectitude also meant that interest rates were lower there than anywhere else—as is the case today in, say, Switzerland or Japan.

Like the present American economy, the late-Victorian economy witnessed a structural shift from manufacturing into services, attended by a widening of the trade deficit in visible goods. But that gap was always covered by the large and swiftly-growing surpluses in invisible trade, due to Britain's earnings as the global banker, insurer, shipper, and commodity dealer, as well as its vast returns on overseas investments.

Until about a decade ago, the United States also enjoyed the position of being the world's greatest creditor nation. Now it has gone to the opposite extreme, with alarming implications for its national prosperity and strength. In that respect, and especially in terms of its soaring budget deficit, the Reagan administration has more resembled the feckless attitude of the Bourbon monarchs of France than the fiscal sobriety of the late-Victorians.

The military position of Great Britain a century or so ago bears many resemblances to that of the United States, which may account for the fact that it is now studied so much at our war colleges. Both nations possessed, relatively speaking, a liberal, laissez-faire political culture which disliked spending large amounts of national income on defense. And yet both had extensive economic and strategical interests overseas which required protection in an unpredictable and often dangerous world.

All this led to earnest debates about "how much is enough," with outside critics complaining about the profligacy of the armed forces, and with the admirals and generals declaring that the monies allocated were insufficient, for the tasks in hand.

On the whole, one has the sense that the British managed the business of balancing needs versus means rather better. Perhaps this is because they had more experience at it, and had learned some lessons from their earlier blunders, such as the Crimean War.

But there was also the fact that Britain had a constitutionally stronger executive branch, in which a Cabinet composed of experienced, senior ministers was usually able to hammer out an integrated national policy while coming under relatively small pressure from domestic lobbies.

This meant in turn that when the British government decided to recognize another power's control of some tropical region, or when it would withdraw from an overexposed position, it could implement such policies without much fear of domestic political obstruction.

Since the U.S. Constitution grants less power to the executive branch than is the case in Britain, there is probably little to be done except to note the differences. It may simply be that when an overextended Great Power faces the need to retrench, controversial alterations in policy can be more easily carried out under a more autocratic constitution than under one featuring a leisurely, eighteenth-century system of checks and balances.

What may be worthy of more attention, however, is the heavy emphasis which Victorian and Edwardian statesmen in London placed upon diplomacy to ease their obligations and close the gap between strategic ends and military means. This, indeed, was the obverse side of that series of strategical contractions made by Britain in the first decade of this century.

By ententes (with France, with Russia), by rapprochements (with the United States), and by new alliances (with Japan), the British eased their obligations in various parts of the world without a total surrender of their interests. This, in turn, allowed a concentration of military and naval power in more critical areas—in the North Sea, for example, where Kaiser Wilhelm II's Germany was building a large and threatening fleet.

To be sure, a policy of diplomatic compromises can only work when foreign powers themselves are also willing to compromise. If such nations are un-appeasable, like the dictator-states of the 1930s, then political deals with them will be flawed. It is as a consequence of those 1930s experiences that, whenever a policy of conciliation towards the Soviet Union is being contemplated today, one will usually be warned of the "lessons of appeasement" by those who prefer a firmer view of Moscow.

But the point about British policy at the beginning of this century is that it did not require concessions to the perceived major threat of Imperial Germany. Rather, it involved a withdrawal of responsibilities in certain regions in favor of third powers—the United States in the Western hemisphere, France in West Africa, Japan in the Far East—which guaranteed stability in return for assuming a larger position. Is such a policy excluded for the United States in the future?

All the long-term indicators suggest that we are shifting from an essentially bipolar world that has existed since 1943 towards a multipolar world with five clusters of power: the United States, the Soviet Union, Japan, China and the European Economic Community. This multipolar world already exists at the economic level—Japan's GNP has now overtaken

5. THE HUMAN PROSPECT

Russia's and the EEC's has overtaken the USA's. In the future, that is likely to translate into a multipolar system at the military level as well.

As we return to the multipolar order of a century ago, diplomacy will be at a premium, especially if a player as subtle as Mikhail Gorbachev is in the field, looking to imitate the role of a Talleyrand or a Bismarck.

Nonetheless, the diplomatic cards are stacked in America's favor. If it can play them properly. It is surely not beyond the wit of American statesmanship to negotiate a redistribution of certain defense burdens towards Western Europe and Japan, and to maintain good relations with the People's Republic of China, which shows every sign of wanting to preserve the status quo in places like Korea.

And if the United States' place as the chief guarantor of order in those regions is somewhat reduced as a consequence, does that bode disaster or merely a redistribution of obligations?

For many reasons outlined above, the British example is not a totally precise one. History never repeats itself exactly. But the way in which Britain adjusted to the altered global conditions around 1900 does suggest policies that leaders in Washington might care to ponder as we move into the post-Reagan era and grapple with America's changed position in the world.

A careful attention to budgetary and trade balances, a check on the rise in the National Debt, an encouragement of greater investment in civilian R & D and in an improved educational system, a greater concern towards evolving a coherent, long-term national military strategy, and a willingness to search for diplomatic solutions to ease the burden of military overextension. That is not a bad catalog of policies for a Great Power to adopt when it confronts relative decline.

HOW THE COLD WAR MIGHT END

*Thinking through a question that has
suddenly become something more than an escapist fantasy*

JOHN LEWIS GADDIS

John Lewis Gaddis is a professor of history at Ohio University. He was born in Texas and attended the University of Texas, graduating in 1963. He received a Ph.D. in history there in 1968. The following year he began teaching at Ohio University. He is the author of several books, including The Long Peace: Inquiries Into the History of the Cold War.

Fata Morgana

IN HIS SPLENDID BOOK *ARCTIC DREAMS: IMAGINATION and Desire in a Northern Landscape*, Barry Lopez describes the most striking of arctic mirages—the fata morgana, in which sharply delineated mountain ranges appear suddenly from a featureless sea, creating the illusion of land where none exists and tempting unwary explorers to set off in search of constantly receding and, in the end, unattainable objectives. Bleak horizons combined with cold climates, he suggests, can alter consciousness and redirect ambitions in wholly unpredictable ways.

What President Ronald Reagan and General Secretary Mikhail Gorbachev saw on the sub-arctic horizon that lay outside Hofdi House, when they met in Reykjavik, Iceland, last October, has not been recorded. But the austere surroundings do appear to have tempted them—briefly, at least—into contemplation of what many would regard as a political fata morgana: the question of how one might rid the world of nuclear weapons and the missiles that carry them. Only at the last minute did astonished advisers manage to pull their bosses back from the abyss that yawned before them: it was, James Schlesinger has written, quoting the Duke of Wellington, "the nearest-run thing you ever saw."

But the view from Reykjavik may yet turn out to have been more than a mirage. The geopolitical ice is shifting beneath our feet these days in unexpected ways. For the first time since the Second World War ended, the superpowers are about to eliminate from their arsenals, by mu-

tual consent, an entire category of nuclear weapons—those carried by intermediate-range missiles. Former opponents of arms control like Richard Perle support this accord, while former supporters like Henry Kissinger oppose it. In a striking reversal of past practice, Moscow appears more willing than Washington to allow intrusive on-site inspection to verify compliance. And all of this is happening under an American Administration that only five years ago was characterizing the Soviet Union as "the focus of evil in the modern world." Familiar verities, it seems, no longer apply; it is difficult to know where one stands.

It would be unwise, therefore, to dismiss the Reagan-Gorbachev discussions at Reykjavik as the aberrant consequence of leaving heads of government alone in the same room, with only their interpreters present. Certainly this attempt to cut through current differences by defining a vision of future harmony will merit more than the puzzled footnote that history books normally accord the summit's only modern analogue: the treaty settling Russo-German differences which Kaiser Wilhelm II and Czar Nicholas II personally negotiated and signed in a single memorable meeting on a German warship in the Baltic in 1905, only to have their horrified governments—and allies—immediately repudiate it.

But the Reykjavik vision of a nuclear-free world implied something larger still: the possibility that the Cold War itself—the occasion for deploying such vast quantities of nuclear armaments in the first place—might one day end, and that some of us might actually live to see the emergence of a new international system capable of moving beyond the condition of perpetual confrontation that has overshadowed our lives for the past four decades. Mirage or not, the view on the horizon was impressive, however fleeting.

But just what would constitute an end to the Cold War, and how might the elimination of nuclear weapons relate to that objective? The question did not come up at Reykjavik, nor has it received very much attention anywhere else: we have so preoccupied ourselves with the bomb and its associated technical, intellectual, and bureaucratic appurtenances that we neglect the larger geopolitical context in which these exist. Would nuclear abolition in fact end the Cold War or simply make it more dangerous? Could the Cold War end with nuclear weapons still in place? And, for that matter, would we even *recognize* an end to the Cold War, should that event someday come to pass?

Precisely because they sound naive, questions like these tend to escape the attention of geopolitical sophisticates. But there are precedents for thinking about how one would like conflicts to end even as one engages in them: in both world wars elaborate postwar-planning exercises were under way in Washington just weeks after the fighting had begun. War, for those who lived through the upheavals of 1917–1918 and 1941–1945, was an exceptional event, to be ended as quickly as possible, but not without careful thought about what victory was supposed to accomplish.

Our generation has had the undeniable advantage of not having to fight a "hot" war on the tremendous scale and at the tragic price that our parents and grandparents had to. But a consequence may be that for us the Cold War has become a way of life: it has been around for so long that it is a thoroughly familiar, if unwelcome, presence. Few of us can remember with much precision how it started; fewer still take the time to consider what the world might look like without the Cold War. We have become so accustomed to this phenomenon—by now the dominant event in the lives of more than one generation of statesmen—that it simply does not occur to us to think about how it might end or, more to the point, how we would like it to end.

The resulting intellectual vacuum violates not only logic and good sense but also a basic Clausewitzian principle, which is that strategy has no rational basis unless it is informed by some awareness of the objective it is intended to achieve: this is what the great Prussian strategist really meant when he described war as the continuation of politics by other means. In our own time, thank goodness, the equation has been reversed: politics has become a way of conducting war by other means, and that is a considerable improvement. But the fact of the reversal hardly lessens the importance of linking the efforts we make to the objectives we seek. It is all very well to think about how one is going to make a trip—in what style, at what speed, and at what cost—but unless one has some idea of what the ultimate destination is to be, then the journey is apt to be long, circuitous, and ultimately unrewarding.

Thinking about destinations requires linking one's direction of travel to the intended point of arrival, a task made trickier in geopolitics than in geography by the fact that such points are often indistinct to begin with, and—like the arctic ice pack—given to shifting their location in unanticipated ways. Still, the future of the Cold War is not wholly concealed: there are a few broad predictions one can make about it that may help us begin to think about how we would like it to come out.

ONE, QUITE SIMPLY, IS THAT THE COLD WAR WILL IN fact end someday, and in some form. Nothing lasts forever in history: even the Hundred Years War had a conclusion, although it took a while to get there. The Cold War may end with a bang or a whimper or—more likely—with something in between, but it will end, as all historical episodes sooner or later do. Whether we, as contemporaries, would recognize that event if it should occur in our lifetimes is, of course, another matter: contemporaries are rarely the best judges of the history through which they live. The great Spanish monarch Philip II, were he able to return four centuries after his reign to read what historians are writing about his era, would be surprised—and not a little annoyed—to see them concentrating on things like sheepherding, the prevalence of malaria, and the Portuguese pepper trade. Historians four hundred years hence, if there are any left by then, will surely view our era from angles of vision quite different from our own; from their perspective, indeed, the Cold War could already have ended, without our even noticing.

It also seems safe to say that when the Cold War does end, it will not do so with the total victory of one side and the unconditional surrender of the other: it will not be a replay of the Second World War. The principal reason for this is obvious: today's Great Powers possess nuclear weapons that preclude, in a manner quite unprecedented in modern history, the absolute imposition of one's will upon the other. But even if nuclear weapons had never been invented, there would still be reason to question the prospects for total domination, because the world these days is less hospitable to hegemonial aspirations than ever before. The day when a single imperial power could, with minimal expenditure of effort and manpower, control vast territories—the Mongols in Russia, or the Spanish in Central and South America, or the British in India—has now most assuredly passed. If Americans and Russians have such difficulties managing inconvenient next-door neighbors—Cubans and Nicaraguans, for example, or Afghans and Poles—then what could ever lead either of us to believe that we could successfully dominate the other? Empires are just not what they used to be.

A third prediction that can be made with confidence is that the end of the Cold War will not bring an end to all international rivalries, or even to all aspects of the rivalry that now exists between the United States and the Soviet

Union. Barring an improbable and necessarily simultaneous change in the mass consciousness of more than 150 nations, conflict in one form or another will remain a prominent feature of the international landscape, much as it was for millennia before the Cold War began.

The Martian Scenario

FROM HERE ON, THOUGH, THINGS GET MURKIER. Consider the question of *what* might end the Cold War. One obvious possibility, of course, is a nuclear war, but there is not a great deal one can say about that, because we have so little basis for anticipating what the results of such a conflict might be. What one can say, though, is that the widespread sense of *inevitability* about a nuclear holocaust that existed during the 1950s and 1960s appears, at least among "experts" on the subject, to be waning. Although public concern about the possibility of a nuclear war remains high, specialists point to the obvious irrationality of starting such a conflict on purpose, to the remarkably low frequency of "accidental" wars in history, to the increasingly effective safeguards against unauthorized use of nuclear weapons which exist on both sides, and to the marked decline in the incidence of both overt and implied nuclear threats which has occurred in recent years, quite independently of shifts in the Soviet-American political relationship from détente to confrontation and back again. There can be, of course, no guarantees. Irrationality in high places will always be a risk, and because Murphy's Law operates in capitalist and socialist societies alike—as the *Challenger* and Chernobyl disasters have recently reminded us—accidents can hardly be ruled out. Still, the record of four decades having passed without *any* nuclear weapon having been used for *any* military purpose whatever is an impressive one. One need only consider how improbable such an outcome would have seemed in the immediate aftermath of Hiroshima and Nagasaki to get a sense of what a remarkable development this has been.

So let us assume—because otherwise there is not much point in discussing the matter—that we will not require the services of the Apocalypse to end the Cold War. History provides more examples than one might think of Great Power rivalries that evolved unspectacularly into something else, without vast conflagrations or annihilations. It is worth looking at some of these to see what they might suggest about our own prospects for undramatic survival.

Great Power rivalries have most often ended peacefully because of the rise of some third power, equally dangerous to both sides. This possibility is known in certain circles as the Martian scenario: Reagan is said to have suggested to Gorbachev at the 1985 Geneva summit that if Martians were suddenly to land, Russians and Americans would settle their differences very quickly.

There are, in fact, a good many historical instances of the Martian scenario. One conspicuous example is the long cold war between Great Britain and czarist Russia that went on for most of the nineteenth century, erupting into actual combat only briefly, during the Crimean War, in 1853–1856. The rise of Germany finally compelled London and St. Petersburg to settle their differences in the decade before the First World War broke out. The same thing was happening at about the same time, and for much the same reason, to an even more ancient antagonism that had produced multiple wars in the past: that between Britain and France. Third-power threats also produced brief but decisive military cooperation between the Soviet Union and its Western allies against Nazi Germany during the Second World War; they have led as well, but this time with the Soviet Union as the perceived danger, to more recent and more durable reconciliations between such bitter former enemies as France and Germany, Japan and China, and Germany, Japan, and the United States.

Is there a third power on the horizon that could compel a resolution of Soviet-American differences? What seems most likely is not that some new rival will emerge, capable of challenging the superpowers militarily, but rather that the standards by which we measure power will begin to evolve, with forms other than military—economic, technological, cultural, even religious—becoming more important. To some extent this is already happening: one superpower, the Soviet Union, will soon be eclipsed by a third power, Japan, in gross national product; another third power, China, has already demonstrated what the Soviet Union has not, which is how a socialist economy can become agriculturally self-sufficient. Nor should Americans be so complacent as to consider themselves exempt from such trends, particularly if we persist in transforming our economy from its traditional industrial and agricultural base into one geared chiefly toward the provision and consumption of "services," the role of which, in the broad calculus of world power, is not at all clear.

The important question, therefore, may be whether the United States and the Soviet Union will continue to divert vast resources into military spending at a time when military strength is beginning to count for less than it has in the past as a determinant of world power. The answer is by no means apparent, but to the extent that both nations face at least a figurative Martian threat (by which I mean a situa-

Would nuclear abolition in fact end the Cold War or simply make it more dangerous? Could the Cold War end with nuclear weapons still in place? Would we even recognize an end to the Cold War should that event come to pass?

tion in which old rules may not apply, one that might force us into new forms of cooperation), this quiet shift in the criteria by which we determine who can do what to whom would appear to be the most likely possibility.

A second way in which Great Power rivalries have traditionally ended has been through the exhaustion of one of the major competitors, while the other remains vigorous. History is not normally so obliging as to arrange for the simultaneous and symmetrical enfeeblement of Great Powers. Consider Spain's long decline in the face of first French and then English hegemony, or the slow erosion of China's strength in the nineteenth century while that of Japan was increasing, or what was by historical standards the remarkably rapid withdrawal of the European colonial powers from Asia and Africa after the Second World War.

But rivalries that end through unilateral decline do not always do so peacefully: Britain's graceful withdrawal from empire after 1945 was the rare exception. More often the fact of decline—or even the appearance of it—has induced desperate actions to reverse the trend. Historians today would hardly describe imperial Germany prior to the First World War as a declining power, but its leaders' perception of waning strength, together with the bumptious way in which their diplomacy and strategy sought to compensate for it, made German fear of decline a major contributor to the outbreak of that great conflict. Japan's attack on Pearl Harbor now appears to have been an act of desperation set off by anxiety over a naval balance of power in the Pacific that seemed to be shifting in favor of the United States. And it is worth recalling that a recurring justification for our disastrous military involvement in Southeast Asia was the concern that if we did not demonstrate the capacity to act we would become, in President Richard Nixon's evocative phrase, a "pitiful, helpless giant."

What this suggests is that some of the most dangerous moments in world politics come when a Great Power perceives itself as beginning to decline—as standing at the top of a slippery slope—and is tempted into irresponsible action against its rival to redress the balance while it still has strength left to do so.

I T IS TOO EARLY TO SAY WHETHER THE UNITED STATES or the Soviet Union will be the first to confront that prospect, although there is reason to suspect that Gorbachev, for one, has not been wholly oblivious of the possibility. But decline on one side or the other will eventually take place: despite the fact that the two superpowers' rivalry—and the geopolitical status that results from it—has lasted for a remarkably long time, nothing in history ensures that it is permanent. Exhaustion, inflexibility, and lack of imagination will eventually take their toll in one or the other of these countries, much as they do among individuals: the problem each country will then confront (and it will be a delicate one, because both are likely still to be sitting atop huge piles of armaments) will be that of managing asymmetrical decline without provoking the vio-

lence that desperation—or, in the case of the unaffected superpower, temptation—so often brings.

But there is a third and more hopeful way in which the Cold War might end: a change in the outlook of its participants. Shifts in attitude do occur from time to time: after all, Russia and the United States abolished their ancient institutions of serfdom and slavery within a decade of each other, in the middle of the nineteenth century. Is it beyond possibility that comparable changes might occur that could bring an end to the Cold War?

Liberals have long wanted to believe that the more democratic states are at home, the less prone they are to initiate the use of force in the world at large: autocracy and aggression, by this logic, go hand in hand. The proposition is questionable on the face of it if one considers how easily a number of scrupulously democratic states—our own included—were able to justify to themselves the virtues of imperialism in the nineteenth century or the necessity for interventionism in the twentieth. But, as the political scientist Michael Doyle has recently pointed out, there is a historical basis for arguing that liberal democracies tend not to go to war with one another. This raises the question: could the extension of democracy—especially within the superpower that has not, until now, had much of it—bring an end to the Cold War?

Stranger things have happened. Both Germany and Japan were, within living memory, autocratic militaristic societies, much given to glorifying the uses of force. The experience of defeat and occupation after the Second World War changed them profoundly, in ways that at times exasperate even former adversaries, who would like them now to become a bit more militant than they are. But war in a nuclear age seems an improbable instrument of social and political reform, nor is there likely to be much call in the future for the services of draconian "reformers" like Generals Lucius Clay and Douglas MacArthur. What if the existence of nuclear weapons should serve, though, as the moral equivalent of a Clay or a MacArthur in reshaping Soviet and American attitudes toward military force? Might such a development help to compensate for the absence in the Soviet-American relationship of compatible domestic institutions and ideologies?

There may be something in this. History prior to 1945 provides little support for the proposition that as military strength increases, the willingness to use it correspondingly decreases. But the United States and the Soviet Union since 1945 have amassed the largest and most powerful military arsenals the world has ever known, without ever having used their weapons directly against each other and, with one or two exceptions, without even having come close to doing so. Where each has sought to challenge the other's position militarily, it has done so through proxies: North Koreans, North Vietnamese, and Cubans in the case of the Russians; Nicaraguan contras, Angolan guerrillas, and Afghan rebels in the case of the Americans. Where each superpower has actually used its military force—as the Americans did in Korea and Indochina and as the Russians have done in Afghanistan—it has consistently been against a third party.

Precisely because they possess nuclear weapons in such quantity and out of fear that any military confrontation between them might escalate, the United States and the Soviet Union have evolved a new kind of Great Power rivalry: a rivalry in which disputes are resolved not through direct combat but, as in certain animal species, through impressive but (so far) non-lethal displays of posturing, threat, and bluff. Such displays may be unnerving. They are hardly a behavior one would like to think characteristic of enlightened nations. But they do reflect a growing pessimism on both sides about what military force can accomplish, and that in itself is a considerable improvement over the old days, when periodic wars between Great Powers were routine events.

The Virtues of Bipolarity

ENDING THE COLD WAR, THEN, COULD BRING BOTH rewards and risks. If the event occurred because of an emerging third-power threat or as a consequence of changing attitudes toward the uses of military force, then the result might be a relationship between Washington and Moscow not too different from the one that exists today between former adversaries like France and Germany, or the United States and Japan. But if the Cold War should seem to be ending as the result of asymmetrical decline, then the danger of a hot war might actually increase. The key to ensuring that the Cold War ends peacefully, therefore, appears to lie in what one might at first glance regard as highly improbable: the emergence of a vested interest among Russians and Americans in the survival and even the prosperity of each other's admittedly very different institutions.

How, though, could such a thing happen in the anarchic, ideologically polarized, and highly competitive international system the two of us have been stuck with since the end of the Second World War? Theorists have long described this system as a zero-sum game, in which gains for one side automatically mean losses for the other. It has never been easy to see how concern for an adversary's interests could arise in such a setting: each state, one assumes, seeks to increase its own power at the expense of the other, thus producing the geopolitical equivalent of a seesaw. Even when one introduces into such a game the possibility that a failure to cooperate might destroy both players, simulations have shown little tendency on either side to sacrifice immediate advantages in the interest of long-term common survival, if only because one can never be sure that one's adversary will do the same.

But curious things have been happening to game theorists lately: their characteristic gloom has quietly been giving way to a measured degree of optimism. Professor Robert Axelrod, of the University of Michigan, has demonstrated that if the same players are allowed to repeat a game several times, they begin to perceive the advan-

tages to themselves of ensuring the other's survival, even in a competitive environment. Perpetuating the game itself becomes a shared interest. The behavior of large corporations tends to confirm Axelrod's findings: they often limit competition where it might endanger the overall market within which they operate. Much the same pattern appears to hold for international banks and even for nations engaged in international trade rivalries. As a result, the possibility of "cooperation under anarchy," together with what such a pattern might imply for Soviet-American relations, is now attracting considerable attention.

International-relations theorists are also rethinking old ideas about bipolarity. For years they assumed that a multipolar world order—a system with three or more Great Powers—had to be more stable than a bipolar one: three or more points of support appeared to provide a greater likelihood of remaining upright than did only two. But now theorists are beginning to ask: Why do the rules of geopolitics have to correspond to those of geometry? International systems are not, after all, pieces of furniture. And, indeed, sophisticated theorists such as Kenneth Waltz, at the University of California, Berkeley, and Robert Gilpin, at Princeton University, have begun to argue that under certain circumstances bipolar international systems can be more stable than their multipolar counterparts.

Bipolarity tends not to require the acrobatics of a Metternich or a Bismarck to sustain itself, which is fortunate, since although acrobats may be plentiful, consistently successful ones are not. By reducing the number of key actors involved, bipolarity also simplifies problems of communication in crises: this helps to explain why the European crisis of July, 1914, involving five roughly equal powers, led to war, whereas the Cuban missile crisis of October, 1962, which involved only two, did not. Finally, bipolarity tolerates defections from coalitions with less damage to the overall balance of power than do more complex and hence more delicately balanced systems. Quarrels over who was to control Morocco could bring Europe to the brink of war in 1905 and 1911; but China could abandon both its American and Soviet allies in the years that followed 1945 without the superpowers' approaching anything like a direct military confrontation as a result.

SO, IN THEORY, COOPERATION IN COMPETITIVE SITUAtions—even in the absence of a referee—is not so implausible as it might seem: given time, a mutual interest in sustaining the system within which they compete can cause even vociferous rivals to develop a stake in each other's survival. But what about the real world of international relations since the end of the Second World War? Four decades of superpower competition has provided more than enough time for the advantages of cooperation to have dawned on both Washington and Moscow. And indeed, if one looks at the actual behavior of Soviets and Americans during this period—as distinct from their frequently deceptive rhetoric—such a pattern does begin to emerge, at times in unexpected ways.

5. THE HUMAN PROSPECT

Cooperation in avoiding nuclear war is the most obvious example. Despite attempts to impress each other by suggesting the opposite, the United States and the Soviet Union have in fact reserved the employment of nuclear weapons for the ultimate extremity of all-out war. They have accepted painful military reverses in limited conflicts—Korea, Vietnam, Afghanistan—rather than resort to such use. They have even shared some nuclear technology: the United States in the early 1960s deliberately leaked to the Russians information on newly developed "permissive action links," control devices intended to prevent the inadvertent or unauthorized detonation of nuclear weapons. Since that time exchanges on how to monitor nuclear tests have become commonplace, even to the point at which the two sides can now seriously discuss proposals for each to explode one of its own warheads at the other's test site.

Cooperation has extended to spheres of influence as well. Despite frequent condemnations of it, the United States has made no sustained effort to "roll back" Soviet control in Eastern Europe. Similarly, the Soviets, with two exceptions, have refrained from directly challenging the much larger, though less restrictive, American sphere of influence in Western Europe, the Mediterranean, the Near East, Latin America, and East Asia. The exceptions were the North Korean attack on South Korea in 1950 (which Stalin presumably authorized) and Khrushchev's decision to place missiles in Cuba in 1962. But both of those adventures followed inadvertent signals from Washington—the withdrawal of American troops from South Korea in 1949, and the failure to overthrow Fidel Castro after the Bay of Pigs landings in 1961—suggesting that it lacked the resolve to defend its interests in those parts of the world. Both probes were conducted cautiously, and the Russians abandoned them soon after the Americans had clarified their determination to resist.

Moscow and Washington have also cooperated, at times through their very competition, to impose order on third parties whose ambitions or rivalries might otherwise have produced war. The superpowers' success in avoiding escalation during a long series of Middle East conflicts provides the most visible example of how such crisis management has been made to work, but there are even more significant—if unacknowledged—instances of Soviet-American cooperation to maintain international order. Would Europe have enjoyed an unprecedented four decades without war had the superpowers—through their mutual suspicions, to be sure—not reversed the 1871 settlement that had imposed upon that continent, with such disastrous results, a unified German state? Would Eastern Europe today be an orderly place if the Soviets should suddenly leave? Or would the Korean peninsula, if the Americans should abruptly withdraw? Even to raise such questions is to induce high states of anxiety on both sides of the superpower relationship, which is why they are so rarely discussed in public. But the very existence of these anxieties suggests how important a stabilizing mechanism the

Soviet-American rivalry has turned out to be in those parts of the world.

The United States and the Soviet Union have even cooperated, within limits, to facilitate espionage. Spying, after all, is what reconnaissance satellites do, even if both governments prefer to cloak their functions behind the euphemism "national technical means of verification." These devices have taken over the role assigned Francis Gary Powers when he flew his U-2 (not very successfully) over the Soviet Union in 1960; today both sides have learned—as the Russians manifestly had not in 1960—the benefits of transparency. These add up to a greatly reduced capability on the part of either for surprise attack, and it is universally acknowledged now that both superpowers feel safer for not having impeded this particular version of an "open skies" inspection plan. Indeed, the principle of remotely conducted espionage had become so thoroughly incorporated into Soviet-American relations by 1979 that the SALT II treaty could provide, with remarkably little public comment, for the configuration of certain weapons systems on each side to ensure that they *would* be visible to the prying—if electronic—eyes of the adversary.

Moscow and Washington have exploited defections from each other's sphere of influence only when it was clear that the rival either could not or would not regain control. Hence the United States took advantage of Yugoslavia's break with the Kremlin in 1948 and, after a long delay, that of the People's Republic of China as well; it was not prepared to challenge reassertions of Soviet authority in Hungary in 1956, or in Czechoslovakia in 1968, or even in Poland in 1981, with the crackdown on Solidarity. The Soviet Union exploited Cuba's break with the United States after 1959, but it made no attempt to contest successful CIA intervention in Iran in 1953 and Guatemala in 1954, or our more overt moves to re-establish control in the Dominican Republic in 1965, or in Grenada in 1983. And although the Russians have provided military assistance to the Sandinistas, in Nicaragua, just as the Americans have done for the Afghan rebels, there is little reason to expect that either superpower would go out of its way to save those distant clients, should their defeat appear imminent.

Finally, Russians and Americans have refrained from obvious attempts to undermine leadership on either side. Both countries have suffered disarray at the top since 1945: in the case of the Soviet Union, the instability that followed Stalin's death in 1953, the erosion of Khrushchev's authority after the Cuban missile crisis, and the illness and death of three Kremlin leaders within as many years during the early 1980s; in the case of the United States, the Johnson Administration's obsessive preoccupation with the Vietnam War, Nixon's self-inflicted Watergate wounds, and, most recently, White House involvement in the Iran-contra scandal. What is striking about these episodes is how rarely the temptation appears to have arisen in the unaffected capital to take advantage of them. There have even been expressions of regret and sympathy—how sin-

What would happen if we were to begin to think of the Soviet-American relationship not as a "cold war" but as a "long peace"—as the most workable set of arrangements for maintaining international order devised in this century?

cere these were is difficult to say—over the difficulties rival leaders were undergoing. Game theorists, to be sure, would find nothing surprising in such a tacit acknowledgment of legitimacy on both sides: otherwise the game might not continue. But students of history will recognize just how unusual such mutual forbearance among leaders of competing Great Powers really is.

An Agenda for Ending the Cold War

NOT ONE OF THESE EXAMPLES OF SOVIET-AMERICAN cooperation originated as the result of formal diplomatic negotiations. They arose instead from patterns of behavior both nations quietly found it in their interests to perpetuate. These patterns have survived shifts of leadership; they have proceeded more or less independent of oscillations between détente and confrontation; they appear now to be so firmly embedded in custom and tradition that it is difficult to conceive of circumstances that might lead either side to depart substantially from them. But there are limits to tacit cooperation. One is never quite sure precisely what has been agreed to, or how long agreements will last. Not all points at issue between the United States and the Soviet Union lend themselves to such informal solutions. It is worth taking a look, then, at just what objects of contention remain, and at what an explicitly negotiated settlement of them might actually require.

First, it would appear, we would have to get around once and for all to ending the Second World War. We would have to resolve certain leftover issues from that conflict, the lifetime of which has been prolonged far beyond what anyone in 1945 would have thought possible. This would hardly be a minor undertaking: it would include finding ways to end the artificial division of Germany and Korea, to withdraw Soviet and American forces from the advanced—and therefore also artificial—positions they still occupy in Central Europe, and quite possibly to dismantle NATO, the Warsaw Pact, and the other multilateral and bilateral alliance structures established during the first tense decade of postwar Soviet-American confrontation.

Second, we would need specific agreements between the United States and the Soviet Union to refrain from projecting their influence—cultural, ideological, and economic, as well as military—elsewhere in the world in order to gain unilateral advantage at the expense of each other. Such accords would have to distinguish between deliberate and inadvertent projections of influence; they would

have to be capable as well of differentiating indigenous shifts in the status quo from those set in motion for their own immediate benefit by Washington, Moscow, or their respective clients.

Third, we would require a clear understanding of what each side considers necessary for its own security. This would of course include mutually verifiable agreements on the control of both nuclear and conventional armaments, but would have to extend as well to such delicate issues as levels of defense spending, the right to maintain military bases on foreign soil, access to critical raw materials, the export and import of sensitive technology, the conduct of ground-based espionage, the question of human rights, and, not least, the extent to which each side's citizens would be free to have contacts with those of the other.

Finally, we would need mechanisms of some sort to counteract the effects, on the perceptions we and the Russians have of each other, of the profound differences between our ideologies, institutions, and cultures. Contrasts between communism and capitalism have had seven decades now to develop. But even if the Bolshevik Revolution had never taken place, there would still be deep institutional and cultural gaps between our ways of life, arising out of centuries of dissimilar historical experience whose impact—even at the most inconvenient moments, as the Daniloff affair demonstrated last year—continues to make itself felt.

One need only run down this list to realize two things, one of them obvious, the other less so. The obvious point is that there is enough here to keep us at the negotiating table for at least the next century, so we should probably not bring out the champagne—or relax restrictions on the consumption of vodka before midafternoon—just yet. The less obvious point is that it is not at all clear, in the event we could ever get agreement on all these issues and thus relegate the Cold War to the history books, that the world would be a safer place as a result.

CONSIDER THE DIFFICULTIES OF RESOLVING ISSUES left over from the Second World War. Germans and Koreans on both sides of the lines that divide them pay lip service to reunification, but neither they nor anyone else has given much thought to the actual political basis upon which such a thing might happen. How, for example, does one "reunite" an entire generation that has never experienced unity? Nor is it apparent what the implications would be of withdrawing Soviet and American forces from Europe. Most Eastern Europeans would welcome such a move, to be sure, but how Soviet security interests could be reconciled with it is as much a question now as it was in 1945. Nor would an Eastern Europe free of Soviet domination necessarily be an orderly place: it certainly was not prior to the Second World War, and long suppressed irredentist grievances still persist in that part of the world. Would Western Europe welcome the dismantling of NATO? European members of the alliance chafe under its demands and resist meeting its obligations, but when opportunities arise for them to become even slightly more self-reliant—as with the prospect this year of a Soviet-American agreement on withdrawing intermediate-range missiles—second thoughts (along with cold feet) abruptly proliferate. There is no way to know, of course, how long the present awkward arrangements in Europe and on the Korean peninsula can last. But awkward though they may be, they have proved to be remarkably durable. No one knows what these areas left to their own devices would be like and, to be perfectly honest about it, there has been no great eagerness in either Washington or Moscow to find out.

What about agreements pledging the United States and the Soviet Union not to seek unilateral advantage at the expense of the other? Here again we have some historical basis for speculation, this time in the form of the ill-fated statement on "Basic Principles" of U.S.-Soviet relations, signed at Moscow in 1972, which promised something very much like that. The accord broke down almost at once, because of disputes over how to apply its vague generalities to specific situations: Did the agreement require the Russians to warn Washington of Egypt's impending attack on Israel in 1973? Was Henry Kissinger justified in freezing Moscow out of the Middle East peace negotiations that soon followed? Which side initiated covert intervention in Angola following the Portuguese withdrawal from the country? Did Moscow do all it could—or, indeed, anything at all—to prevent the final North Vietnamese offensive against Saigon in 1975? The "Basic Principles" promoted more bickering than harmony, and the reason, in retrospect, is not hard to see: when one asks Great Powers to give up the search for unilateral advantage in international relations, what one is really asking them to do is to refrain from pursuing their own perceived interests. That is hardly a realistic thing to expect, and to hold out the prospect of accomplishing it is to invite disillusionment.

Would a world in which each side undertook to respect the other's security requirements be a more orderly place? Perhaps. Certainly it would appear more feasible to attempt to bring divergent superpower interests into approximate congruence with each other than to try to persuade each side of the merits of self-denial. And substantial areas of overlapping interest, as we have seen, already exist. But it is necessary to be realistic here, too, about what more could be achieved: mutually verifiable arms-control agreements might well fall within such a zone of congruence, but up to what point? Would they continue to do so if the effect of bilateral deep cuts in nuclear arsenals were to diminish the *joint* military pre-eminence of the United States and the Soviet Union, and to increase correspondingly the importance of other actors on the international scene? Are we sure that a shift toward multipolarity would enhance stability more than the bipolarity to which we have become accustomed? How would one handle the problem of asymmetrical threats—the fact that what one nation sees as threatening, the other may not? And, perhaps most daunting, how would one take into account the vastly dissimilar domestic systems we and the Soviets have, and the conflicting security requirements these might pose?

That last point suggests, as well, the difficulty of overcoming ideological, institutional, and cultural differences. Well-intentioned efforts to do so date back to the earliest days of the Cold War; today they take a remarkable number of forms, and proceed at a multiplicity of levels. But there remains a lurking uneasiness about "people-to-people" exchanges, "sister-city" contacts, "citizen diplomacy," and the like: Are we really certain, if Russians and Americans had vastly expanded opportunities for contact, that we would actually like each other all that much? Virtually every major war fought during the past century and a half has taken place between nations whose people knew each other from just such intensive contacts all too well, and who came to hate each other vigorously as a result. Even today virulent "people-to-people" animosities survive among Greeks and Turks, Arabs and Israelis, Sunni and Shiite Moslems, Irish Catholics and Protestants, Cambodians and Vietnamese. In contrast, Russians and Americans, who because we inhabit opposite sides of the earth have had so few contacts, almost alone among major nations of the world have never fought a war: the closest we have come are a few confused skirmishes during Allied intervention in Siberia and North Russia shortly after the Bolshevik Revolution.

Peace

ARGUMENTS LIKE THESE TEMPT ONE TO INVOKE what history will record as the Bert Lance Principle: "If it ain't broke, don't fix it." There is, in fact, something to be said for that point of view. Results are difficult to argue with, and it can hardly be denied that the four decades that we think of as the Cold War, years that have seen as high and as protracted a level of international tension without war as any in modern history, have also been four decades of Great Power peace, a period that compares favorably with the longest such periods of coexistence without war in modern history.

But is it not Orwellian to call such a situation "peace," knowing that a nuclear holocaust could break out at any moment? By traditional definitions of the term, it clearly is. We normally think of peace as something that has emerged from a formal process of negotiation around a conference table, and that exists within some clearly worked out and commonly agreed upon international structure, equally binding upon all who have adhered to it: something, in other words, like the system established at Versailles in 1919. But that system lasted only half as long as the present one has, despite the fact that the latter evolved as the result of no peace conference at all and with only a minimum of formal structure to perpetuate it. What has sustained the peace since 1945, many would argue, is precisely the prospect of what might ensue if it should ever come apart—a prospect insufficiently arresting to have impressed itself upon the minds of statesmen in the days before nuclear weapons existed.

We also think of peace as consistent with justice. But history is full of wars that have been fought—with devastating effects—in the interests of justice. The term *just war* itself captures the contradiction neatly. It was indeed largely a preoccupation with justice—and a corresponding neglect of the realities of power—that produced the phenomenon of appeasement in the 1930s, which in turn led so directly and so blindly to the last great war. We might do better not to equate peace and justice so precisely, given the difficulty of defining that latter quality, let alone achieving it. The more feasible approach might be to think of peace, in the way Reinhold Niebuhr suggested, as the condition of order that *precedes* justice, as the compromise with power that has to take place before one can begin to address—as one ultimately still has to—questions of right and wrong.

Finally, we tend to think of peace as something that grows out of harmony between nations, not out of the rivalries that exist among them. But why should that necessarily be so? After all, this nation has long extolled—to the point of having our principles quoted back at us more often than we would like these days—the virtues of competition as the path to economic prosperity and social justice. Is it not at least conceivable that a competitive superpower relationship, if carried on with the requisite degree of caution and restraint, might contribute to the maintenance of order—if not immediately justice—in international relations? The difficulty with traditional schemes for world order is their lack of realism regarding the problem of conflict in international life: they tend to take on the appearance of blurry utopias, more appropriate to some

other world than to the one in which we are obliged to live. There has been nothing utopian about the order the superpowers have imposed since 1945; it has been firmly grounded in the world as it is. Perhaps that is why it has lasted as long as it has.

IT HAS BEEN CHARACTERISTIC OF REVOLUTIONARIES, from the Americans and the French down through the Russians, the Chinese, and even the Vietnamese, that they have sought to confirm the victory of new orders over old ones through the simple expedient of changing names. "Change a name," the historian Crane Brinton observed many years ago, "and you change the thing." It may be that both we and the Russians, heirs of revolution as we are, can learn something from this. What would happen if we were to begin to think of the Soviet-American relationship not as a "cold war" but rather as a "long peace"—as the most workable, if still imperfect, set of arrangements for maintaining international order that the world has devised in this century? Might we gain new perspectives that could make the relationship a safer one, without compromising our vital interests and without losing touch with our principles? Might this be a way to combine the conservative's concern not to sacrifice what has worked in the past with the liberal's insistence upon progress toward a more equitable future? It is difficult to say.

But those who see images on distant horizons are rarely called upon to describe their details with cartographic precision: what is important is whether they are really there or not. The miscalculation that Ronald Reagan and Mikhail Gorbachev made at Reykjavik was not that they looked too far ahead with too little attention to how they might get there: who else, if not the leaders of superpowers, ought to be focusing on long-term objectives? The difficulty was that they did not look far enough. They concentrated on how one might eliminate the Cold War's most conspicuous instruments—nuclear weapons and the missiles that carry them—but not on how one might end the Cold War itself. Had they taken that wider view, they might have discovered yet another curious way in which light can deceive the eye in arctic landscapes: that what appear to be distant objects can, at times, be close at hand. □

The Causes of Wars

Michael Howard

Michael Howard, a Wilson Center Fellow, holds the Regius Chair of Modern History at Oxford University. He was born in London, England. Before receiving his B.A. from Oxford (1946), Howard served in the Cold-stream Guards in Italy during World War II, was twice wounded, and was awarded the Military Cross. He received his Litt. D. from Oxford in 1976. Among his many works, he has written War in European History *(1976) and* War and the Liberal Conscience *(1978), and he has translated, with Peter Paret of Stanford, Karl von Clausewitz's classic study* On War *(1976).*

Since the mid-18th century, many European and American theorists have attempted to explain war as an aberration in human affairs or as an occurrence beyond rational control. Violent conflicts between nations have been depicted, variously, as collective outbursts of male aggression, as the inevitable outcome of ruling-class greed, or as necessary, even healthy, events in the evolutionary scheme. One exception to the general trend was the 19th-century Prussian strategist Karl von Clausewitz, who declared, in an oft-quoted dictum, that war was the extension of politics "by other means." Here, historian Michael Howard argues further that war is one of Reason's progeny—indeed, that war stems from nothing less than a "superabundance of analytic rationality."

No one can describe the topic that I have chosen to discuss as a neglected and understudied one. How much ink has been spilled about it, how many library shelves have been filled with works on the subject, since the days of Thucydides! How many scholars from how many specialties have applied their expertise to this intractable problem! Mathematicians, meteorologists, sociologists, anthropologists, geographers, physicists, political scientists, philosophers, theologians, and lawyers are only the most obvious of the categories that come to mind when one surveys the ranks of those who have sought some formula for perpetual peace, or who have at least hoped to reduce the complexities of international conflict to some orderly structure, to develop a theory that will enable us to explain, to understand, and to control a phenomenon which, if we fail to abolish it, might well abolish us.

Yet it is not a problem that has aroused a great deal of interest in the historical profession. The causes of specific wars, yes: These provide unending material for analysis and interpretation, usually fueled by plenty of documents and starkly conflicting prejudices on the part of the scholars themselves.

But the phenomenon of war as a continuing activity within human society is one that as a profession we take very much for granted. The alternation of war and peace has been the very stuff of the past. War has been throughout history a normal way of conducting disputes between political groups. Few of us, probably, would go along with those sociobiologists who claim that this has been so because man is "innately aggressive." The calculations of advantage and risk, sometimes careful, sometimes crude, that statesmen make before committing their countries to war are linked very remotely, if at all, to the displays of tribal "machismo" that we witness today in football crowds. Since the use or threat of physical force is the most elementary way of asserting power and controlling one's environment, the fact that men have frequently had recourse to it does not cause the historian a great deal of surprise. Force, or the threat of it, may not settle arguments, but it does play a considerable part in determining the structure of the world in which we live.

I mentioned the multiplicity of books that have been written about the causes of war since the time of Thucydides. In fact, I think we would find that the vast majority of them have been written since 1914, and that the degree of intellectual concern about the causes of war to which we have become accustomed has existed only since the First World War. In view of the damage which that war did to the social and political structure of Europe, this is understandable enough. But there has been a tendency to argue that because that war caused such great and lasting damage, because it destroyed three great empires and nearly beggared a fourth, it must have arisen from causes of peculiar complexity and profundity, from the neuroses of nations, from the widening class struggle, from a crisis in industrial society. I have argued this myself, taking issue with Mr. A. J. P. Taylor, who maintained that because the war had such profound consequences, it did not necessarily have equally profound causes. But now I wonder whether on this, as on so many other matters, I was not wrong and he was not right.

■

It is true, and it is important to bear in mind in examining the problems of that period, that before

1914 war was almost universally considered an acceptable, perhaps an inevitable and for many people a desirable, way of settling international differences, and that the war generally foreseen was expected to be, if not exactly brisk and cheerful, then certainly brief; no longer, certainly, than the war of 1870 between France and Prussia that was consciously or unconsciously taken by that generation as a model. Had it not been so generally felt that war was an acceptable and tolerable way of solving international disputes, statesmen and soldiers would no doubt have approached the crisis of 1914 in a very different fashion.

But there was nothing new about this attitude to war. Statesmen had always been able to assume that war would be acceptable at least to those sections of their populations whose opinion mattered to them, and in this respect the decision to go to war in 1914—for continental statesmen at least—in no way differed from those taken by their predecessors of earlier generations. The causes of the Great War are thus in essence no more complex or profound than those of any previous European war, or indeed than those described by Thucydides as underlying the Peloponnesian War: "What made war inevitable was the growth of Athenian power and the fear this caused in Sparta." In Central Europe, there was the German fear that the disintegration of the Habsburg Empire would result in an enormous enhancement of Russian power—power already becoming formidable as French-financed industries and railways put Russian manpower at the service of her military machine. In Western Europe, there was the traditional British fear that Germany might establish a hegemony over Europe which, even more than that of Napoleon, would place at risk the security of Britain and her own possessions, a fear fueled by the knowledge that there was within Germany a widespread determination to achieve a world status comparable with her latent power. Considerations of this kind had caused wars in Europe often enough before. Was there really anything different about 1914?

■

Ever since the 18th century, war had been blamed by intellectuals upon the stupidity or the self-interest of governing elites (as it is now blamed upon "military-industrial complexes"), with the implicit or explicit assumption that if the control of state affairs were in the hands of sensible men—businessmen, as Richard Cobden thought, the workers, as Jean Jaurès thought—then wars would be no more.

By the 20th century, the growth of the social and biological sciences was producing alternative explanations. As Quincy Wright expressed it in his massive *A Study of War* (1942), "Scientific investigators . . . tended to attribute war to immaturities in social knowledge and control, as one might attribute epidemics to insufficient medical knowledge or to inadequate public health services." The Social Darwinian acceptance of the

inevitability of struggle, indeed of its desirability if mankind was to progress, the view, expressed by the elder Moltke but very widely shared at the turn of the century, that perpetual peace was a dream and not even a beautiful dream, did not survive the Great War in those countries where the bourgeois-liberal culture was dominant, Britain and the United States. The failure of these nations to appreciate that such bellicist views, or variants of them, were still widespread in other areas of the world, those dominated by Fascism and by Marxism-Leninism, was to cause embarrassing misunderstandings, and possibly still does.

For liberal intellectuals, war was self-evidently a pathological aberration from the norm, at best a ghastly mistake, at worst a crime. Those who initiated wars must in their view have been criminal, or sick, or the victims of forces beyond their power to control. Those who were so accused disclaimed responsibility for the events of 1914, throwing it on others or saying the whole thing was a terrible mistake for which no one was to blame. None of them, with their societies in ruins around them and tens of millions dead, were prepared to say courageously: "We only acted as statesmen always have in the past. In the circumstances then prevailing, war seemed to us to be the best way of protecting or forwarding the national interests for which we were responsible. There was an element of risk, certainly, but the risk might have been greater had we postponed the issue. Our real guilt does not lie in the fact that we started the war. It lies in our mistaken belief that we could win it."

■

The trouble is that if we are to regard war as pathological and abnormal, then all conflict must be similarly regarded; for war is only a particular kind of conflict between a particular category of social groups: sovereign states. It is, as Clausewitz put it, "a clash between major interests that is resolved by bloodshed—that is the only way in which it differs from other conflicts." If one had no sovereign states, one would have no wars, as Rousseau rightly pointed out—but, as Hobbes equally rightly pointed out, we would probably have no peace either. As states acquire a monopoly of violence, war becomes the only remaining form of conflict that may legitimately be settled by physical force. The mechanism of legitimization of authority and of social control that makes it possible for a state to moderate or eliminate conflicts within its borders or at very least to ensure that these are not conducted by competitive violence—the mechanism to the study of which historians have quite properly devoted so much attention—makes possible the conduct of armed conflict with other states, and on occasion—if the state is to survive—makes it necessary.

These conflicts arise from conflicting claims, or interests, or ideologies, or perceptions; and these perceptions may indeed be fueled by social or psychological drives that we do not fully understand and that one day we may learn rather better how to control. But the problem is the control of social conflict *as such,* not simply of war. However inchoate or disreputable the motives for war may be, its initiation is almost by definition a deliberate and carefully considered act and its conduct, at least at the more advanced levels of social development, a matter of very precise central control. If history shows any record of "accidental" wars, I have yet to find them. Certainly statesmen have sometimes been surprised by the nature of the war they have unleashed, and it is reasonable to assume that in at least 50 percent of the cases they got a result they did not expect. But that is not the same as a war begun by mistake and continued with no political purpose.

■

Statesmen in fact go to war to achieve very specific ends, and the reasons for which states have fought one another have been categorized and recategorized innumerable times. Vattel, the Swiss lawyer, divided them into the necessary, the customary, the rational, and the capricious. Jomini, the Swiss strategist, identified ideological, economic, and popular wars, wars to defend the balance of power, wars to assist allies, wars to assert or to defend rights. Quincy Wright, the American political scientist, divided them into the idealistic, the psychological, the political, and the juridical. Bernard Brodie in our own times has refused to discriminate: "Any theory of the causes of war in general or any war in particular that is not inherently eclectic and comprehensive," he stated, ". . . is bound for that very reason to be wrong." Another contemporary analyst, Geoffrey Blainey, is on the contrary unashamedly reductionist. All war aims, he wrote, "are simply varieties of power. The vanity of nationalism, the will to spread an ideology, the protection of kinsmen in an adjacent land, the desire for more territory . . . all these represent power in different wrappings. The conflicting aims of rival nations are always conflicts of power."

In principle, I am sure that Bernard Brodie was right: No single explanation for conflict between states, any more than for conflict between any other social groups, is likely to stand up to critical examination. But Blainey is right as well. Quincy Wright provided us with a useful indicator when he suggested that "while animal war is a function of instinct and primitive war of the mores, civilized war is primarily a function of state politics."

Medievalists will perhaps bridle at the application of the term "primitive" to the sophisticated and subtle societies of the Middle Ages, for whom war was also a "function of the mores," a way of life that often demanded only the most banal of justifications. As a way of life, it persisted in Europe well into the 17th century, if no later. For Louis XIV and his court war was, in the early years at least, little more than a seasonal variation on hunting. But by the 18th century, the mood had changed. For Frederick the Great, war was to be pre-eminently a function of *Staatspolitik,* and so it has remained ever since. And although statesmen can be as emotional or as prejudiced in their judgments as any other group of human beings, it is very seldom that their attitudes, their perceptions, and their decisions are not related, however remotely, to the fundamental issues of *power,* that capacity to control their environment on which the independent existence of their states and often the cultural values of their societies depend.

■

And here perhaps we do find a factor that sets interstate conflict somewhat apart from other forms of social rivalry. States may fight—indeed as often as not they do fight—not over any specific issue such as might otherwise have been resolved by peaceful means, but in order to acquire, to enhance, or to preserve their capacity to function as independent actors in the international system at all. "The stakes of war," as Raymond Aron has reminded us, "are the existence, the creation, or the elimination of States." It is a somber analysis, but one which the historical record very amply bears out.

It is here that those analysts who come to the study of war from the disciplines of the natural sciences, particularly the biological sciences, tend, it seems to me, to go astray. The conflicts between states which have usually led to war have normally arisen, not from any irrational and emotive drives, but from almost a superabundance of analytic rationality. Sophisticated communities (one hesitates to apply to them Quincy Wright's word, "civilized") do not react simply to immediate threats. Their intelligence (and I use the term in its double sense) enables them to assess the implications that any event taking place anywhere in the world, however remote, may have for their own capacity, immediately to exert influence, ultimately perhaps to survive. In the later Middle Ages and the early Modern period, every child born to every prince anywhere in Europe was registered on the delicate seismographs that monitored the shifts in dynastic power. Every marriage was a diplomatic triumph or disaster. Every stillbirth, as Henry VIII knew, could presage political catastrophe.

Today, the key events may be different. The pattern remains the same. A malfunction in the political mechanism of some remote African community, a coup d'état in a minuscule Caribbean republic, an insurrection deep in the hinterland of Southeast Asia, an assassination in some emirate in the Middle East—all these will be subjected to the kind of anxious examination and calculation that was devoted a hundred years ago to the news of comparable events in the Balkans: an insurrection in Philippopoli, a coup d'état in Constantinople, an assassination in Belgrade. To whose advantage will this ultimately redound, asked the worried diplomats, ours or *theirs?* Little enough in itself, perhaps, but will it not precipitate or strengthen a trend, set in motion a tide whose melancholy withdrawing roar will strip us of our friends and influence and leave us isolated in a world dominated by adversaries deeply hostile to us and all that we stand for?

There have certainly been occasions when states have gone to war in a mood of ideological fervor like the French republican armies in 1792; or of swaggering aggression like the Americans against Spain in 1898 or the British against the Boers a year later; or to make more money, as did the British in the War of Jenkins' Ear in 1739; or in a generous desire to help peoples of similar creed or race, as perhaps the Russians did in helping the Bulgarians fight the Turks in 1877 and the British dominions certainly did in 1914 and 1939. But, in general, men have fought during the past two hundred years neither because they are aggressive nor because they are acquisitive animals, but because they are reasoning ones: because they discern, or believe that they can discern, dangers before they become immediate, the possibility of threats before they are made.

∎

But be this as it may, in 1914 many of the German people, and in 1939 nearly all of the British, felt justified in going to war, not over any specific issue that could have been settled by negotiation, but *to maintain their power;* and to do so while it was still possible, before they found themselves so isolated, so impotent, that they had no power left to maintain and had to accept a subordinate position within an international system dominated by their adversaries. "What made war inevitable was the growth of Athenian power and the fear this caused in Sparta." Or, to quote another grimly apt passage from Thucydides:

> The Athenians made their Empire more and more strong . . . [until] finally the point was reached when Athenian strength attained a peak plain for all to see and the Athenians began to encroach upon Sparta's allies. It was at this point that Sparta felt the position to be no longer tolerable and decided by starting the present war to employ all her energies in attacking and if possible destroying the power of Athens.

You can vary the names of the actors, but the model remains a valid one for the purposes of our analysis. I am rather afraid that it still does.

Something that has changed since the time of Thucydides, however, is the nature of the power that appears so threatening. From the time of Thucydides until that of Louis XIV, there was basically only one source of political and military power—control of territory, with all the resources in wealth and manpower that this provided. This control might come through conquest, or through alliance, or through marriage, or through purchase, but the power of princes could be very exactly computed in terms of the extent of their territories and the number of men they could put under arms.

In 17th-century Europe, this began to change. Extent of territory remained important, but no less important was the effectiveness with which the resources of that territory could be exploited. Initially there were the bureaucratic and fiscal mechanisms that transformed loose bonds of territorial authority into highly structured centralized states whose armed forces, though not necessarily large, were permanent, disciplined, and paid.

∎

Then came the political transformations of the revolutionary era that made available to these state systems the entire manpower of their country, or at least as much of it as the administrators were able to handle. And finally came the revolution in transport, the railways of the 19th century that turned the revolutionary ideal of the "Nation in Arms" into a reality. By the early 20th century, military power—on the continent of Europe, at least—was seen as a simple combination of military manpower and railways. The quality of armaments was of secondary importance, and political intentions were virtually excluded from account. The growth of power was measured in terms of the growth of populations and of communications; of the number of men who could be put under arms and transported to the battlefield to make their weight felt in the initial and presumably decisive battles. It was the mutual perception of threat in those terms that turned Europe before 1914 into an armed camp, and it was their calculations within this framework that reduced German staff officers increasingly to despair and launched their leaders on their catastrophic gamble in 1914, which started the First World War.

But already the development of weapons technology had introduced yet another element into the international power calculus, one that has in our own age become dominant. It was only in the course of the 19th century that technology began to produce weapons systems—initially in the form of naval vessels—that could be seen as likely in themselves to prove decisive, through their qualitative and quantitative superiority, in the event of conflict. But as war became increasingly a matter of competing technologies rather than competing armies, so there developed that escalatory process known as the "arms race." As a title, the phrase, like so many coined by journalists to catch the eye, is misleading.

∎

"Arms races" are in fact continuing and open-ended attempts to match power for power. They are as much means of achieving stable or, if possible, favorable power balances as were the dynastic marriage policies of Valois and Habsburg. To suggest that they in themselves are causes of war implies a naive if not

189

totally mistaken view of the relationship between the two phenomena. The causes of war remain rooted, as much as they were in the preindustrial age, in perceptions by statesmen of the growth of hostile power and the fears for the restriction, if not the extinction, of their own. The threat, or rather the fear, has not changed, whether it comes from aggregations of territory or from dreadnoughts, from the numbers of men under arms or from missile systems. The means that states employ to sustain or to extend their power may have been transformed, but their objectives and preoccupations remain the same.

"Arms races" can no more be isolated than wars themselves from the political circumstances that give rise to them, and like wars they will take as many different forms as political circumstances dictate. They may be no more than a process of competitive modernization, of maintaining a status quo that commands general support but in which no participant wishes, whether from reasons of pride or of prudence, to fall behind in keeping his armory up to date. If there are no political causes for fear or rivalry, this process need not in itself be a destabilizing factor in international relations. But arms races may, on the other hand, be the result of a quite deliberate assertion of an intention to *change* the status quo, as was, for example, the German naval challenge to Britain at the beginning of this century.

This challenge was an explicit attempt by Admiral Alfred von Tirpitz and his associates to destroy the hegemonic position at sea which Britain saw as essential to her security, and, not inconceivably, to replace it with one of their own. As British and indeed German diplomats repeatedly explained to the German government, it was not the German naval program in itself that gave rise to so much alarm in Britain. It was the intention that lay behind it. If the status quo was to be maintained, the German challenge had to be met.

■

The naval race could quite easily have been ended on one of two conditions. Either the Germans could have abandoned their challenge, as had the French in the previous century, and acquiesced in British naval supremacy; or the British could have yielded as gracefully as they did, a decade or so later, to the United States and abandoned a status they no longer had the capacity, or the will, to maintain. As it was, they saw the German challenge as one to which they could and should respond, and their power position as one which they were prepared, if necessary, to use force to preserve. The British naval program was thus, like that of the Germans, a signal of political intent; and that intent, that refusal to acquiesce in a fundamental transformation of the power balance, was indeed a major element among the causes of the war. The naval competition provided a vary accurate indication and measurement of political rivalries and tensions, but it

did not cause them; nor could it have been abated unless the rivalries themselves had been abandoned.

It was the general perception of the growth of German power that was awakened by the naval challenge, and the fear that a German hegemony on the Continent would be the first step to a challenge to her own hegemony on the oceans, that led Britain to involve herself in the continental conflict in 1914 on the side of France and Russia. "What made war inevitable was the growth of *Spartan* power," to reword Thucydides, "and the fear which this caused in *Athens.*" In the Great War that followed, Germany was defeated, but survived with none of her latent power destroyed. A "false hegemony" of Britain and France was established in Europe that could last only so long as Germany did not again mobilize her resources to challenge it. German rearmament in the 1930s did not of itself mean that Hitler wanted war (though one has to ignore his entire philosophy if one is to believe that he did not); but it did mean that he was determined, with a great deal of popular support, to obtain a free hand on the international scene.

With that free hand, he intended to establish German power on an irreversible basis; this was the message conveyed by his armament program. The armament program that the British reluctantly adopted in reply was intended to show that, rather than submit to the hegemonic aspirations they feared from such a revival of German power, they would fight to preserve their own freedom of action. Once again to recast Thucydides:

> Finally the point was reached when German strength attained a peak plain for all to see, and the Germans began to encroach upon Britain's allies. It was at this point that Britain felt the position to be no longer tolerable and decided by starting this present war to employ all her energies in attacking and if possible destroying the power of Germany.

What the Second World War established was not a new British hegemony, but a Soviet hegemony over the Euro-Asian land mass from the Elbe to Vladivostok; and that was seen, at least from Moscow, as an American hegemony over the rest of the world; one freely accepted in Western Europe as a preferable alternative to being absorbed by the rival hegemony. Rival armaments were developed to define and preserve the new territorial boundaries, and the present arms competition began. But in considering the present situation, historical experience suggests that we must ask the fundamental question: *What kind of competition is it?* Is it one between powers that accept the status quo, are satisfied with the existing power relationship, and are concerned simply to modernize their armaments in order to preserve it? Or does it reflect an underlying instability in the system?

My own perception, I am afraid, is that it is the latter. There was a period for a decade after the war when the Soviet Union was probably a status quo power but the

West was not; that is, the Russians were not seriously concerned to challenge the American global hegemony, but the West did not accept that of the Russians in Eastern Europe. Then there was a decade of relative mutual acceptance between 1955 and 1965; and it was no accident that this was the heyday of disarmament/arms-control negotiations. But thereafter, the Soviet Union has shown itself increasingly unwilling to accept the Western global hegemony, if only because many other people in the world have been unwilling to do so either. Reaction against Western dominance brought the Soviet Union some allies and many opportunities in the Third World, and she has developed naval power to be able to assist the former and exploit the latter. She has aspired in fact to global power status, as did Germany before 1914; and if the West complains, as did Britain about Germany, that the Russians do not *need* a navy for defense purposes, the Soviet Union can retort, as did Germany, that she needs it to make clear to the world the status to which she aspires; that is, so that she can operate on the world scene by virtue of her own power and not by permission of anyone else. Like Germany, she is determined to be treated as an equal, and armed strength has appeared the only way to achieve that status.

◼

The trouble is that what is seen by one party as the breaking of an alien hegemony and the establishment of equal status will be seen by the incumbent powers as a striving for the establishment of an alternate hegemony, and they are not necessarily wrong. In international politics, the appetite often comes with eating; and there really may be no way to check an aspiring rival except by the mobilization of stronger military power. An arms race then becomes almost a necessary surrogate for war, a test of national will and strength; and arms control becomes possible only when the underlying power balance has been mutually agreed.

We would be blind, therefore, if we did not recognize that the causes which have produced war in the past are operating in our own day as powerfully as at any time in history. It is by no means impossible that a thousand years hence a historian will write— if any historians survive, and there are any records for them to write history from—"What made war inevitable was the growth of Soviet power and the fear which this caused in the United States."

But times *have* changed since Thucydides. They have changed even since 1914. These were, as we have seen, bellicist societies in which war was a normal, acceptable, even a desirable way of settling differences. The question that arises today is, how widely and evenly spread is that intense revulsion against war that at present characterizes our own society? For if war is indeed now *universally* seen as being unacceptable as an instrument of policy, then all analogies drawn from the past are misleading, and although power struggles may continue, they will be diverted into other channels. But if that revulsion is not evenly spread, societies which continue to see armed force as an acceptable means for attaining their political ends are likely to establish a dominance over those which do not. Indeed, they will not necessarily have to fight for it.

My second and concluding point is this: Whatever may be the underlying causes of international conflict, even if we accept the role of atavistic militarism or of military-industrial complexes or of sociobiological drives or of domestic tensions in fueling it, wars begin with conscious and reasoned decisions based on the calculation, made by *both* parties, that they can achieve more by going to war than by remaining at peace.

Even in the most bellicist of societies this kind of calculation has to be made and it has never even for them been an easy one. When the decision to go to war involves the likelihood, if not the certainty, that the conflict will take the form of an exchange of nuclear weapons from which one's own territory cannot be immune, then even for the most bellicist of leaders, even for those most insulated from the pressures of public opinion, the calculation that they have more to gain from going to war than by remaining at peace and pursuing their policies by other means will, to put it mildly, not be self-evident. The odds against such a course benefiting their state or themselves or their cause will be greater, and more *evidently* greater, than in any situation that history has ever had to record. Society may have accepted killing as a legitimate instrument of state policy, but not, as yet, suicide. For that reason I find it hard to believe that the abolition of nuclear weapons, even if it were possible, would be an unmixed blessing. Nothing that makes it easier for statesmen to regard war as a feasible instrument of state policy, one from which they stand to gain rather than lose, is likely to contribute to a lasting peace.

Plagues, History, and AIDS

Robert M. Swenson

Robert M. Swenson is professor of medicine and microbiology at Temple University Health Sciences Center. As an infectious disease specialist and immunologist, he has had a long interest in the history of epidemics.

The plague bacillus never dies or disappears for good; it bides its time in bedrooms, cellars, trunks and bookshelves; and the day will come when, for the bane and enlightenment of men, it would rise up its rats again and send them forth to die in a happy city.
— The Plague, *Albert Camus*

In December 1981, an article appeared in the *New England Journal of Medicine* describing a curious cluster of seven men who, for no apparent reason, had severe infections with microorganisms that previously infected only profoundly immunocompromised individuals. Soon this became known as Acquired Immune Deficiency Syndrome (AIDS). Since then, the number of cases has increased at a startling rate. By September 1987, more than 40,000 cases had been reported in the United States and an additional 50,000 cases have been recognized in 114 other countries. This worldwide outbreak of a new infectious disease has engendered much fear and apprehension. As a result, there have been frequent references to previous epidemics. Perhaps most frequent are references to the Black Death, the epidemic of bubonic plague that swept through Europe in the middle of the fourteenth century. Despite current fears, there has been little attempt to reexamine previous epidemics for comparisons and insights that may be relevant to the AIDS epidemic. Although it is early in the present epidemic, I believe one can begin to make these comparisons—that is, to place Acquired Immune Deficiency Syndrome in some sort of historical perspective.

There are at least three general ways to examine these questions. First, one can look at previous epidemics and the ways in which they have affected nations, politics, and even the course of history. Second, one can describe the internal "sociological anatomy" of an epidemic, the series of social and political responses that occur during the course of an epidemic. These reactions tend to be somewhat similar in all epidemics and are already occurring during the current outbreak of AIDS. Lastly, since AIDS is a sexually transmitted disease, it is illuminating to compare the response to AIDS with society's responses to other sexually transmitted diseases early in this century. Each of these approaches provides a somewhat different perspective.

Infectious diseases have had a major influence on Western history. Although epidemics have been frequent and devastating, one can categorize easily the small number of different ways in which epidemics have produced these effects. The first of these is through a widespread epidemic affecting the entire population relatively uniformly, resulting in the disruption of social structures and in long-term historical change. The most obvious, and perhaps only, example of this is the epidemic of bubonic plague that occurred in Europe in the fourteenth century. Epidemics may also have markedly different effects on different populations, resulting in significant shifts in the previous balance of power. The importation of smallpox into the Central American Indian population by the Spanish is a dramatic example of this effect. Many military battles, in which one military force is more severely affected than the other, can be viewed as a more common example of this phenomenon. In the last 150 years, many smaller epidemics have produced change through laws enacted in response to the epidemic. Many of our present-day public health laws were enacted during the recurrent cholera epidemics in the United States and England in the mid-nineteenth century. To begin to put AIDS in some historical perspective, it is, I think, helpful to examine some of these epidemics in greater detail.

Bubonic plague struck Europe in 1347, but events of the previous two hundred years had set the stage for this great epidemic. The eleventh and twelfth centuries were politically stable and relatively disease-free, and food production had increased dramatically. As a result, the population, which had been twenty-five million in A.D. 950, had tripled to seventy-five million by A.D. 1250. Around A.D. 1300, a significant drop occurred in the mean temperatures of Europe, and widespread crop failures ensued. The resulting famine forced many peasants to move to the towns, producing severe poverty and crowding. Under these conditions the black rat population also increased greatly.

In urban areas, plague is a disease affecting rats; it is spread by the rat flea. In an epidemic among rats (an epizootic), large numbers of rats die. (In Camus's *The Plague*, the epidemic is heralded by large numbers of dead rats suddenly appearing in the streets.) Infected fleas rapidly leave dead rats for a new host, and if other rats are not available, they will attempt to feed on humans, thereby infecting them. Thus, it is easy to see how, under the appropriate conditions of poverty, crowding, and poor sanitation, an epidemic such as this could occur.

Plague was already established in several areas in Asia. However, not until the mid-fourteenth century was overland travel efficient enough to carry plague westward to the Mediterranean Sea. The epidemic arrived in Marseilles in 1348, and by 1351 all of Europe was afflicted. The immediate effects of the epidemic were devastating. The most accurate estimate for total deaths during this first wave of the epidemic is twenty-five million, or one-third of the population of Europe. No segment of society was spared. Following this epidemic, recurrent waves of plague kept the population at this reduced level for another 150 years. The consequence of this epidemic were far-reaching. Since the population was devastated, real wages increased dramatically. As peasant wages increased, peasants were able to demand a commutation of their services. The population decreased more rapidly than the fall in food supplies, and the resultant drop in food prices made it impossible for landowners to support their large manors. These changes led directly to an end of the old manoral system.

The effects on clergy and the Catholic church were tremendous. The mortality among clerics was greater than 50 percent. Yet the epidemic had even more profound effects on the church and religious thinking. People turned away from traditional religion, which was perceived as having failed totally during the epidemic. Many turned to frenzied, superstitious religion (for example, the flagellants), and, for generations after, much religious thinking focused on the apocalypse. This dissatisfaction with the church contributed in a major way to the Reformation.

Medicine was also profoundly changed by the plague. Most cleric-physicians died. These physicians were viewed as having drastically failed, which resulted in a tremendous rise in the number and popularity of surgeons. New medical texts were developed, and the rudiments of scientific inquiry began. The

initial theories of contagion were developed, and the concept of quarantine was first recognized. This resulted in the first rudimentary hospitals and the development of early public health measures. From this brief outline of the bubonic plague, it should be clear that its effects on Western history were great and long-lasting.

Two additional points were extremely important. Plague could not occur where it did, when it did, or take the form it did until a variety of conditions had occurred to make it possible. For example, the urban population had to reach a certain density, and living conditions and sanitation had to decline to a certain level. The rat population had to reach a certain density and proximity to the human population. And, lastly, travel from Asia had to be sufficiently rapid and frequent to successfully bring the plague bacillus to the European continent. If any one of these had not occurred, the plague epidemic would not have happened. Furthermore, the devastating effects of plague continued because there were recurrent epidemics for the next 115 years. If there had been only a single initial epidemic, however catastrophic, the effects would not have been as great and certainly not as long-lasting.

The most recent worldwide epidemic was the outbreak of influenza A that swept the world in 1918–19. The first cases of influenza were recognized at Camp Funston, Kansas. Two months later massive epidemics began in Spain, France, and England. The attack rates (number of cases per one hundred people) were extremely high, particularly among young adults. Despite massive public health measures, influenza spread rapidly throughout the world. By the time the pandemic ended in 1919, there had been one million deaths in the United States, ten million in India, and an estimated thirty million deaths throughout the world. Despite being the largest epidemic in history, it had little long-term effect, because, unlike the plague epidemic, the influenza epidemic was relatively short-lived and the population losses were rapidly replaced. (It seems callous, but it is true to say that the population itself is our most easily replaced resource.)

Epidemics have a major effect when the disease has a different effect on two populations—what scientists call a "differential impact." The most dramatic example of this is the importation of smallpox into Central America by the Spanish. Humans are the only reservoir for the smallpox virus, and transmission is only from human to human. After surviving infection there is complete, lifelong immunity. Thus, in areas where smallpox has been ongoing, the surviving population is immune, while in other areas where smallpox has not been present, the population remains susceptible. When Asians migrated across the Bering Strait sometime before 10,000 B.C., it appears that they did not take smallpox with them. For this reason, the native populations of the Americas were free of smallpox. By

A.D. 1500, however, smallpox had long been established in Europe, and as a result the adult population was largely immune.

In 1520, a small expedition led by Pánfilo de Narvaez left Cuba and sailed for Central America. When the expedition landed in Mexico, one crewman had active smallpox, and infection was easily established in the susceptible Indian population. From there, smallpox spread rapidly through Central and South America. Epidemics recurred frequently throughout the sixteenth century, eventually complicated by measles epidemics. It has been estimated that out of a native population of twenty-five million, fifteen to eighteen million died of smallpox. Thus, a major factor, if not the major factor, in the Spanish conquest of the Americas was the importation of smallpox into the susceptible native population. (It has also been suggested that the immunity of the Spanish to this devastating disease had great psychological effect on the Indians, making the Spanish appear invincible.)

Throughout history, infectious disease have had a major effect on military battles. Frequently, one army has suffered from disease more severely than the opposing force, drastically altering the outcome of a battle. In general, since the defending forces tend to be more resistant to their own endemic diseases, this differential effect is most marked on the invading force. A dramatic example occurred during Napoleon's invasion of Russia.

In June 1812, Napoleon assembled an army of almost five hundred thousand men to invade Russia. While traveling through Poland and western Russia, almost half of his troops died or were immobilized by typhus. By the time Napoleon began his retreat from Moscow, only eighty thousand able-bodied men remained. These catastrophic losses continued, and by June 1813 only three thousand soldiers remained alive to complete the retreat. The vast majority of deaths were the result of typhus and dysentery rather than battle injuries or exposure to the severe Russian winter. Thus, the power of Napoleon in Europe was broken more by diseases, especially typhus, than by military opposition.

From the mid-nineteenth century to the present, as government bureaucracies became larger and took control of more of society's functions, much smaller epidemics produced change through the legislation enacted in reponse to the epidemics. The cholera epidemics in the United States in 1832, 1849, and 1866 provide excellent examples of these changes.

The largest cholera epidemic began in 1832. The city of New Orleans was hardest hit with five thousand cases. By historical standards, this was a very small epidemic, but it engendered the clear beginnings of public health policy. In early 1832, the New York state legislature passed laws enabling communities to establish local boards of health, and in the summer of 1832

the New York City Board of Health was created. Quarantine regulations were passed and enforced. Cholera hospitals were established. Housing and care for the destitute were set up. Slum clearance was begun, and early efforts of food and drug control were undertaken. As the epidemic subsided, however, the government felt that these measures were no longer necessary, and the New York City Board was disbanded.

In 1854 John Snow demonstrated that cholera was spread through the contaminated water supply. By 1866 few physicians doubted that cholera was portable and transmissible. With the threat of a third cholera epidemic, New York State then passed a law creating the Metropolitan Sanitary District and Board of Health in New York City. This first strong, permanent board of health in the United States exists to this day. The sanitary and public health measures were similar to those employed in 1832 but were more extensive and rigidly enforced. They were also much more effective, as only 591 cases of cholera occurred in New York City during this epidemic. Many of these regulations remain in effect and form the basis of present-day public health policy.

One can also examine what I have referred to as the internal anatomy of an epidemic, by which I mean the behavioral response of both individuals and society to a given epidemic. It soon becomes apparent that there are certain attitudes and behaviors that recur during all epidemics.

First is the denial that the disease in question is even occurring. On June 26, 1832, the first cases of cholera developed in New York City. When the New York Medical Society stated publicly that these nine cases had been diagnosed, the announcement was immediately attacked by New Yorkers who felt it was premature or unwarranted. Business leaders were particularly upset, realizing that even the fear of cholera and a possible quarantine would be disastrous for the city's business. Not until six weeks later, when the evidence of the epidemic could no longer be suppressed, was it officially recognized by the New York Board of Health. Denial also occurs at a national level. Following the initial outbreak of influenza in 1918 at Camp Funston, Kansas, major epidemics occurred two months later in England, France, and Spain. Initially each country attempted to deny the occurrence of influenza within its borders (noting, of course, that influenza was already present somewhere else).

Once an epidemic is recognized, it follows quickly that someone (or something) else is blamed for it. As bubonic plague swept through Europe in 1348, it was claimed that it was caused by Jews who had poisoned wells. As a result, thousands of Jews were burned at the stake. The cholera epidemics in the United States fell disproportionately on the poor. At that time, poverty was viewed as a consequence of idleness and intemperance. The latter was also clearly felt to make one more susceptible to cholera. Since new immigrants were often the most poor, they were blamed for their own susceptibility to cholera, as well as for bringing the disease into the country. Prostitutes were also blamed for the epidemic, even though cholera was not thought to be a venereal disease. Many felt that their "moral corruption" caused them, as well as their clients, to develop cholera. Blame could also be placed at a national level. After the initial outbreak of influenza in the United States, epidemics occurred in Spain, England, and France. In addition to attempting to deny their own epidemics, the countries blamed one another. The French referred to the epidemic as the Plague of the Spanish Lady, and the English called it the French Disease. (Even today we refer to the Asian Flu.)

Epidemics occur in part because old diseases are not yet understood or new disease have arisen. In either case, physicians do not have the knowledge either to prevent the epidemic or to treat its victims effectively. As a result, society views the physicians and medicine of the time as having failed. A corollary of the failure of the existing methods of medicine is the rise of alternative therapies during an epidemic. During the plague epidemic, innumerable remedies and preventatives arose. This is hardly surprising since existing texts provided no effective treatment. During the first cholera epidemic in the United States, physicians routinely employed a limited array of unpleasant, even dangerous, therapies. The most common were calomel (a mercury compound that frequently resulted in mercury poisoning), laudanum (an opium compound), and bleeding. These measures failed to treat cholera and also had numerous untoward side effects. Given the failure and hazards of traditional medicine, it is no surprise that it was surpassed in popularity by botanical medicine during these early cholera epidemics.

A final effect that is common to all epidemics is that they stimulate a variety of new laws. Initially, these laws are viewed as immediately necessary to prevent or control an epidemic, but often they remain in effect long after the epidemic has subsided. For example, many laws were enacted prior to and during the cholera epidemics. Many of these laws continue in virtually their same form one hundred years later.

To understand the AIDS epidemic, it is helpful to review also society's responses to syphilis and gonorrhea in the early part of this century. At that time the organisms causing syphilis and gonorrhea had been identified, and it was clear that these were sexually transmitted diseases. Despite this, there were numerous obstacles to responding effectively these epidemics.

With the realization that these were sexually transmitted diseases with grave health consequences (mental illness and infertility, for example), it was recognized that there was a need for sex education; yet great obstacles existed to what became known as the social hygiene movement. First, the remaining tenets of Victorian respectability made it virtually impossible to discuss venereal diseases. The basic assumption was that men were driven by lust and that discussing sex with them would only make them more uncontrollable. The major question became, How can sex education be presented to men without their recognizing the subject? The answer was to include much talk about plants, birds, bees, and little about sex. Given these subterfuges, there could be little effective sex education. Prince Morrow, a leader of the social hygiene movement, concluded, "Social sentiment holds that it is a greater violation of the properties of life publicly to mention venereal disease than privately to contract it."

It also became clear that large numbers of middle-class wives were being infected by their husbands, who had contracted their infections from prostitutes. With the recognition that gonorrhea was now a common cause of infertility, some feared that the middle class was committing "race suicide." In response to the epidemic of venereal diseases among the middle class, physicians actively promulgated the idea of casual, nonsexual transmission (*sine coitu*) of syphilis and gonorrhea. At that time, it was apparently more important to protect the reputation of middle-class males than to provide a proper understanding of these diseases. The idea of casual transmission remains firmly entrenched to this day, even though there has never been evidence to support that it actually occurs.

As might be expected, prostitutes were blamed for the spread of venereal diseases. They were felt to be not only a moral threat but a health threat to the family as well. Because of this concern, the United States embarked on an effort to eradicate prostitution. Suggestions that prostitution could be regulated, as in France, were entirely unacceptable. As we shall see, all of these ideas have persisted in one form or another throughout the twentieth century with profound effects on our response to sexually transmitted diseases.

With this background, we can now turn to the epidemiology of AIDS. AIDS is the final stage of an infection caused by the human immunodeficiency virus (HIV). HIV, first identified in 1984, is an RNA containing retrovirus. The RNA is used as a template to make a complementary DNA sequence that is incorporated into the chromosome of the infected cell. Once incorporated into the host cell, the virus may remain latent for several years. The host cell infected is the T4 lymphocyte, a white blood cell that has the central role in controlling the entire immune system. Eventually HIV begins reproducing itself within the cell, and new virus particles escape from the cell by literally punching holes in its membrane, producing the death of the T4 lymphocyte. This slow, progressive destruction of T4 cells ultimately impairs the immune system to the point that a person becomes vulnerable to infections with organisms that would never infect someone with a "normal" immune system (that is, "opportunistic infections"). The immune system also carries out surveillance to prevent cancers from arising. As the immune system becomes progressively impaired, various cancers may also develop. The final stage of HIV infection, when opportunistic infections or cancers occur, is recognized as AIDS. It is important to remember that it is the combination of immune dysfunction caused by HIV *plus* the opportunistic infection or cancer that fulfills the definition of AIDS.

Where did HIV come from and how is it transmitted? Retroviruses are very old and have adapted themselves to a variety of animals. Over millions of years they have evolved to survive in higher mammals. Relatively recently they have infected the highest subhuman primates in Central Africa. In most animals they cause no disease and live a harmless, symbiotic relationship. Recently (in an evolutionary sense) the retrovirus has evolved further, so that it can now infect humans *and* destroy the cells it infects. It should be noted that HIV could only develop in an area where the highest subhuman primates are present to allow the gradual adaptation of HIV to a form that ultimately could infect humans.

The first evidence of human infection with HIV is found in serum samples obtained in Central Africa in 1959; the first AIDS cases are believed to have occurred in the late 1960s. By the mid-1970s, changes in modern air travel brought HIV to the rest of the world. Jumbo jets and decreased airfares produced dramatic increases in travel to and from Central Africa, distributing HIV widely. As fourteenth-century travel had to become rapid and efficient enough to bring plague from Asia, modern jet travel had to expand to Central Africa to bring HIV to the rest of the world. The earliest sites were probably central Europe and Haiti. The link to the United States appears to be homosexual males vacationing in the area of Port-au-Prince, Haiti. From there, HIV infection was carried to those areas with the largest concentrations of homosexual males, New York, and San Francisco. Additional factors account for the rapid spread among homosexual males. First, anal intercourse is the most effective sexual means of transmitting HIV. Second, homosexual males are a small "sexually closed community," concentrated in a few major urban areas. Finally, with the Gay Liberation Movement it appears that promiscuity among homosexual males increased dramatically, producing rapid and widespread HIV infection among homosexual males. However, because of the long latent period between HIV infection and the development of AIDS, the first cases of AIDS did not occur in the United States until 1978.

The next group infected with HIV were intravenous drug users. Homosexual drug users, already infected with HIV, infected other intravenous drug users through the sharing of needles for injecting drugs. Drug users are also a relatively small, closed group, and HIV infection has spread rapidly among them. This second wave of the epidemic appears to be two to three years behind the first wave. Despite this, in some areas of New York, 80 percent of intravenous drug users are now infected.

The next wave of the epidemic, which is only barely beginning, is the spread of HIV infection to the sexual partners of bisexual males and intravenous drug users. Recent data indicate that early in the course of HIV infection a person is less infectious than later. This phenomenon has contributed another latent period, so that these cases are just now beginning to appear. The final wave of the epidemic, which has not yet begun, will be when HIV infection is spread widely into the remainder of the population.

A tremendous amount is known about the biology and transmissibility of HIV. The virus is present in large numbers in blood and semen. HIV is also in vaginal secretions and breast milk in smaller but significant numbers. These are the only four fluids capable of transmitting infection. Moreover, transmitting HIV is very difficult. Transmission requires a large volume of blood (as in blood transfusions) or repeated inoculation of smaller volumes (as with intravenous drug users). While males can transmit infection through intercourse with males or females, anal intercourse appears to be more effective than vaginal intercourse. Despite this fact, neither is a particularly efficient method of transmitting HIV infection (less than a one-in-ten chance). The only other modes of transmission are perinatally (at the time of birth) and, perhaps, through breast milk to the newborn infant. HIV is found occasionally in small numbers in saliva, tears, urine, and amniotic fluid, although clearly in numbers too small to transmit infection. Because of this, casual transmission just does not occur. The risk of occupational infection among health care workers caring for infected patients also appears to be extremely low. In a careful study of single needle-stick exposures in health care workers, only one in more than twenty-four hundred has become infected with HIV. (In a similar situation with the hepatitis B virus, more than five hundred people would be infected.) The small number of occupational cases of HIV transmission (approximately eight) all appear to be related to unusual or excessive contact with blood.

There still appears to be a great deal of confusion about the meaning of the antibody test for HIV. Following infection with HIV, the virus begins multiplying within the body. The host's immune system recognizes the "foreign" virus and begins making antibodies directed against it. After three to six months, virtually all who have been infected develop specific antibodies against HIV. Despite this, nearly all people with the

HIV antibody have live virus circulating in their blood; that is, they can transmit HIV infection to others. The presence of the HIV antibody means that the person has been *infected with* HIV (not exposed to HIV) *and* can transmit infection. This differs from other common infections, like measles, where the presence of antibodies means the person has been infected, is now immune, and the virus is no longer present in the body. A positive HIV antibody test means only that a person has been infected with the virus, not that he has AIDS. A diagnosis of AIDS is made only when an opportunistic infection or unusual cancer develops, fulfilling the case definition of AIDS.

A final area of concern is the current extent of HIV infection not only in the United States but also in the remainder of the world. At present, there is very little data from Africa. Two small studies of female prostitutes in Kinshasa and Nairobi revealed that 60 to 80 percent of them are infected. Other data from Kinshasa suggest that 6 percent of the general population are infected, mostly in the twenty- to thirty-five-year age group. In rural areas, less than 0.5 percent of the population are infected. Heterosexual transmission is the major mode of spreading HIV in Africa. Re-use of needles for medical purposes and ritual scarification does not appear to play a significant role. Transmission by mosquitoes or other insects clearly does not occur (although this rumor appears indestructible). The World Health Organization has estimated that ten to twenty million are infected with HIV throughout the world.

The data available from the United States is also incomplete. Approximately 80 percent of a group of homosexual males in San Francisco followed since the late 1970s for the hepatitis B vaccine trials are HIV positive. Seropositivity among homosexuals appears to be highly variable from place to place, and in other areas appears to be significantly less. In some areas of New York City, 80 percent of the intravenous drug users are seropositive, but this falls off dramatically as the distance from New York increases. The only data from the general population are from persons donating blood and from military recruits. Among blood donors with no history of being in a risk group, 4 per 10,000 are seropositive for HIV. As of May 1987, the prevalence of the HIV antibody among applicants for military service is 1.5 per 1,000, though in some urban areas, the prevalence is 5 to 15 per 1,000 among military recruits. Using all of these data, the Centers for Disease Control (CDC) estimates that there are currently 1.5 to 2 million people infected with HIV in the United States.

How many of these people infected with HIV will eventually develop AIDS? The group followed longest has been the cohort of homosexual males in San Francisco. To date, 36 percent of HIV-positive males in this group have developed AIDS. Over the last three years, 5 percent per year have developed AIDS, and the number increases each year. Similar data have been obtained with groups of intravenous drug users. No one yet knows what percentage of HIV-infected individuals will ultimately develop AIDS.

Using these kinds of data, the CDC has estimated that there will be 270,000 cases of AIDS in the United States by 1991. More recent data suggest that there may be as many as 30 percent more cases (350,000). Projections for the rest of the world are as many as seven million cases by 1991. These estimates are minimum numbers based on numbers of people infected now. Even if transmission of HIV were halted today, these numbers of cases will still occur over the next four years. However, there is nothing to suggest that HIV transmission has slackened at all. Thus, it appears that the numbers of HIV-infected people will continue to increase for the foreseeable future.

Several assumptions are necessary in order to discuss fully the effect of the AIDS epidemic. First, it is certain that the number of persons infected with HIV will continue to grow. For now, the only methods of halting the spread of the virus are abstinence from sexual intercourse, "safe sex," or, in the case of drug users, stopping intravenous drug use. The threat of sexually transmitted diseases has never had a significant effect on sexual activity, and it is not likely to now. In less-developed areas, with little in the way of birth control programs, it seems inconceivable that condom use will be widely employed. Similarly, drug abuse programs for intravenous drug users have been notoriously ineffective. Finally, widespread travel will continue to carry HIV infection throughout the world.

Cases among homosexuals will continue to increase. But the next wave of the HIV infection—in intravenous drug users— will show the most dramatic increases. We are just beginning to see the third wave of the epidemic occurring in sexual partners of the first two groups. Since this reflects people infected several years ago, this wave of AIDS cases already seems predestined. The final wave of the epidemic is predicted among the remainder of the heterosexual population. Since all previous epidemics of sexually transmitted diseases have ultimately been spread and maintained by middle-class males (genital herpes and chlamydia are recent examples), there is no reason to suspect that HIV infection will be different. This portion of the epidemic may appear more slowly as infection is diluted into the much larger heterosexual segment of the population.

The fraction of HIV-infected individuals that develops AIDS will also continue to grow. As already noted, 5 percent of those infected with HIV have developed AIDS each year. Two years ago, 25 percent of homosexual males in the cohort had AIDS, last year 30 percent, and this year 35 percent. Next year, it will be 40 percent. No one knows how long this increase will continue.

There are two factors that may interrupt or slow these trends. Azidothymidine (AZT) is a new anti-viral drug that inhibits multiplication of HIV. Although clinically effective, it is limited by significant toxicity. Within five to seven years, safer and more effective drugs will probably be available. These drugs will dramatically alter the progression of HIV infection to AIDS, but they will remain expensive and difficult to distribute widely. Unless some dramatic change occurs, it will be virtually impossible to distribute these drugs to Third World countries. Vaccine development is a slow, tedious process. A safe, inexpensive, widely applicable vaccine will probably not be available for ten to fifteen years. To make a simple, stable vaccine available to Third World countries will take even longer, but both drug therapy and vaccines will be available much earlier for use in high-risk groups in the United States.

With this background information, one can begin to put the AIDS epidemic into some sort of perspective. How does this epidemic compare to the epidemic of plague in the fourteenth century? Simply stated, it doesn't and won't ever. During the first three years of the plague epidemic, one-third to one-half of the population of Europe died. Recurrent waves of plague kept the population at that level for 150 years. The closest contemporary analogy to the plague epidemic would be nuclear holocaust (or better yet, the nuclear winter following something less than total nuclear annihilation). Even if all twenty million people now infected should die, this number would still be less than the mortality during the influenza epidemic of 1918. The lasting effect of the AIDs epidemic will not be in the sheer numbers of lives lost.

There is one important analogy between the AIDS and plague epidemics. As with plague, the specific form of the AIDS epidemic has been determined by a number of specific factors. First, HIV could only arise in Africa where evolution through the highest subhuman primates could occur. Second, the hunting and slaughter of infected monkeys for food provided ample opportunity for the initial infection of humans. Third, the spread of HIV infection to the rest of the world required the development of rapid, frequent, and inexpensive travel to and from Africa. Fourth, it was exceedingly important that HIV was introduced into a smaller, closed community (that is, homosexual males) at a time when sexual activity and promiscuity had increased substantially. This provided the means to amplify dramatically the spread of HIV in this group. Finally, the sharing of needles among drug users was an efficient way of infecting this group, who then became the conduit of HIV infection to the remainder of heterosexual society. As with plague, if any of these had not occurred, the AIDS epidemic would have been changed significantly or perhaps would not even have occurred.

It is much more valuable to ponder the different effects the AIDS epidemic has on various populations. One way to view this phenomenon is to look at areas of the world that may be affected. For example, what effect will this epidemic have on Central Africa? In Africa, HIV infection will continue to increase, spread by heterosexual transmission, particularly in urban areas. The burden of infection will fall on two groups: young men and women, and children born to the infected women. This concentration of AIDS cases among young adults, the potential leaders, will likely have profound effects on the Central African nations. Already, cases of neonatal AIDS are beginning to erode the improvements in infant mortality rates attained over the past twenty years, and all indications suggest that these gains will be wiped out entirely by the AIDS epidemic. The economic drain will be immense and will likely extend far beyond the public health sector in these nations. Since it is unlikely that effective medications and vaccines, even when available, can be supplied to these countries before the end of the century, the consequences of this continuing epidemic will be devastating to these nations.

Since HIV infection is not distributed evenly throughout the population of the United States, it is also possible to look at the different effects on populations within this country. The most obvious group is homosexual and bisexual males. HIV infection is probably most widely spread among these groups. Since the available seroprevalence data tends to be from the most sexually active individuals, the 80 percent seropositivity of some studies cannot be generalized to all of the estimated twelve million homosexual males in the United States. Still, over the next ten years large numbers of homosexual males will die of AIDS. This will have many effects. Homosexual males have already dramatically altered their sexual behavior and will continue to do so. For example, the promiscuity of the recent past will continue to decrease. As long as AIDS is viewed as a homosexual disease, discrimination against homosexuals will increase. As a result, fewer homosexual males will make their sexual preference known. Little is understood about the factors and influences involved in choosing a sexual preference. Therefore, we have no idea what effect fear of this disease will have on young males in the process of choosing their sexual identity, although casual experimentation with homosexuality will probably decrease markedly. Finally, there will continue to be significant effects on those areas in which homosexuals may be concentrated, such as the creative arts. As the fourteenth-century plague epidemic focused writing and art on the apocalypse, this epidemic will alter the concerns of writers and artists of today. In a more general way, we are already reinterpreting contemporary experience in light of the AIDS epidemic and its effects. Almost daily one hears an analysis in some play, book, movie, or other creative work in the perspective of AIDs.

Intravenous drug users make up another group that will be profoundly affected. Currently, this is the fastest growing segment of the epidemic. There is little reason to believe that HIV infection will decrease among these drug users, who are the conduit of HIV infection into the remainder of heterosexual society. Thus, society will soon be faced with the question of spending large sums of money to attempt to rehabilitate drug users or spending similar sums of money to separate them in some way from the rest of society. Based on the experiences of past epidemics, there is little doubt that, faced with this choice, Americans will choose the latter.

Part of the problem is the long lag period between HIV infection and the development of AIDS. Because of this, by the time society recognizes AIDS cases in the heterosexual population, asymptomatic HIV infection will be well established in that segment of the population. When this happens, there will be even less perceived reason to rehabilitate drug users. In fact, the backlash of anger at drug users for spreading HIV infection to the rest of society will most likely result in severe punitive actions against them.

Like the cholera epidemics of the 1800s, AIDS has engendered and will continue to engender numerous new laws and regulations. To date, there has been a struggle between protecting individual rights and protecting the public safety. Some states have passed laws requiring informed consent for HIV antibody testing. Conversely, the federal government requires mandatory testing of some groups. Usually these are disenfranchised groups, such as prisoners or immigrants. (Since HIV infection is already widespread in the United States, there is little reason to deny a person entry into the country because he is infected. This type of law made sense in 1832 to prevent importation of cholera into a country in which it was not yet present.) As in previous epidemics, as the AIDS epidemic grows, concerns for public safety may well erode individual rights, and sentiment favoring mandatory testing will increase. Within a few years, mandatory testing will likely be the rule rather than the exception.

The "internal anatomy" of the AIDS epidemic has been strikingly similar to other epidemics in history. In the first years of the epidemic, it was common to hear statements that AIDS was not a major epidemic—that is, to deny its existence. This soon shifted to a more specific form of denial. As it became apparent that homosexual males and intravenous drug users were primarily affected, people began to deny that the disease would be spread into the rest of society. Although all the epidemiological data still suggests that AIDS will continue to spread gradually into all seg-

ments of society, there continues to be widespread denial or disbelief of this possibility. The slow spread and long incubation period have made it easy to deny the spread of HIV infection. At the moment, more than two million people, including many heterosexuals, are already infected, but the attention remains on the more dramatic AIDS cases occurring, thus far, almost exclusively in homosexual males and drug users.

The AIDS epidemic has provided ample opportunities to cast blame. The rest of the world blames Africa for "starting" the epidemic. In response, Africans deny that AIDS even exists in Africa. Americans blame homosexuals and drug users for starting and continuing the epidemic. For many, it is clearly the moral failings of these groups that have caused them to be infected. For example, some of America's evangelists cite AIDS as a sign of God's wrath on homosexuals and drug users. These attitudes are reminiscent of the nineteenth-century view that poverty was a moral failing and that cholera was God's wrath on the poor. The last feature common to all great epidemics is fear. Clearly, the fear of transmissibility of HIV infection is tremendously exaggerated in the public's psyche. In fact, this paralyzing fear is the single major stumbling block to instituting reasonable, rational public policies. In the fourteenth century, we burned Jews at the stake; today we burn hemophiliacs' houses for fear that they will transmit HIV infection to our children. This is precious little progress in five hundred years.

Even those who have access to more accurate information are tremendously afraid. Just as in the nineteenth century when in New York City no doctors or nurses would care for patients in the cholera hospitals, health care workers today are extremely reluctant, and sometimes refuse, to care for AIDS patients. The administrations of hospitals, as well as physicians, are concerned that if they care for AIDS patients they will be perceived as AIDS hospitals or AIDS physicians. They fear that AIDS patients will be dumped on them and that other patients will flee from them.

As in other epidemics, present-day medicine has been criticized for its failures. With no cure for AIDS currently available, we have seen the rise of numerous alternative therapies. People have grasped at claims of the value of high doses of vitamins, various nutritional remedies, and other unproven remedies. Faced with an incurable illness, it is no surprise that people turn to these alternative therapies. Yet, despite a certain superficial sophistication, many of these alternative therapies seem strikingly similar to the claims of botanical medicine voiced more than 150 years ago during the cholera epidemics.

The current approach to controlling AIDS is similar to that proposed to control syphilis and gonorrhea in the early 1900s. For the vast majority of people, AIDS is, and will be, a sexually transmitted infection. Therefore, the only way to control transmission today is to educate people about this sexual transmission and its prevention—that is, "safe sex." In 1910, the question was, How can we teach men about sex without their recognizing the subject? Now the problem is only slightly different—How can we teach people about AIDS without talking about sex? Apparently most Americans firmly believe that talking to people about sex will cause them to engage in sex. It seems at times as if opponents of sex education would rather have people die from AIDS if the price of saving them is to have them learn about sex. This timidity has resulted in such confusing euphemisms as "exchange of body fluids." People will remain ignorant about HIV transmission until we are able to speak clearly and specifically about sex and sexual transmission.

The idea that sexually transmitted diseases can be spread by casual contact remains firmly entrenched in our culture. Despite the absence of any scientific evidence to support this idea, it has persisted to this day and contributes to the fear of casual transmission of HIV infection. Perhaps at some semi-conscious level, society still feels the need to maintain this belief. People realize it may be needed again when middle-class males begin bringing the HIV infection home to their wives. (There are many difficult things about being a physician caring for AIDS patients, but one of the more difficult is being with a family when a husband's bisexuality is first revealed to the rest of the family. At that moment, everyone firmly wishes that casual transmission did occur.)

All of these factors produce an unfortunate combination of circumstances for the AIDS epidemic in the United States. First, the epidemic is viewed as being confined to two socially unacceptable groups. Add to this the fact that HIV infection is transmitted in such unacceptable ways (that is, sex, particularly "perverted" sex, and illicit drugs), and it is no surprise that there is so little interest in controlling the epidemic among these groups or nervousness about caring for those who are infected. In this regard, it is revealing that very early in the epidemic, while little else was being done for homosexuals or drug users, a major

effort was made to "protect our blood supply" when it was recognized as a potential route for HIV infection into society at large. I am certainly not critical of this important effort, but at the same time funds have been progressively withdrawn from drug abuse programs. This has undermined the only available effort to prevent the spread of HIV infection among drug users. Recent data has indicated the increasing prevalence of HIV infection among prostitutes. Since these women are another potential route for HIV infection into the rest of society, we will soon see increasing attention directed toward them. There are sound public health reasons to focus on groups such as this with a high prevalence of HIV infection. (This is analogous to the strategy of "selective containment" used to eradicate smallpox.) But this effort will also be fueled by the sense of blame and moral outrage already present toward prostitutes and, as a result, we will soon see increasing efforts to identify, test, and quarantine them. Conversely, in all likelihood, little attention will be paid to the middle-class males who provide the demand and economic incentive for their services. All of these developments will be strikingly similar to reactions to the cholera epidemics in the nineteenth century and to venereal diseases during the early part of this century.

Epidemics have recurred throughout history. As scientific understanding has increased and superstitions subsided, much has changed about these epidemics. In very major ways, these changes have made the AIDS epidemic unlike any previous great epidemics. However, as I have tried to point out, in many ways society's responses to the AIDS epidemic thus far have been quite similar to previous societies' responses to epidemics. Although our advanced biotechnology has allowed us to apply sophisticated solutions to the biological problems of AIDS, our human responses have changed little from previous epidemics and hinder us from dealing effectively with many of the social problems that are part of the AIDS epidemic.

Thoughts on Heroism

Larry D. Nachman

Larry D. Nachman is a professor of political science at The College of Staten Island, CUNY, and is a frequent contributor to Commentary *and* Salmagundi.

This is no age for heroes. Circumstance and ethos incline us to be suspicious of heroes. For some, there is something cloying and grating about heroism; it has, for them, too much of a martial air to make them comfortable. For others, it appears to be a trait inappropriate and out of tune with modernity. Heroes are, for them, ridiculously apart from the spirit of the age. Irving Howe has observed that "the characteristic may [be] . . . the same thing [as] the characteristic 'anti-hero' of twentieth-century literature."[1] To confirm Howe's point, one has but to point to the anonymity of urban life which makes it so difficult to win the glory that was classically an object of heroism. Like so much of our contemporary inflated language, the terms *hero* and *heroism* are used so casually and thoughtlessly that it is difficult to know what is meant when we use them. I recently asked a college class to name some contemporary heroes

and to explain why they regarded them as such. This was not a scientific poll, of course, but I thought it interesting when I found they could not name any individuals, but merely suggested types of heroic acts such as rushing into a burning building to rescue a child. That the question is difficult to address may be a reflection of a contemporary belief that heroes are no longer relevant to our culture, that they, like coopers and smiths, belong to another time and another place.

A starting point for an inquiry into the heroic may be found in Alasdair MacIntyre's recent, probing examination of the state of contemporary moral theory, *After Virtue*. In this close critique of the various reigning subjectivist theories on the foundations of morals, MacIntyre turns for contrast to the model offered by heroic societies, that is, to societies where heroic examples are used as

guides for conducting human life. He writes:

> It is not just that [in a heroic society] there is for each status a prescribed set of duties and privileges. There is also a clear understanding of what actions are required to perform these and what actions fall short of what is required. For what are required are actions. A man in heroic society is what he does. . . . To judge a man therefore is to judge his actions.[2]

ACTIONS AND INTENTIONS

This comment suggests three reasons why heroism is so dissonant from the contemporary point of view. First, heroism has to do exclusively with actions. Yet today, we dwell in a psychological universe. It is the motive and intention that capture our attention. In our attempts to grapple with understanding the human condition, we turn our thoughts inward to the tensions and conflicts, known and unknown, that explain the reasons why we are what we are. Our criminal justice system has, for example, been transformed from a process of determining what acts in truth occurred and then measuring those acts by an objective standard of law into a complex diagnostic system in which responsibility becomes diffuse and the goal becomes to transform the inner man by rehabilitation. Action is only one of the many ways in which the reality of a person reveals itself to the world. And like words, actions can deceive. An action may be sincere or hypocritical. That is to say, we test action, not by its results and consequences nor by the meaning of the deed, but by whether or not it is an authentic expression of the self. The luminous and exemplary character of a heroic act vanishes when one seeks its meaning in the character of the person who performs the act.

Secondly, when MacIntyre suggests that "there is for each status a prescribed set of duties and privileges," we feel immediately that we have entered a worldview other than our own. Duties, privileges, and prescriptions have become part of an arcane language that the tongue can say without the words registering on the mind. Like the slang of a previous generation, their use merely dates a person. The obligations imposed by duties, privileges, and prescriptions constitute a standard to which all are held. But it is a characteristic of our time that people do not accept such a standard as a guide to conduct. Alan Bloom, in *The Closing of the American Mind,* has recently reminded us how pervasive moral relativism is in our culture. If there is no common standard of action, heroism becomes merely one person's preference. The hero, like everyone else, is just doing his thing; his acts have worth only for him.

Finally, this flattening of the moral universe conforms well to the egalitarian temper of our times. As Bloom has put it, for those who postulate "the relativity of truth [it] is not a theoretical insight but a moral postulate, the condition of a free society."[3] The hero is an extraordinary person because he does extraordinary acts. The origins of our idea of the hero are

found in aristocratic societies. The hero is he who has better than other people realized the ideal of what a human being is. The hero is both exceptional and a model for others. His acts are an overreaching of what was hitherto considered to be the limits of what humanity can achieve.

THE HERO AND DEMOCRATIC SOCIETY

In an age that has been searching for standards of "minimal competency," the hero would necessarily be

> If there is no common standard of action, heroism becomes merely one person's preference.

a disturbing presence. If heroism is praiseworthy, then cowardice or the unqualified pursuit of self-interest must be blameworthy. Some people, by virtue of their acts, must be better than those whose acts fall short of the mark. In the language of our time, to talk of heroes is to be "elitist." Another word from our new vocabulary comes to mind—judgmental. We find ourselves exhorted not to be judgmental; we are sometimes accused of being judgmental. If we cannot judge, if we say that some acts are better than others, heroism is impossible.

However, I see no necessary contradiction between heroism and democratic values. On the contrary, since its inception in classical Greece and Rome, democracy has demanded a high degree of civic virtue, the willingness of citizens to make considerable sacrifices for the sake of the *res publica*. If the first model tradition offers us for the hero is that given by Homer, a later model of civic sacrifice is associated with the classical republic. Montesquieu regarded civic or public virtue as a necessary condition

for the maintenance of republican government. He explained it tersely: "[Civic] virtue in a republic is a most simple thing; it is a love of the republic."[4] It was, he believed, unnecessary and unlikely to occur in a monarchy.

> [In a monarchy] the state subsists independently of the love of country, of the thrist of true glory, of self-denial, of the sacrifice of our dearest interests, and of all those heroic virtues which we admire in the ancients, and to us are known only by tradition.[5]

The heroic virtues of which Montesquieu spoke are clearly not those of Achilles or Hector. They are rather that willingness to defend the republic and to put its needs before one's own and they are the foundation upon which the survival of this particular political system depends.

The heroic ideal is, therefore, not only consistent with a democratic polity, it is a prerequisite for one. But it is not consistent with what may be called a moral egalitarianism in the form of either the contention that all acts are morally equivalent or the conviction that no person is responsible for his acts. To the extent that this moral egalitarianism has come to be an unexpressed condition for democratic society, to that extent only does the heroic ideal contradict the principles of democracy.

THE HERO AND TOTALITARIAN REGIMES

Democracy is not, to be sure, the only distinctive form of modern political and social life. Totalitarianism, too, is a child of modernity. Totalitarian societies create their own special obstacles to the emergence of heroism. At first sight, it would seem that the sheer weight of evil and moral ugliness in totalitarian regimes and the great peril risked in any kind of opposition to them would be productive of heroism in all walks of life. Any act in opposition to such a system would be unequivocally and undeniably heroic. And such acts have occurred with remarkable frequency. But the frightful power of the regime limits the scope of heroism by dulling the consequences of heroic acts.

MacIntyre can again provide assistance. He writes:

The Subway (1950), George Tooker.

In all those cultures, Greek, medieval or Renaissance, where moral thinking and action is structured according to some version of the scheme that I have called classical, the chief means of moral education is the telling of stories.[6]

Heroism is not a matter of a purely practical calculation of alternatives concluded by the choice of the most beneficial course of action. Often we sense and are moved, by a heroic act that is utterly futile. The heroic sacrifice seemed to do no good; it was impractical. Nevertheless, we admire the act and the actor. Its principal consequences have little to do with the events of which it was part. Rather its importance lies wholly in its effect on those who hear of it. The heroic act is done, in part, for the sake of the story; it is aimed, as MacIntyre suggests, at moral education.

Nothing, then, is further from the spirit of heroism than Christ's admonition that we should "never let the right hand know what the left hand is doing." Although this Christian principle and the heroic ethos have in common a kind of disregard for the consequences of action, there is a great difference between them. Christ wanted to purify the moral act from all contamination of self-interest. His was a morality of intention. Only those acts were good that were done for goodness' sake. If one

did good for any other reason, even merely to seem good in one's own eyes, the act lost its moral quality. Christ's is the most absolute statement of a morality of intentions. But although heroic action demands a disregard both of self-interest and the immediate consequences of the act,

> If we cannot judge, if we cannot say that some acts are better than others, heroism is impossible.

the heroic ethos is a morality of action and consequence. As has been seen, the consequence that matters is, however, not the immediate consequence but the larger results that ensue when the act is held up by others as a model of human conduct. The heroic act must be known, told, and remembered for it to achieve its goal.

THE HERO AS AN EXAMPLE TO OTHERS

It is this element of heroism against which totalitarianism wages a relentless war. A generation ago, Hannah Arendt, who was for our world the great theorist of moral action and interpreter of totalitarianism, examined the threat posed to totalitarian regimes by morally exemplary acts.

> [A] decisive step in the preparation of living corpses is the murder of the moral person in man. This is done in the main by making martyrdom, for the first time in history, impossible.[7]

She proceeds to explain by quoting from David Rousset's memoir of concentration camp life:

> How many people here still believe that a protest has even historic importance? This skepticism is the real masterpiece of the SS. Their great accomplishment. The have corrupted all human solidarity. Here the night has fallen on the future. When no witnesses are left, there can be no testimony. To demonstrate when death can no longer be postponed is an attempt to give death a meaning, to act beyond one's own death. In order to be successful, a gesture must have social meaning. There are hundreds of thousands of us here, all living in

absolute solitude. That is why we are subdued no matter what happens.[8]

Martyrdom, the possibility of a heroic sacrifice, is thwarted in two ways. Totalitarian regimes are ruthless, homicidal, and arbitrary. Their attack is not limited to those who oppose the regime or obstruct its operations. The same fate is frequently shared by the courageous and the cowardly. Arendt traced the consequences of this obliteration of the distinction between innocence and guilt.

> This consistent arbitrariness negates human freedom more efficiently than any tyranny ever had. One had at least to be an enemy of tyranny in order to be punished by it. Freedom of opinion was not abolished for those who were brave enough to risk their necks. Theoretically, the choice of opposition remains in totalitarian regimes too; but such a freedom is almost invalidated if committing a voluntary act only assures a 'punishment' that everyone else may have to bear anyway.[9]

Let me offer a grim and painful example. In Jewish tradition, no one is more honored than he who has performed a *Kiddush Ha-Shem*, a "sanctification of the name." The term is given principally to those who chose to die rather than to renounce God, when their conversion to another religion was demanded as the price for their life. Clearly, under Nazi rule more Jews were slain for being Jews than in their entire history combined. Yet, although commonly they have been accorded the honor due those who martyred themselves for the sake of their faith, it is—and one can observe this only with deep sadness —historically inaccurate to so regard them. Though they deserve to be honored, it is difficult to maintain that they were martyrs; they were, alas, merely victims. It was precisely the essence of the genocidal policy of the Nazis that it did not matter to them whether or not a Jew persisted in his faith. In fact, it did not matter what a Jew did. The issue had been determined by his lineage. The matter was settled at birth. Christians, atheists,

and the most orthodox of Jews were all killed together because they were Jews by blood. Their death was independent of any choice they made or any action they took.

Similarly, in both the Nazi and the communist systems there were many who resisted the regime and died for their resistance. But they died, as Arendt and Rousset noted, alongside others whose every act was directed at keeping themselves out of trouble. In the Gulag there came together Soviet soldiers who had agreed to serve in units sponsored and armed by the Germans to fight against the USSR as well as Soviet soldiers who had fought valiantly against the Germans, been captured and subjected to brutal conditions in German concentration camps. All suffered the same fate.

> The hero is demonstrating with his own life that for human beings there is something more important than life itself.

THE HERO'S STORY

These paradoxes belong to the nature of totalitarian systems. They are the inevitable consequence of the application of uninhibited, arbitrary power. The scope for heroism is further limited by the regime's control of all vehicles of communication. If the story is the basis of moral education, as is the case with heroism as moral example, then the storyteller is indispensable to the heroic ethos. The witness's role is as necessary as the hero's. But witnesses can be killed or silenced. The monopoly of control that totalitarian regimes exercise over the means of communication can be used to alter, distort, and suppress the truth. The Orwellian depiction of how such regimes control the social mem-

ory, the historical record, remains true today. The heroic act may have occurred, but if no trace of it remains, it is as if it never happened.

In the immediate postwar period, this power to erase the historical memory seemed to be novel, absolute, and frightful. The fear of its consequences shaped not only Orwell's classic, *1984*, but Arendt's, *Origins of Totalitarianism*, as well. It seemed that unlimited power had been achieved. The power to control action had always been limited by the courage of individuals to risk their lives. No matter how punitive a dictatorship was all it could do was to exact harsh punishment for proscribed acts. But if people were willing to endure that punishment, the control was to no avail. But if witnesses to those acts of courage were silenced, if all written records were expunged and photographs retouched, then the action, however courageous, lost its meaning. Not only the hero but the heroic act disappeared.

THE STORYTELLER AND THE WITNESS

Neither Orwell nor Arendt foresaw, nor could they have, what we have experienced in the last quarter of a century. Since the publication of *One Day in the Life of Ivan Denisovich*, we have been graced by a succession of works that record and present accounts of those events and those acts which we had thought to be forever lost. The storyteller, who had often been the merely anonymous vehicle of preservation of heroic acts, has come to the foreground of the heroic act. It has been seen that in totalitarian regimes the actors are often mere victims in the sense that they were not willing agents of their fate. It has also been noted that in that dark world the power of the regime has borne down upon the witnesses. In the works of Shalamov, Mandelstam, Solzhenitsyn, and Valladares, it is the act of writing that is heroic. It is the writer who makes choices and takes risks.

Perhaps the archetype for this new figure of the storyteller-hero is Emmanuel Ringelblum. He was a Polish Jew who was attending a World Zionist Congress when the Germans invaded Poland. He elected to return to Warsaw where he formed an under-

Hercules thinking, *Francis Shields.*

ground organization, the *Oneg Shabbot.* This was not a resistance group in the usual sense of the word, rather its function was to gather—at great risk—reports and accounts of what was happening under the German occupation. His hope was that "we may succeed in making sure that not a single fact about Jewish life at this time and place will be kept from the world."[10] The fruit of his courageous labors, *Notes from the Warsaw Ghetto,* gives us an extraordinary account of life at its bitterest. His editor, Jacob Sloan, observed that "in the *Notes* it is the Ghetto that is the hero, and not Emmanuel Ringleblum."[11] But it is nevertheless true that Ringleblum chose his fate in a way that most of those whose suffering he records did not.

That formidable intellect George Steiner has recently argued that the very oppressive force that totalitarian regimes bring to bear on the work of intellectuals gives that work a power, depth, and presence no longer apparent in our own liberal society.

If 'happiness' in the definitions central to the theory and practice of 'the American way of life' seems to [the American writer] the greater good, if he does not suspect 'happi-

ness' in almost any guise of being the despotism of the ordinary, he is in the wrong business. In the world of the Gulag . . . artists, thinkers, writers receive the unwavering tribute of political scrutiny and repression. The KGB and the serious writer are in total accord when both know, when both *act on the*

> What I am referring to is the disclosure that the heroic act is the paradigm and foundation of moral life.

knowledge that a sonnet, . . . a novel, a scene from a play can be the power-house of human affairs, that there is nothing more charged with the detonators of dreams and action than the word.[12]

It is an irony of the modern world that the most repressive political systems known to human history provide a larger field for the heroic than do the freest political systems we have known. This is not merely because, in an obvious way, there is more danger under a totalitarian than under a democratic order. It is also because, as we have seen and as Steiner confirms, there is something in the insistent, sole pursuit of personal goals that makes the heroic act unappealing as a human ideal.

HEROISM AND COURAGE

But what is there in the otherwise valid play of personal ambition that makes it so inconsistent with heroism? One senses that courage is an element of the heroic. Yet courage is frequently an indispensable element of ambition. After all, the classic model of the entrepreneur was that of a risktaker. There are some obvious examples of courageous acts that we would hesitate to call heroic, for example, race-car driving and ski-jumping. Courage and heroism are closely knit, but they are not identical. What is it that distinguishes them?

To ask this question is to seek to confront the definition of heroism. By definition I mean, of course, not a dictionary's account of the meaning of the word but rather a cultural definition, a philosophical explanation of the place of heroism in human affairs. For this kind of explanation, there is, in our literary tradition, a supremely profound and convincing reflection on the nature of heroism; it is to be found in Hegel's *Phenomenology of Spirit*.

In this work, which has helped shaped the modern consciousness, Hegel presents a tableau of cultures, a series of explorations of the modes of Western culture. The first of these representations, the starting point for his attempt to give a philosophical account of the history of civilization, is called, "Lordship and Bondage." In general, Hegel is trying to make sense of distinctively human forms of life, of what he calls, spirit. But how, he asks, does a distinctively human life emerge out of nature? How does man distinguish himself from the rest of nature? How does he fashion, for himself, a way of life that is not given to him by his natural existence?

The work as a whole is an extraordinary probing of what it means to be human. What Hegel posits at the start is a mere possibility, an inchoate, unachieved sense that people have that they somehow are endowed with a worth that is more than the life in their bodies. They feel that they do not merely exist for nature, for the cyclical demands of the preservation of the species. They believe, or they want to believe, that they are here not for nature but for themselves. This more than natural worth Hegel calls, being-for-self. The term is clumsy, but it formulates the basis of the claim that man has a special status in the universe.

But it is only a claim, only a belief. Like other claims, it could be hollow, an instance of self-conceit or self-delusion. It could be that man's only distinction is that he is an animal who brags. Hegel summons up an image of individuals who roam about announcing their superiority to the rest of living creation. They may themselves be convinced; they may be certain of the truth of what they say. But how to prove it? How may they make of their certainty a truth of the world? Hegel's stunning answer is that

It is only through staking one's life that freedom is won; only thus is it proved that for self-consciousness [a human being], its essential being is not [just] being, not the *immediate* form in which it appears, not its submergence in the expanse of life, but rather that there is nothing present in it which could not be regarded as a vanishing moment, that is only pure *being-for-self*.[13]

The language is tightly compacted and abstract, but its meaning is straightforward. If you want to demonstrate that something means more to you than life itself, the way to do it is to show that you are willing to risk

> There is more at stake than first appears in the decline of the heroic ideal.

your life for it. What follows in *The Phenomenology* is a "trial by death," a combat for honor's sake by two individuals who seek to prove to each other that they are willing to sacrifice their lives for their standing in the world. For Hegel, this struggle for honor is the essence of the heroic spirit. The hero is demonstrating with his own life that for human beings there is something more important than life itself.

HEROISM TRANSCENDS THE PRACTICAL NEEDS OF MAN

This exposition of the heroic explains why there is no heroism in pursuing a dangerous occupation or engaging in a risky course of action for the sake of material benefit. The heroic is a category reserved for dangers encountered for the sake of some value unconnected with the exigencies of life. All animals, including man, run risks, place themselves in danger, in

the pursuit of survival. Risks and benefits are calculable, weighed against each other, and reckoned up. The risk and the benefit belong to the same sphere of natural existence. The risks run are, in some sense, necessary risks; they are material means to a material end. But in the heroic act, the risk is unnecessary and avoidable. One can leave the field of combat, cling to life, fully intact, and lose only that nonmaterial value, such as honor, for which one fought in the first place.

For the same reason, courage in defense of others is not necessarily heroic. The issue here does not turn on the distinction between selfishness and altruism. Such a definition sentimentalizes and trivializes heroism. To risk one's life to save others is courageous and always noble, but it is still to remain within the orbit of the exigencies of life. There must be in the act something additional that points to some human ideal for which the sacrifice is offered.

To be sure, in a matter such as this it is all a question of definition. A shift in the terms of the definition will draw different lines, emphasize different qualities, and focus attention on different issues. Hegel's approach has the advantage of illuminating for us a distinctive element of heroism that is in considerable tension with contemporary life.

What I am referring to is the disclosure that the heroic act is the paradigm and foundation of moral life. The hero, by his act, establishes in the world an order of importance that is independent of anything given to us by nature. The hero chooses where instinct dictates that there is no choice to be made. Something as intangible, as evanescent, as impractical as honor, self-worth, or pride in being human is chosen over life itself. The choice makes no sense before it is made. After it is made, something new has entered the world: the status of man as a moral being. The value and importance of that for which the sacrifice is made are established by the sacrifice itself.

The choices here are extreme and total. Achilles could lead a long, happy life in oblivion or win immortal fame at the cost of a short lifespan. That they are so extreme is a reflection of their fundamental character. Once it has been established that choice is possible, that man can devote himself to ends that he himself has created, the choices can be more complex and nuanced. But in all its forms and developments, morality always involves some measure of sacrifice for a good that is not given by nature, a good that human beings bring to the world. The delicate and subtle character of the foundation of the moral life was perfectly and succinctly stated by Thomas Mann in his great tetralogy, *Joseph and His Brothers.*

It is just this indulgence in the superfluous, this submission to artificial hierarchies, and the unashamed wasting of time on their account, which differentiates the civilized from the natural and makes up the sum of human values.[14]

HEROISM AND MORALITY

For heroism and for the category of the moral in general, something must be believed to be and then made to be important. Where people are convinced that nothing matters, there is no place for either heroism or moral choice. A popular anti-Vietnam movie of the last decade ends with the "hero," a paraplegic war veteran, telling an audience of high school students that nothing in the world was worth what he lost. This was not merely a statement rejecting that particular, unpopular war. It was a categorical rejection of taking risks and venturing onto dangerous enterprises for the sake of any human value. In fiction and in fact, such audiences have taken this message to heart. The novel that was one of the emblems of the 1960s, *Catch-22*, carried the message that going into battle, even against the Nazis, was an act that no sane, rational man would choose. *Catch-22* constructs a morally anarchic universe, energized only by cynicism and self-interest, in which those who choose to oppose nazism are pathological or

homicidal and only those who seek to avoid combat are sane and humane.

What we have seen emerge as a kind of distortion of democratic values is a shared sense that no one has a stake in the world, in a public or civic order, in settled traditions and institutions, nor, finally, in a moral order that is shaped by our actions. Again, the issue is not one of altruism pitted against selfishness. For eminently selfish reasons one can determine that the human realm in which one dwells is of such importance that it commands some measure of self-sacrifice. Aristotle, in his *Politics,* sought to explore the separate spheres of human existence by distinguishing the household, which could meet only the day-to-day needs of life, from the *polis,* which was capable of providing man with a field in which he could unfold his purely human traits. For Aristotle, it was clear and evident that the special character of human existence required a view larger and broader than that which could be enclosed in quotidian concerns. By contrast, the slogan of our time and place is to live one day at a time. This vision is not only unheroic and amoral, it is quite simply petty.

By contrast, totalitarian societies fail to provide scope for a heroic or moral life precisely by depriving people of a realm in which choices can be made or where acts can have consequences. Where democratic modernity denies the value and importance of transcendent goods, totalitarian modernity strips the world of such goods by trivializing human life. The human being is regarded as a mere product and instrument of social forces and a bureaucratic structure is installed to direct those social forces, and to shape its human products. The choices of individuals appear futile because no act of an individual can deflect the tide of history. If the characteristic figure of democratic modernity is psychological man, the characteristic figure of totalitarian modernity is socialized

man. But by making war on choice, action, and consequence, totalitarianism confirms their human significance.

I do not wish to appear in any way to support the claim that there is a moral convergence or equivalence between these two forms of social life. Those who take such positions, directly or by implication, are participants in the failure of moral judgment that I am criticizing. Freedom is always preferable to tyranny, even if people misuse their freedom. Rather, what I am pointing to is that there is more at stake than first appears in the decline of the heroic ideal. If we have not left room in our world for heroism, it is not simply because we have rejected the particular character of the hero. It is that we have not left a place for moral choice, for engagements in a world larger than ourselves, and for a view of man that pays proper homage to his moral and ontological dignity.

1. Irving Howe, *Classics of Modern Fiction,* Fourth Edition (San Diego: Harcourt Brace Jovanovich, 1986), 327.

2. Alasdair MacIntyre, *After Virtue,* Second Edition, (Notre Dame, Indiana: University of Notre Dame Press, 1984), 212.

3. Alan Bloom, *The Closing of the American Mind,* (New York: Simon and Schuster, 1987), 25.

4. Baron de Montesquieu, *The Spirit of the Laws* (New York: Hafner Publishing Company, 1949), 40.

5. *Ibid.,* 23.

6. MacIntyre, *After Virtue,* 121.

7. Hannah Arendt, *The Origins of Totalitarianism,* (New York: Harcourt Brace Jovanovich, 1973), 451.

8. Arendt, 451.

9. Arendt, 433.

10. Emmanuel Ringelblum, *Notes from the Warsaw Ghetto: The Journal of Emmanuel Ringelblum,* edited and translated by Jacob Sloan (New York: McGraw-Hill Book Company, Inc., 1958), xxi.

11. Ringelblum, xxii.

12. George Steiner, "The Archives of Eden," *Salmagundi,* Fall 1980-Winter 1981, 88.

13. G. W. F. Hegel, *Phenomenology of Spirit,* translated by A. V. Miller (Oxford: Oxford University Press, 1977), 114.

14. Thomas Mann, *Joseph and His Brothers,* (New York: Alfred A. Knopf, 1971), 104.

A History of the Past: 'Life Reeked with Joy'

"History," declared Henry Ford, "is bunk." And yet, to paraphrase George Santayana, those who forget history and the English language are condemned to mangle them. Historian Anders Henriksson, a veteran of the university classroom, has faithfully recorded, from papers submitted by freshmen at McMaster University and the University of Alberta, his students' more striking insights into European history from the Middle Ages to the present. Possibly as an act of vengeance, Professor Henriksson has now assembled these individual fragments into a chronological narrative that we present here.

Anders Henriksson

Anders Henriksson is assistant professor of history at Shepherd College. Born in Rochester, New York, he received a B.A. from the University of Rochester (1971), and an M.A. (1972) and a PhD. (1978) from the University of Toronto. He is the author of The Tsar's Loyal Germans: The Riga German Community, Social Change, and the Nationality Question, 1855–1905 *(1983).*

History, as we know, is always bias, because human beings have to be studied by other human beings, not by independent observers of another species.

During the Middle Ages, everybody was middle aged. Church and state were co-operatic. Middle Evil society was made up of monks, lords, and surfs. It is unfortunate that we do not have a medivel European laid out on a table before us, ready for dissection. After a revival of infantile commerce slowly creeped into Europe, merchants appeared. Some were sitters and some were drifters. They roamed from town to town exposing themselves and organized big fairies in the countryside. Mideval people were violent. Murder during this period was nothing. Everybody killed someone. England fought numerously for land in France and ended up wining and losing. The Crusades were a series of military expeditions made by Christians seeking to free the holy land (the "Home Town" of Christ) from the Islams.

In the 1400 hundreds most Englishmen were perpendicular. A class of yeowls arose. Finally, Europe caught the Black Death. The bubonic plague is a social disease in the sense that it can be transmitted by intercourse and other etceteras. It was spread from port to port by inflected rats. Victims of the Black Death grew boobs on their necks. The plague also helped the emergance of the English language as the national language of England, France and Italy.

The Middle Ages slimpared to a halt. The renasence bolted in from the blue. Life reeked with joy. Italy became robust, and more individuals felt the value of their human being. Italy, of course, was much closer to the rest of the world, thanks to northern Europe. Man was determined to civilise himself and his brothers, even if heads had to roll! It became sheik to be educated. Art was on a more associated level. Europe was full of incredible churches with great art bulging out their doors. Renaissance merchants were beautiful and almost lifelike.

•

The Reformnation happened when German nobles resented the idea that tithes were going to Papal France or the Pope thus enriching Catholic coiffures. Traditions had become oppressive so they too were crushed in the wake of man's quest for ressurection above the not-just-social beast he had become. An angry Martin Luther nailed 95 theocrats to a church door. Theologically, Luthar was into reorientation mutation. Calvinism was the most convenient religion since the days of the ancients. Anabaptist services tended to be migratory. The Popes, of course, were usually Catholic. Monks went right on seeing themselves as worms. The last Jesuit priest died in the 19th century.

After the refirmation were wars both foreign and infernal. If the Spanish could gain the Netherlands they would have a stronghold throughout northern Europe which would include their posetions in Italy, Burgangy, central Europe and India thus serrounding France. The German Emperor's lower passage was blocked by the French for years and years.

Louis XIV became King of the Sun. He gave the people food and artillery. If he didn't like someone, he sent them to the gallows to row for the rest of their lives. Vauban was the royal minister of flirtation. In Russia the 17th century was known as the time of the bounding of the serfs. Russian nobles wore clothes only to humour Peter the Great. Peter filled his government with accidental people and built a new capital near the European boarder. Orthodox priests became government antennae.

The enlightenment was a reasonable time. Voltare wrote a book called *Candy* that got him into trouble with Frederick the Great. Philosophers were unknown yet, and the fundamental stake was one of religious toleration slightly confused with defeatism. France was in a very serious state. Taxation was a great drain on the state budget. The French revolution was accomplished before it happened. The revolution evolved through monarchial, republican and tolarian phases until it catapulted into Napolean. Napoleon was ill with bladder problems and was very tense and unrestrained.

•

History, a record of things left behind by past generations, started in 1815. Throughout the comparatively radical years 1815–1870 the western European continent was undergoing a Rampant period of economic modification. Industrialization was precipitating in England. Problems were so complexicated that in Paris, out of a city population of one million people, two million able bodies were on the loose.

Great Brittian, the USA and other European countrys had demicratic leanings. The middle class was tired and needed a rest. The old order could see the lid holding down new ideas beginning to shake. Among the goals of the chartists were universal suferage and an anal parliment. Voting was done by ballad.

A new time zone of national unification roared over the horizon. Founder of the new Italy was Cavour, an intelligent Sardine from the north. Nationalism aided Italy because nationalism is the growth of an army. We can see that nationalism succeeded for Italy because of France's big army. Napoleon III–IV mounted the French thrown. One thinks of Napoleon III as a live extension of the late, but great, Napoleon. Here too was the new Germany: loud, bold, vulgar and full of reality.

Culture fomented from Europe's tip to its top. Richard Strauss, who was violent but methodical like his wife made him, plunged into vicious and perverse plays. Dramatized were adventures in seduction and abortion. Music reeked with reality. Wagner was master of music, and people did not forget his contribution. When he died they labled his seat "historical." Other countries had their own artists. France had Chekhov.

World War I broke out around 1912–1914. Germany was on one side of France and Russia was on the other. At war people get killed, and then they aren't people any more, but friends. Peace was proclaimed at Versigh, which was attended by George Loid, Primal Minister of England. President Wilson

arrived with 14 pointers. In 1937 Lenin revolted Russia. Communism raged among the peasants, and the civil war "team colours" were red and white.

Germany was displaced after WWI. This gave rise to Hitler. Germany was morbidly overexcited and unbalanced. Berlin became the decadent capital, where all forms of sexual deprivations were practised. A huge anti-semantic movement arose. Attractive slogans like "death to all Jews" were used by governmental groups. Hitler remilitarized the Rineland over a squirmish between Germany and France. The appeasers were blinded by the great red of the Soviets. Moosealini rested his foundations on eight million bayonets and invaded Hi Lee Salasy. Germany invaded Poland, France invaded Belgium, and Russia invaded everybody. War screeched to an end when a nukuleer explosion was dropped on Heroshima. A whole generation had been wipe out in two world wars, and their forlorne families were left to pick up the peaces.

According to Fromm, indiviuation began historically in medieval times. This was a period of small childhood. There is increasing experience as adolescence experiences its life development. The last stage is us.

Index

Credits/ Acknowledgments

Cover design by Charles Vitelli

1. The Age of Power
Facing overview—National Gallery of Art, Washington, D. C. 16,
18, 19(bottom), 20(bottom)—Giraudon. 19(top), 20 (top)—
Weidenfeld Archives. 31—National Portrait Gallery.

2. Rationalism, Enlightenment, and Revolution
Facing overview—National Gallery of Art, Washington, D. C. 41—
Yale University Library. 42—Bibliothèque Nationale. 43—Scala/
Art Resource. 44—Quesada/Burke, courtesy of Rare Book
Division, Astor, Lenox and Tilden Foundations, New York Public
Library. 45—Rare Book Division, Astor, Lenox and Tilden
Foundations, New York Public Library. 75, 76, 78(top), 78(left)—
Mansell Collection. 78(right)—BBC Hulton Picture Library. 79—by
courtesy of National Maritime Museum.

3. Industry and Ideology
Facing overview—National Archives. 84—From The Textile
Manufactures of Great Britain, by George Dodd, London, 1844.

86—(top) From Book of English Trades, London, 1804; (bottom)
from Cotton Manufacture in Great Britain, by Edward Baines,
London, 1835. 87—(left top and bottom) from The Book of
English Trades; (right top) from Days at the Factories, by G.
Dobb, London, 1843; (right bottom) from Penny Magazine,
November 1944. 88-90—Mansell Collection. 100—Mansell
Collection. 102—Punch, November 1858. 104—Punch, October
1858.

4. Modernism and Total War
Facing overview—138—Library of Congress. 164-169—all photos
for this essay are from The SIPA Press, Paris, France.

5. The Human Prospect
Facing overview—United Nations photo by John Isaac. 205—
Library of Congress.

ANNUAL EDITIONS:
WESTERN CIVILIZATION, VOLUME II
Article Rating Form

Here is an opportunity for you to have direct input into the next revision of this volume. We would like you to rate each of the 37 articles listed below, using the following scale:

1. Excellent: should definitely be retained
2. Above average: should probably be retained
3. Below average: should probably be deleted
4. Poor: should definitely be deleted

Your ratings will play a vital part in the next revision. So please mail this prepaid form to us just as soon as you complete it.
Thanks for your help!

We Want Your Advice

Annual Editions revisions depend on two major opinion sources: one is our Advisory Board, listed in the front of this volume, which works with us in scanning the thousands of articles published in the public press each year; the other is you—the person actually using the book. Please help us and the users of the next edition by completing the prepaid article rating form on this page and returning it to us. Thank you.

Rating	Article	Rating	Article
	1. The Emergence of the Great Powers		19. John Stuart Mill and Liberty
	2. Philip II's Grand Design for the Glory of God and Empire		20. Sarah Bernhardt's Paris
	3. Conflict in Continuity in 17th-Century France		21. How the Modern World Began
	4. Louis XIV and the Huguenots		22. Sarajevo: The End of Innocence
	5. The 17th-Century "Renaissance" in Russia		23. When the Red Storm Broke
	6. Locke and Liberty		24. The Big Picture of the Great Depression
	7. From Boy-King to "Madman of Europe"		25. Munich at Fifty
	8. Galileo and the Specter of Bruno		26. The Nazi State: Machine or Morass?
	9. Meeting of Minds		27. Remembering Mussolini
	10. Prussia & Frederick the Great		28. 1945
	11. The Commercialization of Childhood		29. The War Europe Lost
	12. The First Feminist		30. Thinking Back on May 68
	13. The Shot Heard Round the World		31. Paristroika
	14. Was France the Fatherland of Genocide?		32. Decline—Not Necessarily Fall—of the American Empire
	15. Counter-Revolution? Toulon, 1793		33. How the Cold War Might End
	16. Cottage Industry and the Factory System		34. The Causes of Wars
	17. When Karl Marx Worked for Horace Greeley		35. Plagues, History, and AIDS
	18. Samuel Smiles: The Gospel of Self-Help		36. Thoughts on Heroism
			37. A History of the Past: "Life Reeked With Joy"

(Continued on next page)

ABOUT YOU

Name_____ Date_____

Are you a teacher? ☐ Or student? ☐

Your School Name _____

Department _____

Address _____

City _____ State _____ Zip _____

School Telephone # _____

YOUR COMMENTS ARE IMPORTANT TO US!

Please fill in the following information:

For which course did you use this book? _____

Did you use a text with this Annual Edition? ☐ yes ☐ no

The title of the text? _____

What are your general reactions to the Annual Editions concept?

Have you read any particular articles recently that you think should be included in the next edition?

Are there any articles you feel should be replaced in the next edition? Why?

Are there other areas that you feel would utilize an Annual Edition?

May we contact you for editorial input?

May we quote you from above?

ANNUAL EDITIONS: WESTERN CIVILIZATION, VOLUME II